SOCIALIST
REGISTER
2 0 1 2

SOCIALIST REGISTER 2012

THE CRISIS AND THE LEFT

Edited by LEO PANITCH, GREG ALBO and VIVEK CHIBBER

THE MERLIN PRESS
MONTHLY REVIEW PRESS
FERNWOOD PUBLISHING

First published in 2011
by The Merlin Press Ltd.
6 Crane Street Chambers
Crane Street
Pontypool
NP4 6ND
Wales

www.merlinpress.co.uk

British Library Cataloguing in Publication Data is available from the British
Library

Library and Archives Canada Cataloguing in Publication

Panitch, Leo, 1945–
The Crisis and the Left: Socialist Register 2012 / Leo Panitch, Greg Albo, Vivek
Chibber.
ISBN 978-1-55266-453-7
1. Global Financial Crisis, 2008–2009. 2. Global Financial Crisis, 2008–2009 –
Political aspects. 3. Global Financial Crisis, 2008–2009 – Social aspects.
4. Right and left (Political science).
I. Albo, Gregory II. Chibber, Vivek, 1965– III. Title.

HB3722.P35 2011   330.9'0511   C2011-903277-5

ISSN. 0081-0606

Published in the UK by The Merlin Press
ISBN. 978-0-85036-682-2 Paperback
ISBN. 978-0-85036-681-5 Hardback

Published in the USA by Monthly Review Press
ISBN. 978-1-58367-253-2 Paperback

Published in Canada by Fernwood Publishing
ISBN. 978-1-55266-453-7 Paperback

Printed in the UK on behalf of LPPS Ltd., Wellingborough, Northants.

CONTENTS

SYMPOSIUM ON THE EUROZONE CRISIS
AND LEFT STRATEGIES

CONTRIBUTORS

Elmar Altvater is a professor emeritus at the Otto Suhr Institute for Political Science, Free University, Berlin.

Nicole M. Aschoff is a post-doctoral fellow in the Department of Sociology at Boston University.

Merlin Chowkwanyun is a joint MPH/Ph.D. candidate in public health and history at the University of Pennsylvania.

Adam Hanieh is a lecturer in development studies at the School of Oriental and African Studies (SOAS), London.

David Harvey is professor of geography and anthropology at the Graduate Center of the City University of New York (CUNY).

Ho-fung Hung is associate professor in the Department of Sociology at Johns Hopkins University, Baltimore.

Michel Husson is an economist at the Institut de Recherches Economiques et Sociales (IRES) in Paris.

Ursula Huws is director of the research consultancy Analytica and professor of labour and globalisation at the University of Hertfordshire Business School.

Claudio Katz is a professor of economics at the University of Buenos Aires.

Peadar Kirby is professor of international politics and public policy at the University of Limerick.

Costas Lapavitsas is a professor of economics at the School of Oriental and African Studies (SOAS), London.

Larry Lohmann works at The Corner House, a UK-based solidarity and research organization.

David McNally is a professor of political science at York University in Toronto.

Frances Fox Piven is professor of political science and sociology at the Graduate Center of the City University of New York (CUNY).

Adolph Reed, Jr. is a professor of political science at the University of Pennsylvania.

Jan Toporowski is a professor of economics at the School of Oriental and African Studies (SOAS), London.

PREFACE

Four years after the collapse of 2007–08, it is fair to say that crisis has become the new normal for hundreds of millions of people. Not only have jobs been hard to find, they increasingly fail to provide the income and security that workers had come to expect from employment during the postwar era. Added to the huge numbers of the unemployed is the 'precariat', the growing segment of the working population in jobs that are temporary, low-wage, and without benefits or protection. Conditions that were once associated with the informal sector in the developing world are now becoming truly global.

Meanwhile, there is a lot of talk in the media that we are in the midst of an economic recovery. There is something to this. Banks are flush with cash, profits in manufacturing are on the upswing, and no one can fail to notice that the stock market has bounced back. But while profits are flowing again, the traditional signs of a new cycle of accumulation are hard to find. It isn't entirely surprising, then, that every little bit of bad news sends the markets into a temporary panic – as if everyone is waiting for the proverbial axe to fall. Even within the ruling classes, confidence in this recovery doesn't run very deep. Clearly, if there is a recovery, it is coming in large measure through the transfer of the costs of the crisis to the working class. And this is why the press, even while trumpeting the economic rebound, laments that to most working people, it doesn't feel like a recovery. What it feels like is a crisis that refuses to abate.

As if the structural shift in both the level and the pattern of employment wasn't enough, the crisis for working people is compounded by the political offensive unleashed by the ruling classes. In the advanced capitalist world, unions, pensions, health care, education – virtually every component of welfare capitalism is either being rolled back or dismantled, all in the name of economic necessity. The audaciousness of this programme would be impressive were it not so devastating. It is not just being proposed as a temporary measure to ride out the economic storm. We are witnessing the onset of permanent austerity in the advanced capitalist world. The consistency with which states have turned to this strategy betokens the remarkable degree of consensus within the ruling classes. Across North America and Europe, in state after state, the message is the same – the age of social insurance, of public supports, of protection from the market, and steady wage increases, is well and truly over.

This attack on working people isn't being launched by conservatives alone, though parties of the Right certainly comprise its sharp edge. Wherever they are in office, traditional social democrats have fallen in line with programmatic austerity as the only viable exit strategy from the crisis. And where they are in opposition, they have done little to forge an alternative agenda, much less lead the fightback. If anything, the leaders of social democratic parties have gone out of their way to distance themselves from the mobilizations against austerity. As we write this Preface, their dedication to proving their mettle as managers of the bourgeois order is most conspicuously on display in Greece, but this crisis has clarified that as the main ambition of social democratic leaders everywhere.

The popular resistance that has taken shape on this bleak political terrain is by no means unimpressive. Even while it has not been able to turn the tide, the resistance has been real, and it might be deepening. Who could have imagined that bucolic Wisconsin would be engulfed in a massive social upheaval, which would trigger a weeks-long takeover of the state capital building in Madison, and climax in the largest demonstration in the state's history? No less remarkable are the *Indignes* occupying the city squares in Spain, the strikes and massive demonstrations that have convulsed Greece, and the imaginative sit-ins of the UK Uncut movement as well as the hundreds of thousands of British public sector workers who have taken strike action. Most politically significant of all, of course, has been the wave of rebellions across the Middle East that have broken what appeared to be impenetrable dictatorships. What all of these mobilizations have in common is that they embody a rejection of the neoliberal offensive – whether its latest incarnation, as in Greece, or its accumulated devastation, as in Egypt.

Yet every one of these resistances has only served to reveal the continuing impasse of the Left, and its limited strategic and organizational resources. Defensive resistance alone cannot take advantage of the opportunity that the crisis creates. A common response of the Left when the financial crisis exploded in the US in the fall of 2008 was a Michael Moore-type populist one: *Why are you bailing the banks out? Let them go under.* This was, of course, utterly irresponsible, with no thought given to what would happen to the savings of workers, let alone to the paychecks deposited into their bank accounts, or even to the fact that what was at stake was the roofs over their heads. On the other hand, an even more common response from the Left was about asserting state responsibility: *This crisis is the result of the government not having done its duty: governments are supposed to regulate capital, and they didn't do so.* But putting the issue this way created a fundamentally misleading impression about the role of the capitalist state. The United States has the most regulated financial system in the world, as measured by the number of statutes on the books, pages of administrative regulation, and staff engaged in the supervision of the financial system. But that system is organized in such a way as to facilitate the financialization of capitalism, not only in the US itself, but in fact around the world. Without this, the globalization of capitalism in recent decades would not have been possible.

It was indicative of the Left's sorry lack of ambition in the crisis that calls for salary limits on Wall Street executives and transaction taxes on the financial sector were far more common than demands for turning the banks into public utilities. In fact, most the Left's recommendations were advanced as technocratic policy advice and presented as a means of stabilizing capitalism, rather than using the crisis as an opportunity to educate people on how capitalist finance really works, why it doesn't work for them, and why what we need instead is a publicly owned banking system. Of course, the sort of bank nationalizations undertaken in the wake of the fallout from the Lehman collapse -- with the lead of Brown's New Labour government in the UK being quickly followed by Bush's Republican administration in the US -- essentially involved socializing financial capital's losses while guaranteeing that the nationalized banks would continue to operate on a commercial basis at arm's length from any government direction or control, beyond seeking to maximize the taxpayers returns on their 'investment'. As the essay in last year's volume of the *Register* on 'Opportunity lost: mystification, elite politics and financial reform in the UK' put it, this really represented 'not the nationalisation of the banks, but the privatisation of the Treasury as a new kind of fund manager.'

The most important reason for taking the banks into the public sector and turning them into a public utility is that this would remove the institutional foundation of the most powerful section of capital today, thereby changing the balance of class forces in a fundamental way. But the ultimate point of this, of course, would be to transform the uses to which finance is put. We cannot even begin to think about solving the ecological crisis that coincides with this economic crisis without the Left returning to an ambitious notion of economic planning. The allocation of credit is at the core of economic planning for the conversion of industry as part of directing, in a democratic fashion, what gets invested, where it gets invested, how it gets invested.

This, the 48th volume of the Register, was conceived as a companion to last year's volume on 'The Crisis This Time'. We observed there that economic crises can be turning points which present political opportunities, and pointed to the fact that, so far, it was the ruling classes that were taking advantage of the political opening, not the Left. This volume deepens that analysis in range a ways, not only in terms of broader regional coverage that extends from Latin America to the Middle East to China to Europe, but also by probing the place of the city in capitalist crises, and the new accumulation strategies that feed on both the public sector crisis and the climate crisis, while still portending a new age of austerity. It also takes better measure of the state of the Left in the crisis, not least by a way of a symposium of three essays on what the Left's response should be to the Eurozone crisis. The next volume will take up the challenge of developing socialist strategies for the 21st century.

We want to thank all of the contributors to this volume while as usual indicating that neither they nor we necessarily agree with the various arguments that are presented herein. We also owe thanks to Ruth Felder and Shana Yael Shubs for their translation of Claudio's Katz's essay. Many of the essays in this volume can be traced back to the Socialist Register workshop on the crisis at York University in February 2010, and we are grateful to all those who made that possible and especially to Alan Zuege, Adam Hilton, and Justin Panos for the work they put into this volume in particular. And we are as always very appreciative to Louis Mackay for his cover design, as well as to Adrian Howe and Tony Zurbrugg of Merlin Press for all their efforts on behalf of the Register. Finally, we thank our contributing and corresponding editors for all their help in planning the two Register crisis volumes, and we are delighted to announce that Gilbert Achcar and Adolph Reed are joining the editorial collective.

LP
GA
VC
July 2011

THE URBAN ROOTS OF FINANCIAL CRISES: RECLAIMING THE CITY FOR ANTI-CAPITALIST STRUGGLE

DAVID HARVEY

In an article in the *New York Times* on 5 February 2011, entitled 'Housing Bubbles Are Few and Far Between', Robert Shiller, the economist who many consider the great housing expert given his role in the construction of the Case-Shiller index of housing prices in the United States, reassured everyone that the recent housing bubble was a 'rare event, not to be repeated for many decades'. The 'enormous housing bubble' of the early 2000s 'isn't comparable to any national or international housing cycle in history. Previous bubbles have been smaller and more regional'. The only reasonable parallels, he asserted, were the land bubbles that occurred in the United States way back in the late 1830s and the 1850s.[1] This is, as I shall show, an astonishingly inaccurate reading of capitalist history. The fact that it passed so unremarked testifies to a serious blind spot in contemporary economic thinking. Unfortunately, it also turns out to be an equally blind spot in Marxist political economy.

Conventional economics routinely treats investment in the built environment along with urbanization as some sidebar to the more important affairs that go on in some fictional entity called 'the national economy'. The subfield of 'urban economics' is, thus, the arena where inferior economists go while the big guns ply their macro-economic trading skills elsewhere. Even when the latter notice urban processes, they make it seem as if spatial reorganizations, regional development and the building of cities are merely some on-the-ground outcome of larger scale processes that remain unaffected by that which they produce. Thus, in the 2009 World Bank Development Report, which, for the first time ever, took economic geography seriously, the authors did so without a hint that anything could possibly go so catastrophically wrong in urban and regional development as to spark a crisis in the economy as a whole. Written wholly by economists (without consulting geographers, historians or urban sociologists) the aim was supposedly to explore the 'influence of geography on economic opportunity' and to elevate 'space and place from mere undercurrents in policy to a major focus'.

The authors were actually out to show how the application of the usual nostrums of neoliberal economics to urban affairs (like getting the state out of the business of any serious regulation of land and property markets and minimizing the interventions of urban, regional and spatial planning) was the best way to augment economic growth (i.e., capital accumulation). Though they did have the decency to 'regret' that they did not have the time or space to explore in detail the social and environmental consequences of their proposals, they did plainly believe that cities that provide 'fluid land and property markets and other supportive institutions – such as protecting property rights, enforcing contracts, and financing housing – will more likely flourish over time as the needs of the market change. Successful cities have relaxed zoning laws to allow higher-value users to bid for the valuable land – and have adopted land use regulations to adapt to their changing roles over time'.[2]

But land is not a commodity in the ordinary sense. It is a fictitious form of capital that derives from expectations of future rents. Maximizing its yield has driven low- or even moderate-income households out of Manhattan and central London over the last few years, with catastrophic effects on class disparities and the well-being of underprivileged populations. This is what is putting such intense pressure on the high-value land of Dharavi in Mumbai (a so-called slum that the report correctly depicts as a productive human ecosystem). The World Bank report advocates, in short, the kind of free-market fundamentalism that has spawned both macro-economic disruptions such as the crisis of 2007-09 alongside urban social movements of opposition to gentrification, neighbourhood destruction and the eviction of low-income populations to make way for higher value land uses.

Since the mid-1980s, neoliberal urban policy (applied, for example, across the European Union) concluded that redistributing wealth to less advantaged neighbourhoods, cities and regions was futile and that resources should instead be channelled to dynamic 'entrepreneurial' growth poles. A spatial version of 'trickle down' would then in the proverbial long run (which never comes) take care of all those pesky regional, spatial and urban inequalities. Turning the city over to the developers and speculative financiers redounds to the benefit of all! If only the Chinese had liberated land uses in their cities to free market forces, the World Bank Report argued, their economy would have grown even faster than it did!

The World Bank plainly favours speculative capital and not people. The idea that a city can do well (in terms of capital accumulation) while its people (apart from a privileged class) and the environment do badly is never examined. Even worse, the report is deeply complicit with the policies that lay at the root of the crisis of 2007–09. This is particularly odd, given that the report was published six months after the Lehman bankruptcy and nearly two years after the US housing market turned sour and the foreclosure tsunami was clearly identifiable. We are told, for example, without a hint of critical commentary, that:

> since the deregulation of financial systems in the second half of the 1980s, market-based housing financing has expanded rapidly. Residential mortgage markets are now equivalent to more than 40 percent of gross domestic product (GDP) in developed countries, but those in developing countries are much smaller, averaging less than 10 percent of GDP. The public role should be to stimulate well-regulated private involvement... Establishing the legal foundations for simple, enforceable, and prudent mortgage contracts is a good start. When a country's system is more developed and mature, the public sector can encourage a secondary mortgage market, develop financial innovations, and expand the securitization of mortgages. Occupant-owned housing, usually a household's largest single asset by far, is important in wealth creation, social security and politics. People who own their house or who have secure tenure have a larger stake in their community and thus are more likely to lobby for less crime, stronger governance, and better local environmental conditions.[3]

These statements are nothing short of astonishing given recent events. Roll-on the sub-prime mortgage business, fuelled by pablum myths about the benefits of homeownership for all and the filing away of toxic mortgages in highly rated CDOs to be sold to unsuspecting investors! Roll-on endless suburbanization that is both land and energy consuming way beyond what is reasonable for the sustained use of planet earth for human habitation! The authors might plausibly maintain that they had no remit to connect their thinking about urbanization with issues of global warming. Along with Alan Greenspan, they could also argue that they were blind-sided by the events of 2007–09, and that they could not be expected to have anticipated anything troubling about the rosy scenario they painted. By inserting the words 'prudent' and 'well-regulated' into the argument they had, as it were, 'hedged' against potential criticism.

But since they cite innumerable 'prudentially chosen' historical examples to bolster their neoliberal nostrums, how come they missed that the crisis of 1973 originated in a global property market crash that brought down several banks? Did they not notice that the end of the Japanese boom in 1990 corresponded to a collapse of land prices (still ongoing); that the Swedish banking system had to be nationalized in 1992 because of excesses in property markets; that one of the triggers for the collapse in East and Southeast Asia in 1997–98 was excessive urban development in Thailand; that the commercial property-led Savings and Loan Crisis of 1987–90 in the United States saw several hundred financial institutions go belly-up at the cost of some US$200 billion to the US taxpayers (a situation that so exercised William Isaacs, then Chairman of the Federal Deposit Insurance Corporation, that in 1987 he threatened the American Bankers Association with nationalization unless they mended their ways)?[4]

Where were the World Bank economists when all this was going on? There have been hundreds of financial crises since 1973 (compared to very few prior to that) and quite a few of them have been property or urban development led. And it was pretty clear to almost anyone who thought about it, including, it turns out, Robert Shiller, that something was going badly wrong in US housing markets after 2000 or so. But he saw it as exceptional rather than systemic.[5] Shiller could well claim, of course, that all of the above examples were merely regional events. But then so, from the standpoint of the people of Brazil or China, was the crisis of 2007–09. The geographical epicentre was the US Southwest and Florida (with some spillover in Georgia) along with a few other hot spots (the grumbling foreclosure crises that began as early as 2005 in poor areas in older cities like Baltimore and Cleveland were too local and 'unimportant' because those affected were African-Americans and minorities). Internationally, Spain and Ireland were badly caught out, as was also, though to a lesser extent, Britain. But there were no serious problems in the property markets in France, Germany, the Netherlands, Poland or, at that time, throughout Asia.

A regional crisis centred in the United States went global, to be sure, in ways that did not happen in the cases of, say, Japan or Sweden in the early 1990s. But the Savings & Loan crisis centred on 1987 (the year of a serious stock crash that is still viewed as a totally separate incident) had global ramifications. The same was true of the much-neglected global property market crash of early 1973. Conventional wisdom has it that only the oil price-hike in the fall of 1973 mattered. But it turned out that the property crash preceded the oil price hike by six months or more and the recession was well under way by the fall. The boom can be measured by the fact that Real Estate Investment Trust Assets in the US grew from $2 billion in 1969 to $20 billion in 1973 and that commercial bank mortgage loans increased from $66.7 billion to $113.6 billion over the same period. The property market crash that then followed in the spring of 1973 spilled over (for obvious revenue reasons) into the fiscal crisis of local states (which would not have happened had the recession been only about oil prices). The subsequent New York City fiscal crisis of 1975 was hugely important because at that time it controlled one of the largest public budgets in the world (prompting pleas from the French President and the West German Chancellor to bail New York City out to avoid a global implosion in financial markets). New York then became the centre for the invention of neoliberal practices of gifting moral hazard to the banks and making the people pay up through the restructuring of municipal contracts and services. The impact of the most recent property market crash has also carried over into the virtual bankruptcy of states like California, creating huge stresses in state and municipal government finance and government employment almost everywhere in the US. The story of the New York City fiscal crisis of the 1970s eerily resembles that of the state of California, which today has the eighth largest public budget in the world.[6]

The National Bureau of Economic Research has recently unearthed yet another example of the role of property booms in sparking deep crises of capitalism. From a study of real estate data in the 1920s, Goetzmann and Newman 'conclude that publically issued real estate securities affected real estate construction activity in the 1920s and the breakdown in their valuation, through the mechanism of the collateral cycle, may have led to the subsequent stock market crash of 1929-30'. With respect to housing, Florida, then as now, was an intense centre of speculative development with the nominal value of a building permit increasing by 8,000 per cent between 1919 and 1925. Nationally, the estimates of increases in housing values were around 400 per cent over roughly the same period. But this was a sideshow compared to commercial development which was almost entirely centred on New York and Chicago, where all manner of financial supports and securitization procedures were concocted to fuel a boom 'matched only in the mid-2000s'. Even more telling is the graph Goetzmann and Newman compile on tall-building construction in New York City. The property booms that preceded the crash of 1929, 1973, 1987 and 2000, stand out like a pikestaff. The buildings we see around us in New York City, they poignantly note, represent 'more than an architectural movement; they were largely the manifestation of a widespread financial phenomenon'. Noting that real estate securities in the 1920s were every bit as 'toxic as they are now', they went on to conclude: 'The New York skyline is a stark reminder of securitization's ability to connect capital from a speculative public to building ventures. An increased understanding of the early real estate securities market has the potential to provide a valuable input when modelling for worst-case scenarios in the future. Optimism in financial markets has the power to raise steel, but it does not make a building pay.'[7]

Property market booms and busts are, clearly, inextricably intertwined with speculative financial flows and these booms and busts have serious consequences for the macro-economy in general as well as all manner of externality effects upon resource depletion and environmental degradation. Furthermore, the greater the share of property markets in GDP, then the more significant the connection between financing and investment in the built environment becomes as a potential source of macro crises. In the case of developing countries such as Thailand, where housing mortgages, if the World Bank Report is right, are equivalent to only 10 per cent of GDP, a property crash could certainly contribute to but not totally power a macro-economic collapse (of the sort that occurred in 1997-98), whereas in the United States, where housing mortgage debt is equivalent to 40 per cent of GDP, then it most certainly could – and did in fact generate the crisis of 2007-09.

THE MARXIST PERSPECTIVE

With bourgeois theory, if not totally blind, at best lacking in insights relating urban developments to macroeconomic disruptions, one would have thought that Marxist critics with their vaunted historical materialist methods would have had a field day with fierce denunciations of soaring rents and the savage dispossessions characteristic of what Marx and Engels referred to as the secondary forms of exploitation visited upon the working classes in their living places by merchant capitalists and landlords. They would have set the appropriation of space within the city through gentrification, high-end condo construction and 'disneyfication', against the barbaric homelessness, lack of affordable housing and degrading urban environments (both physical, as in air quality, and social, as in crumbling schools and so-called 'benign neglect' of education) for the mass of the population. There has been some of that in a restricted circle of Marxist urbanists (I count myself one). But in fact the structure of thinking within Marxism generally is distressingly similar to that within bourgeois economics. The urbanists are viewed as specialists while the truly significant core of macro-economic Marxist theorizing lies elsewhere. Again the fiction of a national economy takes precedence because that is where the data can most easily be found and, to be fair, some of the major policy decisions are taken. The role of the property market in creating the crisis conditions of 2007-9 and its aftermath of unemployment and austerity (much of it administered at the local and municipal level) is not well understood, because there has been no serious attempt to integrate an understanding of processes of urbanization and built environment formation into the general theory of the laws of motion of capital. As a consequence, many Marxist theorists, who love crises to death, tend to treat the recent crash as an obvious manifestation of their favoured version of Marxist crisis theory (be it falling rates of profit, underconsumption or whatever).

Marx is to some degree himself to blame, though unwittingly so, for this state of affairs. In the introduction to the *Grundrisse*, he states his objective in writing *Capital* is to explicate the general laws of motion of capital. This meant concentrating exclusively on the production and realization of surplus value while abstracting from and excluding what he called the 'particularities' of distribution (interest, rents, taxes and even actual wage and profit rates) since these were accidental, conjunctural and of the moment in space and time. He also abstracted from the specificities of exchange relations, such as supply and demand and the state of competition. When demand and supply are in equilibrium, he argued, they cease to explain anything while the coercive laws of competition function as the enforcer rather than the determinant of the general laws of motion of capital. This immediately provokes the thought of what happens when the enforcement mechanism is lacking, as happens under conditions of monopolization, and what happens when we include spatial competition in our thinking, which is, as has long been known, always a form of monopolistic competition (as in the case of inter-urban competition).

Finally, Marx depicts consumption as a 'singularity' (a very Spinoza-like conception that Hardt and Negri have been at pains recently to revive). As such it is chaotic, unpredictable and uncontrollable, and, therefore, in Marx's view, generally outside of the field of political economy (the study of use values, he declares on the first page of *Capital*, is the business of history and not of political economy). Marx also identified another level, that of the metabolic relation to nature, which is a universal condition of all forms of human society and therefore broadly irrelevant to an understanding of the general laws of motion of capital understood as a specific social and historical construct. Environmental issues have a shadowy presence throughout *Capital* for this reason (which does not imply that Marx thought them unimportant or insignificant, any more than he dismissed consumption as irrelevant in the grander scheme of things).[8] Throughout most of *Capital*, Marx pretty much sticks to the framework outlined in the *Grundrisse*. He lasers in on the generality of production of surplus value and excludes everything else. He recognizes from time to time that there are problems of so doing. There is, he notes, some 'double positing' going on – land, labour, money, commodities are crucial facts of production while interest, rents, wages and profits are excluded from the analysis as particularities of distribution!

The virtue of Marx's approach is that it allows a very clear account of the general laws of motion of capital to be constructed in a way that abstracts from the specific and particular conditions of his time (such as the crises of 1847–48 and 1857–58). This is why we can still read him today in ways that are relevant to our own times. But this approach imposes costs. To begin with, Marx makes clear that the analysis of an actually existing capitalist society/situation requires a dialectical integration of the universal, the general, the particular, and the singular aspects of a society construed as a working organic totality. We cannot hope, therefore, to explain actual events (such as the crisis of 2007-09) simply in terms of the general laws of motion of capital (this is one of my objections to those who try to cram the facts of the present crisis into some theory of the falling rate of profit). But, conversely, we cannot attempt such an explanation without reference to the general laws of motion either (though Marx himself appears to do so in his account in *Capital* of the 'independent and autonomous' financial and commercial crisis of 1847–48 or even more dramatically in his historical studies of the *Eighteenth Brumaire* and *Class Struggles in France,* where the general laws of motion of capital are never mentioned).[9]

Secondly, the abstractions within Marx's chosen level of generality start to fracture as the argument in *Capital* progresses. There are many examples of this, but the one that is most conspicuous and in any case most germane to the argument here, relates to Marx's handling of the credit system. Several times in volume 1 and repeatedly in volume 2, Marx invokes the credit system only to lay it aside as a fact of distribution that he is not prepared yet to confront. The general laws of motion he studies in volume 2, particularly those of fixed capital circulation and working periods, production periods, circulation times and turnover times, all end up not only invoking but *necessitating* the credit system. He gets very explicit on this point. When commenting on how the money capital advanced must always be greater than that applied in surplus value production in order to deal with differential turnover times, he notes how changes in turnover times can 'set free' some of the money earlier advanced. 'This money capital that is set free by the mechanism of the turnover movement (together with the money capital set free by the successive reflux of the fixed capital and that needed for variable capital in every labour process) must play a significant role, as soon as the credit system has developed, *and must also form one of the foundations for this*.'[10] From this and other similar comments it becomes clear that the credit system becomes absolutely necessary for capital circulation and that some accounting of the credit system has to be incorporated into the general laws of motion of capital. This poses a serious problem because when we get to the analysis of the credit system in volume 3, we find that the interest rate is set by supply and demand and by the state of competition, two specificities that have been earlier totally excluded from the theoretical level of generality at which Marx works.

I mention this because the significance of the rules that Marx imposed upon his enquiries in *Capital* has largely been ignored. When these rules necessarily get not only bent but broken, as happens in the case of credit and interest, then new prospects for theorizing are opened up that go beyond the insights that Marx has already produced. Marx actually recognizes this might happen at the very outset of his endeavours. In the *Grundrisse*, he thus says of consumption, the most recalcitrant of his categories for analysis given the singularities involved, that while it, like the study of use values, 'actually belongs outside of economics' the possibility exists for consumption to react 'in turn upon the point of departure (production) and initiate the whole process anew'.[11] This is particularly the case with productive consumption, the labour process itself. Tronti and those who followed in his footsteps, such as Negri, are therefore perfectly correct to see the labour process as itself constituted as a singularity – chaotic, hard to discipline, unpredictable and therefore always potentially dangerous for capital – internalized within the general laws of motion of capital![12] The legendary difficulties faced by capitalists as they seek to mobilize the 'animal spirits' of the workers to produce surplus value signals the existence of this singularity in the heart of the production process (this is nowhere more obvious than in the construction industry, as we will see). Internalizing the credit system and the relation between the rate of interest and the rate of profit within the general laws of production, circulation and realization of capital, is likewise a disruptive necessity if we are to bring Marx's theoretical apparatus more acutely to bear on actual events.

The integration of credit into the general theory has to be carefully done, however, in ways that preserve, albeit in a transformed state, the theoretical insights already gained. With regards to the credit system, for example, we cannot treat it simply as an entity in itself, a kind of efflorescence located on Wall Street or in the City of London that is free floating above the grounded activities on Main Street. A lot of credit-based activity may indeed be speculative froth and a disgusting excrescence of human lust for gold and pure money power. But much of it is fundamental and absolutely necessary to the functioning of capital. The boundaries between what is necessary and what is (a) necessarily fictitious (as in the case of state and mortgage debt) and (b) pure excess, are not easy to define.

Clearly, to try to analyze the dynamics of the recent crisis and its aftermath without reference to the credit system (with mortgages standing at 40 per cent of GDP in the US), consumerism (70 per cent of the driving force in the US economy compared to 35 per cent in China) and the state of competition (monopoly power in financial, real estate, retailing and many other markets) would be a ridiculous enterprise. $1.4 trillion in mortgages, many of them toxic, are sitting on the secondary markets of Fannie Mae and Freddy Mac in the United States thus forcing the government to allocate $400 billion to a potential rescue effort (with around $142 billion already spent). To understand this, we need to unpack what Marx might mean by the category of 'fictitious capital' and its connectivity to land and property markets. We need a way to understand how securitization, as Goetzmann and Newman put it, connects 'capital from a speculative public to building ventures'. For was it not speculation in the values of land and housing prices and rents that played a fundamental role in the formation of this crisis?

Fictitious capital, for Marx, is not a figment of some Wall Street trader's cocaine addled brain. It is a fetish construct which means, given Marx's characterization of fetishism in volume 1 of *Capital*, that it is real enough but that it is a surface phenomenon that disguises something important about underlying social relations. When a bank lends to the state and receives interest in return, it appears as if there is something productive going on within the state that is actually producing value when most (but not all, as I shall shortly show) of what goes on within the state (like fighting wars) has nothing to do with value production. When the bank lends to a consumer to buy a house and receives a flow of interest in return, it makes it seem as if something is going on in the house that is directly producing value when that is not the case. When banks take up bond issues to construct hospitals, universities, schools and the like in return for interest it seems as if value is being directly produced in those institutions when it is not. When banks lend to purchase land and property in search of extracting rents, then the distributive category of rent becomes absorbed into the flow of fictitious capital circulation.[13] When banks lend to other banks or when the Central Bank lends to the commercial banks who lend to land speculators looking to appropriate rents, then fictitious capital looks more and more like an infinite regression of fictions built upon fictions. These are all examples of fictitious capital flows. And it is these flows that convert real into unreal estate.

Marx's point is that the interest that is paid comes from somewhere else – taxation or direct extractions on surplus value production or levies on revenues (wages and profits). And for Marx, of course, the only place where value and surplus value is created is in the labour process of production. What goes on in fictitious capital circulation may be socially necessary to sustaining capitalism. It may be part of the necessary costs of production and reproduction. Secondary forms of surplus value can be extracted by capitalist enterprises through the exploitation of workers employed by retailers, banks and hedge funds. But Marx's point is that if there is no value and surplus value being produced in production in general, then these sectors cannot exist by themselves. If no shirts and shoes are produced what would retailers sell?

There is, however, a caveat that is terribly important. Some of the flow of fictitious capital can indeed be associated with value creation. When I convert my mortgaged house into a sweatshop employing illegal immigrants, the house becomes fixed capital in production. When the state builds roads and other infrastructures that function as collective means of production for capital, then these have to be categorized as 'productive state expenditures'. When the hospital or university becomes the site for innovation and design of new drugs, equipment and the like, it becomes a site of production. Marx would not be fazed by these caveats at all. As he says of fixed capital, whether something functions as fixed capital or not depends upon its use and not upon its physical qualities.[14] Fixed capital declines when textile lofts are converted into condominiums while micro-finance converts peasant huts into (far cheaper) fixed capital of production!

Much of the value and surplus value created in production is siphoned off to pass, by all manner of complicated paths, through fictitious channels. And when banks lend to other banks, it is clear that all manner of both socially unnecessary side-payments and speculative movements become possible, built upon the perpetually shifting terrain of fluctuating asset values. Those asset values depend upon a critical process of 'capitalization'. A revenue stream from some asset, such as land, property, a stock, or whatever, is assigned a capital value at which it can be traded, depending upon the interest and discount rates determined by supply and demand conditions in the money market. How to value such assets when there is no market for them became a huge problem in 2008 and it has not gone away. The question of how toxic the assets held by Fannie Mae really are gives almost everyone a headache (there is an important echo here of the capital value controversy that erupted and got promptly buried, like all manner of other inconvenient truths, in conventional economic theory in the early 1970s).[15]

The problem that the credit system poses is that it is vital to the production, circulation and realization of capital flows at the same time as it is the pinnacle of all manner of speculative and other 'insane forms'. It is this that led Marx to characterize Isaac Pereire, who, with his brother Emile, was one of the masters of the speculative reconstruction of urban Paris under Haussmann, as having 'the nicely mixed character of swindler and prophet'.[16]

CAPITAL ACCUMULATION THROUGH URBANIZATION

I have argued at length elsewhere that urbanization has been a key means for the absorption of capital and labour surpluses throughout capitalism's history.[17] I have long argued it has a very particular relation to the absorption of overaccumulating capital for very specific reasons that have to do with the long working periods, turnover times and the lifetimes of investments in the built environment. It also has a geographical specificity such that the production of space and of spatial monopolies becomes integral to the dynamics of accumulation, not simply by virtue of the changing patterns of commodity flows over space but also by virtue of the very nature of the created and produced spaces and places over which such movements occur. But precisely because all of this activity – which, by the way, is a hugely important site for value and surplus value production – is so long term, it calls for some combination of finance capital and state engagements as absolutely fundamental to its functioning. This activity is clearly speculative in the long term and always runs the risk of replicating, at a much later date and on a magnified scale, the very overaccumulation conditions that it initially helps relieve. Hence the crisis-prone character of urban and other forms of physical infrastructural investments (transcontinental railroads and highways, dams, and the like).

The cyclical character of such investments has been well documented for the nineteenth century in the meticulous work of Brinley Thomas.[18] But the theory of construction business cycles became neglected after 1945 or so, in part because state-led Keynesian style interventions were deemed effective in flattening them out. The construction business cycle (circa 18 years in the USA) effectively disappeared.[19] But the gradual breakdown of systemic Keynesian contra-cyclical interventions after the mid-1970s would suggest that a return to construction business cycles was more than a little likely. The data suggest that while fluctuations in construction have remained muted, asset value bubbles have become much more volatile than in the past (though the NBER accounts of the 1920s might be taken as contrary evidence to that view). The cyclical movements have also come to exhibit a more complicated geographical configuration, even within countries (e.g. the US South and West exhibiting different rhythms to the Northeast and Midwest).

Without a general perspective of this sort, we cannot even begin to understand the dynamics that led into the catastrophe of housing markets and urbanization in 2008 in certain regions and cities of the United States as well as in Spain, Ireland and the United Kingdom. By the same token we cannot understand some of the paths that are currently being taken, particularly in China, to get out of the mess that was fundamentally produced elsewhere. For in the same way that Brinley Thomas documents contra-cyclical movements between Britain and the United States in the nineteenth century, such that a boom in residential construction in one place was balanced by a crash in the other, so we now see a crash in construction in the United States and much of Europe being counterbalanced by a huge urbanization and infrastructural investment boom centred in China (with several offshoots elsewhere, particularly in the so-called BRIC countries). And just to get the macro-picture connection right, we should immediately note that the United States and Europe are mired in low growth while China is registering a 10 per cent growth rate (with the other BRIC countries not far behind).

The pressure for the housing market and urban development in the United States to absorb overaccumulating capital through speculative activity began to build in the mid 1990s and fiercely accelerated after the end of the high-tech bubble and the stock market crash of 2001. The political pressures put on respectable financial institutions, including Fannie Mae and Freddie Mac, to lower their lending standards to accommodate the housing boom, coupled with the low interest rates favoured by Greenspan at the Fed, unquestionably fuelled the boom. But as Groezmann and Newman remark, finance (backed by the state) can build cities and suburbs but they cannot necessarily make them pay. So what fuelled the demand?

To understand the dynamics we have to understand how productive and fictitious capital circulation combine within the credit system in the context of property markets. Financial institutions lend to developers, landowners and construction companies to build, say, suburban tract housing around San Diego or condos in Florida and Southern Spain. In boom times, construction accounts directly for some 7 per cent of employment and more than double that when building materials suppliers and all the legal/financial services that rotate around the real estate industry are counted in. The viability of this sector presumes, however, that value can be realized. This is where fictitious capital comes in. Money is lent to purchasers who presumably have the ability to pay out of their revenues (wages or profits).

The financial system thus regulates to a considerable degree both the supply of and demand for tract housing and condos. This difference is similar to that between what Marx identifies in *Capital* as 'loan capital' for production and the discounting of bills of exchange which facilitates the realization of values in the market.[20] In the case of housing in Southern California, the same finance company often furnished the finance to build and the finance to buy what had been built. As happens with labour markets, capital has the power to manipulate both supply and demand (which is totally at odds with the idea of the freely functioning markets that the World Bank Report supposes to be in place).[21]

But the relationship is lop-sided. While bankers, developers and construction companies easily combine to forge a class alliance (one that often dominates what is called 'the urban growth machine' both politically and economically[22]), consumer mortgages are singular and dispersed and often involve loans to those who occupy a different class or, particularly in the United States but not in Ireland, racial or ethnic position. With securitization of mortgages, the finance company could simply pass any risk on to someone else, which is, of course precisely what they did, after having creamed off all the origination and legal fees that they could. If the financier has to choose between the bankruptcy of a developer because of failures of realization or the bankruptcy and foreclosure on the purchaser of housing (particularly if the purchaser is from the lower classes or from a racial or ethnic minority) then it is fairly clear which way the financial system will lean. Class and racial prejudices are invariably involved.

Furthermore, the asset markets constituted by housing and land inevitably have a Ponzi character even without a Bernie Madoff at the top. I buy a property and the property prices go up and a rising market encourages others to buy. When the pool of truly credit-worthy buyers dries up, then why not go further down the income layers to higher risk consumers ending up with no income and no asset buyers who might gain by flipping the property as prices rise? And so it goes until the bubble pops. Financial institutions have tremendous incentives to sustain the bubble as long as they can. The problem is that they often can't get off the train before it wrecks because the train is accelerating so quickly. This is where the disparate turnover times, which Marx so cannily analyses in volume 2 of *Capital*, also become crucial.[23] Contracts that finance construction are drawn up long before sales can begin. The time-lags are often substantial. The Empire State Building in New York opened on May Day 1931, almost two years after the stock market crash and more than three years after the real estate crash. The Twin Towers opened shortly after the crash of 1973 (and for years could find no private tenants) and now the downtown rebuilding on the 9/11 site is about to come on line when commercial property values are depressed! Since the realization of the values produced is so crucial to the recuperation of the initial loans then finance companies will go to any lengths to stimulate the market beyond its real capacity.

But there are longer-term issues here that also need to be taken into account. If the NBER papers are correct, the collapse of the construction boom after 1928, which was manifest as a $2 billion drop off (huge for the time) in housing construction and a collapse of housing starts to less than 10 per cent of their former volume in the larger cities, played an important but still not well-understood role in the 1929 crash. A Wikipedia entry notes: 'devastating was the disappearance of 2 million high paying jobs in the construction trades, plus the loss of profits and rents that humbled many landlords and real estate investors'.[24] This surely had implications for confidence in the stock market more generally. Small wonder that there were desperate subsequent attempts by the Roosevelt administration to revive the housing sector. To that end a raft of reforms in housing mortgage finance was implemented culminating in the creation of a secondary mortgage market through the founding of the Federal National Mortgage Association (Fannie Mae) in 1938. The task of Fannie Mae was to insure mortgages and to allow banks and other lenders to pass the mortgages on, thus providing much needed liquidity to the housing market. These institutional reforms were later to play a vital role in financing the suburbanization of the United States after World War II.

While necessary, they were not sufficient to put housing construction onto a different plane in US economic development. All sorts of tax incentives (such as the mortgage interest tax deduction) along with the GI Bill and a very positive housing act of 1947, which declared the right of all Americans to live in 'decent housing in a decent living environment', were devised to promote home ownership for political as well as economic reasons. Homeownership was widely promoted as central to the 'American Dream' and it rose from just above 40 per cent of the population in the 1940s to more than 60 per cent by the 1960s and close to 70 per cent at its peak in 2004 (as of 2010 it had fallen to 66 per cent). Home ownership may be a deeply held cultural value in the United States but cultural values of this sort always flourish best when promoted and subsidized by state policies. The stated reasons for such policies are all those that the World Bank Report cites. But the political reason is rarely now acknowledged: as was openly noted in the 1930s, debt encumbered homeowners do not go on strike![25] The military personnel returning from service in World War II would have constituted a social and political threat had they returned to unemployment and depression. What better way to kill two birds with one stone: revive the economy through massive housing construction and suburbanization and co-opt the better paid workers into conservative politics by homeownership!

During the 1950s and the 1960s these policies worked, both from the political and the macro-economic viewpoints, since they underpinned two decades of very strong growth in the United States and the effects of that growth spilled over globally. The problem was that the urbanization process was as geographically uneven as were the income streams that flowed to different segments of the working class. While the suburbs flourished, the inner cities stagnated and declined. While the white working class flourished, in relative terms the impacted inner city minorities – African-American in particular – did not. The result was a whole sequence of inner-city uprisings – Detroit, Watts, culminating in spontaneous uprisings in some forty cities across the United States in the wake of the assassination of Martin Luther King in 1968. Something that came to be known as 'the urban crisis' was there for all to see and easily name (even though it was not from the macro-economic standpoint, a crisis of urbanization). Massive federal funds were released to deal with it after 1968 until Nixon declared the crisis over (for fiscal reasons) in the recession of 1973.[26]

The side-bar to all of this, was that Fannie Mae became a government sponsored private enterprise in 1968 and, after it was provided with a 'competitor', the Federal Home Mortgage Corporation (Freddie Mac) in 1972, both institutions played a hugely important and eventually destructive role in promoting home ownership and sustaining housing construction over nearly fifty years. Home mortgage debt now accounts for some 40 per cent of the accumulated private debt of the United States, much of which, as we have seen, is toxic. And both Fannie Mae and Freddie Mac have passed back into government control. What to do about them is an intensely debated political question (as are the subsidies to home ownership) in relation to US indebtedness more generally. Whatever happens will have major consequences for the future of the housing sector in particular and urbanization more generally in relation to capital accumulation within the United States.

The current signs in the United States are not encouraging. The housing sector is not reviving. There are signs it is heading for a dreaded 'double-dip' recession as Federal moneys dry up and unemployment remains high. Housing starts have plunged for the first time to below pre-1940s levels. As of March 2011, the unemployment rate in construction stood above 20 per cent compared to a rate of 9.7 per cent in manufacturing that was very close to the national average. In the Great Depression, more than a quarter of construction workers remained unemployed as late as 1939. Getting them back to work was a crucial target for public interventions (such as the WPA). Attempts by the Obama Administration to create a stimulus package for infrastructural investments have largely been frustrated by Republican opposition. To make matters worse, the condition of state and local finances in the US is so dire as to result in lay-offs and furloughs as well as savage cuts in urban services. The collapse of the housing market and the fall of housing prices by 20 per cent or more nation-wide have put a huge dent in local finances which rely heavily on property taxes. An urban fiscal crisis is brewing as state and municipal governments cut back and construction languishes.

On top of all this comes a class politics of austerity that is being pursued for political and not for economic reasons. Radical right wing Republican administrations at the state and local levels are using the so-called debt crisis to savage government programmes and reduce state and local government employment. This has, of course, been a long-standing tactic of a capital-inspired assault on government programmes more generally. Reagan cut taxes on the wealthy from 72 per cent to around 30 per cent and launched a debt-financed arms race with the Soviet Union. The debt soared under Reagan as a result. As his budget director, David Stockman, later noted, running up the debt became a convenient excuse to go after government regulation (e.g. the environment) and social programmes, in effect externalizing the costs of environmental degradation and social reproduction. President Bush Jnr. faithfully followed suit, with his Vice-President, Dick Cheney, proclaiming that 'Reagan taught us that deficits do not matter'.[27] Tax cuts for the rich, two unfunded wars in Iraq and Afghanistan, and a huge gift to big pharma through a state funded prescription drug programme, turned what has been a budget surplus under Clinton into a sea of red ink, enabling the Republican party and conservative Democrats later to do big capital's bidding, and go as far as possible in externalizing those costs that capital never wants to bear: the costs of environmental degradation and social reproduction.

The assault on the environment and the well-being of the people is palpable and it is taking place for political and class, not economic reasons. It is inducing, as David Stockman has very recently noted, a state of plain class war. As Warren Buffett also put it, 'sure there is class war, and it is my class, the rich, who are making it and we are winning'.[28] The only question is: when will the people start to wage class war back? And one of the places to start would be to focus on the rapidly degrading qualities of urban life, through foreclosures, the persistence of predatory practices in urban housing markets, reductions in services and above all the lack of viable employment opportunities in urban labour markets almost everywhere, with some cities (Detroit being the sad poster child) utterly bereft of employment prospects. The crisis now is as much an urban crisis as it ever was.

PREDATORY URBAN PRACTICES.

In *The Communist Manifesto*, Marx and Engels note in passing that no sooner does the worker receive 'his wages in cash, than he is set upon by the other portions of the bourgeoisie, the landlord, the shopkeeper, the pawnbroker, etc.'.[29] Marxists have traditionally relegated such forms of exploitation, and the class struggles (for such they are) that inevitably arise around them, to the shadows of their theorizing as well as to the margins of their politics. But I here want to argue that they constitute, at least in the advanced capitalist economies, a vast terrain of accumulation by dispossession through which money is sucked up into the circulation of fictitious capital to underpin the vast fortunes made from within the financial system.

The predatory practices that were omnipresent within the sub-prime lending field before the crash were legendary in their proportions. Before the crisis broke, the low income African-American population of the United States was estimated to have lost somewhere between $71 and $93 billion in asset values through predatory sub-prime practices. Contemporaneously, the bonuses on Wall Street were soaring on unheard of profit rates from pure financial manipulations, particularly those associated with the securitization of mortgages. The inference is that by various hidden channels massive transfers of wealth from the poor to the rich were occurring, beyond those since documented in the plainly shady practices of mortgage companies like Countrywide, through financial manipulations in housing markets.[30]

What has happened since is even more astonishing. Many of the foreclosures (over a million during the last year) turn out to have been illegal if not downright fraudulent, leading a Congressman from Florida to write to the Florida Supreme Court Justice that 'if the reports I am hearing are true, the illegal foreclosures taking place represent the largest seizure of private property ever attempted by banks and government entities'.[31] Attorneys General in all fifty states are now investigating the problem, but, (as might be expected) they all seem anxious to close out the investigations in as summary a way as possible at the price of a few financial settlements (but no restitutions of illegally seized properties). Certainly, no one is likely to go to jail for it, even though there is clear evidence of systematic forgery of legal documents.

Predatory practices of this sort have been longstanding. So let me give some instances from Baltimore. Shortly after arriving in the city in 1969, I became involved in a study of inner city housing provision that focused on the role of different actors – landlords, tenants and homeowners, the brokers and lenders, the FHA, the city authorities (Housing Code Enforcement in particular) – in the production of the terrifying rat-infested inner-city living conditions in the areas wracked by uprisings in the wake of the assassination of Martin Luther King. The vestiges of redlining of areas of low-income African-American populations denied credit was etched into the map of the city, but exclusions were by then justified as a legitimate response to high credit risk and not supposedly to race. In several areas of the city, active blockbusting practices were to be found. This generated high profits for ruthless real estate companies. But for this to work, African-Americans had also to somehow acquire access to mortgage finance when they were all lumped together as a high credit risk population. This could be done by way of something called the 'Land Installment Contract'. In effect, African-Americans were 'helped' by property owners who acted as intermediaries to the credit markets and took out a mortgage in their own names. After a few years when some of the principle plus the interest had been paid down, thus proving the family's credit worthiness, the title was supposed to be passed on to the resident with help from the friendly property owner and local mortgage institution. Some takers made it (though usually in neighbourhoods that were declining in value) but in unscrupulous hands (and there were many in Baltimore though not, it appears, so many in Chicago where this system was also common) this could be a particularly predatory form of accumulation by dispossession.[32] The property owner was permitted to charge fees to cover property taxes, administrative and legal costs, and the like. These fees (sometimes exorbitant) could be added to the principal of the mortgage. After years of steady payment, many families found they owed more on the principal on the house than they did at the start. If they failed once to pay the higher payments after interest rates rose, the contract was voided and families were evicted. Such practices caused something of a scandal. A civil rights action was started against the worst landlord offenders. But it failed because those who had signed on to the land installment contract had simply not read the small print or had their own lawyer (which poor people rarely have) to read it for them (the small print is in any case incomprehensible to ordinary mortals – have you ever read the small print on your credit card?).

Predatory practices of this sort never went away. The land-installment contract was displaced by practices of 'flipping' in the 1980s (a property dealer would buy a run-down house cheaply, put in a few cosmetic repairs – much overvalued – and arrange 'favourable' mortgage finance for the unsuspecting buyer who lived in the house only so long as the roof did not fall in or the furnace blow up). And when the sub-prime market began to form in the 1990s, cities like Baltimore, Cleveland, Detroit, Buffalo and the like, became major centres for a growing wave of accumulation by dispossession ($70 billion or more nationwide). Baltimore eventually launched a Civil Rights lawsuit after the crash of 2008 against Wells Fargo over its discriminatory sub-prime lending practices (reverse redlining in which people were steered into taking sub-prime rather than conventional loans) in which African-Americans and single-headed households – women – were systematically exploited. Almost certainly the suit will fail (although at the third iteration it has been allowed to go forward in the courts) since it will be almost impossible to prove intent based on race as opposed to credit risk. As usual, the incomprehensible small print allows for a lot (consumers beware!). Cleveland took a more nuanced path: sue the finance companies for the creation of a public nuisance because the landscape was littered with foreclosed houses that required city action to board them up!

THE CHINA STORY

In so far as there has been any exit from the crisis this time, it is notable that the housing and property boom in China along with a huge wave of debt-financed infrastructural investments there have taken a leading role not only in stimulating their internal market (and mopping up unemployment in the export industries) but also in stimulating the economies that are tightly integrated into the China trade such as Australia and Chile with their raw materials and Germany with its high speed rail and automotive exports. (In the United States, on the other hand, construction has been slow to revive with the unemployment rate in construction, as I earlier noted, more than twice the national average.) Urban investments typically take a long time to produce and an even longer time to mature. It is always difficult to determine, therefore, when an overaccumulation of capital has been or is about to be transformed into an overaccumulation of investments in the built environment. The likelihood of overshooting, as regularly happened with the railways in the nineteenth century and as the long history of building cycles and crashes shows, is very high.

The fearlessness of the pell-mell urbanization and infrastructural investment boom that is completely reconfiguring the geography of the Chinese national space rest in part on the ability of the central government to intervene arbitrarily in the banking system if anything goes wrong. A relatively mild (by comparison) recession in property markets in the late 1990s in leading cities such as Shanghai, left the banks holding title to a vast array of 'non-earning assets' ('toxic' we call them). Unofficially, estimates ran as high as 40 per cent of bank loans were non-earning.[33] The response of the central government was to use their abundant foreign exchange reserves to re-capitalize the banks (a Chinese version of what later became known as the controversial Troubled Asset Relief Program – TARP – in the United States). It is known that the state used some $45 billion of its foreign exchange reserves for this purpose in the late 1990s and it may have indirectly used much more. But as China's institutions evolve in ways more consistent with global financial markets, so it becomes harder for the central government to control what is happening in the financial sector.

The reports now available from China make it seem rather too similar for comfort to the American Southwest and Florida in the 2000s, or Florida in the 1920s. Since the general privatization of housing in China in 1998, housing construction has taken off in a spectacular (and speculative) fashion. Housing prices are reported to have risen 140 per cent nationwide since 2007 and as much as 800 per cent in the main cities such as Beijing and Shanghai over the last five years. In the latter city property prices are reputed to have doubled over the last year alone. The average apartment price there now stands at $500,000 and even in second tier cities a typical home 'costs about 25 times the average income of residents', which is clearly unsustainable. One consequence is the emergence of strong inflationary pressures. 'Too much of the country's growth continues to be tied to inflationary spending on real estate development and government investment in roads, railways and other multibillion dollar infrastructure projects. In the first quarter of 2011, fixed asset investment – a broad measure of building activity – jumped 25 per cent from the period a year earlier, and real estate investment soared 37 per cent' according to government statements.[34]

Extensive land acquisitions and displacements of legendary proportions in some of the major cities (as many as 3 million people displaced in Beijing over the last ten years) indicate an active economy of dispossession booming alongside this huge urbanization push throughout the whole of China. The forced displacements and dispossessions are probably the single most important cause of a rising tide of popular and sometimes violent protests. On the other hand, the land sales to developers have been providing a lucrative cash cow to fill local government coffers. Only in early 2011 did the central government demand they be curbed in order to stifle what many commentators saw as the out-of-control property market. The result, however, was to plunge many municipalities into fiscal difficulties.

Whole new cities, with hardly any residents or real activities as yet, can now be found in the Chinese interior, prompting a curious advertising programme in the United States business press to attract investors and companies to this new urban frontier of global capitalism.[35] And as happened in the post–World War II suburbanization boom in the United States, when all the ancillary housing appliances and appurtenances are added in, it becomes clear that the Chinese urbanization boom is playing a highly significant if not driving role in stimulating the revival of global economic growth. 'By some estimates, China consumes up to 50 per cent of key global commodities and materials such as cement, iron ore, steel and coal, and Chinese real estate is the main driver of that demand'.[36] Since at least half of the steel consumption ends up in the built environment, this means that a quarter of the global steel output is now absorbed by this activity alone. China is not the only place where such a property boom can be identified. All of the so-called BRIC countries seem to be following suit. Property prices thus doubled in both Sao Paulo and Rio last year and in India and Russia similar conditions prevail. But all of these countries are experiencing high aggregate growth rates.

Attempts by the Chinese central government to control their boom and quell inflationary pressures by raising step-wise the reserve requirements of the banks have not been too successful. A 'shadow-banking system' is rumoured to have emerged, strongly connected to land and property investments. The result of accelerating inflation has been proliferating unrest. Reports are now coming in of work actions by taxi drivers and truckers (in Shanghai), alongside sudden full-blown factory strikes in the industrial areas of Guangdong in response to low wages, poor working conditions and escalating prices. Official reports of unrest have risen dramatically and wage adjustments have been occurring along with government policies designed to confront the swelling unrest, and, perhaps, stimulate the internal market as a substitute for riskier and stagnant export markets (Chinese consumerism currently accounts for only 35 per cent of GDP as opposed to 70 per cent in the United States).

All of this has to be understood, however, against the background of the concrete steps the Chinese government took to deal with the crisis of 2007-09. The main impact of the crisis on China was the sudden collapse of export markets (particularly that of the United States) and a 20 per cent fall off in exports in early 2008. Several reasonably reliable estimates put the number of jobs lost in the export sector in the 20 million range over a very short period in 2008. Yet the IMF could report that the net job loss in China as of fall 2009 was only 3 million.[37] Some of the difference between gross and net job losses may have been due to the return of unemployed urban migrants to their rural base. But the rest of it was almost certainly due to the government's implementation of a massive Keynesian-style stimulus programme of urban and infrastructural investment. Nearly $600 billion was made available by the central government while the centrally-controlled banks were instructed to lend extensively to all manner of local development projects (including the property sector) as a way to mop up surplus labour. This massive programme was designed to lead the way towards economic recovery. And it appears to have been at least minimally successful in its immediate objectives if the IMF figures on net job loss are correct.

The big question, of course, is whether or not these state expenditures fall in the category of 'productive' or not, and, if so, productive of what and for whom? There is no question that the Chinese national space could benefit from deeper and more efficient spatial integration and on the surface at least the vast wave of infrastructural investments and urbanization projects would appear to do just that, linking the interior to the wealthier coastal regions and the North with the South. At the metropolitan level, the processes of urban growth and urban regeneration would also appear to bring modernist techniques to urbanization along with a diversification of activities (including all the mandatory cultural and knowledge industry institutions, exemplified by the spectacular Shanghai Expo, that are so characteristic of neoliberal urbanization in the United States and Europe). The absorption of surplus liquidity and overaccumulated capital at a time when profitable opportunities are otherwise hard to come by has certainly sustained capital accumulation, not only in China but also around much of the rest of the globe.

In some ways, China's development mimics that of the post-World-War-II United States, where the interstate highway system integrated the South and the West and this, coupled with suburbanization, then played a crucial role in sustaining both employment and capital accumulation. But the parallel is instructive in other ways. United States development after 1945 was not only profligate in its use of energy and land, but it also generated, as we have seen, a distinctive crisis for marginalized and excluded urban populations, that elicited a raft of policy responses during the late 1960s. All of this faded after the crash of 1973, when President Nixon declared in his State of the Union Address that the urban crisis was over and that federal funding would be withdrawn. The effect at the municipal level was to create a crisis in urban services with all of the terrifying consequences of degeneration in public schooling, public health and the availability of affordable housing from the late 1970s onwards.

The investment strategy in China is in danger also of falling into such a lop-sided path. A high-speed train between Shanghai and Beijing is fine for the business people and the upper middle class but it does not constitute the kind of affordable transport system to take workers back to their rural origins for the Chinese New Year. Similarly, high-rise apartment blocks, gated communities and golf courses for the rich along with high-end shopping malls do not really help to re-constitute an adequate daily life for the impoverished masses. The same question is arising in India as well as in the innumerable cities around the world where there are high concentrations of marginalized populations, from the restive suburbs of Paris to social movements agitating in Argentina, South Africa or throughout North Africa. In fact the issue of how to deal with impoverished, insecure and excluded workers that now constitute a majoritarian and putatively dominant power block in many capitalist cities could (and in some instances has already) become a major political problem, so much so that military planning is now highly focused on how to deal with restive and potentially revolutionary urban-based movements.

But in the Chinese case there is one interesting wrinkle to this narrative. In some respects the trajectory of development since liberalization began in 1979, rests on a simple thesis that decentralization is one of the best ways to exercise centralized control. The idea was to liberate regional, local and even villages and townships to seek their own betterment within a framework of centralized control and market coordinations. Successful solutions arrived at through local initiatives then became the basis for the re-formulation of central government policies. Reports emanating from China suggest that the power transition anticipated for 2012 is faced with an intriguing choice. Attention is focused on the city of Chongqing, where a shift away from market-based policies back onto a path of state-led redistribution has been under way for some time, accompanied by 'an arsenal of Maoist slogans'. In this model 'everything links back to the issue of poverty and inequality', as the municipal government 'has turned the market profits of state-owned enterprises toward traditional socialist projects, using their revenues to fund the construction of affordable housing and transportation infrastructure'.[38] The housing initiative entails a massive construction programme designed to provide cheap apartments to a third of the 30 million residents in the city region, where 20 satellite towns are expected to be built, each with a population of 300,000, of which 50,000 people will live in state-subsidized housing. The aim (contrary to World Bank advice) is to reduce the spiralling social inequalities that have arisen over the last two decades across China. It is an antidote to the private developer led projects of gated communities for the rich. This turn back to a socialist redistributive agenda, using the private sector for public purposes, is now providing a model for the central government to follow. It neatly solves the capital surplus absorption problem at the same time as it offers a way to both further urbanize the rural population and to dispel popular discontent by offering reasonable housing security to the less well off. There are echoes of US urban policies after 1945. Keep economic growth on track while co-opting potentially restive populations. The scale of land acquisition entailed in such a programme is, however, already sparking unrest and opposition from those being displaced.

Rival market-based paths exist elsewhere, particularly in the coastal and southern cities, such as Shenzhen. Here the emphasis is more upon political liberalization and what sounds like bourgeois urban democracy alongside a deepening of free-market initiatives. In this case, rising social inequality is accepted as a necessary cost of sustained economic growth and competitiveness. Which way the central government will lean is impossible at this point to predict. But the key point is the role of urban-based initiatives in pioneering the way towards different futures. How then might the left in general relate – both in theory and in political practices – to such a prospect?

TOWARDS URBAN REVOLUTION?

The city is a terrain where anti-capitalist struggles have always flourished. The history of such struggles, from the Paris Commune through the Shanghai Commune, the Seattle General Strike, The Tucuman uprising and the Prague Spring to the more general urban-based movements of 1968 (which we now see faintly echoed in Cairo and Madison) is stunning. But it is a history that is also troubled by political and tactical complications that have led many on the left to underestimate and misunderstand the potential and the potency of urban-based movements, to often see them as separate from class struggle and therefore devoid of revolutionary potential. And when such events do take on iconic status, as in the case of the Paris Commune, they are typically claimed as one of 'the greatest proletarian uprisings' in world history, even as they were as much about reclaiming the right to the city as they were about revolutionizing class relations in production.

Anti-capitalist struggle is about the abolition of that class relation between capital and labour in production that permits the production and appropriation of surplus value by capital. The ultimate aim of anti-capitalist struggle is, quite simply, the abolition of that class relation. Even and particularly when this struggle has to be seen, as it invariably does, through the prisms of race, ethnicity, sexuality and gender, it must eventually reach into the very guts of what a capitalist system is about and wrench out the cancerous tumour of class relations at its very centre.

It would be a truthful caricature to say that the Marxist left has long privileged the industrial workers of the world as the vanguard agent that leads class struggle through the dictatorship of the proletariat to a world where state and class whither away. It is also a truthful caricature to say that things have never worked out that way. Marx argued that the class relation of domination had to be displaced by the associated workers controlling their own production processes and protocols. From this derives a long history of political pursuit of worker control, autogestion, worker cooperatives and the like.[39] Most attempts of this sort have not proven viable in the long run, in spite of the noble efforts and sacrifices that kept them going in the face of often fierce hostilities and active repressions.[40] The main reason for the long-run failure of these initiatives is simple enough. As Marx shows in the second volume of *Capital*, the circulation of capital comprises three distinctive circulatory processes, those of money, productive and commodity capitals. No one circulatory process can survive or even exist without the others: they intermingle and co-determine each other. By the same token, no one circulation process can be changed without changing the others. Workers control in relatively isolated production units can rarely survive, in spite of all the hopeful autonomista and autogestion rhetoric, in the face of a hostile credit system and the predatory practices of merchant capital. The ' power of merchant capital (the Wal-Mart phenomena) has been particularly resurgent in recent years (another arena of much neglected analysis in Marxist theory).

Recognizing this difficulty, much of the left came to the view that struggle for proletarian command over the state apparatus was the only other path to communism. The state would be the agent to control the three circuits of capital and to tame the institutions, powers and class agents that managed the flows that supported the perpetuation of the class relation in production. The problem has always been, of course, that the lifeblood of the state comes from facilitating and tapping into the very flows that the state is supposed to control. That is as true for the socialist state as for the capitalist state. Centralized and top-down management does not work except by way of some liberation of the flows (as the Chinese have proven so expert at doing). And once the flows are liberated, all hell breaks loose because the capitalist genie is out of the bottle. So what are the political prospects for finding a middle path between autogestion and centralized state control when neither of them on their own work effectively as antidotes to the power of capital?

The problem with worker control has been that the focus of struggle has been the factory as a privileged site of production of surplus value and the privileging of the industrial working class as the vanguard of the proletariat, the main revolutionary agent. But it was not factory workers who produced the Paris Commune. So there is a dissident view of that event that says it was not a proletarian uprising or a class-based movement but an urban social movement that was reclaiming the right to the city rather than seeking a revolutionary path towards the building of an anti-capitalist alternative.[41] But why could it not be both? Urbanization is itself produced. Thousands of workers are engaged in its production and their work is productive of value and of surplus value. Why not reconceptualize the site of surplus value production as the city rather than as the factory? The Paris Commune can then be reconceptualized in terms of that proletariat that produced the city seeking to claim back the right to have and control that which they had produced. This is (and in the Paris Commune case was) a very different kind of proletariat to that which Marxists have typically favoured. But at this point in the history of those parts of the world characterized as advanced capitalism, the factory proletariat has been radically diminished. So we have a choice: mourn the passing of the possibility of revolution or change our conception of the proletariat to that of the hordes of unorganized urbanization producers and explore their distinctive revolutionary capacities and powers.

So who are these workers who produce the city? The city builders, the construction workers in particular, are the most obvious candidate, even as they are not the only nor the largest labour force involved. As a political force the construction workers have in recent times in the United States (and possibly elsewhere) all too often been supportive of the large-scale and class-biased developmentalism that keeps them employed. They do not have to be so. The masons and builders played an important role in the Paris Commune. The 'Green Ban' construction union movement in New South Wales in the early 1970s banned working on projects they deemed environmentally unsound and were successful in much of what they did. They were ultimately destroyed by a combination of concerted state power and their own Maoist national leadership who considered environmental issues a manifestation of flabby bourgeois sentimentality.[42]

But there is a seamless connection between those who mine the iron ore that goes into the steel that goes into the construction of the bridges across which the trucks carrying commodities travel to their final destinations of factories and homes for consumption. All of these activities (including spatial movement) are, according to Marx, productive of value and of surplus value. And if, again as Marx argues, maintenance, repairs and replacements (often difficult to distinguish in practice) are all part of the value producing stream, then the vast army of workers involved in these activities in our cities is also contributing to value and surplus value producing investment in the physical infrastructures that make our cities what they are. If the flow of commodities from place of origin to final destination is productive of value, then so are the workers who are employed on the food chain that links rural producers to urban consumers. Organized, those workers would have the power to strangle the metabolism of the city. Strikes of transport workers (e.g. France over the last twenty years and now in Shanghai) are extremely effective political weapons (used negatively in Chile in the coup year of 1973). The Bus Riders Union in Los Angeles and the organization of taxi drivers in New York and LA are other examples.[43]

Consider the flows not only of food and other consumer goods, but also of energy, water and other necessities and their vulnerabilities to disruption too. The production and reproduction of urban life, while some of it can be 'dismissed' (an unfortunate word) as 'unproductive' in the Marxist canon, is nevertheless socially necessary, part of the 'faux frais' of the reproduction of the class relations between capital and labour. Much of this labour has always been temporary, insecure, itinerant and precarious. New forms of organizing are absolutely essential for this labour force that produces and sustains the city. The newly fledged Excluded Workers Congress in the United States is an example the forms that are emerging – an alliance of workers bedevilled by temporary and insecure conditions of employment who are often, as with domestic workers, spatially scattered throughout the urban system.[44]

It is in this light too that the history of the politics of conventional labour struggles requires a re-write. Most struggles that are depicted as focused solely on the factory-based worker turn out, on inspection, to have had a much broader base. Margaret Kohn complains, for example, how left historians of labour laud the Turin Factory Councils in the early twentieth century while totally ignoring the fact that it was in the 'Houses of the People' in the community that much of the politics was shaped and from which much of the logistical support flowed.[45] E.P. Thompson depicts how the making of the English working class depended as much upon what happened in chapels and in neighbourhoods as in the work place. How successful would the Flint sit-down strike of 1937 have been were it not for the mass of unemployed people and the neighbourhood organizations outside the gates that unfailingly delivered their support, moral and material? And is it not interesting that in the British miners' strikes of the 1970s and 1980s, the miners that lived in diffuse urbanized areas such as Nottingham were the first to cave in while the tightly-knit communities of Northumbria remained solidarious to the end? Organizing the community has been just as important in prosecuting labour struggles as has organizing the workplace. And to the degree that conventional workplaces are disappearing in many parts of the so-called advanced capitalist world (though not, of course, in China or Bangladesh), then organizing around work in the community appears to be even more important.

In all these instances, as we alter the lens on the social milieu in which struggle is occurring, then the sense of who the proletariat might be and what their aspirations might be gets transformed. The gender composition of oppositional politics looks very different when relations outside of the factory are placed firmly in the picture. The social dynamics of the workplace are not homologous with those in the living space. In the latter space distinctions based on gender, race, ethnicity, religion are frequently more deeply etched into the social fabric while issues of social reproduction play a more prominent, even dominant role, in the shaping of political subjectivities and consciousness. From this perspective the dynamics of class struggles along with the nature of political demands appear very different. But then when we look backward and reassess, we see that they always were rather different from how the Marxist imaginary wishfully depicted them.

Fletcher and Gapasin thus argue that the labour movement should pay more attention to geographical rather than sectoral forms of organization, that the movement should empower the central labour councils in cities in addition to organizing sectorally.

> To the extent that labor speaks about matters of class, it should not see itself as separate from the community. The term *labor* should denote forms of organization with roots in the working class and with agendas that explicitly advance the class demands of the working class. In that sense, a community-based organization rooted in the working class (such as a workers' centre) that addresses class-specific issues is a labor organization in the same way that a trade union is. To push the envelope a bit more, a trade union that addresses the interests of only one section of the working class (such as a white supremacist craft union) deserves the label *labor organization* less than does a community-based organization that assists the unemployed or the homeless.[46]

They therefore propose a new approach to labour organizing that

> essentially defies current trade union practices in forming alliances and taking political action. Indeed, it has the following central premise: *if class struggle is not restricted to the workplace, then neither should unions be.* The strategic conclusion is that unions must think in terms of organizing cities rather than simply organizing workplaces (or industries). And organizing cities is possible only if unions work with allies in metropolitan social blocks.[47]

'How then', they go on to ask, 'does one organize a city?' This, it seems to me, is one of the key questions that the left will have to answer if anti-capitalist struggle is to be revitalized in the years to come. And actually such struggles have a distinguished history. The inspiration drawn from 'Red Bologna' in the 1970s is a case in point. And it is one of those curious ironies of history that the French Communist Party distinguished itself far more in municipal administration (in part because it had no dogmatic theory or instructions from Moscow to guide it) than it did in other arenas of political life from the 1960s even up until the present day. The struggles fought by the municipalities in Britain against Thatcherism in the early 1980s were not only rearguard but, as in the case of the Greater London Council, potentially innovative until Thatcher abolished that whole layer of governance.[48] Even in the United States, Milwaukee for many years had a socialist administration and it is worth remembering that the only socialist ever elected to the US Senate began his career and earned the people's trust as mayor of Burlington, Vermont.

If the Parisian producers in the Commune were reclaiming their right to the city they had produced, then in what sense might we look to a slogan such as 'the right to city' as a 'cry and a demand' (as Lefebvre put it) around which political forces might rally as a key slogan for anti-capitalist struggle? The slogan is, of course, an empty signifier full of immanent but not transcendent possibilities. This does not mean it is irrelevant or politically impotent. Everything depends on who gets to fill the signifier with revolutionary as opposed to reformist immanent meaning. That is bound to be contested and then, as Marx once put it, 'between equal rights force decides'.[49]

It is indeed often difficult to distinguish between reformist and revolutionary initiatives in urban settings. Participatory budgeting in Porto Alegre, ecologically sensitive programmes in Curitiba or living wage campaigns in many US cities, appear on the surface to be merely reformist (and rather marginal at that). The Chongqing initiative may, despite the Maoist rhetoric, more resemble redistributive Nordic social democracy than a revolutionary movement. But as their influence spreads, so the initiatives reveal other deeper layers of possibility for more radical conceptions and actions at the metropolitan scale. A spreading rhetoric (from Zagreb to Hamburg to Los Angeles) over the right to the city, for example, seems to suggest something more revolutionary might be at stake.[50] The measure of that possibility appears in the desperate attempts of existing political powers (e.g. the NGOs and international institutions, including the World Bank, assembled at the Rio World Urban Forum in 2010) to co-opt that language to their own purposes.

There is no point in complaining at the attempt to co-opt. The left should take it as a compliment and battle for our distinctive immanent meaning, which is simply that all those whose labours are engaged in producing and reproducing the city have a collective right not only to that which they produce but also to decide on what is to be produced where and how. Democratic vehicles (other than the existing democracy of money power) need to be constructed to decide how to revitalize urban life outside of dominant class relations and more after 'our' (the producers of urbanization and urbanism) heart's desire.

One objection that immediately arises, of course, is why concentrate on the city when there are multiple rural, peasant and indigenous movements in motion that can also claim their own distinctive rights? In any case, has not the city as a physical object lost its meaning as an object of struggle? There is of course an obvious truth to these objections. Urbanization has produced a highly differentiated mosaic of communities and interactive spaces which are hard to bring together around any kind of coherent political project. Indeed, there is plenty of rivalry and conflict between the spaces that constitute the city. It was, I suspect, for this reason that Lefebvre changed his focus from the urban revolution to the broader terrain of the production of space, or as I might formulate it, to the production of uneven geographical development as the focus of theoretical analysis and political struggle.

In the pedestrian imaginations of literally-minded academics, such objections sometimes produce the conclusion that the city has disappeared and that pursuit of the right to the city is therefore the pursuit of a chimera. But political struggles are animated by visions as much as by practicalities. And the term 'city' has an iconic and symbolic history that is deeply embedded in the pursuit of political meanings. The city of God, the city on a hill, the city as an object of utopian desire, the relationship between city and citizenship, of a distinctive place of belonging within a perpetually shifting spatio-temporal order, all give it a political meaning that mobilizes a political imaginary that is lost in a slogan such as 'the right to produce space' or 'the right to uneven geographical development'!

The right to the city is not an exclusive right but a focused right.[51] It is inclusive not only of construction workers but also of all those who facilitate the reproduction of daily life: the care givers and teachers, the sewer and subway repair men, the plumbers and electricians, the hospital workers and the truck bus and taxi drivers, the restaurant workers and the entertainers, the bank clerks and the city administrators. It seeks a unity from within an incredible diversity of fragmented social spaces. And there are many putative forms of organization – from workers' centres and regional worker's assemblies (such as that of Toronto) to alliances (such as the Right to the City alliances and the Excluded Workers Congress and other forms of organization of precarious labour) that have this objective upon their political radar. This is the proletarian force that must be organized if the world is to change. This is how and where we have to begin if we wish to organize the whole city. The urban producers must rise up and reclaim their right to the city they collectively produce. The transformation of urban life and above all the abolition of the class relations in the production of urbanization will have to be one, if not the, path towards an anti-capitalist transition. This is what the left has to imagine as constituting the core of its political strategy in years to come.

NOTES

1   Robert Shiller, 'Housing Bubbles are Few and Far Between', *New York Times*, 5 February 2011.
2   *World Development Report 2009: Reshaping Economic Geography*, Washington DC: The World Bank, 2009. See my earlier critique in David Harvey, 'Assessment: Reshaping Economic Geography: The World Development Report', *Development and Change*, 40(6), 1269-77, 2009.
3   *World Bank Development Report*, p. 206.
4   Graham Turner, *The Credit Crunch: Housing Bubbles, Globalisation and the Worldwide Economic Crisis*, London: Pluto, 2008; David Harvey, *The Condition of Postmodernity*, Oxford: Basil Blackwell, pp. 145-6, 169.
5   David Harvey, *The New Imperialism*, Oxford: Oxford University Press, 2003, p. 113; Robert Shiller, *Irrational Exuberance*, Princeton: Princeton University Press, 2000.
6   John English and Emerson Gray, *The Coming Real Estate Crash*, New Rochelle, NY: Arlington House Publishers, 1979; William Tabb, *The Long Default: New York City and the Urban Fiscal Crisis*, New York: Monthly Review Press, 1982; David Harvey, *A Brief History of Neoliberalism*, Oxford: Oxford University Press, 2005; Ashok Bardhan and Richard Walker, 'California, Pivot of the Great Recession', Working Paper Series, Institute for Research on Labor and Employment, University of California, Berkeley, 2010.
7   William Goetzmann and Frank Newman, 'Securitization in the 1920's', *Working Papers*, National Bureau of Economic Research, 2010; Eugene White, 'Lessons from the Great American Real Estate Boom and Bust of the 1920s', *Working Papers*, National Bureau of Economic Research, 2010.
8   Karl Marx, *Grundrisse*, London: Penguin, 1973, pp. 88-100.
9   David Harvey, 'A Commentary on Marx's Method in *Capital*', forthcoming in *Historical Materialism*.
10 Karl Marx. *Capital*, Volume 2, London: Penguin, 1978, p. 357 (my italics).
11 Marx, *Grundrisse*, p. 89.
12 Mario Tronti, 'The Strategy of Refusal', Turin: Einaudi, 1966, available at

http://libcom.org; Antonio Negri, *Marx Beyond Marx: Lessons on the Grundrisse*, London: Autonomedia, 1989.

13 Karl Marx, *Capital*, Volume 3, London: Penguin, 1978, chapters 24 and 25.

14 David Harvey, *The Limits to Capital*, Oxford: Blackwell, 1982, chapter 8.

15 Marx, *Capital*, Volume 3, p. 597; Geoffrey Harcourt, *Some Cambridge Controversies in the Theory of Capital*, Cambridge: Cambridge University Press, 1972.

16 Marx, *Capital*, Volume 3, p. 573. Both Isaac and Emile, incidentally, were part of the utopian Saint-Simonian movement prior to 1848.

17 David Harvey, *The Urbanisation of Capital*, Oxford: Blackwell, 1985 and *The Enigma of Capital, and the Crises of Capitalism*, London: Profile Books, 2010.

18 Brinley Thomas, *Migration and Economic Growth: A Study of Great Britain and the Atlantic Economy*, Cambridge: Cambridge University Press, 1973.

19 Leo Grebler, David Blank and Louis Winnick, *Capital Formation in Residential Real Estate*, Princeton: Princeton University Press, 1956; Clarence Long, *Building Cycles and the Theory of Investment*, Princeton: Princeton University Press, 1940; Manuel Gottlieb, *Long Swings in Urban Development*, New York: National Bureau of Economic Research, 1976.

20 Marx, *Capital*, Volume 3, chapter 25.

21 Karl Marx, *Capital*, Volume 1, London: Penguin, 1973, p. 793.

22 John Logan and Harvey Molotch, *Urban Fortunes: The Political Economy of Place*, Berkeley: University of California Press, 1987.

23 Marx, *Capital*, Volume 2, part 2.

24 'Cities in the Great Depression', *Wikipedia*, available at http://www.wikipedia.org.

25 Martin Boddy, *The Building Societies*, London: Macmillan, 1980.

26 The Kerner Commission, *Report of the National Advisory Commission on Civil Disorders*, Washington, DC: Government Printing Office, 1968.

27 Jonathan Weisman, 'Reagan Policies Gave Green Light to Red Ink', *Washington Post*, 9 June 2004; William Greider, 'The Education of David Stockman, *Atlantic Monthly*, December 1981.

28 Warren Buffett, interviewed by Ben Stein, 'In Class Warfare, Guess Which Class Is Winning', *New York Times*, 26 November 2006; David Stockman, 'The Bipartisan March to Fiscal Madness', *New York Times*, 23 April 2011.

29 Karl Marx and Frederick Engels, *The Communist Manifesto*, London: Pluto Press Edition, 2008, p. 4.

30 Barbara Ehrenreich and Dedrich Muhammad, 'The Recession's Racial Divide', *New York Times*, 12 September 2009.

31 Gretchen Morgenson and Joshua Rosner, *Reckless Endangerment: How Outsized Ambition, Greed and Corruption Led to Economic Armageddon*, New York: Times Books, 2011.

32 Lynne Sagalyn, 'Mortgage Lending in Older Neighborhoods', *Annals of the American Academy of Political and Social Science*, 465(January), 1983, pp. 98–108.

33 Keith Bradsher, 'China Announces New Bailout of Big Banks', *New York Times*, 7 January 2004.

34 David Barboza, 'Inflation in China Poses Big Threat to Global Trade', *New York*

Times, 17 April 2011; Jamil Anderlini, 'Fate of Real Estate is Global Concern', *Financial Times*, 1 June 2011; Robert Cookson, 'China Bulls Reined in by Fears on Economy', *Financial Times*, 1 June 2011; David Barboza, 'Building Boom in China Stirs Fears of Debt Overload', *New York Times*, 7 July 2011.

35   David Barboza, 'A City Born of China's Boom, Still Unpeopled', *New York Times*, 20 October 2010.

36   Anderlini, 'Fate of Real Estate'.

37   International Monetary Fund and International Labour Organization, *The Challenges of Growth, Employment and Social Cohesion*, Geneva: International Labour Organization, 2010.

38   Kathrin Hille and Jamil Anderlini, 'China: Mao and the Next Generation', *Financial Times*, 2 June 2011; Peter Martin and David Cohen, 'Socialism 3.0 in China', available at http://the-diplomat.com.

39   Immanuel Ness and Dario Azzellini, eds., *Ours to Master and to Own: Workers' Councils from the Commune to the Present*, Chicago: Haymarket Books, 2011.

40   Perhaps the single most important exception has been Mondragon. Founded under fascism in Spain in 1956 as a worker cooperative in the Basque country, it now has some 200 enterprises spreading throughout Spain and into Europe. In most of the enterprises the difference of remuneration has been limited until recently to 3 to 1 (compared to the 400 to 1 structure of most US corporations). Mondragon survived in part because it has not only been about production. It created its own credit structures and merchant capital outlets. Its strategy was to work across all three circuits. See George Cheney, *Values at Work: Employee Participation Meets Market Pressures at Mondragon*, Ithaca: ILR Press, 1999.

41   Manuel Castells, *The City and the Grassroots*, Berkeley: University of California Press, 1983; Roger Gould, *Insurgent Identities: Class Community and Protest in Paris from 1848 to the Commune*, Chicago: University of Chicago Press, 1995. For my rebuttal of these arguments see David Harvey, *Paris, Capital of Modernity*, New York: Routledge, 2003.

42   John Tully, 'Green Bans and the BLF: the Labour Movement and Urban Ecology', *International Viewpoint Online*, 357, 2004, available at http://www/internationalviewpoint.org.

43   Michael Wines, 'Shanghai Truckers' Protest Ebbs with Concessions Won on Fees', *New York Times*, 23 April 2011; Jacqueline Levitt and Gary Blasi, 'The Los Angeles Taxi Workers Alliance', in Ruth Milkman, Joshua Bloom and Victor Narro, eds., *Working for Justice: the L.A. Model of Organizing and Advocacy*, Ithaca: ILR Press, 2010, pp. 109-24.

44   Excluded Workers Congress, *Unity for Dignity: Excluded Workers Report*, December 2010, c/o Inter-Alliance Dialogue, New York, available from http://www.excludedworkers.org.

45   Margaret Kohn, *Radical Space: Building the House of the People*, Ithaca: Cornell University Press, 2003.

46   Bill Fletcher and Fernando Gapasin, *Solidarity Divided; The Crisis in Organized Labor and a New Path Toward Social Justice*, Berkeley: University of California Press, 2008, p. 174.

47   Ibid.

48 Max Jaggi et al., *Red Bologna*, London: Writers & Readers, 1977.

49 Henri Lefebvre, *Writings on Cities*, Translated and edited by Elenore Kofman and Elizabeth Lebas, Oxford: Blackwell, 1996; Marx, *Capital,* Volume 1, p. 344.

50 Ana Sugranyes and Charlotte Mathivet, eds., *Cities for All: Proposals and Experiences Towards the Right to the City*, Santiago: Habitat International Coalition, 2010.

51 Henri Lefebvre, *Writings on Cities.*

SLUMP, AUSTERITY AND RESISTANCE

DAVID MCNALLY

The global financial crisis of the late 2000s... stands as the most serious global financial crisis since the Great Depression. The crisis has been a transformative moment in global economic history whose ultimate resolution will likely reshape politics and economics for at least a generation.

Carmen Reinhart and Kenneth Rogoff.[1]

The Great Recession of 2008-9 represents a profound rupture in the neoliberal era, signalling the exhaustion of the accumulation regime that had emerged almost thirty years earlier. Rather than an ordinary recession, a short-lived downturn in the business cycle, it constituted a systemic crisis, a major contraction whose effects will be with us for many years to come.[2] Among those effects are the extraordinary cuts to social programmes, and the resultant impoverishment, announced as part of the Age of Austerity inaugurated by all major states.[3] But another effect, and for socialists ultimately the crucial one, is a new wave of mass working-class insurgency. Since the onset of the Great Recession, factory occupations, general strikes and street-based uprisings have burst forth from Greece to Guadeloupe and beyond. Whether this insurgent wave will be adequate to the task of overturning the ruling-class agenda is far from clear. What is clear is that the age of austerity has raised the bar for movements of resistance, obliging them to undertake much more militant and decisive oppositional practices or risk major defeats.

Illuminating the context of these class struggles is a strategic necessity for any meaningful Left politics. To that end, this article explores the economic dynamics of the Great Recession, the bailout, and the abnormal 'recovery' that followed. It argues that while the recapitalization of banks did stop the financial collapse, monetary policy ('quantitative easing') can no more generate sustained growth today than it has in Japan over the past 15 years. As a result, we can expect a prolonged period of austerity, of food crises in the Global South, and of attacks on public services and working classes – all of which raise key political challenges for the Left.

THE NOT-SO-ORDINARY RECESSION OF 2008-9

By every significant measure, the Great Recession was the deepest and longest decline experienced by global capitalism since the catastrophic collapse of 1929-33. The 30 large economies of the Organization for Economic Cooperation and Development (OECD) underwent a 6 per cent contraction in Gross Domestic Product (GDP) with jobless rates jumping two-thirds higher on average. World industrial output fell 13 per cent; international trade dropped by 20 per cent; global stock markets plunged 50 per cent. A wave of bank collapses swept the United States and Europe, generating a financial panic unlike anything witnessed since the 1930s, and inducing an intense intellectual crisis in ruling-class circles, as confidence in free market nostrums staggered.[4]

Not only was the contraction of 2008-9 deeper than any since the 1930s, it also lasted nearly twice as long as the average recessions of the last 80 years.[5] For the first year, in fact, the downturn closely tracked the patterns of the slump of the early 1930s. As banks toppled across the heartlands of the system, world industrial output and stock markets plummeted at a rate equal to – and often greater than – the stunning meltdown of 1929-30, the first full year of the world depression.[6]

But after a bit more than a year of dizzying collapse, the economic pattern departed from that of the 1930s. Unlike the Great Depression, where the downward movement continued for over three years, in 2008-9 the bottom was reached in half that time.[7] And there can be little doubt that the difference this time was the unprecedented and coordinated intervention by the world's major central banks and treasuries. Together these institutions pumped about $21 trillion (US) into the global financial system, bailing out banks and multinational firms and launching 'stimulus' programmes to revive flagging economies.[8] To put this figure in perspective, it represents an injection of wealth into the world economy equal to one and a half times US GDP. While there was no far-sighted programme involved here – instead it represented a frantic series of *ad hoc* interventions, each tending to throw more money at the crisis than the previous one – the authorities were unrelenting, refusing to stop until the bank collapses were over.

Contrary to a widespread misunderstanding, this intervention did not consist of Ben Bernanke's famous 'helicopter drops' of money into a contracting economy.[9] Rather than mere increases in the general money supply, these were largely targeted rescue packages designed to *recapitalize* collapsing banks and other financial institutions such as AIG, the world's largest insurance company, and government-sponsored mortgage lenders, like Fannie Mae and Freddie Mac in the US, as well as major auto firms. By directly exchanging central bank money for toxic assets, like deteriorating mortgage-backed securities, governments returned these institutions to economic solvency, implicitly acknowledging they were dealing less with an insufficiency of credit in the economy (a liquidity crunch) than with a crisis of insolvency. This is why nothing short of a direct bailout of the financial system could stop the meltdown.

It is true that central bank interventions drove up the monetary *base* of the US financial system (total currency plus bank reserves), which nearly tripled in the course of two and a half years.[10] However, contra the monetarists, there is little evidence that this significantly increased the *supply* of money and credit within the economy. Put differently, the base money underpinning the system may have tripled, but the money circulating throughout the economy did not. Instead, rebuilding of reserves by banks, hoarding of cash by corporations, a decline in the velocity of money (how often it turns over or changes hands), depressed demand for loans from over-stretched consumers, and the reticence of banks to lend all combined to thwart any dramatic expansion of the real money supply. Throughout 2010 and the first half of 2011, in fact, two of the main measures of the money supply (M1 and M2) rose quite slowly. And by some accounts, a broader measure of the money supply (M3) contracted considerably, if not precipitously.[11]

For this reason, while recapitalization of banks and major corporations arrested the financial meltdown, policies devoted largely to 'quantitative easing', i.e. increasing liquidity, have no more proved capable of reviving the US economy than they have of reigniting Japanese growth over the past decade and a half.[12] Moreover, four years since the onset of the Great Recession the recapitalization of banks has not come to an end: a number of nation-states, among them Ireland and Spain, continue to rescue ailing financial institutions. In addition, the persistent bailouts of heavily-indebted states, such as Greece, comprise indirect recapitalizations of banks – and these show no signs of ending any time soon, as we shall see below.

Because coordinated government intercession halted the financial collapse of 2008-9, and alleviated the panic, mainstream economics and the business press anxiously reassured us that the crisis was over and capitalism had returned to vigorous growth. But things are not so simple when we are dealing with a systemic crisis. This is obvious when we examine the peculiar expansion that has followed the recession of 2008-9.

SEARCHING FOR THE ELUSIVE 'RECOVERY'

Just as the Great Recession was no regular contraction, the 'recovery' that began in 2010 has been anything but typical. With the exception of corporate profits – which rebounded sharply, surpassing their previous US peak by the third quarter of 2010 and growing as a share of GDP[13] – the rebound in output, income, employment and investment has been incredibly tepid.

As of mid-2011, for instance, well into the 'recovery', annual economic growth in the US and the more robust parts of Europe was less than 3 per cent, significantly below the average for this stage of a regular business cycle. Indeed, by May 2011 Eurozone growth had slipped beneath 1 per cent, while US growth floundered at less than 2 per cent. More striking, three years after the onset of slump, only Germany and the US of the six largest capitalistically developed economies had topped their pre-recession GDP peaks, leading one influential commentator to suggest that the other four, France, Japan, the UK and Italy, remained in recession.[14]

At this stage of a typical post-war expansion, the economy would be growing two to three times as fast, i.e. by about 5 or 6 per cent a year. Even during the recovery in the middle of the Great Depression, the US economy expanded much more dramatically: by almost 8 per cent in both 1934 and

Figure 1: Employment Recovery following Recessions, 1974–2011

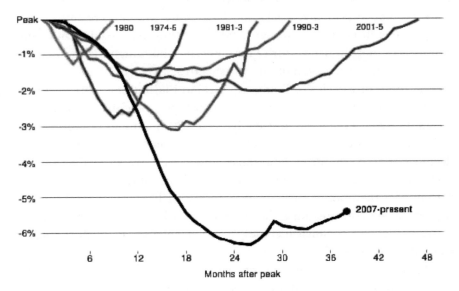

Source: Bureau of Labor Statistics. Chart by Amanda Cox, *New York Times*, 1 April 2011.

1935 and by a stunning 14 per cent in 1936. Yet, so low are rates of expansion today that they are barely making a dent in unemployment. Indeed, in some part of Europe joblessness is on the rise, and in the United States it would take a boom that produced jobs at *twice* the 2010 rate for more than a decade simply to restore the jobs lost during the recession (nearly nine million) and create those required by population growth during the same period (nearly three million).[15] As Figure 1 shows, more than three years after the wave of job losses began, US employment was still more than 5 per cent below its pre-recession level. In the entire period since the Great Depression no recovery has regenerated jobs at such an anaemic rate.

Any serious analysis must also note the racialized character of unemployment and the effects of the Great Recession, the most glaring of which can be found in the data on job loss and poverty. Astonishingly, four out of every ten African-Americans experienced unemployment during the Great Recession of 2008-9. Throughout the first half of 2010, official unemployment among blacks in the US was over 16 per cent, while among Latinos it hovered around 13 per cent. In 35 of America's largest cities, official jobless rates for blacks were between 30 and 35 per cent – levels equal to the worst days of the Great Depression. Factoring in workers who are *involuntarily* under-employed – working part-time because they cannot find full-time work – we arrive at a combined unemployment and under-employment rate in the US of about 20 per cent, and well above 25 per cent for black and Hispanic workers. Not surprisingly, blacks and Latinos are almost three times more likely to live in poverty as whites. And loss of homes is making all of this worse, as more than half of African-Americans who bought homes in 2006 had already been foreclosed upon by early 2010.[16]

The topic of foreclosure brings us back to the housing market, where the first bubble burst. Despite a disastrous collapse, as of this writing it too shows no signs of recovery. Indeed, by spring 2011, American home prices had fallen for 58 consecutive months, with most analysts predicting further declines. Indeed, the drop in average home prices by more than 30 per cent greatly *exceeds* the housing meltdown of the entire period 1925-41.[17] Meanwhile, new home sales are at their lowest level since 1963, further depressing the construction industry. And to make matters worse, growth in retail sales and personal incomes is utterly sluggish across all the major economies of the Global North.

That leaves the recovery in profits as the one silver lining of the rebound from the Great Recession, at least where business is concerned. Significantly, however, the profit improvement has not been driven by investment in new plant and equipment. Instead, it has been a matter of relentlessly squeezing labour, as downsizing and speed-up have enabled companies to get dramatically more output at less cost. This is reflected in unit labour costs in the US – the amount employers spend on labour for each good or service they produce – which fell a whopping 4.7 per cent in 2009, the largest drop ever recorded.[18] While this boosts the corporate bottom line, it does little to revive the overall economy – and cannot do so unless profit growth translates into new business investment. But precisely this – new business spending on plant and equipment – has been the Achilles' heel of recovery from the Great Recession.

Not only has capital investment not roared back, as it typically would have at this point in an ordinary business cycle, it has actually bumped along at historic lows. *The Economist* magazine noted in mid-2010 that, throughout the Global North, 'business investment is as low as it has *ever* been as a share of GDP'.[19] And this remained the case well into 2011.[20] Not only was this the case in the US and European centres, like Germany and Britain; it was also true of states like Canada, which escaped the worst effects of the financial crisis and whose economy has been buoyed by rising prices and increased export demand for raw materials. Business investment in new equipment and machinery in Canada was at just 5.5 per cent of GDP in early 2011, compared to 7.7 per cent in 2000, or to just under 7 per cent in

**Figure 2: Non-financial Corporate Holdings of Cash
and Other Liquid Assets, 2000-2010**

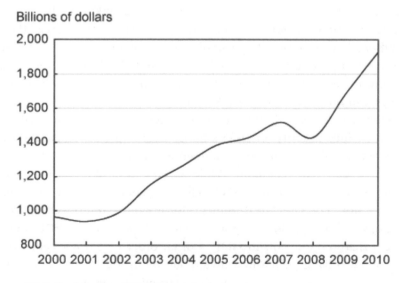

Source: US Federal Reserve Board/Haver Analytics.

2005.[21] As for the United States, business fixed investment remained about 15 per cent below pre-recession levels in late 2010, more than a year into 'recovery'.[22] Put simply, the rise in profits is not translating into new capital accumulation on any meaningful scale. One indicator of this is corporate cash hoarding, which is more pronounced than at any time in the last 60 years. Britain's Chancellor of the Exchequer claimed that as of early 2011 UK firms had cash holdings equal to a remarkable 5 per cent of GDP.[23] Meanwhile, non-financial firms in the US were sitting on about $2 trillion in cash and chequing deposits, an extremely sharp increase in the share of assets held in cash, as Figure 2 illustrates.[24]

One of the obvious reasons for the utterly tepid recovery in business investment is that capacity utilization – the proportion of productive capacity being used by businesses – remains depressed. According to the Federal Reserve, US industry was using 77.4 per cent of its capacity as of March 2011, a rate 3 per cent below the average for the past 40 years.[25] Broadly similar rates, ranging from 73.6 per cent of capacity to about 77.6, can be found in the national economies of Germany, Britain, Canada and France.[26] In such an environment, where demand can easily be met by existing productive capacity, many businesses face a disincentive to invest. Of course, corporations might still make investments if they had good reason to expect a rapid and sustained rise in consumer spending (and related jumps in business investment). But where heavily-indebted consumers are retrenching amidst economic uncertainty and high levels of unemployment, there can be little reasonable expectation of large spikes in demand. To compound matters, as governments attempt to pay for the Great Bailout of 2008-9, they are unwinding stimulus spending and turning to austerity – massive and prolonged cuts to public spending. This amounts essentially to a form of state de-leveraging, which, by eliminating jobs and reducing earnings, can only further depress demand.

Predictably, by early 2011 those governments that had moved most aggressively into austerity, often in a futile effort to placate global investors, discovered that their efforts were hindering recovery, if not driving their economies back into recession. While an economy like Germany's may be able to ride out more than $100 billion in public spending cuts, many others are not. The Greek government, for instance, introduced draconian reductions in hopes of lowering its deficit by 6 per cent in 2010, only to induce a sharp contraction in GDP – of an order of 6.6 per cent for the year – and a collapse of business investment by nearly 20 per cent, but no reduction in public debt.[27] Now, in a desperate effort to keep bailouts flowing from the IMF and the European Central Bank, the Greek government has agreed to a sweeping programme of privatization, involving the selloff of airports, marinas and ports, and has pledged to eliminate 150,000 public service jobs.[28] Portugal meanwhile, having committed to 'savage spending cuts', now anticipates two years of 'deep recession'.[29] Even in the case of a stronger economy, that of Britain, the imposition of the largest spending cuts in history, to the tune of more than $200 billion, and the impending loss of 400,000 public sector jobs, has driven growth rates down to near zero. Combined with tax increases, these policies have chopped about 2 per cent from real household income in the course of a year and, by the first quarter of 2011, had knocked consumer spending to its lowest point since the depths of recession in 2009.[30] And in the US, where fiscal stimulus programmes were responsible for half or more of the 3.5 per cent growth that characterized the best moments of the 'recovery', their removal, never mind the imposition of massive new cuts, can only have a counter-cyclical, i.e. recessionary, effect.[31] In this regard, the austerity agenda risks repeating the American experience of 1937, when large-scale reductions in government deficits helped plunge the economy back into a sharp recession.[32]

But fears of a renewed recession do not explain why governments keep intervening to prevent sovereign debt crises from morphing into debt defaults. Their principal worry, as one mainstream analyst puts it, is that a debt default by Greece, Ireland or Portugal would quickly usher in a new financial crisis and a run on 'zombie banks' that hold private and public debt from these nations. Estimates suggest that eurozone banks would have to absorb losses of $240 billion if those three countries restructured their debt, imposing 'haircuts' on their bondholders, including private banks – and twice that much if Spain too defaulted. Indeed, German banks would be hit by losses equal to a third of their total capital in the event of debt restructurings by Greece, Ireland, Portugal and Spain.[33] So, when the IMF and the European Central Bank draw up a bailout plan for one nation-state or another, it is private banks they are once again rescuing in a process that continues to shift toxic assets from the private to the public sector.[34] At the same time, each ostensible rescue comes with conditions requiring deep cuts to social spending and public service jobs, which in turn push the economies in question back toward recession

In this context, the 'recovery' can only remain shallow, anaemic and prone to collapse into new recessions. This is what I intend in characterizing the period inaugurated by the Great Recession as one of *global slump*. The term is not meant to suggest that there can be no recoveries – as we have seen, these took place during the Great Depression too. Rather, it refers to a period of interconnected crises – sharp recessions, bank bailouts, contractions caused by severe problems of sovereign debt – that, notwithstanding tepid recoveries, fails to generate a robust and enduring upturn in capital accumulation.[35]

HOW WE GOT HERE:
FROM GREAT RECESSION TO AGE OF AUSTERITY

The preceding assessment is based on an analysis that can only be briefly rehearsed here. At its core is the claim that the Great Recession comprised a rupture signalling the end of a quarter-century-long wave of neoliberal expansion (1982-2007). Across that wave three decisive transformations produced an era of sustained expansion *and* laid the basis for a new crisis.[36] The first transformation was a series of critical defeats of labour movements, such as Reagan's crushing of the air traffic controllers' union in the US (1981), the Thatcher government's victory over the National Union of Mineworkers in Britain (1984-85), to name just two of the most momentous events. On a regional level, the smashing of the militant tin miners' union in Bolivia (1986) set a similar tone for workers in Latin America. While the processes differed, the results were depressingly similar: political defeats for labour movements opened up continuing rollbacks of union rights; dramatically curtailed strike activity; facilitated the imposition of tiered workforces (creating larger numbers of 'casual' workers with poorer wages, benefits and labour protections); and shifted the balance of power in the workplaces and the wider society powerfully in capital's favour. Related to this, secondly, were profound processes of industrial restructuring and reorganization that cut the size of workforces (around 300,000 steelworkers lost their jobs in the US for instance), sped up production with new technologies, particularly computerized systems, and thus drove up the rate of exploitation. Under the guise of lean production, just-in-time manufacturing, flexible specialization and so on, capital reaped the gains of rising profitability thanks to increases in the rate of surplus value in the range of 40 per cent. Finally, across this period a major spatial-geographical reorganization of capitalism took place, with the massive development of global sweatshops, many located in low-wage and capital-friendly export processing zones that gave rise to new centres of global accumulation, most notably in China.[37]

By 2006-7, the quarter-century of neoliberal expansion had clearly exhausted itself in a classic process of global over-accumulation and declining profitability on new investment. In fact, the early warning signs of this exhaustion flashed during the acute crisis in East Asia in 1997.[38] Shaken by the latter, central banks responded by driving down interest rates, continuing on this path in 1998 when Russia wobbled and the Long Term Capital Management hedge fund disintegrated. After briefly reversing course, the

US Fed began slashing again when the dotcom bubble burst in 2000-1. Monetary policy thus postponed the day of reckoning, at the cost of inflating asset bubbles in real estate and a multitude of financial instruments. But the bursting of these bubbles did not cause the crash; rather it operated as a trigger. Underlying the crisis was a peaking in business profits, which then turned down, a classic expression of the contradictions of capitalist accumulation, which rendered the system vulnerable to a dramatic financial shock.

Business Week analyst, Michael Mandel, contends that the mass of domestic profits of non-financial firms in the US rose a meagre 6 per cent over the decade 1997-2007, at which point they decisively declined – clear signs of the exhaustion of a cycle of accumulation. Mandel's data also show profits in the financial sector starting a decline in 2006, just prior to the shocks that were to hit banks and hedge funds.[39] In a similar vein, albeit with much greater theoretical and empirical sophistication, Michael Roberts has established that total corporate profits in the US peaked in 2006, commencing a downturn that lasted three years. 'Profits', he notes, 'were falling well before the credit crash began'.[40]

These system-wide tendencies toward a profit slowdown account for the depth and persistence of the Great Recession, as well as explaining why recovery has been so shallow and precarious. Systemic crises that signal the end of an expansionary wave (like that of 1982-2007) can only be resolved via an extended period of capitalist restructuring that is ordinarily accomplished across a cluster of recessions – such as 1929-33 and 1937-39 during the Great Depression, or 1970-71, 1974-75, and 1981-82 during the crisis of the 1970s and early 1980s. But whether capital can successfully drive forward such restructurings depends on the degree of working-class resistance – and in our current case on whether labour and social movements can reverse the austerity agenda of their rulers.

AFTER THE BAILOUTS: AUSTERITY AND FOOD CRISES

In a rare bit of lucidity from a central banker, Mervyn King, the Governor of the Bank of England, observed of the Great Recession that 'the impact of these crises lasts for many years. It is not like an ordinary recession, where you lose output and get it back quickly'. Then, in a remarkably candid comment, he added, 'the price of this financial crisis is being borne by people who absolutely did not cause it'. Given this, he continued, 'I'm surprised that the degree of public anger has not been greater than it has'.[41] Four weeks later, roughly half a million people took to the streets of London to oppose the sweeping cuts announced by Britain's coalition government. Impressive as it was, this show of opposition still fell far short of what will be necessary to reverse the austerity agenda.

To truly understand this agenda, we need to overcome the argument put by a number of Keynesians that the austerity programme to which governments turned in 2010 was an irrational ideological reflex. Rather than the absurd preference of crazed right-wingers, austerity is in significant measure an expression of the *needs of capital* in the aftermath of the Great Bailout, and has been articulated as such by the G20, the IMF and the Bank for International Settlements.[42] The reason for this is quite simple: to finance deficits, governments must be able to sell debt instruments (bonds) to financial investors, both private and public. As with all such investments in debt, buyers assess the risk involved, i.e., the probability that they will get their money back with interest. The riskier they judge the debt instrument to be, the higher return (rate of interest) they will demand.[43] In the aftermath of the huge bailouts that accompanied the Great Recession, financial investors have already judged that some governments, notably Greece, are likely to default on debt payments. That judgement pivots on both an economic and a political risk assessment, the latter having to do with estimations of the capacity of states to tame public opposition to austerity measures. Both calculations determined that Greece had to offer a premium of around 25 per cent on its two-year bonds in spring 2011, an interest rate that is simply not sustainable if it wants to cut its deficits. Rather than a *merely* ideological programme, then, austerity is based on the actual power of global finance to discipline governments via bond markets. In light of that power, deficits do matter: governments must heed the judgements of global financial actors, or run the risk of being priced out of debt markets. So, when the Bank for International Settlements observes, 'total industrialised country public sector debt is now expected to exceed 100% of GDP in 2011 – something that has never happened before in peacetime', it is describing a real problem from the standpoint of capital.[44]

To be sure, there are ways other than austerity to tackle such debt: higher taxes on corporations and the rich, or public ownership of the banking system (and its profits) could be used to eliminate debt without attacking social services and public employees. Similarly, debt defaults can be an entirely rational response, as they were a decade ago in Argentina. But, from the standpoint of capital, these are politically and economically unacceptable.

In this context there is little doubt that political parties of the ruling class have seen an opportunity to deploy the *shock doctrine*. By manipulating the dislocation caused by crisis they seek to garner support for attacks on social programmes, unions and job security.[45] Here, an ideological agenda *does* come into play, as insecurity is mobilized to divide workers, particularly by persuading those in the private sector that public sector wages, pensions and benefits are 'rich' and fiscally 'unsustainable', thereby creating the climate for privatizing public services and/or rolling back the wages, benefits, and union rights of public employees. In a number of national jurisdictions, where public debt levels are far from onerous, austerity programmes carry the imprint of capital's political agenda. Britain, for instance is aggressively pursuing austerity despite carrying an entirely manageable national debt equal to about 60 per cent of Gross Domestic Product, as opposed to Greece, where the government debt/GDP ratio exceeds 150 per cent. In such cases, governments engage in a sort of *competitive austerity* in which deep cuts to social programmes and government borrowing are deployed to weaken unions and reduce corporate taxes, all in an effort to attract international investment.[46]

For both economic and political reasons, therefore, capital and its parties (including social democracy) have united around deficit–reduction, privatization and the shrinking of social programmes. The result is that working–class people face at least 'a decade of pain', to use the term coined by the Institute for Fiscal Studies (IFS) in Britain, which estimates that by 2017-18 the average British family will be more than $4500 poorer due to increased taxes and diminished social services.[47] The consequence will be 400,000 fewer workers in the public sector – fewer nurses, teachers, sanitation workers, hospital orderlies, and social workers – once the cuts are completed.

Shocking as the British reality is, there is more dreadful austerity afoot elsewhere. Already, Latvia has fired one third of all teachers and slashed pensions by 70 per cent. Ireland has chopped 15 per cent from wages of government employees and is warning of further cuts. Meanwhile, Russia is eliminating one out of every five government jobs. In the US, on top of proposed cuts to the tune of $4 trillion in federal spending, tens of billions more are being chopped at state levels, where spending dropped by 7.3 per cent in the 2010 fiscal year, on top of declines the year before.[48] California has cut health insurance for 900,000 poor children, and the state of Michigan has ordered Detroit to close half its schools. Then there is Wisconsin which, notwithstanding impressive resistance, has slashed hundreds of millions from social service budgets and attacked the bargaining and union rights of public sector workers.[49] The Wisconsin experience also serves to underline the *class politics* of austerity, as its governor cut corporate taxes at the same time he slashed state spending and attacked labour unions. Throughout the US, in fact, austerity is being imposed while corporate taxes are falling and seven states have no personal taxes at all, even for their wealthiest citizens.

All of this is just the beginning. The decade of pain has now morphed into an Age of Austerity in which structural adjustment is being visited upon workers in the Global North. Predictably, things are even worse in the Global South. As the World Bank reports, across the planet an additional 64 million people were driven into poverty by the end of 2010 as a direct result of the crisis, the majority of these in the poorest regions of the world.[50] And here neoliberal transformations of agriculture figure prominently, as do the effects of quantitative easing on food prices.

Throughout the neoliberal period, liberalization of world trade, intense competition from heavily subsidised agro-industries in the North and the removal of subsidies for poor farmers in the South have all conspired to drive millions of peasant-farmers off the land from India to Mexico and beyond.[51] So devastating is the crisis in the Indian countryside, that every 30 minutes a farmer commits suicide.[52] To make a horrifying situation worse, in desperate need of foreign earnings, governments have pressured farmers to grow export crops (like cotton or coffee) rather than foodstuffs. Meanwhile, increasing amounts of arable land are being used for the production of bio-fuels rather than food. In Africa alone, at least 50 companies are involved in projects that have already put 3.2 million hectares of land into bio-fuel production, cutting food supplies, and increasing dispossession and landlessness.[53] Similar processes of land-grabbing in Latin America and South Asia, for agribusiness, ecotourism, and real estate development, have led to further displacement and declines in food production.[54]

As a result, fewer countries today are capable of feeding themselves – all of which contributes to import dependency and rising prices and profits for global agro-business. The onset of the global slump briefly arrested the escalation of food prices that had produced a wave of riots in 2008. But now, as the crisis changes form, they are on the rise once again and reaching unprecedented heights. Indeed, by late 2010 the UN Food and Agriculture Organization's food price index hit an all-time high, after rising a staggering 32 per cent in the last half of that year. Food is now more expensive than ever, aggravating economic hardship across the Global South and throwing fuel on the fire of popular resentment.

While speculation by hedge funds has rightly attracted criticism for contributing to spikes in food costs, the causes run deeper. Thanks to new trading platforms for raw commodities, it has become much easier for large investors to move money into financial derivatives based on food. A key turning point in this regard was the 1991 creation of the Goldman Sachs Commodity Index, which made it possible to invest in a bundle of commodities simultaneously. Rather than being tied to a single commodity, like coffee or copper, an investor could now buy a single financial asset that includes a multitude of commodities, among them agricultural products. Then in 2000 the US Commodity Futures Modernization Act deregulated trading in commodity indices and attracted large institutional investors, like pension and managed investment funds, into the market. Not surprisingly, speculative spending via index funds soared 1900 per cent between 2003 and early 2008, and a clear tendency has emerged for food prices to move in tandem with the general movement of financial markets.[55] Finally, with trillions pumped into the banking system and interest rates pushed down to record lows, financial investors have a huge incentive to borrow on the cheap to purchase commodities (and currencies) that look set to appreciate. Oil, gold, minerals, food and other raw commodities have figured particularly prominently in such speculative strategies.[56] In fact, investment bankers and managers of pension and hedge funds have funnelled over $200 billion into bets on food since the financial crisis first broke, driving up prices in a frenzy of speculation.[57] As a result, the global age of austerity has also become one of food insecurity across much of the Global South. And this has decisively shaped patterns of resistance.

RESISTANCE IN AN AGE OF AUSTERITY AND FOOD CRISIS

It has not been uncommon for commentators on the Left to bemoan the lack of resistance to the Great Recession and the Age of Austerity. The lament is misplaced, however. It is not that resistance has been lacking; it is simply that the *modes* of resistance thus far have generally been inadequate to the needs of a new era.[58]

Only a few months into the crisis, a popular upheaval toppled the government of Iceland, where banks had disintegrated with the onset of the financial crisis. As the currency plunged and jobs disappeared, large crowds, led by angry youth, surrounded the parliament buildings and pelted the prime minister's car with eggs and rocks in days and nights of rage. Faced with mass discontent, the government resigned in early January 2009, and a coalition of Greens and Social Democrats won the ensuing election. But when that government too moved to accommodate the demands of foreign lenders, the people of Iceland balked, persistently refusing to accept responsibility for debts to foreign banks.[59]

At the same moment that protests were shaking Iceland, a wave of factory occupations erupted, with the multiracial workforce at Republic Windows and Doors in Chicago leading the way.[60] In the space of a few months, workers at auto parts plants in Britain, Ireland, and Canada seized their workplaces to protest layoffs. In South Korea, metal workers staged a 77-day occupation, defying police attacks and tear gas dropped from helicopters. Notwithstanding the militancy exhibited by these workers, unions generally accepted improved severance agreements that failed to preserve jobs or keep plants open.[61] This was part of a wider pattern in which unions failed to rise to the challenge of the Great Recession and the Age of Austerity. In this context, the uplifting struggle at Republic could not become the launching pad of a mass movement to save jobs and restart production under workers' control – as similar actions did in Argentina in 2001-2.

Where workers did win real concessions on jobs, it required decidedly more militant methods, such as the 'bossnappings' that reverberated across France in 2009. This powerful tactic first emerged when workers at FCI Microconnections in Mante-la-Jolie took over their plant to block layoffs. Seven weeks later, a group of strikers converged on company headquarters in Versailles, set up barricades and prevented the chief executive officer and his staff from leaving. In the face of this mobilization, management eventually agreed to keep the factory open until 2014 and to pay the workers for time they had spent occupying their workplace. In the months that followed, similar bossnappings occurred at French plants owned by Caterpillar, Goss International, 3M, Sony, and Kleber-Michelin.[62]

These creative and audacious tactics by groups of workers in France, Ireland, Scotland, Canada and the US demonstrated a genuine spirit of resistance to the Great Recession. But actions on this scale could not stop the tidal wave of plant closings and layoffs that threw millions out of work, even if they could win local victories. Not even one-day general strikes, which shut down France on several occasions in the early months of 2009 – and enjoyed 75 per cent public support according to polls – have been enough to roll back austerity. Nor has a virtually permanent wave of protests in Greece, perhaps 900 in the course of a single year, including nine one-day strikes, often involving confrontational streets protests.[63] The same was true for the rallies and sit-ins that shut down the work of the Wisconsin legislature for a few weeks in early 2011. So determined is the ruling class to see through the austerity agenda that the dislocation created by day-long general strikes or weeks of disrupting legislative business is simply not sufficient to stop them.

If mass protest by unions forms one key axis of resistance to the Age of Austerity, a rising tide of youth rebellions forms another. In most of the world, young people have been hit disproportionately hard by unemployment, precarious work, and lack of affordable housing. In Egypt, the rate of youth unemployment is 25 per cent. In Tunisia it is 30 per cent.

And in Spain it is a shocking 43 per cent. It comes as little surprise, then, that young activists were a galvanizing force in the popular uprisings in Tunisia and Egypt, and that youth movements have kick-started a powerful wave of urban protest in Spain. The strategic role played by the youth-based April 6th Movement in the mass protests that seized Tahrir Square in Cairo and led to the overthrow of President Hosni Mubarak is widely acknowledged. Months later in Spain, tens of thousands of young people in Spain also occupied town squares, rallying behind groups bearing names like the Lost Generation, Youth Without a Future, The Indignant, and Real Democracy Now.[64] Across North Africa, the Middle East and Europe such militant street-based protests of youth and students have seized city squares, camped out, organized assembly-style democracy, all the while demanding a future beyond austerity and unemployment.[65]

Notwithstanding their inspiring energy and creativity, these youth rebellions also confront a key strategic problem. Only where they have fused with mass protest by organized workers' movements have youth uprisings been capable of overturning governments and transforming the political terrain. As much as they can occupy streets, insurgent movements of youth lack the economic clout of workers' struggles, which can shut off the flow of business profits. If labour movements are frequently too bureaucratic and timid to undertake the determined struggles necessary to curtail the austerity agenda, youth rebellions, while often more audacious and confrontational, regularly discover that occupying public squares does not paralyze capitalist business-as-usual. As a result, the anti-capitalist Left faces the political and organizational challenge of connecting the power of mass strikes by workers with the bold insurgency of street-based youth revolts. Where that has happened, the results have been electric.[66]

The first great example of mass strikes and demonstrations winning victories since the Great Recession – the general strikes and popular uprisings in the French semi-colonies of Guadeloupe and Martinique in the early months of 2009 – displayed just that fusion, as a mass social movement initiated by radical unions united youth, feminists and the unemployed. Guadeloupe and Martinique represent textbook cases of racialized, neo-colonial capitalism. And the intersection of economic hardship, rising food prices, and the dynamics of racialized capitalism gave these strike movements a massive popular resonance.[67]

The battle started on January 20, when a coalition of fifty unions and social movement groups, known as *Stand Up Against Exploitation* (Liyannaj Kont Pwofitasyon, or LKP in the local dialect) initiated a strike demanding a raise of 200 euros ($260 US dollars) per month for the lowest paid workers.

Under the leadership of the General Union of Workers of Guadeloupe, strikers shut down banks, schools, hotels and government offices. Protestors barricaded the main shipping terminal and closed the airport. Alarmed by the power of the movement, the French government sent hundreds of police, but this only further inflamed things, prompting angry youth to occupy the city hall in Sainte-Anne, and others to burn local businesses. By this point, the struggle had taken the form of a joint youth-worker uprising, and had spread to the neighbouring island of Martinique, where 25,000 people (out of a population of 400,000) took to the streets with similar demands.

In the face of unrelenting and escalating opposition, the French government caved in, agreeing on 4 March 2009 to raise salaries for the lowest paid in Guadeloupe by 200 euros, a 40 per cent increase, and to lower water rates, hire more teachers, provide aid to farmers and fishers, fund jobs and training for unemployed youth, freeze rents, and ban evictions. A week later, the government signed a similar agreement with the strikers in Martinique. While the workers of Guadeloupe and Martinique did not win the just society many sought, their militancy, creativity and determination achieved remarkable things, proving that, by uniting workers and discontented youth, it is possible to make major gains in the face of a deep recession. And by striking for more than a month, they underlined the sort of social contestation that will be necessary to derail the austerity agenda. Moreover, their struggles were harbingers of the mass upheavals in Tunisia and Egypt two years later.

There can be little doubt that the sharp escalation of food prices in the second half of 2010 played a detonating role in the outbreak of these rebellions. Throughout the Global South, the average citizen spends a disproportionate share of their income on food: between 20 and 25 per cent in India and Saudi Arabia, and a whopping 40 per cent in Egypt.[68] But detonators are just that. They accomplish nothing unless attached to explosive materials. And such materials are formed through a complex interaction among the accumulated grievances within society and growing hopes for change. Not only are socially explosive materials never traceable to a single cause, their ignition also requires activist networks and organizations that transform basic grievances into effective political protest – and in which the self-activity of the oppressed expands the horizons of possibility and rekindles the radical imagination. So, when the slogan 'Bread and Freedom' echoed across North Africa and the Middle East beginning in December 2010, it was not a question of which of the two was the cause and which the effect. [69] Rather, demands for economic and political justice – for food and freedom, for democracy and dignity – comprise inseparable parts of a singular cry for liberty.[70] As if to illustrate this point, during the upheaval in Egypt, the duo of Bread and Freedom expanded into the triplet of 'Bread, Freedom, Social Justice'.[71]

For the fusion of economic grievances with demands for democracy to generate a popular upheaval, there must be sufficiently robust grassroots networks (independent unions, social movements, student groups) capable of providing organizing hubs of resistance. In Tunisia, a critical role was played by the trade union federation, the General Union of Tunisian Workers (UGTT by its French initials), or more precisely by a layer of militant grassroots activists of the union. Despite the compromised history of the union's national leaders in recent decades, local activists of the UGTT galvanized the movement at crucial junctures, turning union offices into centres of opposition. Having spearheaded independent workers' protest in recent years, these rank-and-file unionists began organizing rallies and general strikes, remaking the UGTT as 'a serious political force with currently unmatched organizing capacity and national reach'.[72] This growing labour insurgency prevented the regime from isolating students and youth while drawing the latter into new oppositional alliances. As one perceptive journalist recounted, 'Fearing student protest, Ben Ali closed all educational establishments. A few hours later, the UGTT finally reacted. Its leadership authorized the regional sections in Sfax, Kairouan and Tozeur to organize a general strike the next day and then in Tunis on 14 January... That evening riots broke out in working class areas of Tunis. This was a turning point'.[73]

Henceforth, the struggle observed a new social dynamic in which '[t]he trade union (UGTT) played the role of momentum regulator and political indicator. It was clear that as long as the trade union kept on declaring strikes the battle was on, and that was the signal to the people to stick to the streets'.[74] Moreover, organized workers' initiatives have continued since the overthrow of Ben Ali. In addition to strikes, activists of the UGTT have waged sit–ins and a 'Caravan of Liberation' that marched on the capital from several cities demanding the removal of all political officials linked to the former dictator. In many towns, union activists have figured centrally in the construction of new structures of local democracy.[75] Nevertheless, conservative as well as radical forces continue to contend over the direction of both the union movement and the revolution – and the outcomes of those struggles will have a huge impact on how far the liberation movement in Tunisia can go.

Although Egypt did not have even a quasi-independent union movement prior to the overthrow of Mubarak in February 2011, it too had a recent history of growing labour insurgence that proved crucial when the mass movement erupted. Beginning in 2002, anti-war, feminist and democratic reform movements had taken to the streets on multiple occasions, helping to create a new climate of opposition. All of these campaigns were initiated and led by intellectuals, professionals and students, though they had much support from ordinary workers.[76] But after 2006, most of these movements ran out of steam. From this point on, the oppositional energies throughout Egyptian society were largely sustained thanks to mass mobilization by workers.

The rising tide of working-class protest can be traced directly to the neoliberal program of 2004 and the accelerated privatization and low-wage export-zones on which it pivoted. As jobs were lost and wages compressed, Egyptian workers engaged in ever more confrontational forms of resistance – strikes, sit-ins and mass rallies and demonstrations – all illegal under the emergency edicts and laws that were in place. In 2006-7 this wave of workers' activism burst into mass protest in the Nile Delta, spearheaded by the militancy of 50,000 workers in textiles and the cement and poultry industries. This was followed by strikes of train drivers, journalists, truckers, miners and engineers. Then 2007-8 saw another labour explosion, with riots at the state-owned weaving factory in Al-Mahla Al-Kobra and widespread strike action elsewhere. By now, workers' protest had become overtly political, with crowds burning banners of the ruling National Democratic Party and defacing posters of President Mubarak. The youth-based April 6th Movement emerged at this point in support of workers' strikes.[77] In all these ways, working-class protest was politicizing wide layers of Egyptian society, creating a culture of resistance, and linking economic and social issues to demands for democratisation.

Over the course of 2004-10, more than two million Egyptian workers undertook thousands of direct actions, prompting one commentator to note that, while other movements had retreated, 'one constituency, the workers' movement, has proved more difficult to control. Successful strikes in both state and private sectors have encouraged the largest and broadest labour movement for more than fifty years.'[78] When excitement over the Tunisian Revolution rolled through Egypt in January 2011, therefore, years of combative working-class protest had laid the groundwork for a movement that would sweep Egypt's President Mubarak from office.

But Mubarak would not leave until workers rose – as workers – once more. To be sure, the vast majority of the millions who were in Egypt's streets after 25 January 2011 were working-class people. But for much of the initial period of the uprising, many workplaces were closed and the action was in the streets. As factories and offices reopened, however, and as activists of the Left called for strikes to topple Mubarak, the situation changed. In the course of the week of 7 February, tens of thousands of workers – Cairo bus drivers, workers at Telecom Egypt, hospital workers, journalists, labourers at textile factories, pharmaceutical plants and steel mills, faculty at Cairo University – launched strikes and sit-ins. Everywhere they called for improved wages, the firing of ruthless managers, back pay, better working conditions and independent unions, and in many cases for the resignation of President Mubarak, shattering any lingering belief the beleaguered leader could ride out the storm without inciting serious threats to Egyptian and foreign capital. And in the months immediately following Mubarak's overthrow, this stream of working-class activism continued to flow on, albeit with ebbs and flows, in mass strikes, demonstrations, and the formation of independent unions, workers' parties and left coalitions.[79]

To be sure, anti-revolutionary forces, including the Egyptian and Tunisian armies, local private capitalists, western governments, and global agencies of neoliberalism like the IMF and the World Bank are working overtime to demobilize the masses and lock in bourgeois property rights and market regulation as the ostensible fruits of revolution. To this end, they are dangling tens of billions of dollars in 'aid', conditional on economic reforms that constitute a new round of neoliberal structural adjustment.[80]

Despite the risks they confront, however, the uprisings in Tunisia and Egypt, like the general strikes in Guadeloupe and Martinique, show that new forms of radical working-class politics can make crucial gains. In each of these cases, we observe the emergence of militant labour activism beyond the constraints of the business unionism that predominates in the Global North. Not only have these union movements been willing to resort to *unlimited* general strikes and mass confrontations with the state, rather than ritualized one-day stoppages; they have also operated as 'tribunes of the oppressed', to use the old socialist term, by fighting for demands that put the needs of the poorest workers to the fore. In so doing, they have put themselves forward as catalysts of 'real peoples' movements', to use Rosa Luxemburg's expression.[81] In linking organized workers, youth, the unemployed, and other oppressed people in common struggle The inspiring events we have described represent *a point of departure*. They create the space for ongoing processes of revolutionary self-activity – for the building of mass movements, cultures of resistance, and meaningful socialist organizations. But all of this will take years of dedicated work, particularly given the defeats and disarray experienced across the neoliberal period. Contrary to some readings, a long-term perspective for the revitalization and renewal of socialist working-class politics is entirely consistent with the notion of *révolution en permanence* – the term Marx used in the aftermath of the revolutions of 1848 to insist on the need for many years of independent working–class politics and organization. 'We say to the workers', he wrote, '"You will have to go through 15, 20, 50 years of civil wars and national struggles not only to bring about a change in society but also to change yourselves, and prepare yourselves for the exercise of political power…"'.[82]

NOTES

1   Carmen M. Reinhart and Kenneth S. Rogoff, *This Time is Different: Eight Centuries of Financial Folly*, Princeton: Princeton University Press, 2009, p. 208.

2   For works that interpret the Great Recession in these terms see Anwar Shaikh, 'The First Great Depression of the Twenty-First Century', *Socialist Register 2011*; and David McNally, *Global Slump: The Economics and Politics of Crisis and Resistance*, Oakland: PM Press, 2011. Leo Panitch and Sam Gindin also assess the Great Recession as a 'structural crisis' of capitalism though their analysis of the dynamics of accumulation and profitability underlying the crisis differs from Shaikh's as well as my own, see Leo Panitch and Sam Gindin, 'Capitalist Crises and the Crisis this Time', *Socialist Register 2011*, p. 4. David Kotz too sees the crisis of 2008 as a systemic one, see his article, 'The Financial and Economic Crisis of 2008: A Systemic Crisis of Neoliberal Capitalism', *Review of Radical Political Economics*, 41(3), Summer 2009, pp. 305-17, although his analysis pivots on the limits of growing economic inequality, rather than overaccumulation and declining profitability. For a mainstream perspective that understands the systemic features of the 2008-9 crisis, albeit in empiricist terms, see Reinhart and Rogoff, *This Time is Different*.

3   The final declaration issued by the G-20 group of the world's wealthiest nations at their June 2010 summit in Toronto included a commitment to 'halve deficits by 2013 and stabilize or reduce government debt-to-GDP ratios by 2016', though Japan, in light of its enduring slump, was explicitly excluded from these commitments. See 'The G-20 Toronto Summit Declaration', 26-27 June, 2011, available at http://www.canadainternational.gc.ca.

4   I document this intellectual crisis in McNally, *Global Slump*, ch. 1.

5   The National Bureau of Economic Research (NBER) in the US dates the Great Recession from December 2007 to June 2009, a duration of 18 months. The NBER has identified 18 recessions since the Great Depression, each lasting ten months on average, see the statement by the Business Cycle Dating Committee, National Bureau of Economic Research, 20 September 2010, available at http://www.nber.org.

6   See Barry Eichengreen and Kevin H. O'Rourke, 'A Tale of Two Depressions: What do the New Data Tell Us?', *Vox*, March 2010, available at http://www.voxeu.org.

7   While the figures used here begin in April 2008, for purposes of this article I work with the NBER dating of the Great Recession as having begun in late 2007, though based on movement of the mass of corporate profits a case can

be made for dating the onset as much as a year earlier.

8   For the sources from which I computed the figure of a $21 trillion dollar intervention see McNally, *Global Slump*, p. 197, n4.

9   Current US Federal Reserve Chairman Ben Bernanke famously used this term in a speech, 'Deflation: Making Sure "It" does not Happen Here', National Economists Club, Washington, DC, 21 November 2002, available at http://www.federalreserve.gov. The term itself appears to have originated in a thought experiment deployed by Milton Friedman, 'The Optimum Quantity of Money', in M. Friedman, *The Optimum Quantity of Money and Other Essays*, Chicago: Adline Publishing, 1969, ch. 1.

10   Richard Koo, 'QE2 has Transformed Commodity Markets into Liquidity Driven Markets', Nomura Equity Research, 17 May 2011; and N. Gregory Mankiw, 'Bernanke and the Beast', *New York Times*, 17 January 2010. Thanks to Anwar Shaikh for drawing Koo's report to my attention.

11   Ambrose Evans-Pritchard, 'US Money Supply Plunges at 1930s Pace as Obama Eyes Fresh Stimulus', *Telegraph*, 25 April 2011.

12   Benjamin Appelbaum, 'Stimulus by Fed is Disappointing, Economists Say', *New York Times*, 24 April 2011.

13   Catherine Rampell, 'Corporate Profits Were the Highest on Record Last Year', *New York Times*, 23 November 2010. Here some caution must be exercised, however, as by many calculations, profits as a share of national income in the US remain dramatically below their post-war heights – in the neighbourhood of 7 per cent today as opposed to 12 per cent in the 1950s and 1960s. See Justin Fox, 'The Real Story Behind Those "Record" Corporate Profits', *Harvard Business Review Blogs*, 24 November 2010, available at http://blogs.hbr.org.

14   Martin Wolf, 'The Road to Recovery Gets Steeper', *Financial Times*, 7 June 2011.

15   Michael Greenstone, 'The Problem with Men: A Look at Long-term Employment Trends', *Brooking Institution Up Front Blog*, 3 December 2010, available at http://www.brookings.edu.

16   Data in this paragraph come from Andrea Orr, 'One in Four Black, Hispanic Workers is Underemployed', Economic Policy Institute, 8 January 2010; Ajamu Dillahunt et al., *State of the Dream 2010: Drained Jobless and Foreclosed in Communities of Color*, Boston: United for a Fair Economy, 2010; Keeanga-Yamahtta Taylor, 'Black America's Economic Freefall', *Socialist Worker*, 8 January 2010, available at http://wwww.socialistworker.org; and Mariko Chang, *Lifting as We Climb: Women of Color, Wealth and America's Future*, Insight Center for Community Economic Development, 2010, p. 5. On the combined unemployment and under-employment rate in the US see Mike Shedlock, 'US Unemployment Rate 10.2%, Underemployment at 20%', *The Market Oracle*, 20 March 2011, available at http://www.marketoracle.co.uk.

17   On the fall in US home prices from 2006 by one third, see Colin Barr, 'Why House Prices Will Keep Falling', *Fortune*, 29 March 2011, available at http://finance.fortune.cnn.com; see also Al Yoon, 'Home Price Drop Exceeds Great Depression: Zillow', *Reuters*, 11 January 2001, available at http://www.reuters.com; Dominic Rushe, 'US Housing Prices Still Falling', *Guardian*, 9 May 2011;

Joanna Slater, 'US Housing: First a Crash, Then a Double Dip', *Globe and Mail*, 1 June 2011.

18   David Parkinson, 'Shrinking Work Force, Rising Profits', *Globe and Mail*, 24 March 2010. See also Jon Hilsenrath and Luca Di Leo, 'Cost-cutting Fuels U.S. Productivity Boom', *Wall Street Journal*, 6 November 2009. On profitable companies and their layoffs, see Andrea Orr, 'Many Highly Profitable Companies Cut Jobs in 2009', Economic Policy Institute, 23 December 2009, available at http://www.epi.org.

19   'Show Us the Money', *Economist*, 1 July 2010.

20   Adam Hersch and Christopher Weller, 'Measuring Future U.S. Competitiveness', Center for American Progress, 9 February 2011, available at http://www.americanprogress.org. For similar issues in Europe into 2011, see 'Business Investment Rate at 20.8 per cent in the Euro Area and 20.3 per cent in EU 27', *Xorte*, 5 May 2011, available at http://www.europe.xorte.com.

21   Karen Howlett, 'Corporate Tax Cuts Don't Spur Growth', *Globe and Mail*, 6 April 2011.

22   Robert Sadowski, 'A Cash Buildup and Business Investment', Federal Reserve Bank of Cleveland, 10 January 2011, available at http://www.clevelandfed.org.

23   Richard Milne and Anousha Sakoui, 'Corporate Finance: Rivers of Riches', *Financial Times*, 22 May 2011.

24   Figure 5 is taken from Sadowski, 'A Cash Buildup and Business Investment'; see also Justin Lahart, 'U.S. Companies Hoarding Cash', *Wall Street Journal*, 10 December 2010. Note that, consistent with my claim that the neoliberal boom was winding down by 1997-98, corporate cash holding start to rise persistently from 2001.

25   Board of Governors of the Federal Reserve System, 'Industrial Production and Capacity Utilization – G.17', 15 April 2011, available at http://www.federalreserve.gov.

26   For Germany, see 'Increased Capacity Utilization in March', 6 April 2011, available from http://www.airberlin.com. For Britain, see 'Capacity Utilization Rate - USD' at http://www.forexpros.com. For Canada, consult Statistics Canada, 'Industrial Capacity Utilization Rates', 14 March 2011, available from http://www40.statcan.ca.

27   Giulio Tremonte, Statement by the Governor of the International Monetary Fund for Italy, 16 April 2011, available at http://www.imf.org; Floyd Norris, 'Inevitability of a Default in Greece', *New York Times*, 6 May 2011.

28   Ralph Atkins and Kevin Hope, 'Greece: Hard to Hold the Line', *Financial Times*, 1 May 2011; Associated Press, 'Creditors May Share Greece's Pain as EU Eyes Debt Repayment', *Globe and Mail*, 18 May 2011.

29   Wolfgang Munchau, 'Political Problems behind a Not-So-Secret Meeting', *Financial Times*, 9 May 2011.

30   Doug Saunders, 'Britain Braces for Sting of Austerity', *Globe and Mail*, 20 October 2010; Landon Thomas Jr., 'British Path: Rocky Result', *New York Times*, 15 April 2011; Helene Mullholland, 'GDP Figures: Cameron Accused of Complacency Over Economy', *Guardian*, 27 April 2011; Julia Kollewe,

'UK Household Spending Slumps to Near Two-Year Low', *Guardian*, 25 May 2011.

31   David Rosenberg, 'Government Intervention Giving Rise to Statistical Mirage', *Globe and Mail*, 6 May 2010.

32   There remains an important debate as to how large a role deficit–reduction played in the recession of 1937, but it can only have been considerable. A detailed account from a Keynesian perspective is provided by Kenneth D. Roose, *The Economics of Recession and Revival, an Interpretation of 1937-38*, New Haven: Yale University Press, 1954; Kindleberger holds that a massive overstocking of inventories in the run-up to 1937 also played a significant role, see Charles P. Kindleberger, *The World in Depression 1929-1939*, London: University of California Press, 1954, ch. 12. On Japan's experience in 1997 see Koo, 'QE2 has Transformed Commodity Markets', p. 7.

33   Martin Wolf, 'The Eurozone after Strauss-Kahn', *Financial Times*, 17 May 2011; Tyler Cowen, 'Euro vs. Invasion of the Zombie Banks', *New York Times*, 17 April 2011; Eric Reguly, 'EU Should Wake from its Dream World and Accept Default', *Globe and Mail*, 7 April 2011.

34   Mario Blejer, 'Europe is Running a Giant Ponzi Scheme', *Financial Times*, 5 May 2011; Costa Lapavitsas, 'Euro Exit Strategy Crucial for Greeks', *Guardian*, 21 June 2011.

35   McNally, *Global Slump*, pp. 8-9.

36   Anwar Shaikh has argued that another key factor was the protracted decline in interest rates after 1983, which raised the rate of profit on enterprise. This appears to be an important point and one neglected by most commentators, including myself in *Global Slump*, and is deserving of further research. See Shaikh, 'First Great Depression', pp. 50-53

37   The preceding paragraph summarizes an argument made at much greater length in McNally, *Global Slump*, pp. 37-57.

38   For an analysis of that crisis in terms of growing problems of world over-accumulations, see my 'Globalization on Trial: Crisis and Class Struggle in East Asia', *Monthly Review*, 50(4), 1998, p. 4; see also World Bank, *East Asia: The Road to Recovery*, Washington, DC: World Bank, 1998, ch. 2

39   Michael Mandel, 'A Bad Decade for Nonfinancial Profits', *Business Week*, Econochat blog, 4 March 2011, available at http://www.businessweek.com.

40   Michael Roberts, 'Profits and Investment in the Economic Recovery', 29 December 2010, available at http://thenextrecession.wordpress.com. This analysis is a confirmation of the data on US profits presented by Anwar Shaikh, 'First Great Depression', p. 48, Figure 1.

41   Phillip Inman, 'Bank of England Governor Blames Spending Cuts on Bank Bailouts', *Guardian*, 1 March 2011.

42   Stephen G. Cecchetti, M. S. Mohanty and Fabrizio Zampolli, 'The Future of Public Debt: Prospects and Implications', BIS Working Paper 300, Bank for International Settlements, March 2010. On the IMF see Alan Beattie, 'Wealthy Nations Urged to Make Rapid Cuts', *Financial Times*, 10 June 2010. For the G20's austerity agenda see Kevin Carmichael, 'G20 Plan's Dilemma: Boosting Growth with Less Spending', *Globe and Mail*, 29 June 2010 and 'The G-20

Toronto Summit Declaration', 26-27 June 2010.

43   The government that issues world money, the dominant international reserve currency and means of payment, will face weaker constraints than do other nations. Today, this refers to the US government. But even America faces some real economic limits on the deficits it can run.

44   Cecchetti et al., 'The Future of Public Debt', p. 1.

45   See Naomi Klein, *The Shock Doctrine: The Rise of Disaster Capitalism*, Toronto: Knopf Canada, 2007. For a sympathetic but at times pointed critique of some parts of Klein's analysis, see Neil Davidson, 'Shock and Awe', *International Socialism*, 124, 2009.

46   I borrow the term 'competitive austerity' from Greg Albo's essay, 'Competitive Austerity and Capitalist Employment Policy', *Socialist Register 1994*. This underlines the continuity of these policies across the neoliberal period; but it does not deny the uniqueness of the current period as a crisis of a neoliberal model that was much more robust at the time of Albo's essay. Whether these policies can contribute to a transcendence of this crisis remains to be seen.

47   The IFS report refers to 'two parliaments of pain', which is the equivalent of a decade. See Steve Schifferes, 'UK Economy Faces Decade of Pain', BBC News, 23 April 2010, available at http://news.bbc.co.uk.

48   Editorial, 'The Looming Crisis in the States', *New York Times*, 26 December 2010.

49   Monica Davey, 'For Wisconsin Governor, Battle Over State Finances was Long in the Making', *New York Times*, 20 February 2011; Konrad Yakabuski, 'Governor Versus Unions: a Battle with National Consequences', *Globe and Mail*, 24 February 2011.

50   *Global Economic Prospects 2010: Crisis, Finance and Growth*, Washington, DC: World Bank, 2010.

51   See McNally, *Another World is Possible: Globalization and Anti-Capitalism*, Second Edition, Winnipeg and London: Arbeiter Ring Publishing and Merlin Press, 2006, pp. 95-108; and McNally, *Global Slump*, pp. 134-40.

52   '"Every 30 Minutes": Crushed by Debt and Neoliberal Reforms, Indian Farmers Commit Suicide at Staggering Rate', Democracy Now, 11 May 2011, available at http://www.democracynow.org.

53   Damian Carrington, 'Biofuels Boom in Africa as British Firms Lead Rush on Land for Plantations', *Guardian*, 1 June 2011.

54   On Latin America, see 'Land Grabbing in Latin America', *Grain*, March 2010. It is true that climate change is also a factor here, but its effects cannot be separated from the social relations of agribusiness, bio-fuels, land-grabbing, and rural dispossession. On the environmental aspects, see Robert Bailey, *Growing a Better Future: Food Justice in a Resource-Constrained World*, Oxfam International, June 2011, available from http://www.oxfam.org.

55   See Institute for Agriculture and Trade Policy, *Commodities Market Speculation: The Risk to Food Security and Agriculture*, November 2008, available at http://www.iatp.org; Christian Aid, *Hungry for Justice: Fighting Starvation in an Age of Plenty*, Christian Aid, 2011, pp. 10-25; and the study by Princeton University economists, Ke Tang and Wei Xiong, 'Index Investment and Financialization

of Commodities', 2010, available at http://www.princeton.edu.

56   For a report on Canadian brokerage houses urging clients to invest in food stocks, see Martin Mittelstaedt, 'A Case for Plowing Funds into Agribusiness', *Globe and Mail*, 13 May 2011. On speculative investment in oil, see Danny Schechter, 'The Scam Behind the Rise in Oil, Food Prices', *Aljazeera.net,* 19 April 2011.

57   Deborah Doane, 'The Threat of Rising Food Prices', *New Statesman*, 11 January 2011. Note that in these cases institutional investors are in part acting as 'speculators'. For a discussion on the underlying dynamics of such speculative flows, see Koo 'QE2 has Transformed Commodity Markets', p. 6.

58   Of course, working-class resistance was also generally inadequate across most of the neoliberal era – which is a key to why capital did so well. And the inadequacies of the movements today are in large part an inheritance of the neoliberal period. It must also be acknowledged, however, that since late 2008 we have seen much more resort to mass street-based protests and general strikes than we did during most of the neoliberal period, and the former in particular have often drawn in whole new layers of youth. But even these heightened modes of resistance have not proved equal to the task.

59   'Icelandic Voters Reject Icesafe Debt Repayment Plan', *Guardian*, 10 April 2011

60   Kari Lyderson and James Tracy, 'The *Real* Audacity of Hope: Republic Windows Workers Stand their Ground', *Dollars and Sense*, January/February 2009; and David Bacon, 'Chicago Workers to the Rest of the Country: Don't let it Die!' *New American Media*, 11 December 2008, available at http://news.newamericanmedia.org.

61   Occasionally, workers did keep a factory open, as at Prisme Packaging in Dundee, Scotland, where a 51-day occupation led to reopening the plant as a workers' cooperative. For background on these struggles, see Immanuel Ness and Stacy Warner Madder, 'Worker Direct Action Grows in Wake of Financial Meltdown', *Dollars and Sense*, November/December 2009; and Alan Sheldon, 'Tools of the Trade: Resistance to the Crisis around the World', *New Socialist,* 66, 2009, p. 24.

62   Jessica Leeder, 'Economic Uncertainty Boils Over in Workplace', *Globe and Mail*, 26 March 2009; David Gauthier-Villars and Leila Abboud, 'Kidnapping the Boss Becoming a Peculiarly French Tactic', *Globe and Mail,* 3 April 2009.

63   On the claim for 900 Greek protests in a year, see Eric Reguly, 'Cue the Protesters', *Globe and Mail,* 6 June 2011.

64   See 'Young, Jobless and Looking for Trouble', *Economist* blog by Schumpeter, 3 February 2011, available at: http://www.economist.com/blogs. On young people and political movements in Egypt, see Tarek Osman, *Egypt on the Brink*, New Haven: Yale University Press, 2010, ch. 7. For good treatments of the dynamics of youth rebellion in Spain, see Suzanne Daley, 'An Awakening that Keeps them Up All Night', *New York Times*, 6 June 2011, and Zach Zill, 'The Uprising over Spain's Future', *Socialist Worker,* 26 May 2011.

65   On assembly-style democracy in Greece, see Costas Douzinas, 'In Greece, We see Democracy in Action', *Guardian*, 15 June 2011; on Spain, see Zill, 'The

Uprising over Spain's Future'.

66   Panagiotis Sotiris argues that such an intersection of youth and worker struggles emerged in Greece in the spring of 2011, see Panagiotis Sotiris, 'Days of Unrest and Hope', *Greek Left Review*, 9 June 2011, available at http://greekleftreview. wordpress.com.

67   In what follows, my account draws from Rudolphe Lamy, 'Price Protests Paralyze Martinique, Guadeloupe', *Associated Press*, 11 February 2009; Angelique Chrisafis, 'France Faces Revolt over Poverty on its Caribbean Islands', *Guardian*, 12 February 2009; United Press International, 'Protests Disrupt Life on French Islands', 13 February 2009; Richard Fidler, 'Guadeloupe: General Strike Scores Victory, Spreads to Other Colonies', *Green Left Weekly*, 3 March 2009 and 'Martinique General Strike Ends in Victory', *Green Left Weekly*, 21 March 2009; 'Grève générale en Guadeloupe: le LKP durcit le ton`, *Afrik. com*, 12 February 2009; and 'Labor Victory in Guadeloupe After Six-Week Strike Reverberates Across French Caribbean and France', *Democracy Now!*, 27 March 2009, available at: http://www.democracynow.org.

68   Christian Aid, *Hungry for Justice*, pp. 29-30.

69   On the emergence of the new food crisis see, Paul Waldie, 'World Food Prices Hit New High, Raising Fears of another Food Crisis', *Globe and Mail*, 6 January 2011; and on the wave of food-related uprisings see 'Food Security: Bread and Freedom', *Guardian*, 1 February 2011; and David McNally, 'A Night in Tunisia: Riots, Strikes and a Spreading Insurgency', available on multiple sites including http://davidmcnally.org. For interesting reflections on the dynamics of revolutionary change in 2011, see Rebecca Solnit, 'The Butterfly and the Boiling Point: Charting the Wild Winds of Change in 2011', March 2011, available at http://www.towardfreedom.com.

70   Just as anger against unemployment, especially for youth, was part of the matrix of grievances that fuelled these revolts, so, as Sadri Khiara points out for Tunisia, was a quest for dignity. See Sadri Khiari, 'Africa: Tunisian Revolution Did Not Come Out of Nowhere', *Pambazuka News*, 26 May 2011, available at http://allafrica.com.

71   Mona El-Ghobashy, 'The Praxis of the Egyptian Revolution', *Middle East Research and Information Project*, 258, Spring 2011, available at http://www. merip.org.

72   'Tunisian Unions Eclipsing Parties as Democratising Force?', *Democracy Digest*, 24 January 2001. See also Eric Lee and Benjamin Weinthal, 'Trade Unions: The Revolutionary Social Network at Play in Egypt and Tunisia', *Guardian*, 10 February 2011.

73   Olivier Piot, 'Tunisia: Diary of a Revolution', *Le monde diplomatique*, February 2011.

74   Dyab Abu Jahjah, 'Notes on the Tunisian Revolution', 14 January 2011, available at http://www.aboujahjah.com.

75   Amanda Sebestyen, 'Tunisia's Brutal Regime May Be Down, But it has Shown it is Not Out', *Tribune Magazine*, May 2011.

76   For a good overview of these movements see Rabab El-Mahdi, 'The Democracy Movement: Cycles of Protest' in Rabab El-Mahdi and Philip Marfleet, eds.,

Egypt: The Moment of Change, London: Zed Books, 2009.

77   For background on the workers' struggles of this period see Hossam El-Hamalawy, 'Egypt's Revolution has been 10 Years in the Making', Guardian, 2 March 2011; Mona El-Ghobashy, 'Egypt Looks Ahead to Portentous Year', Middle East Report Online, 2 February 2003, available at http://www.arabawy.org; Joel Beinin, 'Popular Social Movements and the Future of Egyptian Politics', Middle East Report Online, 10 March 2005; Joel Beinin and Hossam El-Hamalawy, 'Egyptian Textile Workers Confront the New Economic Order', Middle East Report Online, 25 March 2007.

78   Phil Marfleet, 'Act One of the Egyptian Revolution', International Socialism, 130, 2011.

79   See Raphael Kempf, 'Egypt: First Democracy, then a Pay Rise', Le Monde Diplomatique, March 2011; Omar, Mostafa, 'The Spring of the Egyptian Revolution', Socialist Worker, 30 March 2011; Kieron Monks, 'Egypt's Socialist Network Keeps the Spirit of the Revolution Alive', Guardian, 28 April 2011; Mohamed El Hebeishy, 'Five Socialist Parties Unite to Impact Egyptian Politics', Ahram Online, 11 May 2011, available at: http://english.ahram.org.eg.

80   Adam Hanieh, 'Egypt's "Orderly Transition"? International Aid and the Rush to Structural Adjustment', Jadaliyya, 29 March 2011, available at http://www.jadaliyya.com; Austin Mackell, 'The IMF versus the Arab Spring', Guardian, 25 May 2011; 'G8 Leaders Pledge US$20 billion for Post-revolution Egypt and Tunisia', Afriquejet.com, 28 May 2011.

81   Rosa Luxemburg, 'The Mass Strike, the Political Party and the Trade Unions', in Mary-Alice Waters, ed., Rosa Luxemburg Speaks, New York: Pathfinder Press, 1970, pp. 182, 187.

82   Karl Marx, 'Revelations Concerning the Cologne Communist Trial', in Karl Marx and Frederick Engels, Collected Works, Volume 11, London, Lawrence & Wishart, 1979 [1853]. An excellent discussion of the development of Marx's views on permanent revolution is provided by Richard B. Day and Daniel Gaido in their editors' Introduction to Witnesses to Permanent Revolution: The Documentary Record, Chicago: Haymarket Books, 2011, pp. 1-58.

CRISIS AS CAPITALIST OPPORTUNITY: THE NEW ACCUMULATION THROUGH PUBLIC SERVICE COMMODIFICATION

URSULA HUWS

I

This essay argues that 2008 marked a turning point for international capital, with the financial crisis providing an unprecedented opportunity to embark on a new phase of accumulation based, not on what might be called 'primary primitive accumulation' (the generation of new commodities from natural resources or activities carried out outside the money economy) but on the commodification of public services. In this commodification process, which might be regarded as a kind of 'secondary primitive accumulation', activities already carried out in the paid economy for their use value (such as education, or health care) are standardized in such a way that they can be traded for profit and appropriated by capital: use value is thereby transformed into exchange value.[1] This secondary form of accumulation is based on the expropriation, not just of nature or unalienated aspects of life, nor of unpaid domestic labour, but of the results of past struggles by workers for the redistribution of surplus value in the form of universal public services. It thus constitutes a *re*appropriation and, as such, its impacts on working–class life are multiple and pernicious.

For the workers actually delivering public services, new forms of alienation are introduced and there is generally a deterioration in working conditions. However, there are also larger implications for workers in other sectors, because public sector workers are, in most developed economies, the last remaining bastion of trade union strength and decent working conditions, setting the standards for other workers to aspire to. This means that the erosion of the bargaining position of public sector workers also represents a defeat for all workers in their capacities *as* workers. At an even more general level, past gains are snatched from the working class as a whole (including children, the elderly, the sick and the unemployed). This last effect cannot, of course, remain invisible and understandably becomes a focus of opposition. However, a political strategy based only on 'fighting the cuts' risks giving the impression that it is simply the scale of state expenditure that is in contest, rendering invisible the underlying logic of commodification and the new reality that public services themselves have become a site of accumulation that is crucial for the continuing expansion of international capital. The new reality is one in which large sections of capital actually have a vested interest in an *enlarged* public service sector, but one in which services are standardized and capable of being delivered by a compliant and interchangeable workforce, embedded in a global division of labour and subjected to the discipline of that global labour market. This raises new contradictions for the relationship between the state and capital.

It is increasingly difficult, if not impossible, to separate 'finance capital' from 'productive capital' either analytically or empirically.[2] I will not attempt here to disentangle the complex interactions between the lead-up to the financial crisis and the restructuring of transnational organizations, or the ways in which the holding companies that own supposedly non-financial organizations are increasingly behaving like financial ones. Nevertheless, in order to understand this phenomenon, it is necessary to outline some of the background conditions that have led to the emergence of the new breed of multinational corporations currently waxing fat on the commodification of public services.

II

The 2008 financial crisis coincided with a crisis of profitability for international capital which was already undergoing massive restructuring. One aspect of this restructuring was a huge growth in the concentration of capital. 2007 represented a peak in global investment flows, with global FDI flows reaching their highest level ever ($1,833 billion), surpassing the 2000 peak.[3] There was also a record level of cross-border mergers and acquisitions, with the number rising by 12 per cent and the value (some $1,637 billion) up 21 per cent on the previous year.[4] UNCTAD estimated that the total sales of 79,000 TNCs and their 790,000 foreign affiliates amounted in that year to $31 trillion – a 21 per cent increase over 2006 – whilst the total number of their employees rose to some 82 million. The 100 largest TNCs, in particular, strengthened their global grip, with combined foreign assets estimated at $570 billion.[5] However, despite this huge growth, the number of green-field FDI projects actually *decreased* – from 12,441 in 2006 to 11,703 in 2007.[6] This indicates that whilst the process of concentration was accelerating, there was actually a slow-down in the generation of new production. In other words, the largest TNCs were sustaining their profits not so much as a result of new production but through the cannibalization of pre-existing production capacity. Without some new source of commodities from which to generate surplus value, the preconditions were in place for a decline in profitability. When few parts of the world were left outside the scope of global capitalism, where might these new commodities be found?

Associated with this trend was a major reorganization of value chains. Facilitated by a combination of neoliberal trade policies and the widespread introduction of the information and communications technologies that make it easy to relocate economic activities and manage them remotely, the previous decade had seen an acceleration of the trend to modularize business processes in such a way that they could be reconfigured in a variety of different contractual and spatial permutations and combinations. In the late 1990s, 'offshore outsourcing' still seemed something of a risky experiment.[7] A decade later it had come to seem such a normal part of business-as-usual that US and European managers were expected to justify why they had *not* opened call centres in India, shared service centres in Russia or design studios in Vietnam, alongside their production facilities in China. Most large corporations had systematically anatomized their business processes, broken them down into standardized units and, unit by unit, decided whether to concentrate them on a single site or distribute them around the world, whether to keep them in-house or outsource them and whether to search for the lowest price or the highest quality or some complex combination of these things. In aggregate, these decisions had brought about major upheavals. By 2008 a new global division of labour had emerged,[8] with new patterns of regional specialization and new corporate and sectoral configurations. As more and more economic activities became tradable, large companies embarked upon a dual process of disaggregation and aggregation, shuffling and reshuffling these activities into new combinations.[9] Whilst some companies continued to focus on their traditional strengths in manufacturing or the extraction of natural resources, others consolidated their positions as suppliers of services. By 2006, one in five (20 per cent) of the 100 largest non-financial TNCs listed by UNCTAD was a company providing services, compared with only 7 per cent in 1997.

As these huge service companies expanded their markets, the services they supplied became more generic, increasingly developing the character of standard commodities, so standardized that, in many cases, it was possible to supply essentially the same services (for instance IT services, payroll administration or customer services) to client companies regardless of which economic sector they were in: manufacturing, retail, utilities or other sectors. Most of their customer companies were no longer, as they might have been in the past, operating in a buyer's market acquiring bespoke services tailored to their individual needs; rather, they were becoming like shoppers in a chain store, selecting from amongst a range of standard models offered by the seller. Once such a supply reaches critical mass, a harsh economic logic sets in: the larger the market for these services is, and the more that standardization can be achieved, then the lower the price will become. Soon, even customers whose preference might be to continue to produce these services for themselves in-house, or to buy them tailor-made from a small local supplier, are driven by the relentless logic of the market (in which the relative cost of customization has become exorbitantly expensive compared with the purchase of standard products) to realize that such personalization is a luxury, and to follow the crowd to the cheapest supplier. In IT-based business services, in particular, this logic has been given an extra push through the dominance of standard software packages (such as those supplied by Microsoft) or platforms (such as those supplied by SAP Business Management Systems) and the ways that these may be bundled in with the services supplied by global suppliers of telecommunications, energy or other infrastructure services. However, IT-enabled industries are by no means the only examples of sellers' markets in the supply of services; large multinational corporations are also increasingly involved in supplying manual labour, either through labour-only subcontracting by temporary employment agencies or through the outsourced provision of, for instance, security, care or cleaning services. Increasingly prominent amongst the customers of these service companies, over the past decade, have been public sector organizations.

In the early years of the 21st century, these trends reinforced each other, producing a situation whereby large service supply companies (with their own internal global divisions of labour) were desperate to expand. With limited opportunities to grow through acquisition and merger, and markets in many other sectors nearing saturation, the public sector offered a tempting new field for expansion. By 2008, according to a report published by the UK government, outsourced public services accounted for nearly 6 per cent of GDP in the UK, directly employing over 1.2 million people, with a turnover of £79 billion in 2007-08 – an increase of 126 per cent over the estimated £31 billion in 1995-96. The report dubbed this rapidly-expanding sector 'the public services industry' (PSI) and noted that, in terms of value added, it 'is significantly larger than "food, beverages and tobacco" (23bn in 2006), "communications" (£28bn), "electricity, gas and water supply" (£32bn) and "hotels and catering" (£36bn)'. This phenomenon is not peculiar to

Britain. As a share of GDP, the PSI sector was estimated in that year to be even higher in Sweden and Australia. In absolute terms, the UK PSI market, at £79.4bn, was second only to that of the USA (at £393.bn) but the sector was nevertheless significant in scale elsewhere, with an estimated value, for instance, of £44.8bn in France, £32.2bn in Australia and £24.7bn in Spain. If a somewhat broader definition were to be applied, encompassing former public utilities like post, telecommunications, water and energy, these figures would be considerably larger.[10]

Large though these sums are, they represent only a fraction of the total value of public services. Despite the neoliberal anti-'big government' rhetoric of the last quarter-century, despite the very real cutbacks in services that have been experienced by working people as a withdrawal of state support, and despite the sale of public assets,[11] government spending has risen inexorably in all OECD countries both in absolute terms and as a percentage of GDP. Whereas in 1960, government spending was an average 28.4 per cent of GDP across the OECD, by 1980 this had risen to 43.8 per cent since when it has continued to creep up to reach 47.7 per cent in 2009. This varies somewhat by country, with Japan, at 39.7 per cent, the USA at 42.2 per cent and Canada, at 43.8 per cent, relatively near the bottom of the range, and the Netherlands, Sweden, France, Austria, Belgium and Italy near the top, each with government spending between 50 per cent and 54 per cent of GDP. The UK and Germany are close to the average, at 47.2 per cent and 47.6 per cent respectively.[12] An analysis based on government spending per person produces a different ranking, with the USA (where total government spending is estimated at nearly $6 trillion) above Italy, Canada, Britain and Japan, partly because of its much higher military spending.[13] However the figures are broken down, this represents a potential field for expansion which is staggering in its scale, a market which, ironically enough, with the notable exception of the militarized US, is proportionally largest in precisely those countries that, as a result of democratic pressure from below, have built the most comprehensive welfare states. This is how social-democrat Sweden, regarded by Esping-Andersen[14] and others as having achieved the highest degree of decommodification of any developed capitalist economy, contrived to top the list of countries with the largest share of outsourced government services in 2008: the more decommodification, the more scope for recommodification.

III

How has this market been levered open? Procurement of services from external providers is not new, of course. For centuries governments have commissioned buildings, roads, bridges and other 'public works', and purchased goods, ranging from paper-clips to fire engines, from private suppliers. And for just as long there have been scandals relating to the greasing of public servants' palms by suppliers to acquire these lucrative contracts. However it is probably most useful to date the origins of the current wave of outsourcing to the early 1980s. In the UK, the Conservative government pioneered two distinctively different forms of privatization. One of these was the direct sale of public assets, originally promoted as sales to individual citizens rather than to companies. The most high-profile of these were the sales of council houses to their tenants and, starting in 1984, of public utilities – telecommunications, gas and electricity – via widely-publicised share issues, which the general public were invited to buy. Associated with the latter, though less well publicised, was the opening up of telecommunications and energy markets to competition from private companies. The other form of privatization (not involving a total change of ownership) was the government-enforced introduction of 'compulsory competitive tendering', first into local government and then into the National Health Service (NHS). Whilst this did not necessarily mean that the services in question *had* to be carried out by external contractors, in-house departments, employing public servants, were now obliged to compete with private companies in order to be able to continue providing the service in question. This brought downward pressure on wages and conditions and introduced a new precariousness: jobs were no longer necessarily 'for life' but only guaranteed for the duration of the contract.

This first swathe of competitive tendering involved mainly manual tasks such as construction work, waste disposal and cleaning, perhaps not coincidentally also the areas where public sector unions were strong, and had demonstrated this strength in the widespread strikes of the 'winter of discontent' of 1978-79 that directly preceded Thatcher's election victory. Much of the rhetoric surrounding this enforced outsourcing centred, not just on the supposed efficiencies that would be gained through the delivery of services by private companies, unconstrained by the 'restrictive practices' of public sector manual unions, but also on a discourse of 'enterprise': the external provision of these services, it was claimed, would create openings for new small firms. In reality, the majority of the contracts went to large, often multinational companies. In 1984-85, for instance, whilst public attention was focused on the national strike by coal miners – the other group of organized workers directly targeted by Thatcher's Tories – another long-running strike was taking place at Barking Hospital in East London. The striking cleaners at this hospital were employed by a subsidiary of the

Pritchards Services Group, a transnational corporation with 58 subsidiaries in 15 countries, employing 17,000 people in 430 hospitals worldwide, including Saudi Arabia, South Africa, New Zealand, France, Germany and the USA.[15] Interestingly enough, from 1983 to 1994, Thatcher's husband, Denis, was vice-chairman of Attwoods plc, a large international waste management company which stood to gain from precisely this form of privatization. A detailed study of the impact of Compulsory Competitive Tendering in Local Government in the UK carried out in 1993-94 concluded that women were much more adversely affected than men, with female employment in local government declining by 22 per cent compared with 12 per cent for male employment, as well as a much steeper decline in earnings for women than for men. There was also a substantial fall in trade union membership. However the cost implications for the state were actually *negative*. Whilst neoliberal proponents of the policy (in the World Bank, IMF and OECD as well as the UK Government) were claiming that the policy would bring savings of 20-25 per cent, in reality the savings averaged only 6.5 per cent. In the 39 case study authorities studied, this amounted to an estimated £16 million. However the estimated total public costs (taking into account lost national insurance contributions and the cost of related unemployment benefit) were estimated at £41 million (of which £32 million was accounted for by women's employment). Extrapolated to a national level, this was estimated at savings of £124 million and losses of £250 million, leading to a net national loss of £126 million.[16]

Each of these forms of privatization had parallels elsewhere. In Europe, Britain played an important role in pushing through a liberalization agenda which led to the compulsory selling off, first of national telecommunications providers, then of publicly-owned energy companies and the opening up of postal services to the market. There had been EU regulation of public procurement since 1966 (in Directive 66/683, which prohibited rules favouring national suppliers over foreign ones within the single European Market). The turn to neoliberalism brought much broader deregulation in the mid-1980s. The *Single European Act* of 1986 introduced a new regime in which open tendering procedures were established as the norm for all public supplies in the EU and negotiated procedures were allowed only in exceptional circumstances. The first *Utilities Directive* (90/351) removed market access barriers to energy, telecommunications, transport and water, and in 1992 the *Services Directive* (92/50) extended the principles that had governed the procurement of goods, works and public utilities to public services more generally.[17]

Meanwhile, the Uruguay Round of the GATT, which commenced in

1986 and culminated in GATT 1994, brought services (along with capital and intellectual property) within the scope of global trade agreements. 1992, the year in which the International Telecommunications Union (ITU) was established, initiated an era of global telecommunications deregulation which in turn opened up the enabling infrastructure for cheap global transfer of digitised information. This was also the year in which India was able to start exporting its software services freely, through the removal of export barriers that had originally been designed to protect an indigenous industry as part of an import-substitution strategy. In the early 1990s, the stage was therefore set for global companies to provide a range of services across national borders, bulldozing their way through any restrictions that might have been set up to protect national companies or local workforces.[18]

These developments coincided historically with the formal ending of the Cold War after 1989. Not only did this open up the countries of the former Soviet Bloc as new markets for Western capital, it also removed any remaining reasons for employers, in collaboration with national governments, to strike the sort of special deals with labour that characterized the third quarter of the 20th century (variously described as 'Fordism', the 'golden age', the 'post-war Keynesian national welfare state', etc.).[19]

IV

The erosion of these special deals forms part of the context of the development of the new global division of labour practiced by the new business services multinationals. Whether these companies achieve their economies of scale by sending jobs to the places where the skills are abundant and cheap ('offshoring') or by bringing cheap labour to the sites where the work is carried out, for instance through the use of migrant workers, they are adopting what is in effect the same strategy: drawing on a global reserve army of labour. Their choices are not, of course, entirely unconstrained. They have to operate within limits set by, for instance, the supply of suitable skills and qualifications, national regulations which restrict the movements of labour, set minimum wages or impose particular quality standards, and the extent to which the existing labour force is able to put up a fight. Nevertheless, to the extent that employers can draw on alternative sources of labour, this poses a threat to the wages and conditions of existing workforces and acts as a disciplinary force on them.

The existence of this new global reserve army seems directly associated with the long slow unravelling of labour standards in capitalism's privileged core workforce, with its expectations of job security, promotion, employer-provided pension schemes, paid holidays, sickness compensation, maternity rights and the other benefits won by workers in the third quarter of the 20th century. This development cannot, of course, be attributed entirely to the globalization of labour; the direct attacks on organized labour under Thatcher and Reagan, for instance, also clearly played a major role. However the existence of a global reserve army of labour is certainly a major factor in explaining the failure of workers, even workers who have historically been highly-skilled and well-organized, to resist the deterioration in their working conditions and wages of the last two decades, a deterioration that is clearly measurable in terms of longer hours, worsening physical and mental health, lower purchasing power of wages, loss of pension coverage and contractual impermanency. It is hard to escape the conclusion that workers' bargaining position with their employers has been severely undermined by the knowledge that there are other workers out there quite capable of doing their jobs.

It should be noted that, in most developed countries, up to 2008 the major exception to this trend of erosion was among public sector workers. In many countries, during the last two decades public sector workers became, not just the most strongly unionized part of the workforce[20] but also nearly the only remaining carriers of a set of models of what decent work might look like. Public sector workers have taken the lead in, for instance, negotiating equal opportunities agreements, trade-offs between time and money that promote a better work-life balance and the reinforcement of standards that place the quality of service to clients higher than financial considerations.

This is not the place to argue whether a single 'Fordist model' of postwar industrial relations can be said to have existed. Whatever particular compromises had been struck between capital and labour in differing national contexts, and whatever the extent to which neoliberal policies had already begun to dismantle them during the 1980s, it can be safely asserted that 1989 marked a moment when the pressures to move toward a convergent global employment model began, almost universally, to exert greater force than any countervailing pressures from labour to protect or extend previous gains.

This process has not been entirely negative for all workers, of course. Because of huge disparities between countries and the strongly segmented nature of labour markets, as well as the very different degrees with which labour has been able to resist, these levelling processes have represented a relative improvement for some, even whilst they have been experienced as a deterioration in wages and working conditions by others. In particular, women and people from black and ethnic minorities, part-time and temporary workers and workers in countries with a history of very poor employment protection benefited, for instance, from various ILO or European directives against discrimination during the 1990s. Nevertheless, an important part of the context of the opening up of public services to the market has been the simultaneous erosion of employment protection and easing of access to a global pool of labour: a reserve army not just of manual workers but also of 'information workers' who, thanks to the standardization of white-collar work through the introduction of information and communications technologies, are increasingly able to carry out the tasks that had previously formed part of the job descriptions of civil servants or other public sector bureaucrats. Standardization of tasks and the increasingly generic nature of white-collar labour processes (combined with the ease with which digitised information can be transmitted across distance) have rendered office workers newly substitutable for each other, undermining their bargaining power with employers, whether public or private.

V

Far from modifying the more pernicious effects on labour of the marketization of public services of the 1980s and early 1990s, the New Labour government elected to power in the UK in 1997 aggressively pursued further privatization. In local government, for instance, it replaced what the Conservatives had called 'Compulsory Competitive Tendering' with its own 'Best Value' initiative, which placed a legal duty on local councils to secure the most economic, efficient and effective services and demonstrate that they had compared all their services with those of other private and public providers. It also introduced a regime of continuous audit and control, reducing the scope for the exercise of individual professionalism and workers' ability to respond directly to the needs of clients. Whilst there was less apparent and immediate legal requirement to outsource, the general legal obligations were broader (and some of the penalties for failing to demonstrate Best Value, just as punitive, if not more so). Perhaps more importantly, the introduction of this policy involved a change of mindset, with local authorities, of whatever political persuasion, being forced into a process of internalizing the values imposed by the system. Even if services were not outsourced, they had to be managed as if they were, with public servants increasingly placed under the discipline of the market. A precondition for making the required comparisons was that services were defined in standardized ways. Best Value can thus be seen as one of the drivers of a process of routinization and standardization of tasks, accompanied by the introduction of performance indicators and protocols, enabling them to be monitored statistically and providing the basis for quality standards to be inscribed in the contracts or Service Level Agreements (SLAs) that define the terms on which private companies provide these formerly public services.

Since standardization is a prerequisite for commodification, such New Labour policies thus played a crucial role in the commodification of public services that underpins their transformation into units of exchange in a global market.[21] Local government was not the only target: New Labour also introduced major reforms that developed a market for private companies in the National Health Service,[22] education, prisons and legal services.[23] In each case, the process of transforming part of a public service into a tradable commodity passes through the same stages: standardization, the creation of demand, persuading the workforce to accept the changes and the transfer of risk.[24] These developments were not, of course, unique to New Labour, or to the UK. However, their enthusiastic endorsement by social democrats in Britain, as in Scandinavia and elsewhere, played an important role in creating a new common sense, whereby it is seen as both natural and inevitable that norms are set by the market.

In the case of complex personal services (such as teaching, nursing or social work) involving a large body of contextual and tacit knowledge, communication skill and 'emotional work',[25] the standardization processes that underpin commodification are by no means easy to achieve, involving many steps during the course of which: tacit knowledge is progressively codified; tasks are standardized; output measures are agreed; management processes are reorganized; organizations are broken down into their constituent parts; these constituent parts are formalized, sometimes as separate legal entities; and market-like relationships are introduced between them. All this may well be preparatory to a change of ownership or an opening up for external tender. Only when the activity has been actually or potentially transformed into something that can be made or sold by a profit-making enterprise is the ground prepared for further restructuring in ways that form part of the normal practices of multinational companies: mergers, acquisitions, reconfiguration of parts in new combinations and the introduction of a global division of labour.[26]

The decade from 1997 to 2007 saw these standardization and internationalization processes proceeding apace. By 2000, an enormous new array of global protocols and quality standards had been put into place. These include the ISO quality standards.[27] Here, quality management systems requirements grew from 46,571 in 1993 to 1,064,785 in 2009 – a staggering nearly 23-fold increase over a 16-year period.[28] The global growth in environmental standards was equally dramatic – from 13,994 in 1999 to 223,149 a decade later, a 16-fold increase in just ten years. In the meanwhile, millions of workers around the world gained certificates accredited by

Sun, Oracle, Cisco, Microsoft or other IT companies, enabling them to enter a transparent global job market in such a way that their skills were interchangeable with those of others and clearly understood by employers. It is possible for a newly qualified holder of a Cisco Certificate, for instance, to go to a website[29] and discover that it will earn its holder an average annual salary of $69,401 US in the UK or an average of $14,518 US in India. Those who cannot sell their skills to large multinational corporations, can auction them to the highest bidder on websites like oDesk.[30] To give an indication of the scale of the global reserve army created in this way, it can be noted that just one Microsoft certificate, the Microsoft Certified Professional (MCP) was held at the time of writing by 2,296,561 workers.[31] For an occupation that, as recently as the 1980s, was the preserve of an elite few with considerable bargaining power,[32] this number is staggering.

VI

Many of the companies for whose employ these white-collar workers are competing have grown exponentially over the last quarter-century, sometimes with origins in the service divisions of manufacturing companies but sometimes with roots in financial or business services companies. They include Siemens Business Services, Accenture, Capgemini and Capita, with a historical base in Europe or North America. But they also include Infosys, Wipro and Tata Software Consultancy, companies that originated in India, at first providing relatively low-level IT services but soon able to move rapidly up the value chain to become global leaders in the supply of offshore business process outsourcing (BPO). There are also companies that focus more on the supply of manual workers, such as Manpower and Group 4 Securicor and companies that specialise in certain sectors or types of service (such as Vertex, which supplies outsourced call centre services) as well as others that span many types of activity, such as Serco and ISS.

These companies are not passive players in the global economy. They actively market their services to governments and lobby vigorously for an expansion of outsourcing, either individually or through business associations such as, in the UK, the Business Services Association (BSA) and National Outsourcing Association (NOA). Many have consultancy divisions that advise government bodies on how to 'modernize' their services, recommending with one hand the sorts of outsourcing strategies from which they, and other companies, benefit with the other. These consultants are particularly active in emerging markets, such as Vietnam,[33] where the large scale of state services offers rich pickings. Serco has even set up a 'Serco Institute' which describes itself as 'a UK think tank offering research and thought-leadership on the use of competition and contracting in public service reform and the development of sustainable public service markets'.[34] Leys and Player have anatomised the extraordinarily aggressive lobbying of the New Labour and Coalition governments in the UK that shaped the 2011 proposals for NHS reform.[35]

Increasingly, their market relationship with the governments that are their customers is changing from one where the buyers wield the power to a sellers' market. One of the factors bringing about this shift of power is the changing nature, and ownership, of the skills and knowledge of the workforce. Traditionally, many public service workers (including teachers, social workers and health workers) have brought a complex array of skills to their work and have been able to exercise a degree of autonomy in responding individually to their clients. Even in highly bureaucratized rule-driven environments, such as tax offices,[36] many public workers have possessed a considerable amount of specialist knowledge derived from their experience, much of it not written down. The quality of services has therefore depended crucially on the existence of a stable, committed workforce, often with strongly enforced professional and ethical standards developed within communities of practice with a degree of self-regulation.

The processes that form part of the pre-conditions for commodification involve an analysis of these skills and the tasks associated with exercising them, breaking them down into their component parts, setting explicit standards for their performance and, often, introducing an elaborated division of labour whereby the more routine tasks are transferred to less-skilled workers. Internalized forms of control exercised by workers themselves and monitored either by their own motivation or through feedback from colleagues or line managers are thus replaced by externally-dictated ones. This process takes time, often requiring the gradual handover of work to a new, and differently-trained, cohort of workers.

It is not only the workforce that has to be retrained, either: service users also have to become accustomed to being treated as consumers in a mass market rather than individual clients. In the early stages of outsourcing, this process is by no means complete. Considerations both of political expediency and of efficiency demand a smooth and seamless transfer, which is experienced by service users as representing in its early stages no deterioration and, if possible, in some respects an improvement, compared with its 'wasteful' and 'bureaucratic' predecessor. The easiest way to bring about such a transition is to use the same staff to deliver the same service. Thus a typical first outsourcing of any given service (much like a typical corporate takeover) does not involve mass redundancies but rather a transfer of personnel from one employer to another. In Europe, this is eased by TUPE, the EU's Transfer of Undertakings (Protection of Employment) Directive (EC Directive 2001/23). This provides legal protection for transferred employees with respect to their working conditions, including pension entitlements. TUPE's existence has led to a situation where the trade union reaction to outsourcing is often not to resist it outright but to focus on ensuring that transferred employees are fully covered by the TUPE regulations. Industrial action in public sector outsourcing situations is comparatively rare, though by no means non-existent.[37] As a result of successive transfers, in the locations where outsourcing has first taken place, such as the UK, the skilled workforce of the outsourcing multinationals has expanded not so much through new recruitment in the labour market as through transfers. In a department providing IT services, for instance, or a large outsourced call centre, sitting alongside each other, and with very different terms and conditions of employment inherited from their previous employers, may be found workers whose previous employment might have been in a variety of different central or local government departments or in banks, manufacturing companies or service companies. Once employed by the outsourcer, they may find that their work undergoes a further series of changes, with some tasks moved to other branches of the company in other regions or countries and, for those remaining, new performance indicators or targets to be met, and new requirements to be available at what were formerly regarded as unsocial hours for working. Since outsourcing contracts are generally of quite a short duration, each contract renewal will involve further restructuring.

In one case study in the UK, a local government IT department was first outsourced to a large European-based global IT firm (Company A). Some employees took redundancy whilst others transferred their employment to this company. After a few years, the contract came up for renewal and was won by a smaller, UK-based company (Company B). Some of the originally transferred employees remained in Company A, reabsorbed into different roles, some took redundancy and some were employed by Company B. Company B was then bought up by a US-based multinational with a strongly anti-union tradition (Company C). The remaining workforce (still providing the same IT service to the same local authority) had thus been employed by four different employers in less than a decade. Although there did not appear to have been any formal breach of TUPE regulations, there had been a steady decline in the quality of working life and in working conditions over this period. One worker, whose child was dying of cancer, asked permission of the new management at Company C to work from home a couple of days a week (something that would have been normal under the old local authority collective agreement) and was refused permission by a manager who told him that 'If the work can be done from home, it can be done from India'.

Even more invidious for many public sector workers is the shift in values from a public service ethos, where work is felt to have some intrinsic meaning, to a commercial environment where the work leads only to 'filling the pockets of the shareholders', in the words of one IT technician. Many have consciously made a choice to work in the public sector, sacrificing promotion possibilities for what is seen as a secure and rewarding job that makes a contribution to the community.[38] They may make disgruntled employees, refusing to acquire the 'lean and mean' attitudes that command respect in the multinational companies for which they now work, but, to the company, this does not much matter. Once their expertise has been acquired by the company, they can be replaced by a younger, more malleable workforce, grateful for whatever security it can get. In the UK, the Labour government did provide some protection for second-generation employees in outsourced public services, with a 'two-tier' code on terms and conditions in outsourced services that ensured that new employees working alongside former public sector workers received the same pay and pensions. However, this code was withdrawn in December 2010 by the incoming Coalition government.[39] A comparison of working conditions in the same occupations in the public, private and voluntary sectors in the UK, using data from the Labour Force Survey, found that in each case conditions were worse in the private sector. For instance, only 3 per cent of prison officers in the public sector have job tenure of less than a year compared with 11 per cent of those in the private sector and 10 per cent of full-time healthcare and personal service workers in the private sector work more than 48 hours per week compared with only 2 per cent in the public sector.[40]

Once the knowledge of former public sector workers has been stripped and coded and placed in standard databases it can not only be transferred to cheaper employees, it can also be used as an asset by the new employer. For instance, a company that has already gained the experience of running a local government helpline, managing the HR system of a university, supplying the IT to run a tax system or providing the laundry service for a hospital is then able to market this service aggressively to other potential public customers, in other regions or countries. Commodified workers' knowledge thus provides the raw material for expansion.

VII

There is now a sufficient accumulation of such knowledge to propel a huge extension in the scope and scale of outsourcing. In the targets of the PSI companies are a wide range of services with education and health seen as offering the greatest scope for growth.[41] A particularly tempting prize is the British NHS, the third largest employer in the world (after the Chinese Red Army and the Indian State Railways).[42] The aftermath of the 2008 financial crisis has provided exactly the right conditions for such explosive growth. The need to reduce the state deficits (the debts run up by bailing out the banks) legitimates cost-cutting and the search for 'efficiencies' and economies of scale. This is bolstered by a rhetoric of shrinking the state. A new model is being promoted in which the function of government is no long to deliver services but to procure them. This model has already been enthusiastically taken up by some. For instance in October 2010, Suffolk County Council in the UK announced plans to become a 'virtual council' and outsource all its services, including administrative functions, moving from a directly-employed workforce of 27,000 to around 300 employees.[43] Barnet Council is already well-advanced on this path, with its 'Future Shape' policy, announced in 2008, which has been shown to have made few real savings, partly because of the high cost of consultancy, whilst leading to a drastic drop in the quality of services, as well as job losses.[44] (An even more dramatic, though smaller-scale, example is the tiny city of Maywood in Los Angeles County, USA which, since 1 July 2010, has had no employees whatsoever, with all its services provided by independent contractors or staff on loan from the neighbouring city of Bell).[45]

In the UK, whose Coalition government provides an extreme example of this new thinking, the rhetoric surrounding these developments has been confused, on the left, by a focus on 'cuts' that suggests the issue is simply one of the size of the budget devoted to public services, and, on the right, by rhetoric about the 'Big Society'. This rhetoric does not speak of handing public assets over directly to multinational corporations to manage (though this option is not excluded) but suggests that they will be taken over by volunteers. The *Modernising Commissioning* Green Paper published by the UK government in 2010 quotes the Liberal Democrat manifesto commitment to 'support the creation and expansion of mutuals, co-operatives, charities and social enterprises, and enable these groups to have a much greater involvement in the running of public services'. It goes on to say that 'these reforms are fundamental to achieving the *Power Shift* to which this government is committed, transferring power away from central government to local communities'.[46]

To what extent this is a simple smokescreen and to what extent a new role may be opening up for NGOs in the provision of services is a moot point. Globally, the role of NGOs has changed considerably in recent years. Not only are many in partnership with multinational corporations in varying degrees of closeness (for instance, the Aga Khan Foundation providing nursing training in Tanzania funded by Johnson and Johnson),[47] many NGOs are entirely funded by multinationals. For example the *New Citizen Life Centre,* which provides health services and help with finding employment to destitute migrant workers in the Guijing migrant village in Pudong, on the outskirts of Shanghai in China, is entirely funded by Glaxo Smith Kline, where it serves to help promote the company's products as well as to project a positive image of the company in particular, and of capitalism in general.[48] It seems likely that a similar blurring of roles will increasingly take place elsewhere. Even if services are run by NGOs, it is unclear to whom they will be accountable, and how. In the short term, the involvement of voluntary organizations may soften and humanize the impact of the changes; in the longer term, it seems likely that multinational companies will end up taking over the running of any operations likely to be profitable, simply by exploiting the economies of scale they can achieve. There is little question that the main impact of the new approach will be a massive transfer of public assets to corporations that can use them to generate profit. In the process, the public sector workforce will be subsumed into a larger mass of interchangeable labour: dispensable, precarious and – since workers will increasingly be employed by bodies with intermediate positions in shifting global value chains – without a stable framework for collective representation and negotiation.

This situation is not without its contradictions, however. For the state, there are tensions between its role in attracting and controlling capital on its territory on the one hand and, on the other, its role in opening up a new field of expansion for capital. Within national ruling elites, there are tensions between those who want a smaller role for governments *tout court* and those (representing the companies that profit from supplying public services) who would like to see an enlarged public sphere, albeit one that is opened up for profit. There are also contradictions between the national interest in preventing unemployment from reaching unmanageable levels and the interest of global companies in searching out the cheapest workforce, wherever it may be based. What is clear, however, is that if workers are to claw back any returns for the working class from the next wave of accumulation (based as it is on the expropriation of their own past collective efforts at redistribution), new forms of organization will be required: forms of organization that recognize the common interests of a global proletariat, with globally-organized employers.

NOTES

1   Or, perhaps more precisely, it could be said that uncommodified use values are being transformed into commodified use values, giving them exchange value in the market.

2   See Claude Serfati, 'Transnational Organisations as Financial Groups', *Work Organisation, Labour and Globalisation*, 5(1), 2011 for an interesting discussion of the convergence between non-financial and financial TNCs.

3   UNCTAD *World Investment Report*, Geneva: 2008, p. 3.

4   Ibid., p. 4.

5   Ibid., 2008, pp. xv–xvi.

6   Ibid., p. 4.

7   For instance, when it was introduced during the late 1990s in the IT industry for labour-intensive programming tasks such as converting European company accounting systems to cope with the introduction of the euro, or averting the catastrophes it was predicted would be caused by the 'millennium bug'.

8   I have written extensively elsewhere about the long development of this new global division of labour from the 1970s on in, for instance, U. Huws, *The Making of a Cybertariat*, New York: Monthly Review Press, 2003; U. Huws, 'Fixed, Footloose or Fractured: Work, Identity and the Spatial Division of Labour', *Monthly Review*, 57(10), 2006; U. Huws and J. Flecker, A*sian Emergence: The World's Back Office?* IES Report 419, Institute for Employment Studies, 2005.

9   This process is described in more detail in U. Huws, 'The Restructuring of Global Value Chains and the Creation of a Cybertariat', in Christopher May, ed., *Global Corporate Power: (Re)integrating Companies into International Political Economy*, Boulder: Lynne Rienner Publishers, 2006, pp. 65-84.

10   D. Julius, *Public Services Industry Review,* London: Department for Business Enterprise and Regulatory Reform, 2008.

11   Including post and telecommunications, energy and water networks, formerly publicly-owned airlines, state-owned banks and public housing stock.

12   OECD data, quoted in 'A Special Report on the Future of the State', *The Economist,* 19 March 2011, p. 4.

13   IMF data, quoted in 'A Special Report', p. 5.

14   G. Esping-Andersen, *The Three Worlds of Welfare Capitalism*, New Jersey: Princeton University Press, 1990.

15   U. Huws, 'Move Over Brother', *New Socialist,* January 1985.

16   Equal Opportunities Commission, *The Gender Impact of CCT in Local Government*, Manchester: Equal Opportunities Commission, 1995.

17   Subsequently, this process culminated in the 2006 Services Directive (2006/123), which came into force on 28 December 2009, effectively removing any national barriers within the EU to companies wishing to tender for public services.

18 Again, this set the scene for further liberalization of international trade in services under the GATS. In the words of the WTO: 'The Uruguay Round was only the beginning. GATS requires more negotiations which began in early 2000 and are now part of the Doha Development Agenda. The goal is to take the liberalization process further by increasing the level of commitments in schedules'. 'Understanding the WTO: the Agreements', available at http://www.wto.org.

19 B. Jessop, *The Future of the Capitalist State,* Oxford: Polity Press, 2002.

20 Union density is significantly higher among public sector workers than their private sector counterparts in every European country other than Belgium. See V. Glassner, *The Public Sector in the Crisis,* Working Paper 2010.07, European Trade Union Institute, 2010, p. 15.

21 I have written at greater length about this process in, for instance, Huws, *The Making of a Cybertariat*; and Huws, 'The New Gold Rush', *Work Organisation, Labour and Globalisation,* 2(2), 2008.

22 For a detailed anatomization, see S. Player and C. Leys, *Confuse and Conceal: The NHS and Independent Sector Treatment Centres,* London: Merlin Press, 2008.

23 See D. Whitfield, 'Marketisation of Legal Services', *Legal Action,* March 2007.

24 C. Leys, *Market-Driven Politics,* London: Verso, 2003.

25 A. Hochschild, *The Managed Heart: The Commercialization of Human Feeling,* Berkeley: University of California Press, 1983.

26 The question is sometimes raised whether there is any improvement in the quality of services that have been standardized, commodified and outsourced. The implication is that, if this is the case, then the benefits to service users may outweigh any disadvantages to workers. In fact it is extremely difficult to make such comparisons for a number of reasons. First, restructuring is often introduced in situations where services are already deteriorating because of spending cuts. Second, the change processes associated with commodification make it difficult to compare like with like. Third, the obsessive focus on quantitative indicators that is an essential underpinning of commodification renders invisible many of the qualitative changes that may be experienced negatively by service users. Nevertheless, there is a considerable body of research that suggests there is a deterioration (see for example C. Leys and A. Pollock, *NHS plc: The Privatisation of our Health Care,* London: Verso, 2004; Player and Leys, *Confuse and Conceal*; D. Whitfield, *Global Auction of Public Assets,* London: Spokesman, 2009). It is perhaps no accident that John Hutton, Secretary of State for Business Enterprise and Regulatory Reform in the New Labour government in 2008, stopped even arguing that the main advantage of outsourcing was to bring efficiency savings. The Public Services Industry, he said, should be encouraged because 'There is significant export potential in this growth industry. Encouraging and assisting UK firms to make the most of these opportunities will generate substantial benefits not only for UK firms but also for the UK economy. The Review concludes that the best way that government can support the PSI abroad is through maintaining a competitive framework for public services which fosters a dynamic and thriving PSI in the

UK'. See the Executive Summary introduction to Julius, *Public Services Industry Review*, p. v.

27   The International Organization for Standardization, which has 2,700 technical committees, subcommittees and working groups, sets international technical standards for a large range of different industrial processes. The existence of these standards means that it is possible to trade with, or outsource to, an ISO-certified company in the confidence that the outputs will be predictable and standardized, removing the need for detailed supervision, in just the same way that, for instance, electrical standards make it possible to plug an appliance into a standard socket in the confidence that it will function correctly.

28   ISO Survey, 2009, available at http://www.iso.org.

29   In this case: http://www.certificationskit.com/cisco-certification/cisco-certification-salary-statistics.

30   B. Caraway, 'Online Labour Markets: An Enquiry into oDesk Providers', *Work Organisation, Labour and Globalisation*, 4(2), 2010, pp. 111-125.

31   Available at http://www.trainsignaltraining.com

32   I have written in greater depth about the changing occupational identities of IT workers in the context of globalization in U. Huws, 'New Forms of Work; New Occupational Identities', in N. Pupo and M. Thomas, eds., *Interrogating the 'New Economy': Restructuring Work in the 21ˢᵗ Century*, Peterborough, Ontario: Broadview Press, 2010.

33   See C. Dixon, 'The Reformatting of State Control in Vietnam', *Work Organisation, Labour and Globalisation*, 2(2), 2008, pp. 101-118.

34   Available at http://www.serco.com

35   C. Leys and S. Player, *The Plot Against the NHS*, London: Merlin Press, 2011.

36   For a detailed description of the impact on workers' skills on the 'callcenterisation' of the Danish tax system, see Bramming, Sørensen and Hasle, 'In Spite of Everything: Professionalism as Mass Customised Bureaucratic Production in a Danish Government Call Centre', *Work Organisation, Labour and Globalisation*, 3(1), 2009, pp. 114-130.

37   See P. Meil, P. Tengblad and P. Docherty, *Value Chain Restructuring and Industrial Relations – The Role of Workplace Representation in Changing Conditions of Employment and Work*, WORKS Project, Higher Institute of Labour Studies, K. U. Leuven, Leuven: HIVA, 2009.

38   This case study is described in greater detail in S. Dahlmann, 'The End of the Road: No More Walking in Dead Men's Shoes: IT Professionals' Experience of being Outsourced to the Private Sector', *Work Organisation, Labour and Globalisation*, 2(2), 2008, pp. 148-161.

39   H. Reed, *The Shrinking State: Why the Rush to Outsource Threatens our Public Services*, London: A report for Unite by Landman Economics, 2011, p. 13.

40   Ibid., p. 18.

41   Julius, *Public Services Industry Review*.

42   S. Lister, 'NHS is World's Biggest Employer after Indian Rail and Chinese Army', *The Times Online*, 20 March 2004.

43   A. Bawden, 'Suffolk Council Plans to Outsource Virtually all Services', *Guardian.co.uk*, 22 September 2010.

44 D. Whitfield, *Analysis of Development and Regulatory Services Business Case*, London: European Services Strategy Unit, 2011.

45 'There Goes Everybody', *The Economist*, 8 July 2010.

46 Cabinet Office, *Modernising Commissioning: Increasing the Role of Charities, Social Enterprises, Mutuals and Co-operatives in Public Service Delivery*, Cabinet Office Green Paper, London, 2010, p. 5, emphasis in the original.

47 Aga Khan Development Network, 'Upgrading Nursing Studies: Strengthening the Health–Care System in Tanzania', October 2007, available at http://www.akdn.org.

48 B. Neilson, 'Guijing Migrant Village', *Transit Labour*, 2, December 2010, pp. 33–35.

FINANCIALIZATION, COMMODIFICATION
AND CARBON:
THE CONTRADICTIONS OF
NEOLIBERAL CLIMATE POLICY

LARRY LOHMANN

...the exchange of commodities implies contradictory and mutually exclusive conditions. The further development of the commodity does not abolish these contradictions, but rather provides the form within which they have room to move.[1]

Karl Marx, Capital

The contradictions of market approaches to global warming are connected in interesting ways to the contradictions of the neoliberal policy responses to economic crises that set the stage for the 2008 crash. Among these post-1970 'crisis fixes', two have particular relevance to the evolution of climate policy. The first is the increasing privatization and marketization of public goods and of the state and its functions, aimed at redistributing wealth upwards to profit-challenged capital or improving the background conditions for accumulation. This has involved a rollback of health, education and welfare programmes and certain kinds of environmental, financial and social regulation, at the same time as a roll*out* of heterogeneous new state and inter-state mechanisms and regulations.[2] The latter have ranged from trade treaties and host government agreements to public-private partnerships, 'governance' based on cost-benefit analysis, new property rights regimes, licenses for new enclosures, laws promoting offshore tax havens and secrecy jurisdictions and relaxing capital reserve requirements, and – to cite a spectacular culminating example – the allocation of mammoth slices of state treasuries to the 'bail-out' of private financial institutions.

A second, overlapping development reflected in contemporary climate politics is the increased economic and political dominance of finance. Since the 1970s, a transformed and expanded financial sector has promoted new speculation-based hedging opportunities in an uncertain post-Bretton Woods global environment. Financialization has not only channelled more wealth from poor to rich, inflated bubble after bubble, and exacerbated global imbalances. It has also accelerated business's assimilation of cheap labour, land, raw materials and public and smaller private enterprises in new regions and arenas, and, through an enormous extension of finance's traditional role of underwriting present spending with the promise of future production, stimulated demand by offering unsustainable amounts of credit to a labour force whose wages have continued to be under assault from a capital-owning class constantly on the hunt for new sources of profit.

The carbon markets operating today under the aegis of the UN, the EU, and a variety of state and non-state actors reflect, extend and deepen both of these trends. First proposed in the 1960s, pollution markets were developed by economists, 'Big Green' Washington environmental groups, business alliances, and also – tellingly – traders with a background in financial engineering, such as the Chicago Board of Trade's Richard Sandor, the 'father of financial futures'. They then underwent a series of failed policy experiments in the US before being inserted into the country's sulphur dioxide control programme in the 1990s as a business-friendly alternative to more direct regulatory control of polluting technologies. Then, in 1997, the Bill Clinton regime successfully demanded that the Kyoto Protocol – the outcome of many years of public pressure regarding climate change – be converted into a set of carbon trading instruments (Al Gore, who carried the US ultimatum to Kyoto, later became a carbon market player himself). In the 2000s, following the US's about-face on the Protocol, Europe picked up the initiative to become the host of what is today the world's largest carbon market, the EU Emissions Trading Scheme (EU ETS). The project of building liquid global carbon markets worth hundreds of billions of dollars remains the default international approach to the climate crisis. These markets grew rapidly until 2008, when, according to the World Bank, they amounted to US$135 billion, although they have stumbled since, following the financial crash, the 2010 failure of the US Congress to pass proposed carbon trading legislation, uncertainty about the future of UN climate treaties, and a recent spate of criminal and other scandals.[3]

CARBON MARKETS AND FINANCIALIZATION

The development of carbon markets shares many parallels with or links to the markets for financial derivatives that emerged in the 1970s and 1980s and surged into prominence in the 1990s and 2000s. Derivatives and carbon markets, for one thing, are both underpinned by an especially close state-

corporate relationship. The intangible commodities that both markets trade
in depend for their existence on regulation; conversely, in both markets
the state is highly dependent on the private sector for its understanding of
how the relevant trades work. The explosive growth of trade in complex
derivatives owes a great deal to legislation that removes interest rate caps;
allows banks to use derivatives to offload loan risk and extend more
credit on the same capital reserves; removes the divide between ordinary
commercial banking and speculative investment banking; makes limited
liability partnerships possible; accepts banks' own mathematical models as
a way of calculating risk; and exempts derivatives from gambling laws. The
state, in turn, is highly dependent on private sector judgements (from ratings
agencies as well as bankers) about how products should be regulated, and
highly vulnerable to private sector lobbying regarding commodity design.
In carbon markets, conventional divisions between market and regulation
simply disappear. As explained in the following section of this essay,
carbon commodities are created by governments imposing overall limits on
pollution and promulgating and enforcing – with private sector assistance – a
multitude of emissions 'equivalences'.

Carbon markets also display the same extreme dependence of regulators
on the opinions of business figures profiting from the trade. Corporations
collect huge amounts of rent merely by lobbying government regulators
for grants of pollution rights and providing them with the 'expertise' and
information they lack – for example, yearly emissions estimates or new
emissions 'equivalences'. The International Emissions Trading Association
(IETA), a group of 176 transnational financial, law, energy and manufacturing
corporations headed by a former British civil servant, is highly influential in
developing the carbon commodity in ways that would make trading in it
more profitable to the financial sector (some IETA members make money, for
example, by inducing price volatility), while also promoting increased use of
emissions 'equivalences', sweeping standardization of climate commodities,
rubber-stamp regulation, banking and borrowing of carbon pollution credits
across compliance periods, increased participation of financial intermediaries,
no buyer liability for fake products and an unregulated over-the-counter
market that would encourage speculation. Moreover, because many
regulators are themselves buyers or sellers of carbon pollution credits, and
because both buyers and sellers, whether they are from the public or private
sectors, have financial or professional interests in creating as many credits as
possible, there is little incentive on any side to inquire too closely into the
nature and robustness of the commodity.

The distinction between public servants and private profiteers in either market is often little more than a date on a résumé. Just as Goldman Sachs derivatives traders Robert Rubin and Hank Paulson both pushed for regulation promoting the expansion of derivatives markets when they became Treasury Secretaries in the US government, so Christiana Figureres, as Executive Secretary of the UN Framework Convention on Climate Change (a.k.a. head regulator of the Kyoto Protocol carbon market), merely continues the carbon market work she earlier pursued in the private sector at firms such as Endesa Latinoamerica and the Carbon Rating Agency, a company applying credit rating expertise to carbon assets. Ken Newcombe, another leading figure, has moved smoothly from the World Bank's Prototype Carbon Fund to Climate Change Capital (a City of London boutique merchant bank), Goldman Sachs' North American carbon trading desk, and the carbon trading firm C-Quest Capital.

Another connection is the sheer prominence of the financial sector in the carbon business. Among the largest buyers of UN carbon credits today are financial-sector speculators such as Barclays Capital, Deutsche Bank, BNP Paribas Fortis, Kommunalkredit, Sumitomo Bank and – again – Goldman Sachs. Private equity firms and private or public carbon funds are also active. Financial firms can be expected to try to work the same magic with carbon that they deploy with other products. As early as 2008, Credit Suisse put together a US$200 million deal that bundled together carbon credit-manufacturing projects in different stages of completion before slicing them up for sale to speculators. Just as mortgage-backed securities concealed from distant buyers and sellers the economic realities bearing on lower-income neighbourhoods in Detroit or Phoenix, so too such financialized carbon-commodity packages, with their even longer value chains, conceal the heterogeneous climatic and social impacts and conditions of assemblages of, say, hydroelectric projects in India, cookstove projects in Honduras, or schemes burning off methane from coal mines in China and industrial pig farms in Mexico. Integrated into index funds, carbon could come under the influence of speculative activity in other sectors, while also affecting food prices and thus subsistence. Some traders are now even betting on the collapse of the entire carbon credit market, just as many investors once bet on (and hence had incentives to hasten) the collapse of the US housing market. Via the financial sector, climate commodities may also soon be involved in a fresh round of debt-driven expropriation. 'Green bonds' backed by carbon assets are set to create a new Southern debt to the North, backed by Southern land and Southern public funds. In May 2011, for instance, a bond structured by Bank of America Merrill Lynch was announced which would repay investors out of returns from monetized ecosystem services provided by rainforest, including carbon pollution credits.

Perhaps the most fundamental connection between the markets for carbon and for complex financial derivatives, however, is at the commodity level. Originating in a process of especially wrenching abstraction and subsumption of qualitative to quantitative relations, the commodities traded in both markets owe their evolved form to competition-driven mass-production techniques that expand the scope for crisis at every turn.

The new derivative products were created largely by disentangling from their previous contexts uncertainties (ranging from credit risk to default risk, interest rate risk, exchange rate risk and weather risk) so that they could be quantified, sliced, diced, liquefied and circulated around the world as independent, fully-fledged commodities. Contrary to the claims of financiers, these products have little in common with the more context-fettered policies offered by insurance companies, who tend to commodify (un)certainty only where they can attach independent, calculable probabilities to a specific, well-understood set of possible outcomes. Conventional insurance firms, in addition, supply 'safety equivalents' only to people who own the homes and businesses at risk, and only where they can use the law to stop policyholders from activating payouts by treating their own lives, homes and businesses as commodities fully exchangeable for insurance money. Nor, despite the popular critique, do the new financial derivatives have much in common with the limited bets offered by casinos. Casinos, like insurance companies, concentrate on actions whose odds are independent and can be precisely calculated. In addition, they deploy close surveillance of customers, frown on clients betting with other people's money, and remain hemmed in by various legal, moral and geographical restrictions that derivatives traders have successfully struggled to overcome. Nor, finally, did the mortgage-backed derivatives employed in the 'subprime financial system' have much in common with the comparatively conservative punts taken by banks under the old 'originate and hold' mortgage model, in which bankers' evaluation of (un)certainty was a more labour-intensive matter of local, face-to-face evaluation.

In order to expand credit by making it possible to sell certainty commodities to a wide range of cash-flush speculators (who serve as counterparties to hedgers), the mass production of certainty had to be greatly expanded, its labour-intensivity reduced, and various fetters limiting its commodification thrown off. This is where the algorithms introduced by 'quants' or quantitative experts came in. Thus the Black–Scholes equation published in 1973 helped expand the options market by offering a streamlined, academically-sanctioned way of calculating prices for uncertainty using reference sheets, calculators and computers. Physicist David Li's Gaussian copula model, devised in 1999, similarly became the 'combustion engine of the collateralized debt obligation world',[4] making the mass production of structured finance deals possible by displaying how corporate or mortgage defaults might correlate, thus helping to mechanize the manufacture of confidence in ways that made the provision of credit vastly more 'cost-effective'. Key to such processes was, roughly speaking, the 'mystification of uncertainty or contingency as if it were measurable as probability'.[5]

Like the new derivatives, carbon commodities work through a process of radical disembedding – in this case, disembedding the climate issue from the historical question of how to organize for structural, long-term change capable of keeping remaining fossil fuels in the ground. Ominously, however, the valuation paradoxes that afflict climate commodities are even more intractable than those that affect complex financial derivatives, to say nothing of more familiar commodities like ordinary futures or food, energy, and consumer durables. To understand why, it is necessary to explore in some detail the peculiar algebra through which the climate commodity is created.

THE FRAGILE ALGEBRA OF CARBON MARKETS

The climate crisis owes its origin to a variant of what Marx called the 'metabolic rift', in which huge quantities of fossil carbon are taken out of underground deposits to feed industry and subsequently build up in the air and oceans. The amount of carbon still remaining in fossil deposits is enormous compared to the amount that can be quickly absorbed by the above-ground system of atmosphere, oceans, vegetation, soil, fresh water and surface geology. In particular, the earth's living vegetation (today containing perhaps 600–1000 billion tons of carbon) is incapable of absorbing an injection of 4000-plus billion tons of extra carbon from fossil stores built up over millions of years.[6] Because carbon brought to the surface cannot be got safely back underground in the form of coal, oil or gas over human time-scales, and because abruptly stopping the flow of fossil fuels out of the ground would be disruptive to accumulation, 'fixes' analogous to those applied to the original metabolic rift must be sought. The most important current framework for these fixes is carbon markets.[7]

Like other ecosystem services markets, carbon markets aim at 'creating and stabilizing new areas for capitalist activity',[8] but also, more fundamentally, at securing those background conditions for accumulation that are most dependent on fossil fuels and most threatened by calls for emission cuts. In climate-speak, carbon markets' purpose is to 'make climate change mitigation cost-effective'. Both rollout and rollback of state and interstate governance are involved. The rollout side is particularly crucial. State and interstate agencies use neoliberal theory to transform the qualitative problem of climate change mitigation – essentially a question of organizing the long-term, structural political and social changes required to keep most remaining fossil carbon in the ground – into a quantitative field of scarce, ownable items; distribute them among a worldwide grid of proprietors including nation states, companies, communities and individuals; produce the new commodities and stimulate accumulation; and sustain and govern trading systems.

The requirements of commodity creation – accounting, ownership, the possibility of capital accumulation – lead naturally to the framing of the climate problem, and 'climate services', in terms of flows of molecules, especially CO_2 molecules. Since molecules are, in a sense, 'pre-standardized', they can be easily quantified in bulk, and rights to transfer them from one place to another readily owned and commodified, at least in theory. Moreover, in molecular markets, actions and technologies that reduce the emissions of the same number of CO_2 molecules over the short term can be treated as equivalent. This is done regardless of the degree to which they foster structural change away from fossil fuels, and thus lower CO_2 levels, over the long term – which must always be the criterion for effective climate strategy. In molecular markets, a cut of 100 million tons through routine efficiency improvements bears the same value as a 100-million ton cut that comes from, say, strategic investment in non-fossil-fuelled technologies, or from other actions with superior long-term effects on climatic stability. Such markets can operate for a long time without incentivizing long-term strategies for keeping coal, oil and gas in the ground. Rights to molecule flows, therefore, are ideal candidates for climate market commodities under political regimes committed to the unearthing of remaining fossil fuels. Accordingly, carbon markets' foundational equation (as ratified by states and the UN) becomes:

$$\textbf{a better climate = reductions in } CO_2 \textbf{ emissions}$$

But if there is to be a market in these reductions, someone must need to buy them and someone must be on hand to 'produce' or exercise proprietorship over them. (To put it another way, if there is to be a market in greenhouse gas pollution dumps, someone must make them scarce – enclose them – and someone must 'own' and collect 'rent' for them from willing or unwilling customers.) Setting up the necessary apparatus is again, as a rule, the job of states, which both impose demand for reductions and provide means of 'producing' and owning them. Either independently, or under international agreements, governments accomplish the former by imposing 'caps' or limits on emissions on various economic sectors. To create the reduction commodity itself, they then resort to the additional equation:

mandatory reduction of CO_2 emissions to level c within time period p = tradable right to emit CO_2 up to level c by the end of period p

Carbon dioxide reductions (and by inference climate action) can then be achieved by 'production' and distribution of tradable pollution rights, whose scarcity is determined by government fiat.[9] Progressive reductions are accordingly achieved by relying on the equation:

reducing CO_2 emissions progressively = issuing fewer tradable rights to emit CO_2 in period $p + 1$ than were issued in period p

All of this requires a large investment on the part of the state and international agencies in monitoring, reporting and verification, as well as in erecting new legal structures. Government departments, scientists on UN panels, and technical experts of all kinds are delegated to follow and count molecules as they travel from underground hydrocarbons to the smokestacks or tailpipes from which they start cycling among air, oceans, vegetation, soils, rock formations, fresh water, and so on. Politicians, diplomats and officials try to assign responsibility for molecule flows, reductions and savings to various countries and corporations, using the criterion of physical location.

The rentier/producers of CO_2 pollution rights, accordingly, are in the first instance states themselves. European Union Allowances, for example, are 'produced' in a preset amount by strokes of politicians' and bureaucrats' pens under the EU ETS. They are then sold or, more usually, given away free, to large private sector polluters. Once in the hands of polluters, the new rights-to-destroy can then be bought and sold so that pollution is distributed in a way that minimizes aggregate costs. Price signals, it is assumed, will provide sufficient incentive for carbon-inefficient firms to mend their ways. By creating and handing out large quantities of commodified pollution rights, the EU ETS not only moderates pressures to reduce use of fossil fuels, thus protecting general conditions for accumulation, but also directly generates hard cash for the private sector. For example, many European corporations sell or charge their customers for surplus emissions rights that they receive *gratis* under the EU ETS, ploughing the proceeds back into fossil-fuelled business as usual[10] or using them as a slush fund to help them weather the financial crisis. European power companies alone are set to gain US\$127 billion in windfall profits through 2012 through the EU ETS;[11] the handouts given to only ten of Europe's intensive industrial users of fossil fuels exceed the total EU budget for environment.[12] Importantly, what the EU ETS creates rights to and distributes to the private sector is not merely a local or national public good, but a global public good.

Carbon markets' focus on CO_2 molecules also encourages an open-ended dynamic of abstraction that helps expand the scope for accumulation in climate change mitigation still further. By founding carbon markets on the equation 'a better climate = a reduction in CO_2 emissions', market architects in economics departments, trading firms, NGOs – and, ultimately, states and UN agencies – have made possible a cascade of further profit-generating equivalences, for example:

$$CO_2 \text{ reduction A} = CO_2 \text{ reduction B}$$

$$CO_2 \text{ reduction in place A} = CO_2 \text{ reduction in place B}$$

$$CO_2 \text{ reduction through technology A} = CO_2 \text{ reduction through technology B}$$

$$CO_2 \text{ reduction through conservation of biota} = CO_2 \text{ reduction through keeping fossil fuels in the ground}$$

Each such equation encourages capitalists to try to achieve cost savings in 'reduction production' by moving their operations around the globe, switching from one technology to another, avoiding risky investments in low-carbon technologies by annexing cheap carbon-absorbing lands in the global South, and so forth.[13]

Carbon trading's molecular focus also opens up the lucrative possibility of using greenhouse gases other than CO_2 in the manufacture of climate commodities. In response to UN demands to calculate country emissions, the Intergovernmental Panel on Climate Change (IPCC) had early on posited a whole range of CO_2 'equivalents' – including methane, nitrous oxide (N_2O) and various chlorofluorocarbons including the industrial by-product HFC-23 – that were later appropriated by carbon market architects. Although it is a formidable feat of commensuration to quantify the 'global warming potential' of all these compounds in comparison to CO_2, due to their qualitatively different behaviour in the atmosphere over various time spans as well as the different influence the control of each might have on fossil fuel use, the IPCC has not hesitated to stipulate comparative numerical estimates for each gas's effect. It claims, for example, that methane (CH_4) is 72 times more harmful than carbon dioxide over a 20-year time span, 25 times more potent over a 100-year time span, and 7.6 times more potent over a 500 year period. Carbon markets then abstract even from these figures, discarding the 20-year and 500-year time horizons and eliding what are in many cases enormous 'error bands' (in the case of HFC-23, plus or minus 5000). What remains are equations such as

$$CH_4 = 25 \times CO_2$$

$$N_2O = 298 \times CO_2$$

$$HFC\text{-}23 = 14{,}800 \times CO_2$$

Having abstracted from the climate crisis to CO_2 molecules, in other words, the markets now abstract from CO_2 to a highly simplified 'carbon dioxide equivalent', or CO_2e, which represents a common value enabling the exchangeability of a whole range of greenhouse gases. The ratios displayed in the three equations above display clearly the efficiency advantages to be gained by applying mass production techniques to the manufacture of carbon pollution rights. They also demonstrate the importance of climate experts in that process: the slightest revision in estimates of gas 'equivalences' could signify millions of dollars in profit and loss.[14]

In some pollution trading systems – for example, the US sulphur dioxide market invented in the 1990s – governments are the only commodity producers (although they typically quickly sign over ownership to private corporations). However, in most climate markets, other parties are encouraged to collaborate in the production of a second type of commodity for sale in the same markets in order to make more cost savings, investment and speculative opportunities possible. Known as 'offsets', these products are funded by polluters subject to a government 'cap' but are generally manufactured by projects outside the cap. Such projects – which might include, for example, hydroelectric dams or methane-burning operations at landfill sites – are allowed to produce further divisible, measurable, thing-like climate-benefit units if they can satisfy regulators that they result in the emission of less greenhouse gas than would be the case in the absence of the carbon finance they receive. Project funders receive pollution rights that they can use in lieu of emissions reduction obligations under European and Japanese climate laws, sell on to third parties, or speculate with. Such offset commodities, in other words, presuppose the equations

$$CO_2e \text{ reduction under a cap} = \text{offset outside the cap}$$

$$CO_2e \text{ reduction under a cap} = \text{'avoided' } CO_2e$$

The 'avoided emissions' generated by a wind farm in Oaxaca, for example, are made commensurable with the pollution rights handed out by European governments to their high-emitting industrial sectors.

Through this state-sanctioned framework for market exchange, the surplus-generating use of fossil energy by the industrial North is prolonged, while further profits are realized through commerce in a new commodity. For example, routine efficiency improvements at exceptionally dirty, coal-intensive iron works in rural India can generate cheap offsets that help high-polluting electricity generators in Europe – often, as elsewhere, sited in poorer communities – continue business as usual at the lowest possible cost in the face of EU restrictions on emissions. Like some other ambitious forms of market environmentalism, carbon offset trading not only morphs existing environmental regulation toward ineffectiveness (for example, by punching holes in emissions 'caps' and letting in offset credits from outside, thus 'rolling back' part of the regulation that underpins cap and trade schemes). It also helps head off demand for other regulatory measures more capable of addressing the fossil fuel problem in all its political complexity. It is probably not too much to say that since the 1980s, one of the unvoiced mottos of carbon markets' more sophisticated supporters in government and the private sector has been to stop effective climate action before it starts.

Bringing to bear IPCC-sanctioned 'equivalences' between CO_2 and other greenhouse gases further multiplies the 'efficiencies' that offset trading bestows on big business at the expense of climatic stability. For instance, merely by destroying a few thousand tons of HFC-23, the Mexican chemical manufacturer Quimobasicos is set to sell over 30 million tonnes of carbon dioxide pollution rights to Goldman Sachs, EcoSecurities and the Japanese electricity generator J-Power.[15] Assuming that destruction of HFC-23 can be carried out for US\$0.25 per tonne of CO_2e, and that a ton of CO_2 offset pollution rights can command \$19.50 on the EU ETS spot market (May 2011 prices), both the company and the financial sector intermediaries it sells to can realize super-profits. Industrial buyers of the permits can in turn save $128.50 a ton by using the rights in lieu of paying fines for not meeting their legal emissions requirements, while industrialists and speculators alike can turn to advantage the $6 price differential between cheap Kyoto Protocol offsets (known as Certified Emissions Reductions or CERs) and more expensive European Union Allowances (or EUAs). Such 'industrial gas' offsets – generated at a handful of industrial installations in China, India, Korea, Mexico and a few other countries – still account for the bulk of Kyoto Protocol carbon credits, helping to keep carbon pollution rights so cheap that they approach the status of a second 'free allocation' of pollution rights to fossil-intensive European industry.[16] And if such offset projects help keep the wheels on fossil-fuelled industries in the North, neither do they interfere in any way with the further entrenchment of coal, oil and gas in the global South.

Relentless competition and the lure of new profit opportunities drives a similar process of continual, creative elaboration of the equation

$$\text{actual } CO_2e \text{ reduction} = \text{'avoided' } CO_2e \text{ emission}$$

to maximize the number and type of activities that can be 'avoided'. The greater the range and volume of 'baseline' pollution sources that can be imagined and quantified, and the higher that counterfactual emissions 'baselines' can be set, the more emissions that offset buyers and sellers can then claim to have 'avoided' and the more capital they can accumulate. Thus JP Morgan, BNP Paribas, and the World Bank are avid proponents of a prospective multi-billion-dollar market in 'avoided deforestation', in which projects can produce carbon credits even if they allow an *increase* in deforestation, as long as the increase is less than what regulators agree 'would have happened' in the absence of capitalist agency. The Optimum Population Trust is even selling carbon pollution credits from its family planning operations on the voluntary market, claiming that they generate a calculable number of 'avoided' humans and the greenhouse gas molecules they generate.

In general, carbon businesses wanting to get the jump on rivals have no choice but to 'mechanize' such number wizardry as much as possible, as well as to appropriate the maximum amount of unpaid quantification labour. Lobbying for standardized accounting methodologies that can be applied in project after project, they also seek highly-capitalized means of tallying molecules, such as satellite measurements of biotic carbon, which promise higher returns than labour-intensive, context-sensitive ground measurements. As a rule, only investors and producers with the capital to hire expert, computer-equipped consultants with easy familiarity with government and UN regulation will succeed in the offset market.[17] Investors tend to shun low-yield offset projects requiring labour-intensive accounting and hands-on work with communities and to outsource as much as possible of any menial accounting labour that may be required to states or nonprofit bodies hoping to finance their operations through carbon markets, such as conservation or development NGOs or even Indigenous Peoples' organizations. With the correct accounting techniques, a company investing in overseas 'carbon-saving' projects can increase emissions both at home and abroad on the pretext of reducing them, while also generating novel opportunities for financial speculation. For example, in net terms, the European corporate sector does not need to take any domestic action at all to reduce its emissions before 2017, 12 years after the onset of the EU ETS, partly because of the 1.6 billion tons of offset credits it is entitled to use. So far, over three-quarters of these have come from a few industrial gas projects, which even EU Climate Action Commissioner Connie Hedegaard admits have a 'total lack of environmental integrity'.[18]

Such techniques of 'internalizing the climate externality' are key to new appropriations of surplus. For example, the mere prospect of 'avoided deforestation' credits (much in the news at the 2010 Cancun climate talks) is already encouraging land grabs in Africa, Asia and Latin America whose vast extent is directly proportional to the high-energy intensity and high carbon dioxide production of fossil fuels.[19] Unavoidably, this emerging market attributes to a narrow range of human agents – typically investors, professional forest managers, environmental organizations and police – a process of carbon conservation which is usually an outcome of millennia of inextricably interwoven relations between humans and their natural environment. Even if, as is exceedingly unlikely, a large share of the revenue from transactions in 'avoided deforestation' carbon credits were ever channelled to Indigenous communities with histories of forest protection, the result would still be a stupendous extraction of surplus value from generations of painstaking labour. The Wall Street firm McKinsey, for example, calculates that 2 gigatons of CO_2e could be reduced globally from 'slash and burn agriculture conversion' at a cost of less than €2 per ton. The figures (which have had a major influence on the governments of Brazil, Indonesia, Guyana, Democratic Republic of Congo and Papua New Guinea, as well as the World Bank and UN) are based on the opportunity cost of not deforesting or degrading land, which in the case of small-scale agriculture, much of whose yield is not sold on the market, can be very low. They thus favour climate action being taken on land controlled by people who are the poorest in economic terms, who are then likely to be displaced at high human cost (not included in the calculations) and to see their store of knowledge of low-carbon subsistence livelihood provision depleted as a result (also not included in the calculations). In general, accumulation in the carbon markets takes place not through 'decarbonization' or 'defossilization' but through the algebra of expropriation.

Thus just as complex derivatives markets lost touch with what they were advertised as being 'about' (the provision of certainty), carbon markets have taken the climate issue and decontextualized, reengineered, and mathematized it until little of relevance to global warming is left. Worse: in their efforts to make certainty and climate benefit 'economizable', and to deploy mass production techniques, both markets have increasingly interfered with delivery of the very social goods their proponents claimed they were providing. One reason is what George Soros calls 'reflexivity', which in the financial markets involves investors' observations, biases and calculative machinery disrupting the 'economic fundamentals' they are supposed to describe, leading, if ignored, to crisis. In the carbon markets, nations or corporations aware that they can be credited with 'reducing' more greenhouse gas emissions in 2020 if they fail to clean up today have an incentive to stay dirty, or even to roll back pollution regulation.[20] Firms may set up new factories to produce HFC-23 or N_2O in order to cash in on the carbon market[21] or start up new commodity production lines by persuading governments not to enforce or promulgate environmental laws. In Nigeria, for instance, Western oil companies (with the collaboration of UN carbon market regulators) have contracted to sell carbon credits to Italy and Norway for avoiding gas flaring activities that have been stipulated as the 'baseline' in spite of the fact that they are illegal and unconstitutional.[22] All of this, of course, reinforces a trend toward additional emissions that can then, in turn, also be lucratively 'avoided'. Yet trying to 'fix' the contradiction by recalculating the baseline against which savings are measured in order to take account of perverse incentives merely creates another perverse incentive to change the new baseline as well. As in the derivatives markets, the calculative machinery necessary for a novel market is itself undermining the possibility of market calculation as well as engendering systemic instabilities.[23] Just as the risk markets wound up ultimately increasing risk, their drive for expanded liquidity resulting in a catastrophic drying up of liquidity, so too the Kyoto carbon markets 'might so far even have contributed to increasing global emissions'.[24] Internalization has increased the number and severity of externalities; 'modelling' has expanded the scope and dangers of the unmodelable.

Both markets' claims to be helping the poor to mobilize assets have also come to less than nothing. The expanded credit offered to the US poor on the strength of the predicted future prices of their houses, while attractive to a government eager to maintain effective demand, turned out to be poisoned. The carbon market's claim to be able to offer the world's poor a lucrative opportunity to sell pollution rights to the rich, similarly, has wound up concealing resource grabs and scams disproportionately benefiting the wealthy in both South and North.[25]

In notable respects, the contradictions of carbon commodities are even more explosive than those affecting complex financial derivatives. In the world of finance, even collateralized debt obligations (CDOs), although their underlying asset has been sliced, diced, and mixed in ways that make it virtually untraceable and unassessable, are, in the end, based on real, specifiable mortgages on actual houses. But the basis for a climate commodity that includes offsets cannot be specified, quantified or verified even in principle. To manufacture offsets by counting 'avoided CO_2 emissions', a baseline must first be established with which to compare current molecular activity. This baseline must be unique, since a single value, however arbitrary, is required for exchange to be possible. Hence the calculation of 'avoided emissions' not only demands the sort of knowledge human beings have never before attained, attempted, or believed possible. (Which of all the scenarios that counterfactual historians and novelists have imagined might have followed a Nazi invasion of Britain is the 'true' one?) It also demands, impossibly, that this knowledge come in the form of an extremely precise quantification of the associated hypothetical molecular movements. This impossibility of verification – and thus of regulation – gives corporations a licence to print climate money without much fear of sanction, since the distinction between counterfeit and legitimate currency is meaningless. As the Munden Group, a Wall Street consultancy, writes with respect to forest offsets, an 'opaque set of variable standards' creates 'a tremendous incentive to create (or destroy) supply as it suits the participants in the market'. In a carbon bubble characterized by continuing pressures to spin out fanciful equivalences involving climate and CO_2e molecules, the resulting asset valuation crisis and loss of confidence – some analysts use the term 'subprime carbon'[26] – could trigger severe economic effects. Not only does (temporary) success in commodity formation mean failure in climate action; the functioning of the commodity itself is ultimately in question.

However, having acquiesced in the growth of carbon markets for a decade and a half, most governments, with the possible exception of a few smaller Southern countries such as Bolivia, are now no more likely to want to abolish them voluntarily than financial regulatory authorities worried about credit default swaps or CDOs were inclined to abolish these products in the years leading up to the financial crash. As Slavoj Zizek paraphrases Marx: 'They know very well how things are, but still they are doing it as if they did not know. They no longer believe, but the things themselves (commodities) believe for them.'[27]

CONCLUSION: FETISHISM AND IDEOLOGY

The CO_2 molecules used to build the global warming commodity are comfortably conceptualized as entities without a history, whether human or climatic. As such, they are representative of the wholly external yet universal 'nature' of post-18th century capitalist ideology described by Neil Smith in his lead essay in the 2007 Socialist Register on *Coming to Terms with Nature*.[28] As apolitical objects seemingly susceptible to manipulation, management and mastery by experts, they are easily treated, fetishistically, as 'the' cause of global warming.[29] The carbon market's use of them in disembedding climate change from the history of fossil fuel use and re-embedding it in the movements of molecules emitted 'by' bounded nation states and corporations is accordingly an ideological as well as an economic operation. The equations that compose the algebra of carbon markets not only raise profit rates, but also run together, in a seemingly 'apolitical' and 'self-evident' way, activities with disparate effects on climate history. Thus ex-World Bank executive Robert Goodland, noting that methane released by domesticated animals causes '32 billion tons of carbon dioxide equivalent, more than the combined impact of industry and energy', can effortlessly draw the conclusion that 'replacing livestock products with better alternatives' would have 'far more rapid effects on greenhouse gas emissions ... than actions to replace fossil fuels with renewable energy'.[30]

Similarly, it is an unavoidable part of the day-to-day technical methodology of carbon offset accounting that carbon project sponsors and managers are pictured as creating value (it is they who 'avoid' emissions that otherwise were 'inevitable'), while nonprofessional actors in already low-emitting contexts or social movements actively working to reduce use of fossil fuels are demoted into passive objects of deterministic calculation or even global warming culprits. The task of building singular, calculable scenarios around 'what would have happened' to the world in the absence of each of thousands of particular carbon projects meanwhile leaves little room for debate about broader social and industrial change. Political conflicts over 'whether another world was possible' – and hence over how large industrial entitlements to the earth's carbon dumps are to be – are attributed, as a matter of methodology, to one side or the other having made a calculation error. As Marx showed, ideology goes all the way down into, and rises up from, the 'metaphysical subtleties and theological niceties' of the technical features of the commodity itself.

Yet the ideological moves embedded in carbon market structure are as contested and uncompletable as the rest of the commodification process. For instance, the accounting framework according to which anthropogenic climate change is caused by molecules emitted by bordered 'geobodies'[31] like 'Pakistan' or 'Canada' has often provoked conflict at international climate negotiations due to the way it occludes the history of fossil fuel use, its connection with surplus extraction and imperialism, questions of ecological debt and so forth. Thus the Chinese government has questioned whether all the molecules emanating from Chinese smokestacks are really 'Chinese', or should in part be attributed to the Western countries that consume the wage goods China produces – a particularly pressing issue given that in recent years Europe's statistical claims to be making 'progress' on climate change, based on tabulating physical locations of molecules, conceal the fact that it has offshored much of its emissions.[32] Taking an opposite tack, the aviation company United Continental recently warned that forcing all airlines flying into Europe to control their emissions in accordance with the EU ETS would 'exceed the legal authority of the European Union' by, for example, allowing Brussels to regulate molecules emanating from machines that are used to start jet engines in Los Angeles.[33]

Supplementing what Zizek calls the 'cynical' fetishism through which officials and technocrats 'no longer believe, but the commodities believe for them'[34] is a scapegoating style of ideology. Apologists for carbon markets typically blame their negative climatic results not only on 'carbon cowboys' and 'corruption', but, more importantly, on 'inadequate regulation' or 'market design flaws'. As in the financial markets, enormous efforts are put into imagining, defining and policing boundaries between corruption and regulation and between fraud and normal market activity.[35] The state-corporate nexus necessary for the formation of the climate commodity is read as a 'potential' conflict of interest, reflexivity as a 'flaw in market design' rather than as part of the design itself, erosion in the rule of law as accidental rather than inherent. The carbon market's decade-long failure to achieve climate results is attributed to 'insufficiently tight emissions caps', and thus failed 'governance', rather than as flowing from a structure in which the caps' function is to create a new commodity without affecting general price stability or fossil fuel dependence, as well as to keep other climate initiatives at bay. What with its own ever-renewed failures, a self-perpetuating carbon market reform industry need never rest idle. To borrow the words Michel Foucault applied to the prison, the carbon market has 'always been offered as its own remedy: the reactivation of [its] techniques as the only means of overcoming [its] perpetual failure ... the supposed failure [is] part of [its] functioning'.[36]

Scapegoating ideology, however, is as double-edged as its cynical variety, or as the climate commodification process itself. Depending on political circumstances, calls for 'better regulation' or 'crackdowns on corruption' can intersect fruitfully with the more strategic, long-term campaigns for decommodification of the earth's carbon-cycling capacity being undertaken by grassroots movements and groups such as Via Campesina, the California Movement for Environmental Justice, and movements in Ecuador, Canada and Nigeria opposing fossil fuel extraction.[37] Useful information on patterns of subsidies provided to fossil fuel polluters by the EU ETS, or on the perverse incentives associated with HFC-23 projects, often come from groups clinging to the fetish of reform, and important analyses of the contradictions of the climate commodity from Wall Street consultants who would be horrified at the extent to which their contributions are aiding the understanding of radical movements against the trade. Thus while frank discussion of the consequences of the continuing unfolding of the contradiction between exchange-value and use-value in carbon markets is more politically productive when undertaken with affected publics than with fetish-constrained state officials and technocrats, or in the pages of the financial press, political spaces for breaking the trance that carbon markets have imposed on climate policy can be, and are being, opened at many levels.

NOTES

I am grateful for comments and discussion to Andres Barreda, John Saxe Fernandez, Steve Suppan, Jutta Kill, Ricardo Coelho, Hendro Sangkoyo, Martin Bitter, Oscar Reyes, Raul Garcia, Matthew Paterson, Gar Lipow and Arief Wicaksono.

1   Karl Marx, *Capital*, Volume 1, London: Penguin, 1990, p. 198.
2   Jamie Peck and Adam Tickell, 'Neoliberalizing Space', *Antipode*, 34(3), 2002.
3   After a slight uptick to nearly $144 billion in 2009, total market value declined to $142 billion in 2010. The EU ETS's share of world carbon markets stood at about 97 per cent in 2010, including the EU's purchase of carbon credits manufactured in the global South under the Kyoto Protocol (see World Bank, *State and Trends of the Carbon Market 2011*, Washington: World Bank, 2011). Worldwide, it is mainly EU allowances and Kyoto Protocol credits that are bought and sold through trading platforms and over the counter. However,

there exist many other carbon markets. Some of these are, like the EU ETS, 'compliance' markets – components of government regulatory programmes for greenhouse gases. An example is the Regional Greenhouse Gas Initiative set up to regulate emissions from the electricity sector in some states in the Northeastern US – which also slumped in 2010. Other such schemes exist in New Zealand and New South Wales. Plans for yet other compliance markets in Japan, Australia, Korea, some regions of China, California and some other western US states are meanwhile facing delays and obstacles. So-called 'voluntary markets' selling unofficial carbon commodities have seen large increases in trading volume but remain relatively small at less than 0.3 per cent of global carbon markets. They too have suffered some setbacks, notably the collapse, in late 2010, of the Chicago Climate Exchange's cap and trade program among volunteering corporations. Carbon market proponents, however, remain hopeful that the markets will eventually grow into the trillions of dollars.

4   Gillian Tett, *Fool's Gold: How Unrestrained Greed Corrupted a Dream, Shattered Global Markets and Unleashed a Catastrophe*, London: Abacus, 2009, p. 121.

5   Stephen Gudeman, *Economy's Tension: The Dialectics of Community and Market*, London: Berghahn, 2008, p. 141.

6   See P. Falkowski, R. Scholes et al., 'The Global Carbon Cycle: A Test of Our Knowledge of Earth as a System, *Science,* 290(5490), 2000. The equivalent of the earth's entire production of plant and animal life for 400 years is today burned every year in the form of fossil fuels. See H. Haberl, 'The Global Socioeconomic Energetic Metabolism as a Sustainability Problem', *Energy* 1(1), 2006 and J. S. Dukes, 'Burning Buried Sunshine: Human Consumption of Ancient Solar Energy', *Climatic Change* 61(1-2), 2003.

7   Also important are expedients such as carbon capture and sequestration, which would liquefy fossil-origin carbon dioxide emitted by power plants and transfer it to a new 'waste frontier' in leaky geological formations. Such 'fixes', of course, open new metabolic rifts. For example, just as, in the original rift Marx described, cities accepted one-way shipments of soil nutrients from depopulated and privatized rural lands in the form of food and fibre, a carbon-constrained industrial sector is now engendering a new country-city contradiction by attempting to seize biotic carbon for its own use, again without any prospect of 'giving it back' to the rural areas from which it comes.

8   Morgan M. Robertson, 'The Neoliberalization of Ecosystem Services: Wetland Mitigation Banking and Problems in Environmental Governance', *Geoforum*, 35(3), 2004, p. 362.

9   It is essential to clarify the nature of these rights, since their status is a source of perpetual confusion among progressives as well as market actors in the climate debate. The pollution rights issued to the North and Northern industry under the Kyoto Protocol and the EU ETS are not exclusionary in the sense that ordinary private property rights are (nor are they permanent, since the number of rights given out can be reduced over time). Under Kyoto, nations and industries in the global South are allowed to continue using global carbon sinks without restriction. This has led to the popular belief that Kyoto is 'progressive' in that it allows special privileges to the South while imposing

binding limits on the North, in accordance with the principle – enshrined in the UN Framework Convention on Climate Change – that South and North have 'differentiated responsibilities' for global warming. This superficial account leaves out four crucial facts. First, while Kyoto does not enclose the earth's carbon-cycling capacity in the classical sense of excluding others from access to it, it does exclusively provide nation states and private firms in industrialized countries with legal and economic guarantees protecting their power to harm others by overusing that capacity. Second, Southern nations' permission to continue greenhouse gas pollution, unlike that accorded to Northern nations and industries, does not come in a lucrative *commodity form*. In other words, Kyoto, like the EU ETS, awards assets to the North but not to the South. Third, even if, as now seems unlikely, Southern nations were brought under a global 'cap' and issued commodities, it would only be in an amount proportional to their much smaller historical use of fossil fuels. Finally, the primary function of caps is not to limit emissions (from the point of view of most climate scientists, the Kyoto Protocol's caps are derisory) but rather to fulfil the conditions for commodity creation. Caps are likely to continue to be set at a level lax enough to allow fossil fuel-based accumulation to proceed smoothly in the North, but just strict enough to create a climate commodity – also for the benefit of the North – at the same time. In all of these senses, a regime of emissions restrictions that appears formally to favour the South in fact favours the North.

10 Michael Pahle, Lin Fan and Wolf-Peter Schill, 'How Emission Certificate Allocations Distort Fossil Investments: The German Example', *Energy Policy*, 39(4), 2011.

11 Oscar Reyes, 'The EU Emissions Trading System: Failing at the Third Attempt', Corporate Europe Observatory and Carbon Trade Watch, Barcelona, April 2011. Free handouts to the private sector may be cut back somewhat after 2012, but will continue in key industrial sectors.

12 Sandbag, 'The Carbon Rich List: The Companies Profiting from the EU Emissions Trading Scheme', London, February 2010.

13 Nicholas Stern, an ex-World Bank economist, carbon businessman and author of the British government's influential Stern Report, calls the latter a 'very good deal'. See *The Global Deal: Climate Change and the Creation of a New Era of Progress and Prosperity,* New York: Public Affairs, 2009, p. 166.

14 Donald MacKenzie, 'Making Things the Same: Gases, Emission Rights and the Politics of Carbon Markets', *Accounting, Organizations and Society*, 34, 2009, pp. 440-455.

15 United Nations Risoe Centre, 'CDM Pipeline Overview' 2011, available at http://cdmpipeline.org.

16 In January 2011, EU member states approved a proposal to ban HFC-23 and N_2O offsets effective 1 January 2013. Industry then lobbied for the date to be pushed back to April 2013. The delay effectively nullifies 1-2 years' worth of emissions reductions within Europe. See Corporate Europe Observatory, 'Laughing All the Way to the (Carbon Offset) Bank: Collusion between DG Enterprise and Business Lobbyists', April 2011.

17   A small handful of consulting firms dominate the sector, including Det Norske Veritas, TUV Sud, SGS, and Deloitte, collecting large fees and working closely with UN regulators.

18   Reyes, *The EU Emissions Trading System*, p. 1.

19   In October 2010, for instance, Liberia's president demanded the extradition of a British carbon businessman on charges of bribery in connection with a deal to lease a substantial percentage of the country as carbon offsets worth up to US$ 2.2 billion. See www.redd-monitor.org for many other examples.

20   Michael Szabo, 'Kyoto May Push Factories to Pollute More: UN report', *Reuters*, 2 July 2010; 'EU Lawmakers Wade into HFC Debate', *Point Carbon*, 15 July 2010; Herbert Docena, *The Clean Development Mechanism in the Philippines: Costly, Dirty, Money-Making Schemes*, Focus on the Global South, Bangkok, 2010, available at http://www.thecornerhouse.org.uk. The World Bank, similarly, by lowering its efficiency standards for thermal power plant loans, has been able to ramp up production of carbon credits and thus boost revenues from the 13 per cent brokerage fee it charges for the offset transactions it mediates, see Daphne Wysham, 'Nothing More than Hot Air', *Earth Island Journal*, Summer 2011. In May 2011, carbon traders expressed opposition to a new European directive proposing cuts in energy consumption in buildings, vehicles and industry on the ground that it would reduce demand for carbon pollution rights and depress carbon prices; see Pete Harrison, 'EU Energy Plan Threatens Carbon Billions', Reuters, 30 May 2011. It is no surprise that a large proportion of Kyoto Protocol carbon offset projects that claim to be 'reducing' emissions in fact directly support the expansion of fossil fuel use, which exacerbates global warming. Carbon offsets are providing extra finance for gas pipelines, fossil fuel-fired generating plants, coal mines and oil wells. See United Nations Risoe Centre, 'CDM Pipeline Overview'.

21   Fred Pearce, 'Carbon Trading Tempts Firms to Make Greenhouse Gas', *New Scientist*, 16 December 2010.

22   Isaac Osuoka, 'Paying the Polluter? The Relegation of Local Community Concerns in "Carbon Credit" Proposals of Oil Corporations in Nigeria', in S. Böhm and S. Dabhi, eds., *Upsetting the Offset The Political Economy of Carbon Markets*, London: MayFlyBooks, 2009; United Nations Risoe Centre, 'CDM Pipeline Overview'. Osuoka's investigation of Nigerian carbon offsets devised by Western oil companies and carbon consultant firms found that it was nearly impossible to determine whether the gas that the companies claimed will be diverted from flaring to productive use would not in fact come from dedicated gas extraction operations, whose production is not flared.

23   George Soros, *The New Paradigm for Financial Markets: The Credit Crisis of 2008 and What it Means*, New York: Public Affairs, 2008; Edward Li Puma and Benjamin Lee, *Financial Derivatives and the Globalization of Risk*, Durham: Duke University Press, 2004, p. 36.

24   Dieter Helm, 'Government Failure and Rent-Seeking and Capture: The Design of Climate Change Policy', *Oxford Review of Economic Policy*, 26(2), 2010, p. 189.

25   See Herbert Docena, *The Clean Development Mechanism in the Philippines* and

various issues of the Indian climate change magazine *Mausam,* available at http://www.thecornerhouse.org.uk.

26   Michelle Chan, *Subprime Carbon: Rethinking the World's Largest New Derivatives Market*, San Francisco: Friends of the Earth, 2009. As argued above, however, the difficulties are more profound that those associated with the so-called subprime crash, although the economic stakes are, so far, not so high.

27   Slavoj Zizek, *The Sublime Object of Ideology,* New York: Verso, 1989, p. 31.

28   Neil Smith, 'Nature as Accumulation Strategy', *Socialist Register 2007:Coming to Terms with Nature*, Monmouth: Merlin Press, 2006, pp. 16-36.

29   For example, the well-known US climate activist Bill McKibben has characterized the climate change issue as a 'fight between human beings on the one hand, and physics and chemistry on the other'. See 'Bless Bolivia for Recharging the Fight to Rescue Our Climate', *Huffington Post,* 1 April 2010, available at http://www.huffingtonpost.com. The global activist network McKibben is associated with, 350.org, embodies the CO_2 fetish in its very name, referring to the '350 parts per million' atmospheric concentration of CO_2 target.

30   Robert Goodland and Jeff Anhang, 'Livestock and Climate Change', *Worldwatch,* November/December 2010, pp. 10-19.

31   The term is from Thongchai Winichakul's seminal *Siam Mapped: A History of the Geo-Body of a Nation*, Honolulu: University of Hawaii Press, 1994.

32   An increase in 'imported' emissions in mining and manufactured goods from the global South wipe out the (insignificant) emissions cuts Northern countries promised to make under the Kyoto Protocol. For example, the UK's claimed emissions cut of 11 per cent from 1990 to 2008 turns into a 6 per cent increase when 'offshored' emissions are included. See G. P. Peters, J. C. Minx, C. L. Weber and O. Edenhofer, 'Growth in Emission Transfers via International Trade from 1990 to 2008', *Proceedings of the National Academy of Sciences,* 108(21), 2011.

33   Pilita Clark, 'United Warns EU on Emissions Scheme', *Financial Times,* 3 April 2011.

34   The markets' dominant players and architects typically do not even bother trying to defend them against charges that they are environmentally ineffective. See, for example, Organization for Economic Cooperation and Development, 'Scaled-Up Market Mechanisms – What is Needed to Move Forward? A Summary of Recent OECD/IEA Analyses', November 2010, available at http://www.oecd.org.

35   Thus financial journalists' coverage of the sensational scandals that now wash over the carbon markets every few months – massive electronic thefts, double-selling, fraudulent accounting, land swindles, billion-dollar tax cheats, and so on – serves partly to reiterate the idea that better 'regulation' will be able to tackle future problems. Just as no effort is too great when it comes to investigating a Madoff or a Rajnaratnam if it helps to draw a distinction between what they do and what is 'normal' or unproblematic in financial markets, so too no effort is too great in probing the shenanigans of 'carbon cowboys' selling obviously bogus products if it helps to consign any deeper inquiry into the structure of

carbon markets to the trash pile of 'anticapitalist ideology'. This is one reason why some of the best news coverage of corruption in carbon markets, as in financial markets, is to be found in publications such as the *Financial Times* and *Bloomberg*.

36   Michel Foucault, *Discipline and Punish: The Birth of the Prison*, London: Penguin, 1979, pp. 268, 271.

37   For documentation on such emerging movements, which are beyond the scope of this article, see Tamra Gilbertson and Oscar Reyes, *Carbon Trading: How it Works and Why it Fails,* Uppsala: Dag Hammarskjold Foundation, 2009; Patrick Bond, 'Carbon Trading, New Enclosures and Eco-Social Contestation', *Antipode*, forthcoming; and websites such as http://www.carbontradewatch. org, http://www.viacampesina.org, http://www.durbanclimatejustice.org and http://www.ejmatters.org, http://www.thecornerhouse.org.uk. Such 'decommodification' movements typically align themselves with related movements against commodification of water, electricity, health services and fossil fuels, as well as land rights, labour, tax reform, alternative energy, alternative transport and food sovereignty movements and victims of the 'dispossession through algebra' that became visible with the recent financial crash.

THE NEW AMERICAN POOR LAW

FRANCES FOX PIVEN

Early in 2011, the US Census Bureau reported that 14.3 per cent or 47 million people – 1 in 6 of Americans – were living below the official poverty threshold, currently set at $22,400 annually for a family of four. Some 19 million people are living in what is called extreme poverty, or on incomes below half the poverty line. More than a third of those extremely poor people are children. Indeed, over half the children younger than six living with a single mother are poor.[1] Extrapolating from this data, Isabel Sawhill of the Brookings Institution estimated that the poverty rate will increase to nearly 16 per cent by 2016, and the child poverty rate will increase to 26 per cent.[2] No one will be surprised to learn that minorities are substantially overrepresented among the poor, but so are women.[3]

The situation of the poor in the United States is actually considerably worse than these numbers suggest. In the US, the official poverty line is an absolute measure of subsistence needs, simply three times the minimal food budget created in 1959, adjusted for inflation in food costs. This means that the poverty threshold takes no account of increases in tax, or housing, or fuel, or transportation, or healthcare costs, all of which are rising more rapidly than the costs of basic foods. So the poverty measure understates the basic costs of subsistence. Moreover, in 2006 interest payments on consumer debt put over 4 million people who were not officially in poverty below the line, making them 'debt poor'.[4] Similarly, if childcare costs, estimated at over $5,000 a year in 2002, were deducted from gross income, many more people would be counted as officially poor.[5]

Moreover the very idea of using a measure of absolute necessities should be questioned. Most countries measure poverty in relative terms, generally those below half the median income, thus taking into account the overall rise in living standards in the society in assessing the circumstances of those at the bottom. When comparable measures are used, the United States has far higher poverty rates than other rich countries.[6] Indeed, poverty rates in the United States may match rates in some parts of the global South. New York

City, the global centre of American neoliberalism, is also the international capital of finance, and its poverty rate is just under 20 per cent. The result is that 'If New York City were a nation', reports James Parrott, 'its level of income concentration would rank 15th among 134 countries, between Chile and Honduras'. He adds that Wall Street is only 15 miles from the Bronx, the nation's poorest urban county.[7]

High levels of poverty in the United States preceded the economic meltdown of 2007–09. Between 2001 and 2007, poverty actually increased for the first time on record during an economic recovery, from 11.7 per cent in 2001 to 12.5 per cent in 2007.[8] Poverty rates for single mothers in 2007 were 50 per cent, higher in the US than in 15 other high-income countries.[9] Black employment rates and income were declining *before* the recession struck in 2007. And there is simply no evidence to support the familiar bromide that poverty in the US today is a temporary condition associated with youth or hard luck or economic crises. Preconceptions notwithstanding, the US is a low mobility society.[10]

That said, these trends worsened sharply with the onset of the Great Recession that began in 2007. The Economic Policy Institute reported that the typical working-age household, which had already seen a sharp decline of roughly $2300 in income from 2000 to 2006, saw another decline of $2700 from 2007 to 2009.[11] Higher and mid-wage industries accounted for most of the job losses, while lower-wage industries accounted for nearly half of such growth as occurred in the uncertain recovery.[12] Manufacturing contracted, and overall the labour market lost 6.1 per cent of payroll employment. New investment, when it occurred at all, was much more likely to be in machinery than in new workers, so unemployment levels remain alarmingly high.[13] In other words, the recession accelerated ongoing market trends toward lower-wage and insecure employment.[14]

A decade ago it was widely thought that the next phase of welfare innovation would be something called 'workfare'. Although workfare programs on the ground varied considerably, the basic idea was simply to make the receipt of welfare benefits conditional on work by the recipient, sometimes work for wages, sometimes in exchange for a welfare check; sometimes the work was in the public sector, and sometimes for private employers. Jamie Peck studied these innovations as they were being developed in the US, Canada and Great Britain, and proposed that, local variations notwithstanding, the 'policy orthodoxy of flexibly deregulated labour markets now [had] a social policy analogue in the concerted advocacy of workfare programs'.[15] But Peck was also keenly aware of the limits of workfare, which depended on buoyant labour markets. And in fact, the welfare-to-work policies did not become dominant, just as in an earlier era the workhouse did not become dominant. Particularly in the United States, an older strategy of impoverishment and insult has prevailed, except that it has been imposed with particular vigour on women and minorities.

REGULATING THE POOR

In *Regulating the Poor,* Richard Cloward and I argued that the treatment of the poor in modernizing western societies could only be understood in relation to the problem of enforcing and regulating labour, a problem that became more salient as labour markets supplanted traditional and largely agricultural arrangements that had shackled people to the soil and the lord. Of course, for much of our history, the majority of working people were in fact poor. But we meant a stratum of people worse off than the main body of workers, and distinct from them in that they were also stripped of social respect. As traditional labour relations lost ground to markets, this was accomplished in significant part by the creation of a new institution, a system of discipline and assistance usually called poor relief. The Webbs wrote of the widespread creation of relief systems in commercializing Europe as the development of 'a new statecraft relative to destitution'.[16] The inauguration of relief systems was usually provoked by outbreaks of disorder by people who were starving. But the management of relief over time was more importantly shaped by its role in disciplining workers. From its early beginnings, the new statecraft gave meagre assistance to those who turned to it, and the terms of that assistance were harsh. Just as important, those who turned to the parish or the county were subject to sustained rituals of public humiliation. That harsh treatment and especially the humiliation has always constituted a dramatic warning to the mass of working people trying to survive on their earnings. The practices of relief or the workhouse or welfare sent the message that there was a worse fate than low wage work, and that fate was to fall into abject poverty and become a pauper.

Poverty and its institutionalized insults have been used to divide and terrify working people for centuries. It stands to reason that with the intensification of labour exploitation in the neoliberal period, with shrinking wages, the spread of insecure and irregular work, and the escalation of the war against unions, that extreme poverty would also increase, and so would its uses as a social drama to intimidate workers who were still managing to stay afloat. It also follows that the strategy would be boldest in the United States where other neoliberal labour policies were so aggressively promoted. But while there are striking continuities in the law and practice of poor relief across time and across borders, the institution has also been periodically overhauled, sometimes to take account of shorter-term problems of popular rebelliousness, and sometimes in reflection of deep-seated changes in labour markets. Recent developments in the United States suggest to me that the ancient institution of relief has been adapted to take account not only of the deteriorating terms of wage labour generally in a neoliberal era, but also of vast changes in the composition of the American labour market.

These changes were historic. We talk a lot about the 'race to the bottom' resulting from the fact that American workers now compete with low-wage workers everywhere. But there have also been system-wide changes in the American labour market resulting from the massive incorporation of women, as well as the incorporation of previously agricultural African Americans and Latinos.[17] I am arguing that poverty policy was reconstructed as a reaction to these developments. For a brief time during the more liberal period of welfare in the 1960s and 1970s, a good many single mothers had been permitted to live on the dole while their children were young, and even to live at levels not worse than low wage workers. The expansion of the imperative of wage labour to include women, as well as African-Americans and Latinos who had laboured in the agricultural South or Latin America, often under feudal terms, came to be reflected in policies that created a class of disrespected poor people that was not only becoming more numerous and worse off, but in which women and minorities were disproportionately prominent. Between 2000 and 2009, the percentage of mothers in the labour force increased, even as the percentage of women with an income less than half the poverty level rose, and the percentage of poor children receiving welfare assistance fell.[18] When the Great Recession hit, 77 per cent of low-income women reported living paycheck to paycheck, a 17 point jump from the previous year.[19] Similarly, when unemployment rose overall, it rose much more among Blacks and Latinos, who are also far more likely to find themselves among the long-term unemployed, and far less likely to receive unemployment benefits.[20]

Part of the cause for high and rising poverty levels in the United States is the inevitable result of the decades-long business mobilization to reduce labour costs and weaken labour organizations in the workplace. The mobilization began in the 1970s, and took form in changing workplace labour relations, where employers trying to hold down wages became much more intransigent in negotiations, and deployed strategies of union busting and restructuring of the labour process to make work more insecure. And business also mobilized to change public policies bearing on workers and their unions, with the result that National Labor Board decisions became much less favourable to workers and unions, workplace regulations were not enforced, the minimum wage lagged far behind inflation, and safety net programs for the unemployed or the unemployable became more restrictive and benefit levels fell (although the Earned Income Tax Credit which effectively provides a taxpayer subsidy to low-earning workers and their employers expanded enormously). Inevitably, the overall impact of the campaign to reduce labour's share of national earnings also had the effect of increasing the proportion of the population unable to earn even a poverty level livelihood.[21] But that is not the whole of it. The poor and the programs that assisted them were also the object of a large-scale campaign of direct attack.

THE CAMPAIGN

Neoliberalism is variously defined, but most commentators would agree that it involves the increased penetration and domination of the state by capitalist interests. The project of state domination in an electoral-representative democracy depends not only on lobbyists, but also on winning public opinion, at least enough to win elections. And the first phase of the attack on the poor does seem to have originated as an electoral strategy. This began even while the Black Freedom Movement of the 1960s was still in full throttle, and was evident in the presidential campaign of Republican Barry Goldwater, as well as the recurrent campaigns of sometimes Democrat George Wallace, the segregationist Alabama governor. Richard Nixon's presidential bid in 1968 picked up the theme. As many commentators have pointed out, Nixon's campaign strategy tapped the rising racial animosities not only of white southerners, but also of the white working–class people who were now locked in contests with newly urbanized African-Americans over jobs, public services, and housing and school desegregation. The racial theme was instantly merged with talk about the poor, with the steady rise of political propaganda targeting the poor and contemporary poor relief programs. Indeed, poverty became a kind of metaphor for Blacks, along with other metaphors, like welfare and unwed mothers, and crime.

Much of the energy for the campaign came from electoral politics as resurgent Republicans tried to defeat Democrats by associating them with Blacks and policy liberalism. But whatever the immediate impetus, the bold outlines of the message were classical invocations of the call for excluding and demeaning the very poor that in short order were to result in a 'War on Drugs' that largely ignored the major traffickers in favour of the lowest level offenders,[22] massive prison incarceration and the wholesale 'reform' of the main means-tested cash assistance program, Aid to Families of Dependent Children.[23] This politically driven attack on the American poor was an important opening drama in the decades-long campaign launched by business and the organized Right against workers.[24]

In fact, the neoliberal campaign to dominate the state had a much larger agenda than regulating the poor or attacking African-Americans. The bigger goals were soon apparent: massive redistribution of the burden of taxation, deregulation, the cannibalization of government services through privatization, wage cuts and enfeebled unions. At this stage, the poor, and Blacks, were a rhetorical foil, a propagandistic distraction to win elections and make bigger gains. Still, the rhetoric was important. A host of new think tanks, political organizations and lobbyists in Washington D.C. carried the message that the country's problems were caused by the poor whose shiftlessness and sexual promiscuity were being indulged by a too-generous welfare system. Moreover, big cuts in the means-tested programs followed in short order. The staging of the cuts was itself propaganda, but the cuts also accumulated to erode the safety net that protected both the poor and workers, especially low wage workers, and that meant especially women and minorities. By 1980 and the election of Ronald Reagan, propaganda had smoothed the path for huge cuts in programs for poor people. Means-tested programs were cut by 54 per cent, job training by 81 per cent, housing assistance by 47 per cent.[25] By the 1990s, the Republican campaign against the poor, and Blacks, came to be inflected back on the Democrats as they floundered for electoral strategies to ward off the assault, and to raise business money. It was Bill Clinton who campaigned with the slogan 'end welfare as we know it'.

The campaign at the federal level was soon matched by the activities in the state capitols of organizations like the American Federation for Children, the American Legislative Exchange Council, the Institute for Liberty, and the State Policy Network. Their agenda was also big, eventually calling for large-scale privatization of public services, business tax cuts, the rollback of environmental regulations and consumer protections, crippling public sector unions, and measures (like requiring photo identification) to restrict access to the ballot by students and the poor. In other words, the agenda was and is the capture of the American governmental apparatus. But from the beginning of the neoliberal mobilization in the 1970s, the poor were a main public target, and the main policy consequences were welfare cutbacks, particularly in the Aid to Families with Dependent Children (AFDC) and state-level General Assistance programs, coupled with a law and order campaign that resulted in draconian sentencing practices, a huge prison expansion, and the massive incarceration of Black men.

Much of this effort was played out in state politics. AFDC was a federal grant-in-aid program targeted to impoverished lone mothers and their children that ceded considerable authority to the states, and often the counties, in determining eligibility and setting benefit levels. When Black insurgency escalated in the 1960s, the federal government issued a series of rulings that restrained state and local governments from their customary restrictive welfare practices. Not surprisingly, the rolls rose and benefit levels reached their peak in the late 1960s. Then, as the protests subsided, federal oversight was withdrawn. Between 1970 and 1996, the real average level of maximum benefits fell by more than half, providing income for a family of three of only a fraction of the poverty line. Finally, in 1996, the program was eliminated, to be replaced by Temporary Assistance to Needy Families (TANF), a block grant that gave the states a good deal of leeway to limit assistance for a variety of reasons, and a remarkable incentive to do just that since the states received the full grant no matter how many people they actually assisted. The law also eliminated or greatly reduced the eligibility for federal safety net programs of legal immigrants during their first five years of US residence.[26] Subsequently, noncitizen eligibility for Food Stamps and Supplemental Security Income was restored, but not for TANF or Medicaid.[27] The industry of policy researchers studying the effect of this reform all agree that, not surprisingly, the rolls have fallen dramatically and that at least for a time, work effort by recipients increased. As Stephen Pimpare points out, evaluations of the effects of the new program either on labour markets or family well-being are less conclusive, perhaps, he says, because benefits had already been reduced sharply by the time TANF was introduced so few families actually counted on welfare for a large portion of their income.[28]

In any case, the significance of the large changes that occurred in welfare policy over these decades cannot be properly assessed by research that fastens narrowly on the impact on a relatively small population of recipients. A more informative study is provided by Soss, Fording and Schram in a forthcoming book.[29] Their data show that at the beginning of the 1960s, state-to-state variations in welfare benefit levels were closely correlated with differences in state retail wages, and remained substantially lower than those wages, averaging 60 per cent. Then as Black insurgency forced the expansion of the rolls and the raising of benefit levels along with the introduction of food stamp benefits, the relationship between wages and benefit levels weakened, and in some states benefits actually exceeded the value of wages. After the mid-1970s, as insurgency disappeared, the real value of benefits declined, although not as much as wages in the low-wage sectors that Soss, Fording and Schram track.[30] Not, that is, until the introduction of a new welfare policy in the 1990s simply eliminated benefits for most recipients.

Soss, Fording and Schram think that the policy introduced in 1996 created a welfare regime of supervision and discipline, one that stresses the civic primacy of the market roles of consumer, worker and customer, and imposes those roles through state-level programs organized according to a business model, and indeed incorporating businesses into the bureaucracy by means of contracts for administering parts of the program.[31] They may be right that something quite new is at work here in the eager adaptation of a business model by welfare bureaucracies. What may be more important, however, is the public celebration by the welfare establishment of the business model and the noisy application of wage work imperatives to the mothers of young children.

The recession has now prompted further cutbacks in welfare programs. Because cash assistance has been so crippled by welfare reform, the federal food stamp program became very important in providing assistance to the poor. The program, which has been renamed the 'Supplemental Nutritional Assistance Program', was boosted by stimulus funds provided in the 2009 Recovery Act, and benefits temporarily rose in that year and so did participation, which increased from 34.4 million people to 40.8 million, most of whom were below the poverty line.[32] That program has been the target of repeated attempts at cuts by the Congress, including attempts to tap the program's funds for farm subsidies, and now an effort is under way to deny food stamps to any family that includes a worker on strike.[33]

But the biggest setbacks in assistance programs are occurring on the state and local levels. The developments which have made the federal arrangement of American governance so important in the policies that affect the poor deserve note. First, in the 2010 midterm elections the Republicans made large gains in the state capitols, and they are using their new majorities to continue to cut state taxes on business and the wealthy, invoking the mantra of 'job creation'. As a result, since states usually cannot legally run deficits, cuts in assistance programs to the poor and the unemployed seemingly become necessary. Moreover, the supplemental federal funds for TANF that were included in the Recovery Act of 2009 are running out. Thus the states have been the stage for a kind of manufactured austerity, a seeming structural imperative resulting from both the accumulation of past policies such as recurrent tax cuts for business and the affluent, and the complex allocation of authority in the federal system. I should also note that federalism in the American system has always nurtured the business strategy of threatening to exit, to move across the state line (or across national borders) if their policy demands were not met. In response, states are cutting the TANF caseload and benefit levels and shortening lifetime limits on assistance. The percentage of single mothers receiving benefits fell from 16 per cent in 2001 to 11 per cent in 2007 and then to 10 per cent in 2010.

The mechanisms through which this was accomplished are not unfamiliar. In New York City, the onerous application process introduced with welfare reform includes 'two interviews, fingerprinting, presumptive fraud investigations, home visits conducted by case investigators and mandatory workforce orientations and up-front job search activities'.[34] No wonder that the rate at which applications are denied, usually on the grounds of noncompliance with one or another of the unbelievably complex program rules, creeps upward as the recession continues. Those denied face eviction and homelessness, food insecurity and health problems. Meanwhile, unemployment insurance, basically a state program supplemented by emergency federal provisions for the longer-term unemployed, is also under attack by the states. Indeed, some states never accepted the federally funded long-term insurance extensions.[35] Michigan has already reduced the state-paid unemployment benefit from 26 to 20 weeks, and Florida followed suit despite a state unemployment rate of over 11 per cent by reducing state benefits to 23 weeks. Some four million workers have run out of all unemployment benefits.[36] A hotel housekeeper in Indiana, a mother with four children, describes the parallel changes in her working conditions: 'When I started 10 years ago we'd clean 14 to 15 rooms a day. Now we clean 40.... Its always run, run, run. I don't eat lunch anymore. If I don't finish in time, they'll cut my hours the following week'.[37]

There are also signs on the horizon that, as the fiscal problems created by tax cuts and recession shortfalls roll through the federal system, deeper organizational changes to facilitate spending cuts are being contemplated. State and local governments are both the single largest employer in the US and the main providers of a range of social supports. Fiscal stresses are an opportunity to attack on both fronts. The *New York Times* reported that state policy makers are 'working behind the scenes to come up with a way to let the states declare bankruptcy and get out from under crushing debts, including the pensions they have promised retired public workers'.[38] And some states are moving to create arrangements for 'emergency financial management' that are reminiscent of the state takeover of New York City finances during the fiscal crisis of 1975-76.[39]

These are not random moves. To the contrary, the path has been prepared by groups like the American Legislative Exchange Council, which claims a membership of 2,000 state legislators and sees the recession as an opportunity to move forward on its mission of shrinking government, lowering taxes, and promoting free market fiscal policies.[40]

POLICY AS PROPAGANDA

In the 1960s, the poor – usually personified in the welfare mother (who became Ronald Reagan's imaginary welfare queen by the 1980s), or the homeless vagrant, or the crack addict – emerged as a central reference in American political discourse. At first, this was largely the result of the equation of poverty, and liberal programs to ease poverty, with race and the indulgence of Blacks, an equation made easier by the fact that so many Blacks were indeed poor, and that Black insurgency had prompted the Great Society programs to ease poverty. The Republican strategy of stirring up racial antagonisms to wean white southern Democrats and the white northern working-class voters away from their traditional Democratic allegiances was perhaps obvious. Nor was this just a matter of campaign appeals. The organized Right, including rightwing foundations, politically engaged corporate leaders and the Christian Right, built a vast propaganda machine that wove together poverty, race and sex in appeals that helped to incite right-wing populist movements for four decades.[41]

The growing complexity of governance makes the public acutely susceptible to propaganda, especially propaganda that takes the form of stories that give simple explanations, usually pointing to particular villains who are ostensibly to blame for what is going wrong in their society. After all, it is nearly impossible to decipher what is going on in the centres of power. Can the public track debates about 'credit default swaps' or 'debt-to-GDP ratios' or can they disentangle proposals for health care reform or financial regulation? Stories, slogans and sound bites can make a rough sense of a very complicated, even inscrutable, political world. But it was by no means the message machine alone that made the poor a target. Government policies and the bureaucrats and politicians that hover over them create a reality through their design and communication about public programs. In other words, government programs are themselves also a message machine.

I can make my point easily by pointing to the program called social security, or more accurately Old Age Survivors and Dependents Insurance. The program has only superficial resemblance to the private insurance policies that most people have been led to think of when they think of social security. An insurance policy is an individual contract where regular fees accumulate to guarantee payments when the event insured against occurs. Social security taxes do not accumulate to be paid out when old age or disability strikes. Benefits to the aged or disabled are drawn from the payroll taxes of current workers. The reformers of the 1930s were eager to define their program as a nationwide insurance program because they thought that people accustomed to private insurance would find that more appealing, more 'American'. They probably were right, at least in the shorter run. After all, social security is so popular that it has foiled a series of attempts to privatize it. But the price has been that Americans don't understand that the program they love is a government venture that collectivizes risk and is even modestly redistributive.

In a curious commentary on the success of the social security deception, Stuart Butler and Peter Germanis, both from the Heritage Foundation, published an article in 1982 on how to 'prepare the political ground' for the privatization of social security in the face of the 'political power of the elderly' which 'will only increase in the future'. Their article, entitled 'Achieving a "Leninist" Strategy', proposes a series of incremental changes that will benefit and attract the support of the financial and business community in particular, while assuring the elderly that their benefits will remain intact, meanwhile expanding Individual Retirement Accounts as a private prototype, and requiring the Social Security Administration to establish individual accounts revealing 'the inter- and intra-generational distribution that occurs under the current system'. The elderly 'might then come to realize that they have not purchased an earned annuity but instead are receiving a tremendous welfare subsidy'.[42] Or perhaps the elderly would then realize that they also were 'dependent' on a collective, and governmental, effort. In any case, program as propaganda is clearly a game that both the Right and the Left can play.

Social security has provided a measure of economic security for many people, and has dramatically reduced old age poverty, so one might applaud the shrewdness of the policy experts who designed the program to mislead the public. However, many policies that are not so benign, that work to the benefit of the better-off, or promote the profitability of particular industries, are also designed to mislead the public, largely by hiding the policies from view. Suzanne Mettler sees these policies as part of the 'submerged state ... [which] eludes most ordinary citizens: they have little awareness of its policies or their upwardly redistributive effects, and few are cognizant of what is at stake in reform efforts'. Federal guarantees to banks for student loans, tax-deferred savings accounts, home mortgage interest deductions are examples. Mettler reports the remarkable finding that majorities of those who enjoy each of these government benefits think that they have not used a government social program.[43]

Not so with programs that reach the poor. These programs are typically very visible, the targeted beneficiaries (or victims) are usually loudly announced or more likely denounced by politicians, a good many people know or think they know about the programs, indeed often seem obsessed with them, and so do most of those who benefit know they have used a government social program. Mettler reports that in 2008, large majorities of those who benefited from social security for the disabled, supplemental security income, Medicaid, welfare, subsidized housing and food stamps knew in each case that they had in fact used a government program.[44] Note for example that the welfare-to-work 'demonstration' programs that preceded the elimination of AFDC in favour of TANF, and the state TANF programs as well, often made the participating poor very visible indeed, outfitting them in orange day-glow vests as they picked up trash in the parks or on the parkways.

PENALIZING THE POOR

The criminal justice system is at least as visible. Indeed, beginning in the 1960s, the problem of law and order became a central theme in electoral politics, a theme invoking a Durkheimian drama about race, poverty, deviance and punishment. I said earlier that some of this can be traced to the Republican electoral campaigns of the 1960s which featured rhetoric about the poor, welfare, and crime as virtual synonyms for race and especially for Blacks. Over time, poverty politics resulted in first the steady erosion of safety net benefits, and then the overhaul of the main cash assistance program. Parallel to these developments, criminal sentencing became much harsher, especially but not only in connection with 'the war on drugs' and mandatory sentencing policies. Millions of men, most of them minorities, have been incarcerated. Even after serving their sentence or sentences, they are permanently stigmatized. They are usually effectively stripped of their right to vote, diminishing the importance of the African-American vote overall, and since they are unlikely to secure stable employment, they are consigned to the economy of the streets. Douglas Glasgow describes the life:

> Being broke, hustling, jiving, stealing, rapping, balling; a fight, a bust, some time; no job, lost a job, a no-paying job; a lady, a baby, some weight; some wine, some grass, a pill; no ride, lost pride, man going down, slipping fast, can't see where to make it; I've tried, almost died, ready now for almost anything.[45]

The expansion of the penal system that accompanied welfare reform is central to the argument made by Loic Wacquant. He sees the prison as an analogue to the ghetto, which also warehouses and marginalizes populations. '[T]he poverty of the social state', he writes, 'against the backdrop of deregulation elicits and necessitates the grandeur of the penal state'.[46] And he thinks the creation of the penal state is propelled by the political logic of neoliberalism, 'namely the construction of a post-Keynesian, "liberal-paternalistic" state suited to institute desocialized wage labour and propagate the renewed ethic of work and "individual responsibility" that buttress it'.[47] Much of what Wacquant has to say about the penal system is true. It is huge, processing many millions of people, most of them poor minority men. It is expensive, absorbing ever larger shares of public budgets. And the expansion of the system has been rapid and precipitous. Still, I wonder about the economic logic, or whether there is any unitary logic propelling the expansion of the penal system? And does that logic in fact reflect the imperatives of neoliberalism? In systemic terms, is massive incarceration logical at all?

Clearly there is or was an electoral logic. Much of the fuel that fed the drive for tough drug laws, mandatory sentencing, and prison construction was generated by electoral politics, and particularly by the Republican strategy mentioned earlier of demonizing African-Americans in order to draw white voters away from the Democratic party with which Blacks had come to be associated. Some of that played itself out in national politics, and was evident in law and order initiatives as early as the Nixon administration. It also came to be mimicked by the Democrats. Bill Clinton used his 1994 State of the Union address to advertise his support of 'three strikes and you're out' legislation which condemned repeat offenders, including non-violent ones, to lifetime imprisonment, and then threw his support behind the Violent Crime Control and Law Enforcement Act.[48] Moreover, the electoral uses of crime and punishment were by no means confined to national politics. State prisons grew as candidates in gubernatorial races jumped into the fray trying to take advantage of the backlash politics fostered by national races by making campaign promises about tough anti-crime initiatives and prison building projects. Indeed, without the fuel of electoral contests organized around the backlash, it is hard to imagine that incarceration would have spiralled up as it did.

But I disagree with Wacquant's argument that the penal system functions much like welfare or workfare 'to push its clientele onto the peripheral segments of the deskilled job market... continually (re)generating a large volume of marginal laborers who can be super- exploited at will'. The evidence we have about the actual consequences of incarceration does not support this explanation. Quite aside from the vast budgets commanded by the penal system which could of course be directed to arguably more successful training programs, are the wasted people and wasted labour that result from mass incarceration in fact functional for neoliberal labour markets?

A prison record hardly equips those released for wage labour, desocialized or otherwise. One-third of released prisoners are reincarcerated within six months, and nearly half within a year.[49]

There is another grim possibility, that mass incarceration reflects the fact that the neoliberal labour market, having already incorporated women and immigrants on its own terms, and with vast numbers of potential workers in the southern hemisphere and China ready to be recruited with a click of the mouse, simply has little use for rebellious African-American men.

I think we are at a pivotal moment, not only in the United States but also across the planet, if only because what happens in the US has widespread repercussions. Even putting aside the 'end-times' wonderings about climate change, food scarcity and nuclear disaster, the neoliberal juggernaut in the US is on a roll, calling for union busting state laws, ever greater clawbacks in the form of tax cuts for business and the affluent, and budget cuts for everyone else, but especially for the worst-off, coupled with court-rulings that open the electoral system even wider to the influence of money while other changes are introduced into electoral administration that make voting more difficult for the growing populations of naturalized citizens, youth, and the poor.

Still, the corporate wealthy have been on a roll before, and they have been slowed, and in some respects even reversed, by the rise of protest movements that threatened to make the factories, the cities, and even the country ungovernable. Maybe the sheer boldness of the business Right, encouraged by their Tea Party allies, is a kind of overreach, and the sheer bravado of their demands is making evident what the Left has failed to make evident. This is the hope of Wisconsin, when thousands of students, workers, and community sympathizers gathered and occupied the capital to protest the right-wing Governor's proposals to cut social spending by roughly the same amount as business taxes had been cut the previous month, adding for good measure a proposal to sharply limit the collective bargaining rights of public sector unions and threatening to call out the National Guard if the unions made trouble. Wisconsin does, I think, point the way, but it's also the case that in Wisconsin the protestors have not yet won and, in the aftermath of the protests, the Wisconsin Senate is actually considering the reversal of child labour laws.

The juggernaut will be hard to stop. It will take a bigger and bolder movement than Wisconsin and, both for moral and strategic reasons, it must include the worst-off whose circumstances are so closely bound to the circumstances of working people generally. So far, the rhetoric of resistance is uncomfortably fastened on the idea of saving the 'middle class'. Leaving aside that what is meant is the working class, a movement large enough and threatening enough to roll back the juggernaut will have to be inclusive. Most especially, it will need the armies of poor women, African–Americans and Latinos who are the foil for the broader attack on working people. Our future depends on it.

NOTES

1   See Greg Kaufmann, 'US Poverty: Past, Present and Future', *The Nation*, 22 March 2001; Kathryn Ann Edwards, 'Another Look at Poverty in the Great Recession', Economic Policy Institute, 5 January 2011, available at http://www.epi.org.

2   The extrapolation is based on the known relationship between the unemployment rate and the poverty rate. See Isabel V. Sawhill, 'An Update to "Simulating the Effect of the 'Great Recession' on Poverty"', The Brookings Institution, 7 October 2010.

3   On female poverty see Heidi Hartmann, 'Women, the Recession, and the Stimulus Package', *Dissent*, 56(4), pp. 42-47.

4   Steven Pressman and Robert H. Scott III, 'Consumer Debt and Poverty Measurement', *Focus,* Institute on Research on Poverty, Summer 2010.

5   See Women's Legal Defense and Education Fund, 'Reading Between the Lines: Women's Poverty in the United States', 2009, available at http://www.legalmomentum.org.

6   See Pamela Wiepking and Ineke Maas, *Gender Differences in Poverty: A Cross-National Research,* Luxembourg Income Study Working Paper, No. 389, October 2004.

7   Quoted in Tom Robbins, 'Eat the Rich', *The Village Voice*, 2 February 2011; see also James Parrott, 'As Incomes Gap Widens, New York Grows Apart', *The Gotham Gazette,* 18 January 2011.

8   See LaDonna Pavetti, Danilo Trisi and Liz Schott, 'TANF Responded Unevenly to Increase in Need During Downturn', Center on Budget and Policy Priorities, 25 January 2011.

9   Legal Momentum, 'Poverty Rates for Single Mothers are Higher in the U.S. than in Other High Income Countries', June 2011, available at http://www.legalmomentum.org.

10   See Doug Henwood's review of a series of studies by the Pew Charitable Trusts Economic Mobility Project, 'Mobility Today', *Left Business Observer,* 132, 24 April 2011.

11   See Economic Policy Institute (EPI), *The State of Working America 2011,* available at http://www.stateofworkingamerica.org.

12   Catherine Rampell, 'Higher-Paying Jobs Lost, but Lower-Paying Jobs Gained', *Economix*, 23 February 2011.

13   Catherine Rampell, 'Companies Spend on Equipment, Not Workers', *New York Times,* 10 June 2011. The replacement of workers by machinery and new organizational methods continues a several-decades trend, as Kim Moody

documents in *U.S. Labor in Trouble and Transition*, London: Verso, 2007.

14 EPI, *The State of Working America 2011*.

15 See Jamie Peck, *Workfare States*, New York: The Guilford Press, 2001, p. 56.

16 Sidney Webb and Beatrice Webb, *English Poor Law History Part I, The Old Poor Law*, Hamden: Archon Books, 1963, p. 29.

17 Monthly labour force participation rates have declined slightly for men, but have risen robustly for women in the past three decades. See Hartmann, 'Women, the Recession, and the Stimulus Package', Figure 3, p. 45.

18 See Deepak Bhargava et al., 'Battered by the Storm: How the Safety Net is Failing Americans and How to Fix It', Institute for Policy Studies, December 2009; The Women's Legal Defense and Education Fund, 'Single Mothers Since 2000: Falling Further Down', Legal Momentum, 13 January 2001, available at http://www.legalmomentum.org.

19 'Women Bear Brunt of Economic Crisis', *Minority News*, 6 May 2011.

20 See Andrew Grant-Thomas, 'Why Are African Americans and Latinos Under-Represented Among Recipients of Unemployment Insurance and What Should We Do About It?' *Poverty and Race*, 20(3), May/June 2011.

21 The Economic Policy Institute reported in 2005 before the recession that workers getting the minimum wage earned less than a third of the average hourly wage. See Lawrence Mishel, Jared Bernstein, and Sylvia Allegretto, *State of Working America 2008/2009*, Ithaca: Cornell University Press, 2009.

22 See Eric Sterling, 'Time for a Change: 40 Years of Drug War Hasn't Worked', *Alternet*, 15 June 2011. Sterling was counsel to the House Judiciary Subcommittee and had the main responsibility for the writing of the law.

23 Agamben's discussion of 'bare life' that is included in the legal regime for the purpose of being excluded is pertinent here. See Julie A. Nice, 'Poverty as an Everyday State of Exception', in Shelley Feldman, Charles Geisler, and Gayatri A. Menon, eds., *Accumulating Insecurity: Violence and Dispossession in the Making of Everyday Life*, Athens: University of Georgia Press, 2011; see also Giorgio Agamben, *Homo Sacer: Sovereign Power and Bare Life*, Stanford: Stanford University Press, 1998.

24 This was not the first time that a focus on poverty and relief policy was paired with a focus on crime. During the late eighteenth and early nineteenth centuries in England, relief expanded in response to protests precipitated by enclosure and modernizing changes in the terms of rural labour. But so did repression, as the Parliament moved to elaborate the criminal codes, and troops were deployed across the country. See John Lawrence Hammond and Barbara Bradby Hammond, *The Town Labourer, 1760-1832: The New Civilization*, London; Longmans, Green & Co., 1917, pp. 37-94.

25 See Sheldon Danziger, 'Budget Cuts as Welfare Reform', *American Economic Review*, 73(2), 1983, p. 65.

26 See Philip Kretsedemas and Ana Aparicio, eds., *Immigrants, Welfare Reform, and the Poverty of Policy*, Westport: Praeger, 2004; see also Amanda Levinson, 'Immigrants and Welfare Use', Migration Policy Institute, August 2002.

27 See Audrey Singer, 'Welfare Reform and Immigrants: A Policy Review', Brookings Institution, 20 June 2011; see also Audrey Singer, 'Immigrants, Welfare Reform and the Coming Reauthorization Vote', Migration Policy Institute, August 2002.

28   Stephen Pimpare, 'In the Wake of Reforms: Unclear Outcomes and the State of Welfare Policy Analysis, 1996-2008', unpublished manuscript, Silver School of Social Work, New York University.
29   Joe Soss, Richard C. Fording and Sanford F. Schram, *Disciplining the Poor: Neoliberal Paternalism and the Persistent Power of Race*, Chicago: University of Chicago Press, 2011.
30   Ibid., ch. 4.
31   See Sanford F. Schram, Joe Soss, Linda Houser and Richard C. Fording, 'The Third Level of US Welfare Reform: Governmentality under Neoliberal Paternalism', *Citizenship Studies*, 14(6), 2010, pp. 739-754.
32   See FRAC Alerts, 26 April 2011, The Food Research and Action Center, available at http://www.frac.org.
33   Editorial, *New York Times*, 25 March 2011.
34   Federation of Protestant Welfare Agencies, 'Policy Matters', January 2011.
35   These states are Arkansas, Louisiana, Mississippi, Montana and Utah and Arizona is currently resisting a renewal of federal long-term benefits. See Catherine Rampell, 'For Want of a Word, Arizona's Jobless Lose Checks', *New York Times*, 18 June 2011.
36   See William M. Welch, 'Long-term Jobless See Reduction in Benefits', *USA Today*, 17 May 2011.
37   Quoted in Editorial, 'Unfair Working Conditions: Blame Greed, Not the Economy', *Los Angeles Times*, 11 June 2011.
38   Mary Williams Walsh, 'A Path is Sought for States to Escape their Debt Burdens', *New York Times*, 20 January 2011.
39   See Rania Khalek, 'Coup d'état Coming Soon to a City Near You', *Common Dreams*, 20 April 2011, available at http://www.commondreams.org.
40   See Leonard Gilroy and Jonathan Williams, eds., *State Budget Reform Toolkit*, Washington, DC: American Legislative Exchange Council, 2011.
41   See Lewis H. Lapham, 'The Tentacles of Rage', *Harper's Magazine*, September 2004.
42   Stuart Butler and Peter Germanis, 'Achieving a "Leninist" Strategy', *Cato Journal*, 3(2), Fall 1983.
43   See Suzanne Mettler, 'Reconstituting the Submerged State: The Challenges of Social Policy Reform in the Obama Era', *Perspectives on Politics*, 8(3), September 2010, Table 3, p. 809.
44   Ibid., p. 809.
45   Douglas Glasgow, *The Black Underclass: Poverty, Unemployment, and the Entrapment of Ghetto Life*, San Francisco: Jossey-Bass Publishers, 1980, p. 104.
46   Wacquant, Loic, 'Ordering Insecurity: Social Polarization and the Punitive Upsurge', *Radical Philosophy Review*, 11(1), Spring 2008, pp. 9–27.
47   See Loic Wacquant, 'The Place of the Prison in the New Government of Poverty', in Mary Louise Frampton, Ian Haney Lopez and Jonathan Simon, eds., *After the War on Crime: Race, Democracy, and a New Reconstruction*, New York: New York University Press, 2008, pp. 23-37.
48   See Timothy Black, *When a Heart Turns Rock Solid*, New York: Pantheon Books, 2009, p. 217.
49   Ibid., p. 268.

A TALE OF TWO CRISES:
LABOUR, CAPITAL AND RESTRUCTURING
IN THE US AUTO INDUSTRY

NICOLE M. ASCHOFF

Much of the global auto industry went into a well-documented free fall following the 2007 financial meltdown. The US market was hit particularly hard. The collapse in credit for dealers and consumers combined with skyrocketing fuel prices and wary consumers led to an evaporation of demand. US assemblers saw sales drop 50 per cent and foreign assemblers 40 per cent in 2009 to settle at an almost 30 year low of 10.4 million vehicles in the US.[1] Chrysler and General Motor's (GM) bankruptcy filing that year seemed to signal the long prophesied downfall of Detroit. Citing the negative economic repercussions of the industry's collapse, the US state threw the assemblers a lifeline, trading financial assistance for reorganization. GM and Chrysler emerged from bankruptcy with fewer plants, dealerships and brands, a new ownership structure, and a mandate to produce smaller 'greener' vehicles. In the process unionized autoworkers became partial 'owners' of the 'new' automakers and agreed to sweeping concessions in wages and benefits that put them on par with non–union assembly workers in the US.

While the financial crisis and ensuing auto crisis did force significant change upon the industry, these changes do not represent a fundamental break from the past. Instead, the primary consequence of the crisis has been to accelerate and reinforce ongoing processes of capitalist restructuring, largely at the expense of autoworkers. In fact, GM, Chrysler and Ford have benefited from the recent crisis. It allowed the Detroit Three to rapidly regroup after their competitive strategy of the last two decades failed. This pattern of crisis followed by restructuring is endemic to the auto industry, particularly in big, competitive markets like the US. Assemblers have enacted multiple waves of restructuring in the US since the 1980s that combined with increasing foreign investment have resulted in a constantly evolving industry. The recent crisis represents a continuation of these dynamics. Thus, from the perspective of capital, the present crisis can be largely situated within the ongoing process of restructuring occurring in the industry.

The same cannot be said for unionized autoworkers in the US. The Detroit Three in partnership with the US government exploited the doomsday atmosphere surrounding the crisis to push through concessions that fundamentally undermine the power of the United Auto Workers (UAW) to protect and improve the working lives of its members. While US autoworkers' fortunes have oscillated in synch with the booms and busts of the industry, their overall trajectory during the past three decades has been one of decline and disorientation. Long-term trends of de-unionization, concessions, and isolation have paved the way for unprecedented concessions. The recent crisis has essentially erased the post-war gains of unionized autoworkers in the industry.

Hence, the crisis has had divergent consequences for capital and labour. For capital it has triggered a rapid restructuring and the restoration of profits, while for workers it has compounded the precarious position of unionized autoworkers by reversing decades of hard-won gains. To better understand the crisis and its differing consequences for capital and labour, it is necessary to situate it within an historical context. Doing so allows us to gain a clearer perspective on the nature of the crisis and, importantly, explore possible avenues for workers to regroup and fight back.

CRISIS FOR CAPITAL

In the fall of 2008, the US auto industry looked like it was headed for disaster. Chrysler and GM reported losses for the year totalling $8 billion and $31 billion respectively. The turmoil in financial markets beginning a year earlier caused the market for asset-backed securities to dry up. Almost overnight consumers found it difficult to finance vehicle purchases and dealers were unable to get credit to purchase inventory from assemblers. Detroit was affected more severely than foreign assemblers because of its overreliance on both the SUV (sport utility vehicle) segment (which had contracted because of skyrocketing fuel prices) and, in the case of GM and Ford, their finance subsidiaries. But the crisis was not confined to US assemblers. The industry is tightly interlinked with complex, overlapping supply chains. For this reason, the collapse in credit markets rapidly generated a chain reaction that threatened the survival of assemblers, suppliers, dealers, workers and the communities who depend on them, particularly in states like Michigan, Kentucky, Ohio, Indiana, Alabama and Tennessee.[2]

GM and Chrysler announced in late 2008 that they would not have enough cash to continue running operations by 2009 unless they received financial support from the US government. Despite widespread public opposition, in December 2008 the Treasury Department established the Automotive Industry Financing Program (AIFP) under the Troubled Asset Relief Program (TARP). Through the AIFP, the Treasury extended loans of $4 billion and $13.4 billion respectively to Chrysler and GM. The loans were conditional and required the assemblers to submit viability plans to cut costs and streamline operations in line with their declining market share. The assemblers submitted these plans in February 2009 and requested additional financial support because they continued to burn through cash. In March of that year the Obama administration rejected their proposals as 'not sufficient to achieve long-term viability' and demanded the assemblers 'take more aggressive action as a condition of receiving additional federal assistance'. GM and Chrysler were given 60 and 30 days to achieve Obama's restructuring goals or else declare bankruptcy and be forcibly restructured by the US state. Both firms failed to meet their deadlines and declared bankruptcy.[3] Ford had sufficient cash reserves and negotiated a $9 billion emergency credit line, and so managed to avoid bankruptcy.

The bankruptcy process for both firms was classified as a 'court-supervised asset sale'. GM and Chrysler both sold their 'good' assets – the parts of their companies that they wanted to keep – to the 'new' GM and Chrysler. Undesirable assets and debt remained at the 'old' companies and were liquidated through a longer bankruptcy process. The goal of the court-supervised asset sale was to get the companies out of bankruptcy quickly, thus accelerating their turnaround.[4]

Chrysler, already majority owned by Cerberus Capital Management (CCM), was divided between Fiat, the UAW Voluntary Employment Benefits Agreement (VEBA) fund and the US and Canadian governments, who would be minority stakeholders.[5] Eight assembler and supply plants were slated to close. To create the 'new' GM, fourteen assembly and parts plants and three warehouses were slated to close, the Hummer, Pontiac, Saab and Saturn divisions were sold or discontinued, and GM was divided between the US government, the UAW and Canadian Auto Workers, the Canadian government, the provincial government of Ontario and unsecured GM bondholders. Although Ford didn't declare bankruptcy it also restructured. It sold its Jaguar and Rover divisions to Tata in 2008, reduced its share in Mazda to just 3 per cent, and in 2010, discontinued its Mercury brand and sold Volvo to Geely.[6]

The automotive crisis and forced bankruptcy restructuring of GM and Chrysler were significant events for both the industry and the individual firms. The state's intervention and financial assistance allowed the assemblers to rapidly streamline operations and decrease capacity, allowing them to focus on profitable divisions. But the crisis was not the culmination of an overall pattern of decline, nor was it a game-changing event that forced abrupt change on the industry. Instead, the restructuring that occurred was part of an *ongoing* re-organization of the global automobile industry, especially in 'replacement' markets like the US. For years global assemblers have been overhauling operations and designing new strategies to cope with increased competitive pressures. In this section we will situate this restructuring within a broader historical context to shed light on the significance of the crisis for capital.

US assemblers have been reorganizing their operations almost continually in the US market since the 1980s, in an attempt to maintain market share in the face of growing competition from foreign assemblers located in the US and abroad. With the emergence of Japanese and European competitors in the 1960s US assemblers gradually lost their monopoly over the global auto industry, especially as imports began to encroach on their home market in the 1970s. To cope they first began to move production of parts and some assembly to the US South and Mexico as a way to cut costs. However, as imports continued to increase, US assemblers pressured the Reagan administration for import restrictions on foreign cars. The resulting 'voluntary' export restrictions catalyzed a wave of investment by Japanese assemblers and suppliers into the US during the 1980s. Foreign firms first moved into the Midwest to take advantage of existing supply networks. However, beginning in the late 1980s foreign supplier investment in the US increased significantly, allowing foreign assemblers to migrate investment southward to take advantage of lower-cost labour.

In response to growing competition on their home soil, US assemblers spent billions restructuring operations during the 1980s. They closed coastal assembly plants and reopened plants in the country's interior to be close to the country's transportation nerve centre, while simultaneously moving more low value-added production to low-wage sites in Mexico.[7] US firms also moved away from producing smaller cars, ceding these segments to Japanese and European manufacturers and focusing on large cars and light trucks.[8] During the late 1980s US assemblers expanded into other brands and segments to improve profitability. For example, GM spent billions acquiring the niche brands Lotus and Saab, Ross Perot's computer company EDS and Hughes Electronics, as well as other ventures in financial services and defence contracting.[9]

The geographical dynamism of the 1980s continued in the 1990s and

2000s. As Figures 1 and 2 show, investment during the last two decades was spatially dynamic, with growth and decline in investment occurring simultaneously, especially in the Midwest.

Figure 1: Reported Assembler Investment, 1988-2006

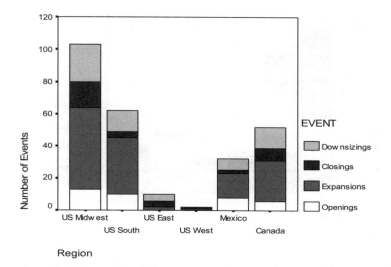

Source: Data is from the Automotive Investment Patterns (AIP) database constructed by the author.[10]

Japanese assemblers expanded production in the US and were joined by European assemblers and global suppliers, mainly from Europe and East Asia. This influx of production was coupled with strategies undertaken by US assemblers and some parts suppliers to lower costs by moving to Mexico and re-tool existing production in the Midwest. Rather than a uni-directional movement of production from traditional manufacturing regions to low-wage sites in the US South and Mexico, the investment pattern in the North American auto industry during the past three decades has been characterized by a reorganization of production, resulting in an 'auto alley' stretching from the Great Lakes to the Gulf of Mexico.[11]

Investment patterns have also been temporally dynamic with no overwhelming trend of decline during the last two decades, but rather a cyclical pattern of growth and decline. As Figure 3 illustrates, reported investment by assemblers and suppliers has experienced peaks and troughs over time in line with broader trends in the economy, but has consistently showed a mix of growth and decline.

Much assembler investment during the past two decades is characterized

Figure 2: Reported Supplier Investment, 1988-2006

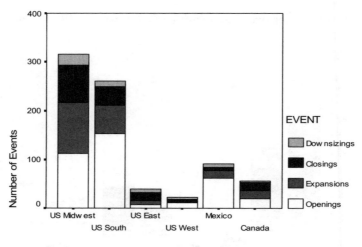

Source: AIP database.

Figure 3: Reported Investment by Assemblers & Suppliers, 1988-2006

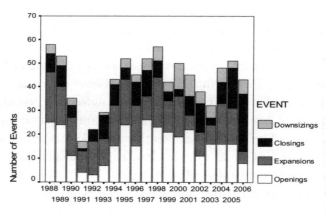

Source: AIP database.

by re-tooling existing plants or opening new plants to produce trucks (light trucks, SUVs and minivans). While the US market is generally considered a stagnant 'replacement' market because market saturation is high, its market for trucks has exhibited high growth rates, especially in the 1990s. Light trucks accounted for more than half the total value of all US auto sales by the late 1990s.[12] The widespread popularity of trucks combined with their only marginally higher input demands made them a very profitable offering for assemblers. As shown in Table 1, both US and foreign assemblers shifted their product mix definitively toward trucks between 1995 and 2005. US assemblers decreased cars and increased trucks, while foreign assemblers increased both kinds of investment.

Table 1: Automobile Production in North America by Region (1995, 2005)

1995	US MIDWEST	US SOUTH	US EAST	US WEST	MEXICO	CANADA	TOTAL
US CARS	2,812,610	1,335,068			339,798	679,057	5,166,533
US TRUCKS	3,362,022	1,111,537	436,725		61,716	961,350	6,033,350
JV CARS	367,093			229,393		116,610	713,096
JV TRUCKS				123,257		59,258	182,515
ASIAN CARS	1,233,261	333,236			54,700	196,269	1,817,466
ASIAN TRUCKS	99,514	132,554					232,068
EURO CARS		11,876			156,422	7,588	175,886
EURO TRUCKS							0
TOTAL	7,874,500	2,924,271	436,725	352,650	712,636	2,020,132	14,320,914
2005							TOTAL
US CARS	1,709,434	354,493			408,805	982,403	3,455,135
US TRUCKS	3,794,246	1,699,974	14,489		483,395	759,159	6,751,263
JV CARS	272,632			248,471			521,103
JV TRUCKS				158,927		189,997	348,924
ASIAN CARS	1,236,663	383,252			343,684	424,560	2,388,159
ASIAN TRUCKS	481,130	745,448			66,111	266,952	1,559,641
EURO CARS		124,846			300,386		425,232
EURO TRUCKS		95,558			1,009		96,567
TOTAL	7,494,105	3,403,571	14,489	407,398	1,603,390	2,623,071	15,556,024

Note: Vehicles are non-commercial. 'Trucks' includes light trucks, SUVs, and minivans. Chrysler is considered a US firm in 1995. J.V. refers to East Asian/US joint-venture assembly plants. Source: Production data compiled by author from Automotive News Market Data Book (1996; 2006).

In addition to re-tooling for increased truck production, during the 1990s and early 2000s GM and Ford tried to improve market share and profitability through internal restructuring. Ford bought Volvo, Rover, Aston Martin, Jaguar, and increased its control over Mazda, and GM bought Hummer, Daewoo and a controlling share of Isuzu. US firms also reshuffled their existing structures during the 1990s: GM sold Lotus, EDS and Delphi, while Ford spun off Visteon.[13] As GM and Ford 'de-verticalized' their supply operations, independent suppliers found the need to expand, and former in-house suppliers developed new partnerships with foreign assemblers, pushing them to open new plants.[14] As illustrated above in Figure 2, many suppliers, both foreign and of North American origin were pressured to follow assembly plants in order to retain or get contracts. Tier 1 suppliers also evolved to take on more responsibility for manufacturing and design.[15] For example, in the late 1990s Delphi was asked to coordinate Mercedes' entire supply chain stretching 1500 miles from Juarez, Mexico to Tuscaloosa, Alabama.

Restructuring in North America during the 1990s was part of a global process of restructuring. Whereas new assembly capacity in the 1980s was mostly of Japanese origin, in the 1990s American, European and Korean firms began rapidly increasing investment in emerging markets. Global assemblers looked to corner new growing markets in countries like Vietnam, China, India, Pakistan and the Philippines where market saturation rates were very low. Trade barriers were also relaxed in many countries during the 1990s, and with Triad (North America, Western Europe and Japan) market competition increasing rapidly, global assemblers hoped to develop new avenues of future growth. However, the potential of these markets seemed uncertain after the Asian economic crisis. By the end of the nineties many analysts suggested that firms had overestimated demand in emerging markets, and global assemblers and suppliers continued to rely on profits from Triad markets, particularly the US market.[16]

At the same time Ford and GM evolved to rely more heavily on their finance divisions (Ford Credit and GMAC) as a source of revenue and to compensate for their difficulty generating profits outside of truck production. The cost of credit was relatively low during the late nineties, allowing Ford and GM to gain huge profits from finance. In a highly competitive and cyclical industry like auto, revenue from credit activities is attractive because it represents a more steady income stream than profits from productive activities. Profits from their finance subsidiaries enabled GM and Ford to prop up unprofitable segments (like existing car models) worldwide while simultaneously acquiring new firms and expanding into developing markets. It is estimated that finance contributed 54 per cent of Ford's net income in 1996,[17] and in the 1989-2006 period 93 per cent of GM's consolidated net income was produced by GMAC.[18] While these statistics tend to overstate the role of finance because the finance subsidiaries were subsidized by the automakers through purchase incentives, GMAC and Ford Credit were nonetheless an important source of profit. For example, between 2001 and 2006 GM received over $8 billion in cash dividends from GMAC.[19]

The rise of finance also supported the industry as a whole during this period. As Krippner argues, free-flowing credit – a result of US state policies in the 1980s and 1990s – 'fueled asset price bubbles in financial markets and real estate markets'.[20] These bubbles, particularly the housing bubble, created a consumption boom as homeowners took advantage of declining interest rates to re-finance their homes, often borrowing additional funds to spend on home improvement, debt, and luckily for the auto industry, new vehicles.[21] Ford and GM were able to use easy credit conditions to offer substantial incentives to new customers, maintaining sales for US assemblers in the face of growing competition. The housing boom also provided an additional revenue stream for GM and Ford because GMAC and Ford Credit were heavily entrenched in mortgage markets. By 2006 GMAC's ResCap operation was servicing $412 billion of mortgages and owned $69 billion in mortgage loans, totalling almost 40 per cent of GMAC's receivables.[22]

GM and Ford's strategy of relying on trucks and finance to support their global operations was successful during the nineties. They regained the market share they had lost during the 1980s because SUVs delivered excellent margins and credit was cheap. But, because US firms used earnings from trucks and finance to prop up unprofitable segments rather than develop new offerings in other segments, they were left vulnerable to decreasing market share. Asian (and European) manufacturers took advantage of the product gap and at the same time started offering more vehicles in the segments where US assemblers were popular. As the market slowed down after 2000, US firms' market share continued to slide and factories were kept running by huge rebates and fleet sales. The subprime mortgage crisis put an end to this dead-end strategy. Ford Credit and especially GMAC's (majority owned by CCM after 2006) exposure to the imploding housing market, in combination with the industry slowdown and Detroit's sliding market share, created a perfect storm for the subsidiaries and all but locked them out of the credit markets when the financial crisis hit.[23]

Broadly speaking, the crisis showed the limits of growth in replacement markets like the US, Europe and Japan. The ten year production and sales boom in the US from 1995 to 2005 simply heightened competition in a market already characterized by overcapacity. With demand stalled in the US and Europe, and future sales uncertain, US firms began to ramp up efforts to expand faster into developing markets, especially those that were relatively unscathed by the downturn like China and India. In 2009 total new car sales in BRIC nations amounted to 20 million units, roughly one-third of the global total, and it is estimated that by 2050 half of all cars worldwide will be sold outside the Triad region. China overtook the US in 2009 as the largest domestic market for automobiles in the world, and is currently GM's largest market. Toyota, Ford and Honda are all increasing productive capacity in China, scrambling to catch up with Volkswagen, GM, and Hyundai, who invested early and have a firm grasp on the market. VW alone controls nearly 20 per cent of the Chinese market. Smaller assemblers are also keen to expand in China because of its large appetite for luxury vehicles. China is now BMW's second largest market and the third largest market for Jaguar Land Rover.

India has also seen extremely rapid growth – in 2009 its domestic market for passenger cars grew by over 25 per cent. In the past two years Ford, Nissan, GM, Toyota, Honda and Volkswagen have all expanded their productive base in India, building new assembly plants and expanding their supplier networks. Ford has recently announced that India will be its new small-car hub and has begun exporting Ford Figos from India to South Africa. Recent investments combined with the massive presence of Subaru in India have pushed India ahead of Japan as the largest global producer of 'basic' low-cost cars. Thailand and Indonesia have also seen a surge in new investment. Ford has designated Thailand as its export hub to the ASEAN region and is in the process of constructing a new assembly plant there, and Volkswagen is constructing its first assembly plant in Jakarta.

However, while new growth is likely to be concentrated in countries like China, India and Brazil, most experts agree that the lion's share of automotive production and sales will take place in North America, Western Europe and Japan for the near future. The clustering of skilled labour, sunk capital, and well-established supply-bases in combination with political pressure push assemblers and suppliers to continue investing in or near traditional manufacturing regions. Indeed, after a brief hiatus following the automotive crisis, new productive investment has resumed in the US. Kia opened a plant in West Point, Georgia in 2009 to produce Sorento cross-overs and is currently expanding the plant to build sedans. After decades of producing exclusively in Mexico, Volkswagen is opening an assembly plant and supplier park in the US. VW's complex in Chattanooga, Tennessee will start producing mid-size sedans in 2011. And Toyota has restarted production of Corollas at its new plant in Tupelo, Mississippi.

The Detroit Three are also building new capacity. GM is investing $336 million to retool its Detroit-Hamtramck plant to produce the Volt as part of its new 'green' strategy.[24] Chrysler is investing $600 million to retool its Belvidere, Illinois plant, replacing the Dodge Caliber with a new small car. Detroit assemblers also remain heavily invested in SUVs. With demand spiking for these vehicles once again, particularly for smaller cross-overs, assemblers are restarting production at shuttered plants. GM is currently developing the next generation Cadillac Escalade and Chevy Suburban, because it argues there are still few major players in this segment of the auto industry. More recently, in December 2010 Ford announced it was investing $600 million in its Louisville, Kentucky plant to build small SUVs.

In addition to new investment, US assemblers have been raking in profits since the crisis. Ford actually gained market share in 2009 and 2010, posting its highest profit in a decade to become the world's most profitable auto company last year. GM's November 2010 IPO illustrates perhaps best of all the upswing of the industry. It pulled in over $20 billion in the offering, signalling a growing investor confidence in the future of the company, and the US auto industry. GM is also developing a new finance subsidiary called GM Financial to offer leases, and sub-prime loans in an effort to sell more vehicles and compete with its former subsidiary GMAC (now called Ally).[25]

So then, what has been the impact of the automotive crisis for the Detroit Three? The crisis forced the industry to regroup after the boom of the 1990s fizzled and easy credit conditions disappeared. US firms in particular have had to readjust after their trucks and finance strategy proved unable in the long run to prop up the rest of their operations. But this evolution has not been earth-shattering – the 'new' US auto manufacturers are essentially slimmer versions of the old ones. Using the financial assistance and authority of the US state, they've simply eliminated some unprofitable lines and cut their costs faster than they would have otherwise, allowing a rapid turnaround to profitability. Although credit is less available, US firms will continue to rely on finance as a source of profit and cushion against the cyclicality of the industry. They are also moving slowly into the (notoriously unprofitable) small car market and will continue to focus on SUVs with a slight shift toward smaller SUVs.

Recasting the recent crisis in a historical context shows that it is part of a continual process of 'creative destruction' in the auto industry over the past three decades, with firms opening plants, closings plants, buying companies and then spinning them off later. Rather than an overall pattern of decline, or an abrupt shift after the crisis, the dynamics of the industry are better understood as a continual process of reorganization. The inherent cyclicality of the industry combined with rising competition both in the US and globally suggests this kind of restructuring will be a permanent feature of the industry.

CRISIS FOR LABOUR

When Chrysler and GM asked the US government for financial assistance in late 2008 the public response was unenthusiastic to say the least. A wide spectrum of voices blamed the industry crisis on high-cost labour, with the general sentiment: 'US taxpayers should not bail out the UAW.'[26] This perspective was echoed by the US government. When it did finally agree to extend Treasury money to GM and Chrysler, one of its main conditions was that the assemblers restructure their labour agreements to match those at non-union assemblers in the US. This is ultimately what has occurred. By the spring of 2009 the UAW had agreed to implement a tiered wage system for all new hires in which wages were cut in half to around $14.50 an hour, a six year wage freeze on all new GM and Chrysler hires, a strike ban until 2015 for Chrysler and GM workers, the elimination of the Jobs Bank, and a host of other concessions.[27]

This victory of capital over the UAW was a long time coming. While the industry has been cyclical with its upswings and downswings in sales and production, and constant restructuring, the situation for autoworkers since at least the 1980s has been a steady downward trend in terms of unionization rates, bargaining power, and workplace rights. Just as the recent financial crisis allowed US assemblers to quickly restructure their productive operations, it also gave them an opportunity to speed up the dismantling of their labour agreements. They used the shock of the financial crisis and swift downturn in the auto industry to extend concessions originally applied only to certain groups of the UAW to the whole membership. In this section we will embed the recent crisis and its impact in the broader narrative of decline and disorientation experienced by US autoworkers over the past three decades.

A crucial factor in the weakening position of US autoworkers has been the restructuring of the industry described above. The influx of new, non-union investment, coupled with significant movement of production to low-wage sites in the US South and Mexico, has put a great deal of pressure on unionized workers. The influx of non-union, foreign suppliers has been particularly damaging. By the 1990s, US assemblers could for the first time legitimately threaten to outsource components, modules and even whole systems away from their in-house parts suppliers and workers to new companies often located only a short distance away. In the 1970s and increasingly in the 1980s the Detroit Three began sourcing many low-value added products, like wiring harnesses and spark plugs, from low-wage plants in the US South or Mexico, but remained dependent on in-house parts manufacturers for more complex and higher value-added components. The influx of Tier 1 suppliers like Bosch and Denso in the 1990s and 2000s, and rising competition amongst supplier firms, allowed US firms to shift the power dynamic and demand major concessions from workers (and suppliers) at the local level in exchange for the 'right' to continue making a product.[28]

De-verticalization has been compounded by the inability of the UAW to organize new investment by assemblers and suppliers. While the total number of jobs in the US auto industry stayed relatively constant from 1950 to 2005, dropping in the years since, the number of unionized workers has declined sharply over the past three decades. This is partly a result of dramatic productivity gains at the Detroit Three – they simply need fewer workers to produce the same number of cars – and partly a result of outsourcing and Detroit's decreased market share. Although estimates vary, the US auto industry today is between 30 and 50 per cent unionized, compared with 90 per cent in the early 1980s. UAW membership dropped from 1.5 million in 1979 to just 557,099 at the beginning of 2006. Today it is less than 350,000 with about two-thirds of membership actually employed in the auto sector. New investment simply hasn't been unionized. Suppliers created 200,000 jobs between 1990 and 2000 alone, but the number of these jobs that are union is negligible. Fewer than 30 per cent of suppliers are unionized despite the fact that over 70 per cent of production workers in the industry are employed by suppliers.[29]

Rising numbers of non-union jobs combined with decreasing numbers of union members has isolated unionized auto workers, making them more vulnerable to concessions, particularly at the local level. UAW attempts to stem trends of outsourcing and attrition through the development of cooperative relationships with the Detroit Three have proven ineffective. This has pushed local unions to negotiate directly with assemblers to save jobs. Throughout the 1990s unionized locals agreed to reorganizing production, implementing work teams and flexible 'production cells' in exchange for promises of investment in plants and new products. But these moves have rarely prevented outsourcing and have ultimately undercut the union's power in a classic divide-and-conquer scenario.

The dismantling of worker gains at Delphi is an important example of the weakening of the UAW because it served as a template for concessionary bargaining prior to and during the recent auto crisis for the workers at the Detroit Three.[30] Delphi is the former in-house parts manufacturer for GM. It was consolidated during the 1990s and spun off as an independent entity in 1999, making it for a time the largest supplier in the world. Delphi workers were members of the UAW and at the time of the spin-off were covered under the same contract as GM.

With Delphi's primary customer GM's market share sliding and the UAW national contract up for renegotiation in the fall, in early 2003 Delphi began publicly complaining about its labour costs, citing high wages and legacy costs as major impediments to future growth. The company had readily matched the GM contract in the 1999 negotiations and had even given hourly workers a raise, but by 2003 it was calling for a new order. It argued that if it could cut its workforce by 5000 and implement a tiered wage structure it would be competitive with non-union suppliers in the US like Johnson Controls and Lear.[31] The UAW agreed. Using an undemocratic 'supplemental agreement' to the national contract, Delphi and the UAW executive board negotiated the tiered structure in 2004 in which new workers would be paid half the wage of existing workers. In return for its cooperation Delphi promised to keep open three 'threatened' plants in Michigan, Alabama and Kansas.[32]

A year later, after Delphi was charged with fraud by the Securities and Exchange Commission (SEC) for systematically 'overstating its assets and understating its liabilities', the company again demanded concessions.[33] It brought in Steve Miller – the CEO known for taking Bethlehem Steel into bankruptcy, dumping its pensions onto the Pension Benefit Guaranty Corporation and cutting off health insurance for retirees – to pressure workers to reopen their contract. Miller argued that if Delphi couldn't reach agreements with GM and the UAW to cut its labour costs substantially it would not last until the 2003 UAW contract expired.[34] It proposed cutting wages to $10 an hour, eliminating cost of living allowances (COLA) and the Jobs Bank, and reducing benefits, vacations and holidays.[35] The company also wanted greater leeway to hire temporary workers. Miller famously quipped: 'Globalization has taken away the ability to have someone who mows the lawn or sweeps the floor to get $65 an hour.'[36]

When Delphi declared bankruptcy in the fall of 2005 the message to workers was the more cuts the union provided, the more factories Delphi would keep open and vice versa. The Delphi bankruptcy was the biggest bankruptcy to date in the auto industry and workers (and the UAW) were under enormous pressure to make concessions. As the editor of *Automotive News* presciently opined:

> Whether the unions willingly negotiate or the bankruptcy court voids Delphi's labour agreements…wages and benefits will be cut, plants will close and workers will lose their jobs. It is inevitable… [T]here is no way to stop what is part of the natural order because protectionism cannot work…Once the new competitive equilibrium is set during the Delphi reorganization, it will become

the standard for other suppliers and the bogey for the Big 3 when they head into bargaining in 2007.[37]

The UAW yielded to the pressure, negotiating a 'Special Attrition Program' in which 24,000 jobs were cut, and all new hires were temporary or second-tier workers. After the agreement the company went on a hiring spree of temporary workers in places like Milwaukee and Alabama. Delphi went further with its demands, filing a request with the bankruptcy judge to cancel its labour agreements with the remaining workers unless they agreed to additional concessions. The UAW ultimately approved the elimination of COLA, the Jobs Bank, defined pensions, and agreed to the sale or closure of 24 plants in the US.

Although various industry and bankruptcy experts challenged the validity of the filing and the financial crisis at Delphi, the company's actions elicited little opposition from the UAW leadership.[38] In fact, the UAW didn't even show up to court on the day of the filing. The union accepted that previous gains were no longer sustainable. Speaking to rank-and-filers in 2006, UAW President Ron Gettelfinger argued: 'This isn't a cyclical downturn. The challenges we face aren't the kind that can be ridden out. They're structural changes, and they require new and farsighted solutions.'[39]

These 'farsighted solutions' have since become apparent. The UAW's failure to resist Delphi's concessionary demands laid the groundwork for an almost identical scenario at the Detroit Three. As predicted, during the 2007 contract negotiations Detroit made a push to extend the Delphi concessions to unionized assembly workers across the industry. Again the UAW went along, agreeing to tiered wages and a separate health and pension plan for new 'non-core' workers such as materials movers, general stores managers, and finished vehicle drivers. Wages for non-core work were modelled after the second-tier wages negotiated at Delphi. The UAW also agreed to take on healthcare responsibility for workers and retirees through a voluntary employment benefits agreement (VEBA), removing the costs from Detroit's books.[40] Despite these concessions, when GM and Chrysler asked the US government for financial assistance in late 2008, the UAW was publicly excoriated. According to the White House press secretary, Detroit had 'unworkable labour contracts' and was operating under an 'obsolete business model'. Politicians argued that unionized labour 'had brought the industry to its knees', its 'affluent wages and benefits prevent[ing] the Detroit automakers from successfully competing'.[41]

A key condition for receiving financial assistance from the US state was that GM and Chrysler 'make every effort to achieve labour cost parity with the [non-union] transplants'.[42] In particular it demanded that GM and Chrysler:

> (1) achieve total compensation packages (wages and benefits) competitive with transplants, (2) apply work rules that are competitive with transplants, and (3) eliminate any compensation or benefits, other than customary severance pay, to employees that have been fired, laid off, furloughed or idled.[43]

These demands by the state put the UAW in a very tough position. By saying that worker concessions were the only way GM and Chrysler would survive, the US state made it nearly impossible to construct an alternative that wouldn't isolate the UAW further.

The UAW ultimately agreed to concessions in May 2009 that expanded the 2007 give-backs.[44] The new concessions extended second-tier (half-pay) wages to all new hires, loosened restrictions on the use of temporary workers, cut supplemental unemployment benefits (SUB pay), eliminated COLA, froze wages for new workers at GM and Chrysler for six years and barred GM and Chrysler workers from striking until 2015. Despite these concessions the Treasury determined that the companies had still not implemented satisfactory viability plans and must declare bankruptcy. The bankruptcy restructuring compounded the concessions by closing plants and forcing workers to compete for the remaining jobs. The bankruptcy restructuring also deepened autoworkers' dependence on Detroit's profitability because it transformed the UAW and the VEBA into a partial 'owner' of GM and Chrysler.

While the industry has rebounded in the two years since the crisis, the situation for autoworkers has only worsened. The experience of workers at GM's Lake Orion, Michigan plant is telling. As part of its post-bankruptcy agenda to develop profitable small cars, GM decided to re-tool the idled plant to build the subcompact Aveo and compact Verano. However, GM and the UAW Executive negotiated a secret agreement in which only 60 per cent of laid-off employees would be brought back at Tier 1 wages. The rest of the workforce would be forced to come back at a second-tier wage of $14.50 an hour, stay on layoff, or transfer 250 miles to GM's Lordstown plant. This came as a shock to workers who voted in 2009 to extend second-tier wages only to new hires. The justification for this new arrangement was that in order to produce a profitable small car the UAW and GM had agreed to 'work together…to arrive at innovative ways to staff these operations' in the 2009 contract.[45] Apparently 'innovative' staffing is code for low-cost labour.

These trends are likely to continue. GM and Ford recently announced that they will hire at least 36,000 new workers over the next few years, all at a second-tier wage. With demand having rebounded, factories are running all out with workers clocking maximum overtime. Under the current national contract Detroit can hire up to 25 per cent of their total workforce at second-tier wages.[46] In addition, Detroit is implementing strategies targeted at individual plants to lower labour costs and expand its second-tier workforce. For example, at a parts plant in Saginaw GM workers voted to 'buy down' their wages. Workers would receive a $40,000 pay-out if they agreed to decrease their wages from $18.50 to $12 an hour.

And with many workers making half what they used to, GM has announced that it will invest more in labour-intensive production because its costs are more manageable now that the UAW allows a range of employment options including Tier 1 and Tier 2 workers, flex workers who work two to three days a week, temporaries and workers on 'temporary assignment'.[47] GM has also opened a non-union plant in Brownstone, Michigan near Detroit to produce lithium-ion batteries. It is GM's first non-union plant in over three decades. Of the thousands of laid-off workers in the area, none were called in to the plant. This is significant because GM claims to be channelling its resources toward this kind of technology in the future. Is non-union production its future too?

One thing is certain. The recent crisis has meant something very different for workers and capital. After years of complaining about the drag of labour costs, US assemblers have finally managed to downgrade their working conditions to match non-union plants. After the concessionary model proved easy to implement at Delphi – not a single workday was lost in opposition – it was only a matter of time before it was extended to workers at the Detroit Three. When the industry hit the skids in 2008 Detroit and the US government seized the opportunity, reversing nearly every gain unionized autoworkers made in the post-World War II period.

Thus, instead of conditions at non-union foreign assemblers improving over the years to match those of US assemblers, US assemblers in partnership with the US state have simply pushed down working conditions to match those of non-union firms. GM now pays only $2 more per hour in labour costs than Toyota, compared with industry estimates of over $30 an hour in recent years.[48] And new assemblers feel little pressure to offer wage parity. Wages at the Hyundai plant in Alabama and the Kia plant in Georgia start at about $15 and max out at $21 an hour. Volkswagen's Chattanooga workers will start at $14.50 and top out at $19.50 with workers in the supplier park making about $10 an hour. But non-union autoworkers aren't complaining. West Point, Georgia – the site of Kia's new assembly plant – was once a textile town until textile firms abandoned the town in favour of low-wage sites outside the US. Kia jobs are a godsend compared with available service jobs. The plant received 43,000 applications for the original 1,200 assembly jobs.

While Detroit has been working toward this outcome for years, it's worth emphasizing that the US government played a direct role in the restructuring and forced concessions. Its demand for work rules and wages to match non-union firms effectively negates the right of workers to collectively bargain to better their wages and working conditions. Work in the auto industry is dangerous, gruelling and alienating. The gains that autoworkers achieved over the years mitigated the difficulties of the job to a small degree and allowed workers to support a family and send their kids to college. On second-tier wages UAW families are eligible for food stamps. The dismantling of autoworker gains in recent years has also opened the door to similar moves by other manufacturers. Harley Davidson, Mercury Marine and Kohler have all erected two-tier systems.[49]

BEYOND THE CRISIS

Needless to say the atmosphere at unionized assemblers and suppliers is tense, especially with contract negotiations between the UAW and Detroit coming up in September 2011. Despite the renewed profitability of Detroit, reversing the tiered wage system is not on the agenda for the UAW. The union believes lower wages are essential to Detroit's survival. According to UAW President Bob King: 'We know it's pretty hard to support a family and everything on a $15 an hour wage, but we also know that we have to keep General Motors and Ford and Chrysler competitive.'[50]

With tiered wages off the table, the UAW is planning a push to organize non-union plants in the US instead. But it won't try to organize from the ground up as in past failed attempts to organize non-union assemblers. This time the union will borrow a tactic from the SEIU and try to convince non-union assemblers like Nissan and Toyota to voluntarily sign a 'non-disparagement agreement' in which each side agrees not to censure the other during the campaign, thus promoting a fear-free election environment. The UAW believes that workers are afraid to join the union because the company will move to a low-wage, non-union site if they do. By establishing neutrality and emphasizing the UAW's mission to 'add value' and promote the employer's success, the union believes both auto manufacturers and workers will see the benefit of the union. If auto manufacturers do not agree to neutrality agreements, the UAW plans to pressure them through a political smear campaign highlighting assembler abuses in the US and abroad.[51]

The deep-seated, anti-union attitude of foreign assemblers in the US makes the viability of this plan doubtful. Foreign assemblers like Nissan and Honda have taken great pains to avoid unions. It seems highly unlikely that now, when their market share is strong, their brands are popular, and the UAW is the weakest it has been in decades, that they will voluntarily invite the union in. But, whether the plan is practical or not, the nature of the strategy indicates a deeper problem within the UAW. The underlying premise is that workers are too afraid of capital flight to organize, so instead, the union will bypass the rank-and-file and go directly to management to ask its permission to unionize the plant. This not only destroys the potential of empowering rank-and-file workers, but also justifies management's use of capital flight and plant closure to repress workers.

While the threat of plant closure is real – workers do lose jobs to capital mobility and imports – it is necessary to put globalization and capital mobility in perspective. As we showed in the first part of this essay, the restructuring of the auto industry over the past three decades is not a simple globalization story of investment leaving for low-wage sites. Instead, it has been a story of constant restructuring with growth and decline occurring simultaneously in time and space. By not challenging popular accounts of globalization and capital mobility in the US auto industry, the UAW gives support to management threats to move if workers unionize or try to protect their rights from concessions. And as the recent crisis highlighted, concessionary bargaining has no end. The more the union gives, the more it is asked to give, dividing workers, undermining solidarity, and destroying the viability of the UAW. The message to both union and non-union autoworkers should be that the auto industry is here to stay, so workers across the industry must fight to rebuild solidarity and put an end to fear-based repression.

The first place this rebuilding must occur is within the UAW itself. The tiered wage structure in combination with expanding numbers of temporary workers has greatly undermined solidarity within the union. Rank-and-filers in the UAW recognize this fact and have taken the lead in rebuilding solidarity since the crisis. At an Indianapolis stamping plant last year GM workers, despite heavy pressure from GM and the UAW International, voted overwhelmingly against reopening their contract to allow buy-downs and tiering. And in an historic turnaround, in the fall of 2009 Ford workers voted against a national contract demanding additional concessions. After GM and Chrysler emerged from bankruptcy in 2009 with more concessions than Ford, the company argued that its workers should agree to further concessions to even the score and make Ford more competitive. In particular it demanded limits on the right to strike, a wage freeze, and the removal of restrictions on entry-level hires. But Ford workers had had enough. When Bob King gathered workers together on the shop floor of Dearborn Truck to convince them to vote in favour of the concessions he didn't get past his first sentence. According to UAW activists, when King asked members if they could hear him, a worker shouted 'No!' sparking a chorus of 'No's', foot stomping, and clapping. King left without another word. The contract was rejected by over 70 per cent of membership in production and 75 per cent in skilled trades, with some locals rejecting it by 90 per cent.[52]

The recent crisis demonstrates that the UAW's strategy to battle neoliberalism and globalization through concessions is untenable. Concessions have been unable to preserve jobs, wages, or benefits, and in the long run have ultimately threatened the very survival of the unionized auto sector. As Marx and Schumpeter emphasized long ago, capital continually re-invents itself. Auto manufacturing in the US will evolve and continue to experience cycles of decline and growth, but it is here to stay. If auto unions are to recover from the crisis they must also reinvent themselves and fight back against fear-based repression. Rank-and-file workers are taking the lead in this process, even as they face opposition from the UAW leadership. To succeed workers must rebuild solidarity within the union by reversing the tiered wage system and demanding equal pay for equal work. And rather than looking for 'big' victories like unionizing the foreign assemblers, workers should start organizing drives at the hundreds of non-union suppliers in the US where workers are desperate for a union. At the same time, workers and the union must also look to the future of the industry and become advocates of more sustainable transportation, placing themselves in the vanguard of green technology development. Doing so will restore the power of autoworkers and in the process help to revitalize the US labour movement.

NOTES

I would like to thank Sam Gindin and Pankaj Mehta for commenting on an early draft of this paper.

1   In this essay, use of the term 'foreign' generally refers to firms not of US-origin that operate or invest in the US.
2   United States Government Accountability Office (USGAO), 'Summary of Government Efforts and Automakers' Restructuring to Date', *Report to Congressional Committees*, GA-09-553, 2009.
3   Ibid.

4   Ibid.

5   In June 2011 Fiat bought the US government's share of Chrysler and began negotiations to buy out both the Canadian government's and the UAW VEBA's share.

6   Ford sold Aston Martin in 2007.

7   James M. Rubenstein, *A Changing U.S. Auto Industry: A Geographical Analysis*, New York: Routledge, 1992.

8   Carl H. A. Dassbach, *Global Enterprises and the World Economy: Ford, General Motors, and IBM, the Emergence of the Transnational Enterprise*, New York: Garland Publishing, 1989.

9   Stan Luger, *Corporate Power, American Democracy, and the Automobile Industry*, Cambridge: Cambridge University Press, 2000; Alex Taylor, 'The Death of the Sport-Utility Vehicle Foretold', *Fortune*, 8 July 1996, p. 22.

10   The data tracks all openings, expansions, closings and downsizings reported in every issue of the weekly trade journal *Automotive News* from 1988 to 2006. The AIP database is intended to illustrate *trends* in investment over time and space rather than a census of all events. Nicole M. Aschoff, *Globalization and Capital Mobility in the Automobile Industry*, Ph.D. Thesis, Johns Hopkins University, Baltimore, 2010. Refer to Chapter 2 and Appendix 1 for a detailed discussion of the AIP database.

11   Aschoff, *Globalization and Capital Mobility*; Thomas Klier and James Rubenstein, *Who Really Made Your Car: Restructuring and Geographic Change in the Auto Industry*, Kalamazoo: W.E. Upjohn Institute for Employment Research, 2008.

12   Julie Froud, Sukhdev Johal, Adam Leaver and Karel Williams, *Financialization and Strategy: Narrative and Numbers*, New York: Routledge, 2006.

13   Restructuring in the auto industry rarely follows a coherent long-term plan because competition and the cyclicality of the industry force assemblers to please the markets through frequent, high-visibility restructuring programs. As Froud et al. argue: '[T]he stock market can often change its shallow, collective mind much more rapidly than giant firms can change their strategies. Thus, in a first period, the market may encourage or even demand supposedly value-creating moves by individual firms which may then in a second period provide the basis for general condemnation of the industry and a call for strategy reversal.' Froud et al., *Financialization and Strategy*, p. 44.

14   De-verticalization refers to the process by which vertically integrated firms such as GM and Ford outsourced in-house production to independent suppliers.

15   The automotive industry is commonly divided into the categories of original equipment manufacturers (OEMs) who manufacture cars and their original equipment suppliers. Parts that are installed on cars outside the factory, after the sale, are considered part of the aftermarket (AM) production network. Original equipment suppliers fall into three tiers. Tier 3 suppliers are generally the smallest and produce individual parts such as hoses, gaskets, etc. Tier 2 suppliers are larger and produce a range of products that include more complicated components and sometimes modules. Tier 1 suppliers are the largest suppliers and produce a wide range of parts, components, and modules. Tier 1 suppliers

are now often delegated responsibility for organizing Tier 2 and 3 suppliers by assemblers, and sometimes produce entire systems for cars.

16   Timothy Sturgeon, and Richard Florida, 'Globalization and Jobs in the Automotive Industry', A Study by Carnegie Mellon University and the Massachusetts Institute of Technology, Final Report to the Alfred P. Sloan Foundation, March 2000.

17   Froud et al., *Financialization and Strategy*.

18   Richard J. Anderson, Cristina Muise and David Gancarz, 'Partial Divestitures as an M&A Alternative: The Case of GMAC', *The Journal of Corporate Accounting & Finance*, 21(January/February), 2010.

19   Anderson et al., 'Partial Divestitures'.

20   Greta Krippner, *Capitalizing on Crisis: The Political Origins of the Rise of Finance*, Cambridge: Harvard University Press, 2009, p. 224.

21   Gerald F. Davis, *Managed by the Markets: How Finance Reshaped America*, Oxford: Oxford University Press, 2009.

22   Anderson et al., 'Partial Divestitures'.

23   Ibid.

24   As US assemblers adjust their plants and products in line with their decreasing market share, investment seems to be shifting away from Canada and back toward the US, reversing investment trends of the 1980s when Canada was a favoured destination of new investment.

25   David Welch and Dakin Campbell, 'Why Ally Financial and GM, Once Family, Are Now Rivals', *Markets & Finance*, 24(February), 2011.

26   James Sherk, 'Auto Bailout Ignores Excessive Labour Costs', *Heritage Foundation*, 19 November 2008, available at http://www.heritagefoundation.org; Sven Gustavson, 'Auto Bailout Shifts to Political Assault on UAW', 2009, available at http://www.mlive.com.

27   The far-reaching concessions agreed to by the UAW put a great deal of pressure on Canadian autoworkers to agree to similar give-backs. In March 2009 the CAW agreed to a wage freeze and other concessions but has thus far resisted a tiered wage structure such as the one adopted by the UAW.

28   In March 1996 Delphi workers went on strike in Dayton, Ohio at two GM brake plants, shutting down 61 Delphi plants within a week. Two years earlier, the union had agreed to reorganize production, implementing work teams and flexible 'production cells' in exchange for a promise of substantial investment in the plant by GM. GM failed to keep its part of the agreement, outsourcing new brake contracts for the 1998 Chevrolet Camaro and Pontiac Firebird to Robert Bosch instead.

29   Office of Aerospace and Automotive Industries, 'US Automotive Industry Employment Trends', *US Department of Commerce*, 30 March 2006.

30   See Aschoff, *Globalization and Capital Mobility* for a detailed case study of Delphi.

31   Delphi cut 5,000 jobs shortly after it was spun-off from GM in 1999.

32   This illustrates the short term thinking of the union. The company decided to close these plants anyway (just two years later), but achieved an historic feat of the tiered wage system.

33   Form 8-K Current Report, Securities and Exchange Commission, 1 March 2005; Form 8-K Current Report, Securities and Exchange Commission, 8 June 2005.

34   Joseph B. White, 'Delphi Negotiates with GM, UAW about Big Revamp', *Wall Street Journal*, 5 August 2005.

35   Jeffrey McCracken and Lee Hawkins Jr., 'Delphi Asks Union for Deep Cuts as Chapter 11 Deadline Nears', *Wall Street Journal*, 7 October 2005.

36   Jeffrey McCracken, 'Delphi Seeks Further Concessions: In Addition to Wage Cuts, Greater Leeway is Requested to Hire Non-union Workers', *Wall Street Journal*, 28 October 2005.

37   Edward Lapham, 'Delphi's Wage War Will Reshape U.S. Labour Market', *Automotive News*, 14 November 2005.

38   The only challenge from labour the company faced was from a group of dissident workers inside the UAW called the Soldiers of Solidarity whose efforts achieved the few benefits Delphi workers received during the bankruptcy proceedings.

39   Jeffrey McCracken, 'In Shift, Auto Workers Flee to Health-Care Jobs', *Wall Street Journal*, 11 September 2007.

40   The VEBA was a boon for Detroit automakers. In 2007 the UAW agreed to take on the cost (and risk) of health care for workers and retirees in exchange for a lump sum and company stock. The nature of the transfer, especially the agreement to receive payment in the form of stocks, made UAW members extremely vulnerable to the ups and downs of share prices in a notoriously cyclical industry. During the 2009 bankruptcy restructuring GM and Chrysler were able to decrease their financial obligations to the VEBA in exchange for an increase in preferred stock, decreasing the likelihood that the VEBA will be able to cover the health care costs of UAW members and retirees in the years to come.

41   Sherk, 'Auto Bailout Ignores'; Steve Finlay, 'Kiss Babies, Bash Auto Industry', *Ward's Auto World*, 1 June 2008; Clive Crook, 'Does Obama Still Want Stronger Unions?', *National Journal*, 22 November 2008.

42   USGAO, 'Summary of Government Efforts', p. 26.

43   Ibid., p. 27.

44   The concessions were negotiated first at Ford and then expanded at GM and Chrysler prior to bankruptcy. The Jobs Bank was also eliminated in late 2008.

45   Jane Slaughter, 'UAW Members Protest 50% Wage Cut at GM Plant, Demand a Vote', *Labor Notes*, 21 October 2010.

46   David Barkholz, 'Detroit 3 are Expected to Add 36,000 Tier 2 Jobs by 2015', *Automotive News*, 12 April 2011.

47   Detroit has been slowly increasing the number of temporary workers it employs, especially since 2007. See Jane Slaughter, 'Auto Workers Stuck in Two-Tier System', *Automotive News*, May 2011, p. 8.

48   While GM and Toyota have historically paid comparable wages in the US, GM's total compensation costs have been much higher than Toyota because of its large number of retirees. This cost disparity worsened as GM's active working population decreased over the past three decades due to productivity

gains and decreased market share, while its retiree pool increased. However, recent concessions in combination with the VEBA have largely eliminated this cost differential.

49   Louis Uchitelle, 'Unions Yield on Wage Scales to Preserve Jobs', *New York Times*, 19 November 2010.

50   Dee-Ann Durbin, 'GM, Chrysler Investing in New Small Cars', *Associated Press*, 31 October 2010.

51   Jane Slaughter, 'UAW says it will go "All In" to Organize Foreign-Owned Auto Plants', *Labor Notes*, 24 January 2011.

52   Brent Snavely, 'UAW Members Defeat Proposed Changes to Ford Contract', *Detroit Free Press*, 2 November 2009; Brett Hoven, 'Ford Workers Reject New Concessions – Build a Movement to Change the UAW', 5 November 2009, available at http://www.socialistalternative.org.

RACE, CLASS, CRISIS:
THE DISCOURSE OF RACIAL DISPARITY
AND ITS ANALYTICAL DISCONTENTS

ADOLPH REED, JR.
AND MERLIN CHOWKWANYUN

A Harvard University study of more than 2,500 middle-income African American families found that, when compared to other ethnic groups in the same income bracket, blacks were up to 23 percent more likely. 'Our data would seem to discredit the notion that black Americans are less likely', said head researcher Russell Waterstone, noting the study also found that women of African descent were no more or less prone than Latinas. 'In fact, over the past several decades, we've seen the African-American community nearly triple in probability'. The study noted that, furthermore, Asian-Americans.

The Onion, 30 November 2010

The only thing that hasn't changed about black politics since 1965 is how we think about it.

Willie Legette (ca. 1999)

The 2008-09 economic crisis hit black Americans and other populations classified as nonwhite in the United States hard in relation to whites. This differential impact was no surprise to anyone who pays attention to patterns of inequality in the United States. Nonwhites, especially blacks and Latinos, are on the average poorer and economically less secure than whites. It was predictable, therefore, that those populations in the aggregate would experience the hardships of bad economic times in disproportionate measure. That likelihood underlies the inclination to inquire into the issue of racially differential impacts in the first place. And, unsurprisingly, as the studies and reports discussed here demonstrate, that prediction has generally been affirmed by empirical examination.[1]

Research precisely specifying racial disparities in the distribution of advantages and disadvantages, well-being and suffering has become common enough to have generated a distinctive, *pro forma* narrative structure. Quantitative data, usually culled from large aggregate data sets, is parsed to generate accounts of the many facets of apparent disparity along racial lines with respect to barometers of inequality such as wealth, income and economic security, incarceration, employment, access to medical care, and health and educational outcomes. However, as *The Onion* parody suggests, they tend not to add up to much beyond fleshing out the contours of the disproportionate relations, which are predictable by common sense understanding. Explanations of the sources of disparities tend to dribble into vague and often sanctimonious calls to recognize the role of race, and on the left, the flailing around of phrases like 'institutional racism' that on closer examination add up to little more than signifying one's radical credentials on race issues.

So what, then, do researchers assume they are doing in rehearsing versions of the same narrative with slightly different variations on the punch line? What are its conceptual foundations and premises? How should we assess the strengths, limits and significance of its perspectives on race, class and inequality and their connections, especially to understand American capitalism's social and ideological reproduction in the current period?

This essay is an initial attempt to answer those questions and, through doing so, to assess the deeper significance of the discourse of racial disparity that has taken shape in American social science and policy research during the last decade and a half. We consider what the findings of disparate impact at the level of gross racial groups mean and do not mean and examine ambiguities within this literature concerning race as a significant element in the reproduction of durable inequalities. In doing so, we identify several interpretive pathologies.

Among those pathologies are a schematic juxtaposition of race and class that frequently devolves into unproductive either–or debates; the dilution of class into a cultural and behavioural category or a static (usually quantitative) index of economic attainment that fails to capture power relations; sweeping characterizations of white Americans' racial animus and collective psyche; ahistorical declarations that posit a long and unbroken arc of American racism and that sidestep careful dissection of how racism and, for that matter, race have evolved and transformed; and a tendency to shoehorn the United States' racial history into a rhetorically powerful but analytically crude story of 'two societies', monolithic and monochromatic. Our overall concern is the extent to which particular inequalities that appear statistically as 'racial' disparities are in fact embedded in multiple social relations and how the dominant modes of approaching this topic impede the understanding of this larger picture. We believe that too much writing, including that on the crisis of 2008, is laced with generic, *a priori* assumptions about the role of racial categorization that then straitjackets research and tempts researchers, in Ian Shapiro's words, to 'load the dice in favor of one type of description', in this case, characterizing disparities in outcome as strictly 'racial' and thus resulting in the ho–hum and one–dimensional research conclusions we have mentioned.[2]

II

Initial accounts of the crisis have mostly come from major left–liberal think–tanks and magazines and often carry provocative titles like 'Mortgage Industry Bankrupts Black America' or 'Drained: Jobless and Foreclosed in Communities of Color'. The overall narrative is the same. First, authors select an undesirable phenomenon for study, such as unemployment, foreclosure, personal bankruptcy, and increasingly unmanageable subprime mortgages. Next, using quantitative data from a variety of sources, they cross–tabulate or run regressions against race (and sometimes other variables) and find that for minorities, the percentage of the group experiencing the adverse phenomenon is substantially greater than it is for white counterparts. When regressions are used, non–white race yields greater odds ratios and greater coefficients for the undesirable outcome, usually even if other variables are held constant. Some reports identify additional manifolds to this basic story – for example, a positive association between racial segregation and higher rates of subprime loans issued or greater likelihood of traditional mortgage denials for minorities than for whites.[3] In short, whites may have it bad in the recession, but minorities have it far worse. Thus the authors of these reports conclude, in some form or another, there are really two recessions and that one's ascriptive status determines which one a person will experience, and by extension, the severity of the pain.

Anyone who recalls the controversy over the Boston Federal Reserve's 1992 study on racial discrimination in the mortgage market and racial disparity in loan denials knows that claims over the magnitude of a variable's effects can quickly morph into methodological ping pong.[4] Defenders, critics, and those in between filled hundreds of pages and edited volumes with careful, if often arcane, dissection of the study.[5] Our intent for this essay is not to develop a critique along these technical lines; let us assume the findings of these studies, in their basic outline, are correct. Rather, we wish instead to assess, from a left perspective, the analytical payoff (or lack thereof) in this framework.

Common among these reports is a tautological reference to one racial disparity to explain another while avoiding concrete exploration of either's roots. And like their counterparts in the larger racial disparities field, the overall takeaways often simply exhort readers to register the historical and enduring impact of race and racism. So, to take one example, a typical report notes that 'for communities of color, the crisis is intensified', while another reminds the reader that 'economically, blacks and Latinos have suffered disproportionately because of structural racism and the web of policies that evolved from it'.[6] Policy proposals, too, sometimes take this form, such as a call for 'expand[ing] the use of Racial Equity Impact Assessments for public planning and policy so that racial inequities can be anticipated and prevented prior to the adoption of new policies and practices'.[7] More frequently, they are reasonable, and unobjectionable and include calls for better regulation of lending markets, especially of independent mortgage brokers who sell subprime loans; targeted metropolitan job creation programs, particularly in minority-heavy areas hit hard by the crisis; support for affirmative action to combat demonstrable ongoing discrimination; and foreclosure moratoriums. Thus after much rhetorical buildup and table after table of statistics showing pervasive racially disparate crisis outcomes, we are left with a plate of levelheaded, if technocratic and hardly novel, liberal policy solutions.

But the greatest pitfall to this writing is its limited potential for providing left analysts with a holistic causal account of the forces behind the bleak figures. At its most simplistic, the reader is simply left with figure after figure illustrating disparity and not much else, or only slightly better, a series of plausible just-so stories that attempt to fill in the explanatory blanks *post hoc*. One study, for example, spotlights unemployment disparities that vary in severity by region but tells us little about what specific characteristics of those regions – local history, institutions, labour market changes, political regimes, redevelopment initiatives, gentrification, and others – might account for these differences. A comparative examination of Sacramento and Minneapolis featured in the report would seem to encourage such analysis, but like most reports of the sort, its author does not undertake it.[8]

Simplistic use of race as the key analytic category, moreover, suggests intra-racial class uniformity and encourages thinking in monochromatic dyads. Much of the problem rests with the almost exclusive reliance on quantitative data sets, which usually limits researchers to pre-defined administrative and demographic variables while ignoring consideration of forces not captured by that data. This is not to say that analytically sophisticated quantitative work is completely absent. An Institute of Race and Poverty report on prime loan denials and subprime mortgage issuances in the Twin Cities, for instance, carefully uncovers egregious racial disparities in lending alongside a sophisticated dissection of the financial web linking predatory subprime mortgage brokers, debt collectors, and financial institutions who bundle and securitize loans. It identifies clearly discernible geographic patterns in subprime lending, with the highest rates in North Minneapolis and its 70 per cent black population, while noting that subprime mortgage rates are also not exclusive to the neighbourhood, and thus invites more precise inquiry into the role of neighbourhood boundaries and how they (along with race and a host of other considerations) influence the calculations and behaviour of all sociological actors in the real estate industry.[9]

In general, however, this research is far more flatfooted. Why, then, in light of its tedious quality has the focus on racial disparity become the default frame for characterizing inequality? One answer is that it is because it is. That is, in part something like a bandwagon effect is at work. Douglas Massey and Nancy Denton's *American Apartheid* and Melvin Oliver and Thomas Shapiro's *Black Wealth/White Wealth* were field-shaping books in the mid-1990s; the attention that they generated helped to establish racial disparity discourse as *lingua franca* of inequality studies in the United States. To that extent people operate within it automatically, as the presumptive common sense frame within which academic and policy scholars approach inequality.[10] This frame congeals around institutional and material imperatives. Funding streams make some lines of inquiry more commonsensical than others, and formulation of inequality in terms of racial disparities appeals to funders in part because doing so conveniently sidesteps potentially thorny causal questions about the foundation of racially asymmetrical distribution of costs and benefits in contemporary American capitalism's logic of systemic reproduction. Therefore, assessment of the discourse of racial disparity requires, as an element of making sense of the sources of its proliferation and assumed explanatory power in the absence of substantive interpretive payoff, reconstructing the historical dialectic through which it has taken shape.

III

The roots of racial disparities discourse reach back to key debates, texts and political tendencies over the past 40 years and more. These include the 1968 *Report of the National Advisory Commission on Civic Disorders* – more popularly known as the *Kerner Report* – which gave official sanction to identification of 'white racism' as the generic source of the manifest racial inequalities made visible by the civil disturbances of the mid-1960s. The *Report* declared famously that 'Our Nation Is Moving Toward Two Societies, One Black, One White – Separate and Unequal'. The appeal of black power sensibility and a Third Worldist rhetoric of 'domestic colonialism', reflected and reinforced a perspective in which racism is the main impediment to black aspirations and combating it is the definitive objective of black politics. Robert L. Allen's 1974 volume, *Reluctant Reformers: The Impact of Racism on American Social Reform Movements,* which argued that all major progressive movements in American history have been undone by white racism, became something of a bible for those who insisted that combating racism should take priority over all other political objectives.

More direct precursors include the debate in the late 1970s and 1980s around William Julius Wilson's *Declining Significance of Race,* which occurred in the context of intensifying controversy over affirmative action and other 'race-targeted' social policy initiatives; the status of claims concerning the extent to which black inequality stemmed from existence of a black urban underclass defined by behavioural and attitudinal pathologies; the highly publicized mid-1990s rightist ideological intervention condensed around anti-egalitarian texts like Dinesh D'Souza's *The End of Racism* and, especially, Charles Murray and Richard Herrnstein's *The Bell Curve: Intelligence and Class Structure in American Life,* which repackaged three-quarters of a century of hereditarian sophistries about I. Q. and 'natural' hierarchy, and the resurgence of significant legislative and judicial challenges to affirmative action and racial set-asides in the early years of this century.

Important as those earlier debates and tendencies are for a nuanced understanding of the intellectual and ideological genealogy of disparity discourse, it is impossible to examine that history here in requisite detail. We will provide that more elaborate account elsewhere, but for now we will assert that seen against those contexts, the rise of a growth industry around racial disparities is easier to understand. Moreover, taking into account the recurring anti-egalitarian challenges to racial equality highlights the many useful functions that research emerging from the disparity focus performs. For one, its authors call attention (though often in broad brush strokes rather than precise ways) to the connections between past historical developments and their residual consequences and role in shaping present-day racial inequality. Further, documenting the existence and consequences of current impediments to black and Latino economic mobility, especially ongoing discrimination, calls into question analyses that explain that lack of mobility by recourse to individual behavioural traits. Lastly, the work simultaneously challenges narratives that acknowledge racial inequality's existence but suggest that it is withering away – and that government measures not only do not help this process and are unfair but may in fact hinder it.

But the difficult political context surrounding this writing's production has discouraged criticism of its assumptions and analytical deficits. In order to understand the drawbacks of 'racial disparity' as a lens for interpreting the fallout of the crisis of 2008, it is useful to review two canonical racial disparities texts, Massey and Denton's *American Apartheid* and Oliver and Shapiro's *Black Wealth/White Wealth*, that capture the *modus operandi* of present-day approaches to racially disparate impacts.[11]

IV

Advocates of a disparities framework will often list a number of domains that exhibit egregious racial disparities; residential segregation, along with the standard book on the subject, *American Apartheid*, frequently tops this list. Published in 1993, *American Apartheid* argues that social scientists have insufficiently studied segregation's persistence and its role in perpetuating black economic disadvantage. The study impressively compiles indices (mostly from the 1980 United States Census) documenting black–white segregation and substantial black spatial isolation. Most usefully, it highlights five distinct dimensions of black population settlement – unevenness, isolation, clustering, concentration, and centralization – whose simultaneous manifestation comprised 'hypersegregation', a concept the book introduced.[12] Its authors argue for a 'persisting significance of race', and stress the particularity of black residential patterns, pointing out that segregation of other minority groups exists to a much lower degree.[13] They accentuate the tragedy of persistent segregation in an era after the formal legal dismantlement of Jim Crow and the fair housing laws passed in its direct wake, concluding that 'in the south, as in the north, there is little evidence of substantial change in the status quo of segregation'.[14]

It is impossible to deny Massey and Denton's empirical findings. Even as metropolitan settlement patterns since their work have become increasingly complex such that spatial categories like 'city' and 'suburb' tell us far less about racial composition than they once did, there is no doubt that for many blacks, residential options are greatly and uniquely constrained.[15] Thus *American Apartheid* was and remains an important counterweight against the politics of racial backlash. Documenting hypersegregation and its short-circuiting of economic channels for those caught within it called into doubt the highly individualistic analyses of the time. Why, then, does the analysis in *American Apartheid* fall short? Put simply, despite the empirical heft and political utility, its analysis barely advances that of the *Kerner Report's* 'two societies' trope or the raft of studies written around the same time on residential segregation. Though written nearly three decades apart, 'white racism' and its psychologistic gloss remain the key causal dynamics behind the racially disparate outcomes that Massey and Denton so ably chronicle. The authors draw repeatedly from considerable survey research on whites' aversion to living alongside black neighbours, especially as black composition rises, and whites' tendency to move away from or avoid moving to neighbourhoods as a result.[16]

There are, of course, commendable nuances to the account. Throughout the text, Massey and Denton draw a careful distinction between 'prejudice' and 'discrimination'. The first refers to the racial animus displayed by individual whites. The second refers to a set of institutionalized mechanisms and repertoires that actually restrict more neighbourhood integration. Explaining the distinction and relationship between the two, they write that 'although white prejudice is a necessary precondition for the perpetuation of segregation, it is insufficient to maintain the residential color line; active discrimination against blacks must occur also'.[17] The book then lists mechanisms behind this 'active discrimination'. Chief among them is the sleaze and chicanery of realtors who hide home listings from blacks or only steer them to segregated neighbourhoods and away from ones with substantial white residency. Another is the lending behaviour of financial institutions, which consistently offer fewer home loans to those in neighbourhoods that are integrated or primarily black, a disparity that holds even at an individual level.[18] Massey and Denton write that 'although each individual act of discrimination may be small and subtle, together they have a powerful cumulative effect in lowering the probability of black entry into white neighborhoods'.[19]

At first glance, the distinction between prejudice and discrimination seems to separate *American Apartheid* (and the dozens of studies influenced by it) from mid-century social science that saw individual prejudice as the fundamental mechanism behind racial inequality.[20] But when one asks what exactly motivates the institutionalized discrimination that Massey and Denton identify, the only answer derivable from the volume takes one back to individual prejudice. The behaviour of realtors and financial institutions is portrayed as a response to a collective prejudicial white psyche averse to black-white residential proximity. That Massey and Denton ultimately anchor their institutional account in collective psychology – while at points seeming not to do so – is reinforced by phrases such as 'the link between prejudice, discrimination, and segregation', 'strong link between levels of prejudice and discrimination and the degree of segregation and spatial isolation that blacks experience', and other instances where the resulting phenomenon (segregation), an institutional pattern (discrimination), and individual attitudes (prejudice) are clumped together.[21]

We hardly deny that these links exist, require condemnation, and should be legally constrained. The book's policy prescriptions centre around strengthening lax enforcement of fair housing laws and improving monitoring of the real estate industry. But the explanatory aspect of the work is another matter, and it can take us only so far analytically. It inadequately anchors the story of race and residence within the urban political economy – the drive to accumulate, the relationship among value, race, and space, or the role of property as speculative capital and in the derivation of exchange-value. This theme receives little attention in the book except for all too quick and scattershot references to white fears of depressed property values and bank fears of neighbourhoods in racial transition. This reasserts the psychologistic reflex that has underlain much interpretation of racial inequality since the 1950s. Yet a deeper causal account must be propelled by something besides white psychology, even if it certainly plays a role. The book's basic outlines, alas, differ only slightly from *Kerner*-era studies of residential segregation, like Karl Taeuber and Alma Taeuber's *Negroes in Cities* or Rose Helper's *Racial Policies and Practices of Real Estate Brokers*, both of which Massey and Denton briefly reference, and the *Kerner Report*'s 'white racism' frame itself.[22]

Notably, it is only in the chapter providing historical exposition where *American Apartheid* briefly departs from a framework rooted in collective psychology. Among others, Massey and Denton draw from Arnold Hirsch's *Making the Second Ghetto* and Kenneth Jackson's *Crabgrass Frontier*, two historical monographs on mid-century urban renewal (and its forced relocation of many black residents) and racially exclusionary suburbanization. While hardly ignoring the role of hostile white attitudes, each underscores the centrality of state and local government actions. Hirsch is especially attentive to the catalytic role of Chicago's private urban development interests, and the ghetto formation that he documents is motivated *both* by its imperatives and racial animosity.[23] More recent urban histories, covering a number of periods within the 20th century, have followed this lead, including Robert Self's *American Babylon*, Beryl Satter's *Family Properties*, and Samuel Roberts's *Infectious Fear*. Roberts, for example, traces the early twentieth century razing of a black Baltimore district not only to racist fears of the black population as unclean disease vectors, but crucially to the urbanization of Baltimore capital and the commitment to preserving and increasing property values as well.[24]

Such supple analyses of class and race's interstitial operation do not carry over into *American Apartheid's* examination of contemporary trends, the book's central focus. In rightly rejecting the right-wing fiction of free-standing market forces and autonomous residential choices, Massey and Denton end up dismissing the role of underlying market imperatives altogether.[25] At one point, they explicitly reject the relevance of class as an analytic. But they do so by perpetuating the unproductive class and race dichotomy and operationalizing class in a static, quantitative way (namely, by equating it with household income). In doing so, they find that the upper-income black population still experiences high rates of segregation; ergo, race trumps class.[26] This is true enough, but only as long as one accepts such a reductionist definition of class in the first place. That reductionist view also closes off the holistic analyses that might more fruitfully explore the relationship between political economy and racial attitudes and their spatial consequences.

Taking racial disparity as a starting point can subtly coerce a univariate view that precludes attention to many overarching class dynamics. One of these is intra-racial inequality. On residential segregation, a recent study by Sean Reardon and Kendra Bischoff shows that *income* segregation *among* blacks in the 100 largest metropolitan statistical areas 'grew rapidly in the 1970s and 1980s, at a rate more than three times faster than the corresponding growth of white income segregation', during the exact time span that is *American Apartheid*'s focus.[27] This concurrent development does not invalidate *American Apartheid*'s overall findings, especially its authors' emphasis that upwardly mobile blacks who move to suburbs still tend to end up in ones that are more segregated.[28] But it does suggest that a bifurcated 'two societies' model tells us little about what goes on *within* the two nodes themselves. Strictly racial interpretation prevents careful consideration of other forces shaping social life.

Published two years later, Jonathan Yinger's *Closed Doors, Opportunities Lost* covers much of the same territory as *American Apartheid* (and contains many of the same weaknesses), but discuses a much wider range of influences in its account of motivations for white avoidance and exit of neighbourhoods.[29] Yinger cites two local studies on Chicago and Cleveland wherein respondents' perceptions regarding safety and crime, education, and quality of city services greatly reduced or eliminated racial considerations in white residential choice. Of course, these considerations are often inextricably bound up with attitudes about race, and the constricted quality of survey research can make disentangling them difficult, but Yinger's point is that 'racial and ethnic attitudes are not so strong for most people that they cannot be overcome by other neighborhood factors'.[30]

Methodologically, identifying these 'neighborhood factors' and detailing how exactly they operate requires more than large-scale aggregate analysis (in this case, the metropolitan statistical area). That approach is necessary and undeniably useful for seeing general macro-level trends, but there are many micro-level trends that it cannot pick up, including urban redevelopment initiatives, suburban heterogeneity (however limited), and economic exploitation and gentrification (by both blacks and whites). Black-on-black gentrification, in particular, tends to occur in small corridors, and thus can easily be masked by these conventional quantitative analyses of segregation.[31] Moreover, when cast in the language of racial disparity, such aggregate analysis takes the larger percentage of blacks who are residentially segregated as a marker of little black political and economic power altogether. But this birds' eye view cannot capture the small but influential number of blacks who defy residential constraints, and in turn, play influential roles in the 'black urban regimes', the constellation of black elected officials, political appointees, and pro-growth business interests that exert an enormous impact on urban development.[32] Just as a robust aggregate GDP figure (to take just one example) can mask the economic stress experienced by the bulk of the population, so too can the depressing aggregate figures on minority outcomes – like those in *American Apartheid* and much racial disparities research – mask the affluence of a handful. Considered this way, the thematic maps periodically trucked out to show pervasive segregation may in fact obscure more subtle trends. For this work and others, then, method and choice of data obscure as much as they illuminate.[33]

V

Massey and Denton's portrait represents the dominant mode of left thinking about residential segregation. It is indeed the sort of book one wields when making the case that we live in a society that is not 'post-racial', where 'race matters', and 'racism' still exists. Published two years later in 1995, Oliver and Shapiro's *Black Wealth/White Wealth* reinforces this view but uses wealth, rather than housing, as its focus. Though its general template resembles *American Apartheid* and various disparities predecessors, the work may be even more influential. Reliably invoked by those using the racial frame, it and its political prescriptions have been embraced by major policy think-tanks and foundations with decidedly non-leftist, non-progressive political orientations. To understand the implications of this widespread impact and its resulting strange policy bedfellowism, it is important to examine *Black Wealth/White Wealth*'s core approach and assumptions.

On one level, *Black Wealth/White Wealth* is a very important intervention in stratification research that critiques the limits of conventional social scientific measures of socioeconomic status (SES), principally occupational group, education level, and income. Pioneered by Edward Wolff and Michael Sherraden, this work pointed out the inadequacy of orthodox SES measures for predicting life chances insofar as they failed to take into account the critical role of assets like stocks and bonds, inheritances, and real estate holdings.[34] By not accounting for wealth, stratification researchers therefore ignored a crucial dimension of economic inequality. Two households with identical annual incomes, for example, might still be quite unequal if one sat on an additional $50,000 or held a cashable portfolio of securities that the other did not. For crucial life events like medical emergencies, first home-purchases, college tuitions, seed money for a business, and spells of unemployment, this wealth leverage is crucial, and it is obvious how incorporating wealth into stratification research adds considerable complexity.

Oliver and Shapiro extend this insight to racial inequality, drawing from the Survey of Income and Program Participation (SIPP), a cross-sectional dataset that interviewed 11,257 households eight times between 1987 and 1989 about their occupational histories, educational backgrounds, parental characteristics, income levels, and wealth holdings. The empirical heart of *Black Wealth/White Wealth* is comprised of tables showing clear black-white wealth disparities. These hold across income levels, educational level, occupational category, and household structure – and regardless of whether one measures total net worth (NW) or net financial assets (NFA), the latter of which excludes equity, principally in homes and vehicles, not easily transformable into usable funds. A number of the results are dramatic and alarming. For example, one table displaying wealth disparities between 'middle-class' whites and blacks (defined as those making between $25,000 to $50,000 a year) shows that whites in 'white-collar' jobs have median NFA of $11,952, while blacks in the same kind of occupational category have median NFA of zero.[35] Even when black median NFA is positive, it is only a fraction of white median NFA in the same category under examination. And when specific types of assets are compared, black asset figures reflect far lower value.[36] Summarizing the implications of this data, like Massey and Denton, Oliver and Shapiro harken back explicitly to the Kerner Report. Their results are evidence 'that whites and blacks constitute two nations'. [37]

This compilation proved hugely useful in the 1990s debates referenced earlier, especially when mobilized against opponents of race-specific affirmative action who cynically appealed to ideals about preserving consideration on 'merit' while ignoring gross inequalities of resources conferred to swaths of applicants at birth. On this score, like *American Apartheid*, *Black Wealth/White Wealth* deserves praise and recognition for providing a counterweight to right-wing narratives. But like its counterpart on residential segregation, its actual analysis of how race structures a disparate outcome and fits into the larger American political economy is less satisfying.

Unlike *American Apartheid*, Oliver and Shapiro root their causal account less in 'white racism' and collective psychology than in the long historical arc of American racial exclusion. In *American Apartheid*, history is dispensed with in an obligatory chapter on early- and mid-century ghetto formation. In *Black Wealth/White Wealth*, history powerfully exerts its effects at all times, from the creation of racial wealth gaps through their persistence to the present. Specifically, the authors identify three historically durable mechanisms. The first, 'the racialization of state policy', refers to various racially exclusionary policies of the American welfare state that have 'impaired the ability of many black Americans to accumulate wealth' and denied to blacks a host of government-backed avenues of economic security available to whites, including 'homesteading, land acquisition, home ownership, retirement, pensions, education, and asset accumulation'.[38] Second, 'the economic detour' prevented accumulation of start-up capital for African-American entrepreneurial activity and relegated that which existed to largely segregated markets.[39]

The third, and most durable, of these mechanisms, is presented in the form of geological metaphor: 'the sedimentation of racial inequality', or the 'central ways the cumulative effects of the past have seemingly cemented blacks to the bottom of society's economic hierarchy'. Throughout American history, according to this account, 'generation after generation of blacks remained anchored to the lowest economic status in American society' while those on the other side of the sediment (whites) simultaneously benefited.[40] The wealth gap tables throughout the text reflect the cumulative consequences of this racial sedimentation. At the start, the reader is treated to a breezy, impressionistic, and stagist historical tour that proceeds from slavery, emancipation, racially exclusionary homesteading, the lost promise of Reconstruction (from lack of post-Civil War land redistribution to Redemption); mid-century suburbanization and housing policy that fuelled white homeownership, denied the same to blacks, and created segregated housing and real estate markets; and finally 'contemporary institutional racism' on the part of discriminatory institutions that impedes the accumulation of assets, particularly access to fair home loans.[41] Oliver and Shapiro declare that 'structural disadvantages have been layered one upon the other to produce black disadvantage and white privilege'.[42]

Having outlined this ostensibly historical framework, Oliver and Shapiro zoom in on two specific features contributing to racial wealth gaps. The first is housing. Historical Jim Crow social welfare policy, particularly racially exclusionary FHA home loans, surely account for some of the higher white rates of present-day homeownership, NW, and home value that Oliver and Shapiro observe. Surveying literature on racial disparities in housing prices and residential segregation (including *American Apartheid*), they show aggregate housing value appreciation for whites has been consistently greater.[43] They suggest persuasively that this is due to racially disparate access to mortgage markets, fairly rated loans, and residential choice.

They then examine inter-generational transfers of assets, including monetary gifts, informal loans, securities, and inheritances, especially of homes. Because whites historically have not faced barriers (formally codified and otherwise) that prohibited blacks from procuring certain assets, it is plausible that this would be reflected in racial wage gap figures of the present. Oliver and Shapiro argue as much via interspersed interviews in which white respondents repeatedly report more frequent and substantial assistance from parents and relatives in the form of tuition and wedding assistance, down payment money for homes, and substantial inheritances of wealth. (By contrast, among black interviewees, only two expect 'large inheritances'.[44]) They supplement these personal accounts with cross-tabulations that explore the effects of family occupational background – 'upper-white-collar', 'lower-white-collar', 'upper-blue-collar', and 'lower-blue-collar' – on one's subsequent income, NW, and NFA. They discover that for those who manage to increase their occupational mobility, all three measures are much higher for whites than they are for blacks. For example, for an 'upper-white-collar' white person who has ascended from 'upper-blue-collar' origins, NW is $89,898 and NFA is $29,199, compared to $11,162 and $0, respectively, for blacks experiencing the same mobility.[45] Regression analyses show that factors one might think would aid in accumulating more NFA – including increasing age (often associated with more earnings and assets), and high occupational job status – are statistically significant only for whites, not blacks. Whites, meanwhile, garner $1.34 in NFA per income dollar compared to $0.62 for blacks.[46]

The picture that emerges is one in which racial disparity endures within and across time periods. That is, blacks historically have been unable to accumulate certain assets, and when they have, they have been of less value and therefore less significant (in purely quantitative terms) to those who might inherit them. By contrast, whites historically have had a much easier time acquiring such assets – with no small assist from the racialized mid-century welfare state, to say nothing of discriminatory private institutions – and white descendants have therefore benefited enormously from a chain of hand-me-down wealth that most blacks did and do not enjoy. Above all, it is this chain that seems to be the most powerful determinant of the persistent wealth gap. The 'historical transmission of inequality', continues onward, inertia unimpeded, as Oliver and Shapiro remind readers in *Black Wealth/ White Wealth* that 'between 1987 and 2011 the baby boom generation stands to inherit approximately $7 trillion', and that 'for the most part, blacks will not partake in divvying up the baby boom bounty', for 'America's racist legacy is shutting them out'. A recent 2010 policy brief by Shapiro examining this exact period reveals that the racial wealth gap during this period quadrupled.[47]

Who could quarrel with this? The language of sedimentation, legacy, and history certainly separates *Black White/White Wealth* from pedestrian research that simply describes another disparity *du jour* with little else. But this may amount more to rhetorical genuflection than substantive historical analysis. Rigorous invocation of the past to shed light on present conditions (in this case, the racial wealth gap) must not only identify a persistent social mechanism in the past (in this case, unequal asset accumulation and later inheritance) but also carefully consider when it changes or even stops and to what degree. And it is here where the historical framework falters. Racialized inheritance no doubt explains much of what Oliver and Shapiro observe, but as they note, the 'bounty' comes mostly from the parents of white 'baby boomers'. That generation, in retrospect, is more an aberration than a norm. Its (white) members attained the assets that *Black Wealth/White Wealth* identifies during a period of welfare state expansion, re-distributive policies, rising labour compensation and benefits, and a booming domestic economy.

By the mid-1960s, however, this 'affluent society' began showing signs of destabilization before devolving a decade later into what Robert Brenner, Judith Stein, Robert Pollin, and Jacob Hacker have memorably characterized, respectively, as 'the long downturn', 'the great compression', 'the hollow boom', and 'the great risk shift'.[48] These formulations refer to a 40-year-period that has seen a decline in American manufacturing and global trade competitiveness; undercutting of organized labour; persistent wage stagnation; exponential growths in income and wealth inequality; mounting consumer debt; and the marketization, reduction, or elimination of public and private benefits, social services, and welfare programmes – in short, what we on the left understand as neoliberalism.[49] This shredding of the mid-century public and private welfare state thus renders questionable the claim that inter-generational transfers will continue in as widespread a manner as they have, at least among those not fortunate enough to be in upper economic tiers.[50] The economic crisis of 2008 throws this into even greater relief, given the ongoing havoc it continues to wreak on home ownership, housing prices, retirement accounts, and savings that would have been more abundant in prior times and thus more available for inter-generational transfer, by whites or blacks.

One interpretive goal should therefore be to think hard about whether mechanisms that have perpetuated racial wealth gaps in the past will take the same form in the future. This is the task, in other words, of concrete periodization and historicization rather than reliance on self-satisfying but overly elastic, transhistorical phrases like 'America's racist legacy'.[51] Yet some of the linkages between *Black Wealth/White Wealth*'s wide-spanning historical arc and the authors' findings are apparent only in very generic ways. Take, for example, the authors' first historical stage, that from slavery to the early 20th century. Here, *Black Wealth/White Wealth* makes much of white homesteading and the lost promise of Reconstruction, waxing counterfactually for a black yeomanry that never was. But it is unclear how consequential widespread petty black landownership would have been for contemporary wage gaps given the restructuring and dislocation in the southern agricultural economy from the immediate post-bellum period into the mid-20th century.[52] The wind-up historical narrative we get might more simply be summed up as an elaborate way of saying that race in history has 'mattered'. And? Despite the spectre of history in *Black Wealth/White Wealth*'s opening pages, the account we get ends up being far less complex and multi-factorial than promised.

This leaves us with a more typical stratification study than we might expect, one that suffers from methodological constraints similar to what we have identified in both the initial crisis studies and *American Apartheid*. Oliver and Shapiro's quantitative orientation leaves them with a treatment of class that takes the form, to use Barbara Fields's words, of the 'diffuse definitions of applied social science – occupation, income, status'.[53] Class is alternately operationalized here as income tiers, college degree attainment, and the schematic occupational categories referenced earlier. But the danger here is that such static conceptualizations often can become 'unwieldy catch-all unit[s] of analysis' and 'overly inclusive'.[54] For one, they do not allow situation of the wealth tabulations in a social context to understand how the transformation of certain job sectors (for instance, the steel or mining industries) has affected wealth in different ways than others (like public sector work or banking). This inattentiveness to the more fine-grained intra-racial gradients in social position prevents exploration of whether some of the black population does not fall quite as easily into the general pattern that Oliver and Shapiro document, even though the overwhelming majority no doubt does.

Notably, Dalton Conley's *Being Black, Living in the Red*, another book on the racial wealth gap that uses a more recent prospective data set, the Panel Study of Income Dynamics (PSID), is aware of these issues (even if the nature of the data necessarily results in a constricted definition of class). Through a series of regression models, Conley notes that, however uncommon, for those households where white wealth and black wealth (along with other economic measures he studies) *do* reach parity, a host of black outcomes associated with those gaps decline significantly or disappear altogether. Whereas Oliver and Shapiro take us up to the black wealth disparity – and posit through the sedimentation metaphor that it will persist – Conley takes us beyond to consider part two, when intra-racial class heterogeneity closes the wealth gap for some, and examines the consequences of this intra-racial class restructuring.[55] His findings deserve more follow-up. And beyond individual households, class analysis leads to consideration of how the social relations of production alter localities and regions, transformations that greatly affect the life chances – and self-understandings or pragmatic identities – of those within them. In the wake of the 2008 crisis, such an approach is crucial to understanding who precisely has been hit hardest, where, and why without resorting simply to shortcut indexical use of race.

VI

To return to our original question, then, why, despite its serious limitations, does the focus on racial disparity persist as the principal interpretive frame for discussing apparently racialized inequality? The policy recommendations that follow from the disparitarian perspective point to part of the answer. Like *American Apartheid*, most of *Black Wealth/White Wealth*'s recommendations are sound, including re-vamped anti-discrimination policy in lending or changes in the taxation of assets commonly held by the affluent. It is telling, though, that what have arguably gained the most traction are more dubious proposals for 'asset-based' social policy – such as Individual Development Accounts (IDA)[56] – that focus on encouraging start-up individual wealth accumulation. Such stratagems represent détente with rather than commitment to changing capitalist class relations, including those that contribute to intra- and inter-racial disparities in the first place. Among other limitations, they accommodate, rather than uproot, a key determinant of wealth gaps (racial or otherwise): the entrenched credit and debt regime, chronicled brilliantly by historian Louis Hyman's *Debtor Nation*.[57] Focus on wealth building as strategy and analytical lens for understanding inequality thus is not nearly as progressive as some think, since turning attention away from income is to ignore what it fundamentally reflects: the nature of a capitalist wage-labour relation.

It is telling as well that this focal shift has occurred at precisely the time incomes have skyrocketed for a single-digit percentage of the population while remaining flat for everybody else. Hegemonic chestnuts like 'equal opportunity', 'American Dream', 'awarding achievement and merit, not birth', 'level playing field' abound in *Black Wealth/White Wealth* and Shapiro's own follow-up volume, *The Hidden Costs of Being African-American*, published in 2004. These red flags confirm that the agenda at work here stems from a concern to create competitive individual minority agents who might stand a better fighting chance in the neoliberal rat race rather than a positive alternative vision of a society that eliminates the need to fight constantly against disruptive market whims in the first place. This is a notable and striking reversal from even the more left-inclined of War on Poverty era liberals, who spoke without shame about moving beyond simply placing people on an equal starting line – 'equality of opportunity' – but also making sure they ended up closer to an equal finishing line.

Within the racial context specifically, such proposals exude more than a whiff of racial communitarianism and collective racial self-help, along with a dollop of republican nostalgia. Although Oliver and Shapiro are careful to note that they advocate 'penetration into the newest and most profitable sectors of the wider economy' alongside the 'development of local community-based entrepreneurs', the involvement of financial institutions or 'community-based' institutions in these policy proposals and their actual execution is perfect fodder for a bourgeois racial brokerage or machine politics, or more likely, a reinforcement of one that already exists.[58] This focus only serves to affirm a racialized class politics from above.

The discourse of disparity also accommodates a strain of stigmatizing behavioural argument that stretches back at least to Kenneth B. Clark's 1965 study, *Dark Ghetto*.[59] This strain, in varying ways, has characterized the economically marginalized segment of the black population – the most common focus of racial disparities research – as culturally deviant and bereft of role models, typically reasserting a politics of black petit bourgeois racial noblesse oblige that originated in the late 19th century rubric of racial 'uplift'.[60] These claims often have relied on a narrative anchored in racialized geography ('ghetto-specific culture'). *American Apartheid,* for example, contains lurid and impressionistic sections – in disturbingly racialized language bordering on vicious stereotype – on ingrained, 'concentrated' social deviance and cultural pathologies supposedly engendered and exacerbated by constricted, segregated space. These ideas have shaped the policy consensus around the racialized notion of 'concentrated poverty', one that holds that these spatial configurations perpetuate poverty, foreclose economic opportunities, breed undesirable behaviours and require dispersal through varied policy initiatives, from the destruction of high-rise public housing to vouchers for moving into mixed-income neighbourhoods. In the name of a progressive-sounding anti-racism, policy discussion has come to focus on technocratic initiatives to rearrange space that in this way grant causal primacy to a spatial consequence rather than to more fundamental dynamics of metropolitan economies, particularly those linked to the political economy of land use, labour markets and the politics of social service distribution.[61]

It should give us pause that these decidedly non-leftist policy prescriptions flow from the leftist frame of choice for analyzing the racial minority experience in the crisis of 2008. In choosing that frame, rather than fundamentally rethinking default approaches in the face of changing historical circumstances, the left has simply dusted off, rinsed, and repeated. This reflex is reinforced by commitment to a *pro forma* anti-racism that depends on evocations – as in Michelle Alexander's widely noted recent book, *The New Jim Crow*[62] – of regimes of explicitly racial subordination in the past to insist on the moral primacy of simplistic racial metaphor for characterizing inequality in the present. Most charitably, this tendency arises from intensified concerns to defend racial democracy in debates over the legitimacy of race-targeted social policy that have recurred since the late 1970s. Less charitably, it is an expression of an at best self-righteous and lazy-minded expression of the identitarian discourse that has increasingly captured the left imagination in the United States since the 1990s.[63] This is moreover an antagonistic alternative to a politics grounded in political economy and class analysis, despite left-seeming defences that insist on the importance of race *and* class. Its commitment to a fundamentally essentialist and ahistorical race-first view is betrayed in the constantly expanding panoply of neologisms – 'institutional racism', 'systemic racism', 'structural racism', 'colour-blind racism', 'post-racial racism', etc. – intended to graft more complex social dynamics onto a simplistic and frequently psychologistic racism/anti-racism political ontology. Indeed, these efforts bring to mind Kuhn's account of attempts to accommodate mounting anomalies to salvage an interpretive paradigm in danger of crumbling under a crisis of authority.[64] And in this circumstance as well the salvage effort is driven by powerful material and ideological imperatives.

The discourse of racial disparity is, when all is said and done, a class discourse. Even the best of the studies analyzing the racial impact of the crisis, for example, in focusing on racial disparity in subprime mortgage markets and foreclosure rates, sidestep a chance to interrogate the very limitations of the hegemonic commitment to homeownership altogether. More generally, automatic adoption of the racial disparities approach avoids having to conduct the detailed work that would situate ascriptive status within the neoliberal regime of accumulation that mitigates its influence. Repetitiously noting the existence of segregated neighbourhoods and how they decrease property value (real and perceived) and increase the likelihood of subprime mortgage is to identify a *result*, albeit one that is surely repellent. It does not tell us with much exactitude what institutions, policies, actuarial models, and systems of valuation produce those results, or more generally, what sociologist Mara Loveman describes as the 'extent a particular essentializing vocabulary is related to particular forms of social closure and with what consequences'.[65] It substitutes in its place pietistic hand-wringing and feigned surprise over results that can hardly be surprising.

Ironically, it is authors who operate from outside of that frame, and in some cases outside the left entirely, that currently have the most to offer us. Gretchen Morgenson and Joshua Rosner's *Reckless Endangerment* traces the short-term roots of the crisis, detailing how a 1990s consensus on pushing homeownership led to a system of tax credits, perverse incentives, refinancing, risky (and often fraudulent) loans, lax regulation, and debt securitization that exploded a decade and a half later. To cast the story primarily in terms of racial disparity is to capture only a sliver of what some have labelled the 'real estate financial complex'. Doing so misses as well the legitimizing role that disparities rhetoric played in pushing minority homeownership. Focusing so robotically on racially disparate home financing and credit access obscures how these injustices, repugnant as they are, fit into a larger picture of income stagnation and welfare state instability, which gave rise to the increasing need, documented by Hyman, for significant household debt, protracted mortgages, and accelerated re-financing in the first place, all simply to stay afloat. In the accounts we reviewed here, the *Kerner Report's* 'white racism' remains the enemy, while the Big Kahuna, financialization, wobbles in the background, meriting more an obligatory mention than focused inquiry on how it impacts other phenomena. The misdirection strategies can take if predicated on such an analysis are obvious.

Our call to transcend this stifling frame is absolutely *not* a call to ignore racial exclusion or to declare in abstract terms, as Ellen Wood has, that race is not 'constitutive of capitalism' the way class is.[66] Rather, we advocate that in analyzing the current situation and how it fits into historical context, left analysts ought to conduct what Ian Shapiro has labelled 'problem-driven' research, in his words, 'to endeavor to give the most plausible possible account of the phenomenon that stands in need of explanation', in this case racially disparate impacts, instead of forcing it into a stifling, ready-made narrative.[67] Doing so will break away from analytical sloth and widen strategic options. Doing so also requires jettisoning the hoary, mechanistic race/class debate entirely. We believe that our critique here demonstrates the virtues of a dynamic historical materialist perspective in which race and class are relatively distinct – sometimes more, sometimes less, sometimes incoherently related or even interchangeable – inflections within a unitary system of capitalist social hierarchy, without any of the moralizing, formalist ontological baggage about priority of oppression that undergirds the debate. From this perspective insistence that race, or any other category of ascriptive differentiation, is somehow *sui generis* and transcendent of particular regimes of capitalist social relations appears to be, as we have suggested here, itself reflective of a class position tied programmatically to the articulation of a metric of social justice compatible with neoliberalism. That is a view that both obscures useful ways to understand the forces that are intensifying inequality and undermines the capacity to challenge them.

NOTES

1   See, for instance, Charles Bromley et al, *Paying More for the American Dream V: The Persistence and Evolution of the Dual Mortgage Market,* California Reinvestment Coalition, 2011; Barbara Ehrenreich and Dedrick Muhammad, 'The Recession's Racial Divide', *New York Times,* 13 September 2009; Kai Wright, 'Mortgage Industry Bankrupts Black America', *The Nation,* 24 July 2008; Wright, 'The Assault on the Black Middle Class', *The American Prospect,* 4 August 2009; and the series of studies by Algernon Austin, Gregory Squires and their colleagues for the Economic Policy Institute as well as those by Amaad Rivera, Ajamu Dillahunt, Mazher Ali and their colleagues for United for a Fair Economy from 2008 to 2011.

2   Ian Shapiro, 'Problems, Methods, and Theories in the Study of Politics', in Shapiro, *The Flight from Reality in the Human Sciences,* Princeton: Princeton University Press, 2007, p. 188.

3   Debbie Gruenstein Bocian, Wei Li, and Keith Ernst, *Foreclosures by Race and Ethnicity: The Demographics of a Crisis,* Center for Responsible Lending, 18 June 2010; Seth Wessler et al., *Race and Recession: How Inequity Rigged the Economy and How to Change the Rules,* Applied Research Center, May 2009; *Communities in Crisis: Race and Mortgage Lending in the Twin Cities,* Institute on Race and Poverty, February 2009.

4   Alicia Munnell et al., 'Mortgage Lending in Boston: Interpreting HMDA Data', Working Paper No. 92-7, Federal Reserve Bank of Boston, October 1992, available from http://www.bos.frb.org.

5   For the debate that it generated, see, for example, John Goering and Ron Wienk,

eds., *Mortgage Lending, Racial Discrimination, and Federal Policy*, Washington, DC: Urban Institute Press, 1996; Stephen Ross and John Yinger, eds., *The Color of Credit: Mortgage Discrimination, Research Methodology, and Fair-Lending Enforcement*, Cambridge: MIT Press, 2002. An otherwise excellent account of both the study and the events leading up to the subprime crisis in general is Gretchen Morgenson and Joshua Rosner, *Reckless Endangerment: How Outsized Ambition, Greed, and Corruption Led to Economic Armageddon*, New York: Times Books, 2011, is unfortunately too dismissive of the study and the careful and serious methodological debates that occurred over its findings.

6   Wessler et al., *Race and Recession*, p. 7; Amaad Rivera et al., *The Silent Depression: State of the Dream* 2009, Boston: United for a Fair Economy, 2009, p. iii.

7   Wessler et al., *Race and Recession*, p. 47.

8   Algernon Austin, *Uneven Pain: Unemployment by Metropolitan Area and by Race*, Issue Brief No. 278, Economic Policy Institute, 8 June 2010.

9   *Communities in Crisis*, pp. 26-34.

10   There has been an interesting critical discussion of this phenomenon in public health and epidemiological research. See Dawn R. Comstock, Edward M. Castillo and Suzanne P. Lindsay, 'Four-Year Review of the Use of Race and Ethnicity in Epidemiologic and Public Health Research', *American Journal of Epidemiology*, 159, 2004, pp. 611-619 and Camara Phyllis Jones, 'Invited Commentary: "Race", Racism and the Practice of Epidemiology', *American Journal of Epidemiology*, 154, 2001, pp. 299-304. Also see Merlin Chowkwanyun, 'The Strange Disappearance of History from Racial Health Disparities Research', *Du Bois Review: Social Science on Race*, 8, 2011, p. 253.

11   Douglas Massey and Nancy Denton, *American Apartheid: Segregation and the Making of the Underclass*, Cambridge: Harvard University Press, 1993; Melvin Oliver and Thomas Shapiro, *Black Wealth/White Wealth: A New Perspective on Racial Inequality*, New York: Routledge, 1995.

12   Massey and Denton, *American Apartheid*, pp. 74-78.

13   Ibid., p. 112.

14   Ibid., p. 81.

15   Katz et al., 'Immigration and the New Metropolitan Geography', *Journal of Urban Affairs* 32(5), 2010, pp. 523-547; Richard Alba and John Logan, 'Variations on Two Themes: Racial and Ethnic Patterns in the Attainment of Suburban Residence', *Demography*, 28(3), 1991 and 'Minority Proximity to Whites in Suburbs: An Individual-Level Analysis of Segregation', *American Journal of Sociology*, 98(6), 1993.

16   Massey and Denton, *American Apartheid*, p. 93.

17   Ibid., p. 97.

18   Ibid., p. 107.

19   Ibid., p. 98.

20   Ellen Herman, *The Romance of American Psychology: Political Culture in the Age of Experts*, Berkeley: University of California Press, 1996 and Leah Gordon, 'The Question of Prejudice: Social Science, Education, and the Struggle to Define the "Race Problem" in Mid-Twentieth Century America, 1935-1965', Ph.D. Thesis, University of Pennsylvania, Pennsylvania, 2008.

21   Massey and Denton, *American Apartheid*, pp. 109–110.

22   Karl Taeuber and Alma Taeuber, *Negroes in Cities*, Chicago: Aldine, 1965; Rose Helper, *Racial Policies and Practices of Real Estate Brokers*, Minneapolis: University of Minnesota Press, 1969.

23   Kenneth Jackson, *Crabgrass Frontier: The Suburbanization of the United States*, New York: Oxford University Press, 1987, chs. 11–12; Arnold Hirsch, *Making the Second Ghetto: Race and Housing in Chicago, 1940-1960*, Chicago: University of Chicago Press, 1983, ch. 4.

24   Robert Self, *American Babylon: Race and the Struggle for Postwar Oakland*, Princeton: Princeton University Press, 2003; Beryl Satter, *Family Properties: How the Struggle Over Race and Real Estate Transformed Chicago and Urban America*, New York: Picador, 2010; Samuel Roberts, *Infectious Fear: Politics, Disease, and The Health Effects of Segregation*, Chapel Hill: University of North Carolina Press, 2009, p. 136. It is notable that Roberts maintains this class analysis while writing about the age of Jim Crow, during which a strictly racial interpretation might be more justifiable, though hardly adequate.

25   Massey and Denton, *American Apartheid*, pp. 10–11.

26   Ibid., pp. 84–88.

27   Sean Reardon and Kendra Bischoff, 'Income Inequality and Income Segregation', *American Journal of Sociology*, 116(4) January 2011, pp. 1115–16.

28   Massey and Denton, *American Apartheid*, p. 69.

29   Jonathan Yinger, *Closed Doors, Opportunities Lost: The Continuing Costs of Housing Discrimination*, New York: Russell Sage Foundation, 1995, pp. 120–21.

30   Ibid., p. 121.

31   This may partly explain why the topic has received such little attention. An important exception is Michelle Boyd's account of a Chicago neighbourhood revitalization project in the late 1980s and early 1990s. See Boyd, 'The Downside of Racial Uplift: The Meaning of Gentrification in an African American Neighborhood', *City and Society*, 17(2), December 2005, pp. 265–88; Boyd, 'Defensive Development: The Role of Racial Conflict in Gentrification', *Urban Affairs Review*, 43(6), July 2008, pp. 751–76; and Boyd, *Jim Crow Nostalgia: Reconstructing Race in Bronzeville*, Minneapolis: University of Minneapolis Press, 2008, chs. 2–5. Peter Kwong has called attention to intra-racial exploitation between Chinese employers and Chinese workers in the United States. See Kwong, *The New Chinatown*, Second Edition, New York: Hill and Wang, 1996.

32   See Adolph Reed, Jr., 'The Black Urban Regime: Structural Origins and Constraints', in Reed, *Stirrings In The Jug: Black Politics In The Post-Segregation Era*, Minneapolis: University Of Minnesota Press, 1999, ch. 3; John Arena, 'Race and Hegemony: The Neoliberal Transformation of the Black Urban Regime and Working Class Resistance', *American Behavioral Scientist*, 47(3), November 2003, pp. 352–380.

33   Chowkwanyun has criticized a parallel quality in racial health disparities research that results from its similar reliance on large, aggregated data sets and repeated uncovering of statistical associations between race and adverse health outcomes.

Constrained by methodology and type of empirical base, such research thus rarely penetrates a level deeper than these macro-level quantitative portraits to tell us what concrete policies; institutions, phenomena and actors are causing them. More generally, Robert Aronowitz identifies a similar phenomenon in post-war epidemiology and identification of quantifiable 'risk factors'. See Chowkwanyun, 'Strange Disappearance'; Aronowitz, 'The Social Construction of Coronary Heart Disease Risk Factors', in Aronowitz, *Making Sense of Illness: Science, Society, and Disease,* New York: Cambridge University Press, 1998.

34   See Edward Wolff, *Top Heavy: The Increasing Inequality of Wealth in America and What Can Be Done About It,* Second Edition, New York: New Press, 2002 [1995]; Michael Sherraden, *Assets and the Poor: A New American Welfare Policy,* New York: M.E. Sharpe, 1991 for single-volume summations of these authors' views.

35   Oliver and Shapiro, *Black Wealth/White Wealth,* p. 94.

36   Ibid., p. 106.

37   Ibid., pp. 91, 125.

38   Ibid., p. 4.

39   Ibid., pp. 4-5.

40   Ibid., p. 5.

41   Ibid., pp. 11-52.

42   Ibid., p. 51.

43   Ibid., pp. 147-151.

44   Ibid., p. 156.

45   Ibid., p. 166.

46   Ibid., pp. 130-133.

47   Ibid., pp. 6-7; Thomas Shapiro, Tatjana Meschede, and Laura Sullivan, 'The Racial Wealth Gap Increases Fourfold', Institute on Assets and Social Policy, May 2010. In addition to lax taxes on inheritances, Shapiro identifies persistent disparities in the labour and housing market as other culprits.

48   Robert Brenner, *The Boom and the Bubble: The US in the World Economy,* New York: Verso Books, 2002, ch. 1; Judith Stein, *Pivotal Decade: How the United States Traded Factors for Finance in the Seventies,* New Haven: Yale University Press, 2011, ch. 1; Robert Pollin, *Contours of Descent: U.S. Economic Fractures and the Landscape of Global Austerity,* New York: Verso Books, 2005 [2003], chs. 2-3; Jacob Hacker, *The Great Risk Shift: The Assault on American Jobs, Families, Health Care and Retirement and How You Can Fight Back,* New York: Oxford University Press, 2006.

49   David Harvey, *A Brief History of Neoliberalism,* New York: Oxford University Press, 2006, p. 2.

50   Shapiro advances such a claim even more forcefully in *The Hidden Cost of Being African-American: How Wealth Perpetuates Inequality,* New York: Oxford University Press, 2004, ch. 3.

51   Kenneth Warren has urged a similar approach for African-American literature, arguing for constricting its definition to works produced between the beginning and end of federally sanctioned legal segregation. This stands in contrast to all encompassing definitions that include black American writing

from the antebellum era to the present. See Warren, *What Was African American Literature?* (Cambridge: Harvard University Press, 2011), ch. 1.

For two other considerations of how race's operation has changed over time that consider the limits of strictly using race as a marker of social position, see Adolph Reed, Jr., 'The "Color Line" Then and Now', in A. Reed and K. Warren, eds., *Renewing Black Intellectual History: The Ideological and Material Foundations of African American Thought,* Boulder: Paradigm, 2010 and Michael Katz, Mark Stern, and Jamie Fader, 'The New African-American Inequality', *Journal of American History,* 92(1), June 2005, pp. 75-108.

52   A considerable body of work chronicles this restructuring and the political mobilization against it, including Steven Hahn and Jonathan Prude, eds., *The Countryside in the Age of Capitalist Transformation,* Chapel Hill: University of North Carolina Press, 1985, chs. 6-7; Hahn, *The Roots of Southern Populism: Yeoman Farmers and the Transformation of the Georgia Upcountry, 1850-1890,* New York: Oxford University Press, 1983; Jack Temple Kirby, *Rural Worlds Lost: The American South, 1920-1960,* Baton Rouge: Louisiana State Press, 1987. It is worth noting that this counterfactual on the lost opportunity for land redistribution in the immediate wake of the Civil War plays a central role in much pro-reparations discourse, which also mobilizes a similar long narrative of American history by highlighting cross-generational racial disadvantage. But like the one presented in this work, it is more impressionistic outline than detailed exploration of contemporary inequality's historical roots. For one example, see Raymond Winbush, ed., *Should America Pay?: Slavery and the Raging Debate on Reparations,* New York: HarperCollins, 2003.

53   Barbara J. Fields, 'Ideology and Race in American History', in James McPherson and Morgan Kousser, eds., *Region, Race and Reconstruction: Essays in Honor of C. Vann Woodward,* New York: Oxford University Press, 1982, p. 150.

54   Adolph Reed, Jr., 'Review: *The New Black Middle Class',* *Political Science Quarterly,* 103, Spring 1988, pp. 159-161.

55   Dalton Conley, *Being Black, Living in the Red: Race, Wealth, and Social Policy in America,* Berkeley: University of California Press, 1999. Curiously, both volumes are frequently cited next to one another, even though their analytical missions are quite different. In the second edition of their book and a separate volume by Shapiro, Conley is mentioned but not engaged. See Oliver and Shapiro, *Black Wealth/White Wealth: A New Perspective on Racial Inequality,* Second Edition, New York: Routledge, 2006, p. 232; Shapiro, *The Hidden Cost,* p. 96. Conley explores the role of class dynamics in blunting the racial wealth gaps' deleterious effects. Oliver and Shapiro state that this is not a primary goal when they write that they 'do not intend here to engage in a discourse about class in modern American life; the concept is important but not entirely germane to our purposes', which is to show the endurance of the racial wealth gap whatever class measure they use (p. 70).

56   Largely due to Sherraden's *Assets and the Poor,* IDAs emerged as an attractive policy idea in the 1990s. They entitle low-income applicants who promise to save an agreed upon sum of money to matching funds from local municipalities, community organizations, or financial institutions who partner

up to participate in the program, sometimes in an amount many times more than the original principal. These transfers, in turn, come with no stipulations that they be paid back but are restricted to certain usages, such as paying for college, making a down payment for a home, or starting a small business, and they usually require recipients to attend workshops on wealth management and financial responsibility. IDAs have attracted a broad spectrum of neoliberal support, including the Democratic Leadership Council, the Aspen Institute, Bill Clinton, and George W. Bush.

57   Louis Hyman, *Debtor Nation: The History of America in Red Ink,* Princeton: Princeton University Press, 2011.

58   Oliver and Shapiro, *Black Wealth/White Wealth,* First Edition, p. 193. The literature on such politics and its close ties with community development efforts remains thin, but see Nicole Marwell, *Bargaining for Brooklyn: Community Organizations in the Entrepreneurial City,* Chicago: University of Chicago Press, 2007; Karen Tani, 'The House that "Equality" Built: The Asian American Movement and the Legacy of Community Action', in Annelise Orleck and Lisa Hazirjian, eds., *The War on Poverty and Struggles for Racial and Economic Justice: Views from the Grassroots,* Athens: University of Georgia Press, 2011; Kent Germany, *New Orleans after the Promises: Poverty, Citizenship, and the Search for the Great Society,* Athens: University of Georgia Press, 2007.

59   Kenneth B. Clark, *Dark Ghetto: Dilemmas of Social Power,* New York: Harper & Row, 1965.

60   On the politics of racial uplift, see Kevin Gaines, *Uplifting the Race: Black Leadership, Politics and Culture in the Twentieth Century,* Chapel Hill: University of North Carolina Press, 1996; Michele Mitchell, *Righteous Propagation: African Americans and the Politics of Racial Destiny after Reconstruction,* Chapel Hill: University of North Carolina Press, 2004; Touré F. Reed, *Not Alms but Opportunity: The Urban League and the Politics of Racial Uplift, 1910-1950,* Chapel Hill: University of North Carolina Press, 2008; Wilson J. Moses, *The Golden Age of Black Nationalism, 1850-1925,* Oxford: Oxford University Press, 1988; August Meier, *Negro Thought in America, 1880-1915: Racial Ideologies in the Age of Booker T. Washington,* Ann Arbor: University of Michigan Press, 1963.

61   For rare critiques against this consensus, see Larry Bennett and Adolph Reed, Jr., 'The New Face of Urban Renewal: The Near North Redevelopment Initiative and the Cabrini-Green Neighborhood', in Reed, ed., *Without Justice for All,* Boulder: Westview Press, 1999; David Imbroscio, '"(U)nited and Actuated by Some Common Impulse of Passion": Challenging the Dispersal Consensus in American Housing Policy Research', *Journal of Urban Affairs,* 30(2), April 2008, pp. 111-30; Herbert Gans, 'Concentrated Poverty: A Critical Analysis', *Challenge,* 53(3), May-June 2010, pp. 82-96.

62   Michelle Alexander, *The New Jim Crow: Mass Incarceration in the Age of Colorblindness,* New York: New Press, 2010.

63   For a class and institutional analysis of the emergence of this identity discourse and its reach (with even the labor movement increasingly forsaking the language of class in favour of it), see Adolph Reed, Jr., *The Lesson of Obamamania: There*

Is No Substitute for an Anti-Capitalist Politics, London: Verso, forthcoming, 2012.

64   Thomas S. Kuhn, *The Structure of Scientific Revolutions*, Chicago: University of Chicago Press, 1962.

65   Mara Loveman, 'Is "Race" Essential', *American Sociological Review*, 64, December 1999, p. 896.

66   Ellen Meiksins Wood, 'Class, Race, and Capitalism', *Political Power and Social Theory*, 15, 2002, p. 276. Wood's comment is part of a symposium on the race/class controversy. See also in the same issue: Adolph Reed, Jr., 'Unraveling the Relation of Race and Class in American Politics'; Maurice Zeitlin, 'On the "Confluence of Race and Class" in America'; Steven Gregory, 'The "Paradoxes" of Misplaced Concreteness'; and Reed, 'Rejoinder'.

67   Donald Green and Ian Shapiro, 'Revisiting Rational Choice', in Shapiro, *Flight from Reality*, p. 95n146.

FINANCE, OIL AND THE ARAB UPRISINGS: THE GLOBAL CRISIS AND THE GULF STATES

ADAM HANIEH

A particularly striking feature of the 2011 Arab uprisings has been the prominent role of the six states of the Gulf Cooperation Council (GCC) – Saudi Arabia, Kuwait, United Arab Emirates, Qatar, Bahrain and Oman. During the course of the uprisings, these states launched a range of conspicuous political and diplomatic initiatives, acting as the single most important Arab conduits of US and European Middle East policy and working to undermine and pacify the radical orientation of the struggles across the region.[1] Three of these states – Saudi Arabia, Oman and, most notably, Bahrain – experienced their own uprisings, which were met with violent state repression and a stunning media silence. Western governments refrained from any severe condemnation of this repression, explicitly prioritizing the *status quo* and seeking to block any possibility of 'regime change'. The paramountcy placed on supporting the Gulf monarchies – and the Gulf's own essential role in backing US and European interests in the region – signals once again the centrality of the GCC to understanding the politics of the modern Middle East.

This central political role intersects with the ever-widening regional differentiation that arose in the wake of the recent global economic crisis. In the GCC itself, although there were a few high profile financial casualties due to the heavy indebtedness of some large conglomerates, the crisis had the principal effect of strengthening the position of the Gulf's dominant classes. The nature of class formation in the GCC permitted the spatial displacement of crisis onto migrant workers and, coupled with state support to the largest Gulf financial and industrial entities, meant that Gulf elites were largely shielded from the worst impacts of the economic downturn. This strengthening of GCC capitalism contrasts with the dramatically worsening living standards in the rest of the Middle East. In countries such as Egypt, Tunisia, Yemen and Jordan, the global crisis has had – and continues to have – a severe impact. A plunge in commodity exports, worker remittances and financial flows, combined with rising food and energy prices, meant the poorest populations of the Middle East were hit very hard. This differentiated experience of the crisis across the region indicates not only the relative strengthening of the GCC elites within the Gulf itself, but also the widening gap between GCC and other Middle East states. The Gulf's dominant position within the region as a whole was thus sharply accentuated in the wake of the crisis.

Nonetheless, and despite the primacy of the GCC states in the strategic calculations of imperialism, a thorough analysis of the Gulf's complexities has been largely absent from radical accounts of the uprisings. This is a highly problematic lacuna. The GCC forms the core of capitalism in the Arab world; it is both the central zone of accumulation and the region's principal articulation with the global economy. The GCC's pivotal position in the affairs of the area reminds us that the Middle East cannot be treated as a simple agglomeration of distinct nation-states separate from the regional and global scales. Rather, each of the states that constitute the region are linked within a wider reproduction of capitalism, which, in turn, is located in – and must be understood through – its interaction with the world market. This nested hierarchy of states, centred around the GCC bloc, is the frame through which to interpret Western policy towards Egypt, Tunisia, Libya or any of the other states in the Middle East. [2]

The GCC's enormous oil supplies – estimated to surpass one-quarter of the world's production in the coming decades – clearly give the region a central importance to the strategic calculations of the leading capitalist states. But this essay attempts to step behind the question of oil as such, and contends that the reasons for the GCC's centrality to the hierarchies of the world market are ultimately found in two immanent tendencies of capitalism – the internationalization and financialization of capital. These tendencies give the Gulf's commodity exports and financial surpluses a particular significance within the global political economy. They have materialized the Gulf *as* a region within the world market – incorporating it into the specific power configuration that has characterized the global political economy over the last decade. A US-led world order, marked by internationalized circuits of capital stretching from the production of value in Asia to its realization in the advanced capitalist core, has rested to a considerable extent upon the way that the Gulf region has been both incorporated into this structure and dominated by US power.

As part of this framework, this analysis aims to go beyond both Marxist and mainstream analyses that treat the Gulf as simply a giant oil spigot, and refocus attention upon the region's own processes of class and state formation.[3] It will be shown that the particular insertion of the GCC into the world market has precipitated a process of class-formation in which a section of the Arab world has become ever-more closely tied to the continued maintenance of capitalism at a global scale. This has meant that the interests of the ruling classes in the Gulf are directly counterposed to those of the poor in the Middle East as a whole – a process reinforced by both the increasing imbrication of Gulf capital with the economies of other Middle East states and the deepening alignment of the Gulf states with the projection of US military and political power. This is the context in which the Arab uprisings have unfolded, and the ultimate reason for the GCC's central role in buttressing imperialist interest in the region.

INTERNATIONALIZATION, FINANCE AND THE WORLD MARKET

A central theme of contemporary Marxist debates over the nature of the global economy is how to understand the mutual interaction of hierarchically organized states and their relationship to the capitalist world market. A range of scholars have convincingly argued that Marx's own thought shows a deep pre-occupation with this theme and – contrary to a widely held belief – his starting point was not the 'closed national economy' but a theorization of the capitalist world market as a whole.[4] It is through an understanding of the abstract motion of accumulation at the level of the world market that national capitalist development is best interpreted. Integral to such an approach is a conception of imperialism – where the circuit of capital interlocks across national borders and reproduces hierarchies through value transfers between different geographical spaces.

One of the implications of placing the world market at the heart of any theoretical assessment of the nation-state is a necessary focus upon capital's tendency to internationalize.[5] Marx famously noted this tendency, commenting that capitalism acted to 'tear down every spatial barrier to intercourse, i.e. to exchange, and conquer the whole earth for its market … [as capital develops] the more does it strive simultaneously for an even greater extension of the market'.[6] This process describes the way in which social relations are increasingly intermeshed across the globe as capitalism expands its spatial reach. In its drive to augment value, capitalism necessarily pushes to expand the spatial boundaries in which it operates while simultaneously attempting to reduce the circulation time between different moments of its circuit (such as the moments of the production of value itself or that of its realization). Internationalization is thus not *external* to capital (i.e. the result of policies, laws or institutional factors) but immanent to the way in which capital *exists as capital*.

Internationalization is closely linked to a second feature of the circuit of capital, financialization. Like internationalization, finance arises as an immanent feature of capital's movement through its circuit. In this case, finance acts to overcome the potential barriers that emerge due to the fact that capital's movement is based upon phases that are 'separate in time and space, and appear as particular, mutually indifferent processes'.[7] These barriers indicate that the movement of capital is a necessary feature of its existence (value must first be produced and then realized) and, simultaneously, is a negation of that same existence (while capital is moving value is not being produced).[8] By re-directing money-capital from one part of the circuit to another, finance acts to supersede this discontinuous nature of the circuit of capital itself.

The role of the financial circuit in promoting and deepening internationalization has become particularly important over the last two decades. The specific hierarchical structure of the global economy that developed under neoliberalism acted to tightly integrate all nation-states into complex production chains – subordinating countries in the South, and necessitating ways to link circuits of capital across the world market. Money flows and new financial instruments were a key factor in overcoming the barriers to the circulation of capital that arose in this process, helping to knit together different moments of production, realization and speculation. Moreover, financial instruments such as derivatives enabled capitalists to manage (and speculate) on the risk associated with fluctuations in value that occur across time and space.[9] This process was reflected through the rapid increases in portfolio and FDI flows across borders, as well as the global expansion of stock markets and private firms dealing in financial instruments. The money-capital form thus acted to bridge varying turnover times of fixed and circulating capital, interlock the production and realization of value across different circuits, and tie together the past and future creation of value. As these circuits of capital intertwine across different spaces the reproduction of capital within a specific geographical space becomes more closely tied to the reproduction of other capitals at the international scale.[10] In short, the expansion of finance in the recent period can be seen as a *necessary* component of the deepening process of internationalization under neoliberalism.

THE GULF'S LOCATION IN THE WORLD MARKET

The interlinked processes of internationalization and financialization are important to understanding the significance of oil as 'circulating constant capital' and thereby the ways in which the Gulf has been integrated into the world market. In the post-Second-World-War period, internationalization proceeded rapidly as US companies expanded overseas and oriented their production towards international exports. Between 1959 and 1964, US companies set up international subsidiaries at the rate of more than 300 per year, more than ten times the pre-war rate.[11] New industrial sectors emerged at this time, most significantly the petrochemical industry, led by US multinationals such as Dow, Union Carbide and Standard Oil. The petrochemical sector substituted manufactured commodities such as plastics, synthetic fibres, pesticides, fertilizers and detergents, for naturally-occurring materials.[12] The internationalization of capital also necessitated a fundamental reconfiguration of the transport sector. Large-scale commercial land and air transit grew rapidly in the immediate post-war period as the first 'global' markets began to take shape. Mass automobile production developed as factories were built throughout Europe under US-backed reconstruction plans.

All of these developments were predicated on an increasing demand for inputs of energy and raw materials. Internationalization – precisely because it was premised upon *globally-oriented* production circuits – demanded large increases in energy use. Oil had become, in the words of Simon Bromley, a 'strategic commodity'.[13] It had a greater energy density than any other rival energy source, and its derivatives were ideal for powering automobiles and airplanes. Oil and natural gas supplied the necessary energy for industrial production and also formed the basic feedstock for new industries such as petrochemicals and transport. Initially, the bulk of the world's oil production had been located in Europe and the US, but following a wave of discoveries during the 1920s and 1930s, it was clear that the Gulf region of the Middle East – Saudi Arabia, Kuwait, Iraq, Iran and the smaller Gulf states – held the world's largest supplies of cheap and easily accessible hydrocarbons. By 1969 the Middle East had surpassed North America and Europe as the world's major supplier of oil, and by the mid-1970s, production in the Middle East was the same as their combined totals.[14]

The internationalization of capital thus rested upon the integration of the Gulf region into global capitalism. For this reason, the underlying basis of US power led inexorably towards US domination of the Middle East and, in particular, the incorporation of the Gulf states into a US-led global order. The story of this domination has been recounted in many places,[15] but, for the purposes of this essay, what is important to emphasize is that while oil was the proximate cause of US policy towards the region – behind the oil commodity lay the transformation of the world market itself. The 'internationalisation of the self-expansion of social capital' as Palloix described it, rested to a very great extent upon oil as circulating constant capital (both as energy and as a feedstock). It is this transformation of the social relations underpinning the character of the world market that explains how the Gulf was, in essence, formed by the world market itself.

THE GULF AND US FINANCIAL POWER

This process of internationalization became even more marked during the 1970s and it is at this time that the Gulf's importance to financialization definitively emerged. Policy shifts such as the development of offshore financial markets in Europe, the so-called Euromarket, Nixon's break with the dollar-gold standard in 1971, and the liberalization of foreign investment laws enabled financial flows to increase rapidly.[16] These changes in financial markets helped to further deepen internationalization as North American, European and Japanese companies borrowed prodigious amounts to finance overseas expansion and in doing so became truly 'multi-national'. The rising prominence of finance had very significant implications for the oil-producing Gulf countries. By the early 1970s, countries such as Saudi Arabia and Kuwait had negotiated better deals with US and European oil companies that gave them a greater share of oil revenues.[17] Following a steep rise in the price of oil in 1973 and again in 1979, these countries had begun to receive large amounts of money – which became known as petrodollars – that were redirected through new financial markets in Europe and elsewhere to multinational companies and banks and thus provided a key source of the credit that underpinned internationalization.[18] Furthermore, with poorer countries in Latin America, Africa and Asia facing massive deficits in the wake of the oil price rises, US banks extended loans to them from recycled petrodollars. In turn, this debt became a weapon used by international financial institutions such as the World Bank and IMF to compel these countries to open their productive, financial and commercial sectors to foreign ownership and thereby accelerate the internationalization of capital.[19]

These processes did not happen spontaneously. They were led and directed, by the special role of the US state that 'bore the burden – and had the accompanying capacity and autonomy – to take on the task of managing the system as a whole'.[20] The Gulf was critical to the strengthening of US power in this period in a number of different ways. First, by guaranteeing that the world oil trade would be denominated in US dollars, the US government ensured that its currency underlay trade in the world's most important commodity. In March 1978, US Treasury Secretary Michael Blumenthal secretly flew to Saudi Arabia in order to negotiate a deal with the Saudis to sell their oil solely in US dollars.[21] In return, the US offered Saudi Arabia extensive military and political support. The Saudis then used their influence as the world's largest producer to prevent the cartel of oil producing nations, OPEC, from pricing oil in a diversified basket of currencies.[22]

Furthermore, the US ensured that petrodollars accruing in the Gulf were invested in US dollar-denominated bank accounts, equities and treasury bonds. As David Spiro has documented, in 1974 an agreement was reached between the Saudi government and the US Treasury that saw Saudi Arabia deposit billions of dollars in the US Federal Reserve through a secret arrangement to buy US treasuries outside the normal auction for such securities.[23] Spiro notes that: 'Having agreed to invest so much in dollars, the Saudis now shared a stake in maintaining the dollar as an international reserve currency... dollars constituted 90 per cent of Saudi government revenues in 1979, and ... Saudi investments were, roughly at the same time, 83 per cent dollar denominated'.[24] At the level of OPEC as a whole, reserves held in US dollars increased from 57 per cent of total reserves to 93 per cent from 1973 to 1978.[25] In this manner, firstly as the world's chief supplier of oil and gas, and secondly as the source of prodigious amounts of surplus capital, the Gulf became a decisive geographical zone to the overall development of contemporary capitalism.

'GLOBALIZATION' AND THE POST-2000 PERIOD

The ways in which capitalism's tendencies of internationalization and financialization are materialized in the Gulf's relationship to the contemporary world market were strikingly demonstrated in the post-2000 period. The defining characteristics of this period – specifically, the shift of much of global manufacturing to Asia and the role that consumer and corporate debt played in maintaining consumption levels in the advanced capitalist countries – were profoundly linked to the Gulf's location in the global political economy and, simultaneously, have helped to transform the Gulf itself. This was illustrated in two main respects. First, the Gulf's commodity exports were essential to facilitating the new patterns of internationalization signified by the expansion of Asian manufacturing. Second, financial flows from the Gulf to US markets were critical to sustaining the uneven, debt-based consumption that characterized the post-2000 period.

With the internationalization of much of global manufacturing to Asia,

Middle East oil and gas exports began to turn eastwards. The world's energy consumption rose by nearly one-fifth from 2000-2006; with China alone making up 45 per cent of the global increase.[26] By 2006, China had become the third largest oil importer at a global level, despite the fact it held its own large reserves and was the sixth largest oil producer in the world. Essential to meeting the enormous Chinese demand for oil were exports from the Gulf region. Nearly one half of China's crude oil imports were coming from the Middle East in 2006, with Saudi Arabia the largest source of imports (around 16 per cent) and Oman and the UAE also significant sources.[27] These levels have continued to increase and, in early 2010, a spokesperson for Saudi Arabia's oil producing company, Aramco, revealed that Saudi oil exports to China had surpassed those to the US.[28]

The eastward shift of Gulf trade was not restricted to crude oil and gas; it was also reflected in Gulf petrochemical exports that provided a critical feedstock for Asian factories. In 2004, China imported about 42 per cent of globally traded polyethylene, 44 per cent of polypropylene, 45 per cent of PVC and 48 per cent of polystyrene.[29] Much of these basic petrochemical products were sourced from the Gulf region; the Saudi Arabian Basic Industries Company (SABIC), the most important petrochemical firm in the Middle East, was sending half its exports to Asia by the end of 2009.[30] All industry expectations expect these patterns to continue; indeed, the president of Exxon Mobil has predicted that the Middle East would be supplying three-quarters of the world's petrochemical exports in the next decade.[31]

PETRODOLLAR FLOWS

These shifts in the Gulf's energy and petrochemical exports thus underpinned the expansion of Asian-centred manufacturing in the post-2000 period. The Gulf region was the fulcrum around which this new phase of the global economy consolidated − its commodity exports providing the energy and raw materials that girded the expansion of internationalization. At the same time, the Gulf's role in enabling the new patterns of internationalization was paralleled by its significance to global financial processes, as the eastward shift of the Gulf's energy and commodity exports was matched with a massive increase in its pools of surplus capital.

A nearly ten-fold rise in the price of oil from 1999 to November 2007 ($9.76 per barrel to $90.32 per barrel) was the first phase in the growth of these petrodollar flows − with the revenues of oil exporting countries estimated to have risen at an annual rate of 27 per cent from 2002-2007. The second phase occurred in the wake of the 2007-08 global financial crisis, with the oil price dramatically reaching a peak of $145 a barrel in July of 2008 and revenues rising by a further 50 per cent.[32] These new waves of petrodollars were to largely flow westwards into US financial markets where they were recycled as credit for US consumers and businesses. They were thus a pivotal feature of the particular form that financialization of the global economy took in the post-2000 period.

David Lubin, an analyst with Citigroup, has measured what he calls the 'petrodollar effect' – the difference between the level of petrodollars in the global economy during the 1990s, and the increase following the meteoric rise in the world oil price. According to Lubin, from 2002-06 the extra liquidity arising from countries producing more than one million barrels/day of oil amounted to USD$1.02 trillion. For the Gulf alone, over USD $510 billion of extra liquidity was generated in the 2002-06 period.[33] This liquidity was reflected in the rapid increase in the current account surpluses of the Gulf countries, which the IMF estimated to be 22 per cent of GDP in 2007, the highest of any region in the world.[34]

Much of these surpluses were used to purchase foreign assets in the advanced capitalist core such as equities, bonds and real estate. The Institute for International Finance estimates that foreign assets of GCC central banks and government-related funds increased from $0.5 trillion at the end of 2002 to $1.6 trillion at the oil price peak in July 2008.[35] These figures, however, only include state-owned foreign assets. At the close of 2007, it was estimated that if the private investments held by GCC-based companies, individuals or ruling families were also included the total amount of foreign assets reached $2.2 trillion.[36] This figure was more than the assets held by China's central bank and exceeded the combined GDP of Australia and India for 2008.

Some caution is needed in attempting to determine the scale and nature of foreign asset ownership by the Gulf states. It was estimated in 2007, for example, that only 27 per cent of asset purchases by Middle East oil investors were identifiable.[37] The main reason for this opacity is the investment patterns of sovereign wealth funds (SWFs), large quasi-government agencies that have been established by many countries to manage natural resource revenues. The amount of money controlled by SWFs is huge: in 2007, the world's top 20 funds were estimated to control USD$2.1 trillion, bigger than the amount invested in both hedge funds and private equity funds.[38] The world's largest SWF, the Abu Dhabi Investment Authority, is located in the GCC. Estimates for its wealth ranged from $500 billion to almost $900 billion at the end of 2007 (the latter figure was equivalent to 461 per cent of UAE GDP or US$207,000 per UAE citizen).[39] In addition to the lack of clarity around SWF asset purchases, many individuals and private companies in the GCC own significant quantities of foreign assets but do not reveal them publically. Moreover, in some cases, different accounting methods are used by GCC government agencies to measure the value of assets held.[40]

Despite the difficulties in measuring these new Gulf petrodollar flows, it is clear that they were a major element in sustaining the high debt levels that characterized the US economy in the post-2000 period. Alongside the surpluses of Asian countries, they enabled the US to run a growing current account deficit and continue as the main zone of consumption for the mass of commodities produced in China and other low-wage areas across the globe. US Treasury data shows that Middle East oil exporters placed between 50-70 per cent of their identifiable petrodollars in US equities and bonds from 2002-2007.[41] From June 2005 to June 2006, GCC holdings of US securities increased by 50 per cent – more than any other country or region of the world.[42] Indeed, from 1998, petrodollar flows essentially switched places with Western Europe as the second major origin of global savings – matching those from East Asia.

IMPLICATIONS FOR THE GULF

The reconstitution of the global scale that underpinned the Gulf's insertion into contemporary capitalism has, contemporaneously, transformed social relations within the Gulf itself. In this sense, the GCC is best seen as 'internally related' to the capitalist world market – the interpenetration of the GCC's social relations with the motion of the world market is not external to those relations, but part of what actually constitutes them.[43] This means that the deepening of internationalization and financialization at the global scale is, itself, materialized in the ways that the GCC's own social relations develop.

This is confirmed concretely by the nature of class formation that typifies the GCC states.[44] The Gulf productive circuit is, in essence, oriented towards the production of circulating constant capital that feeds into internationalized circuits of accumulation; the productive circuit may be physically located in the Gulf but it is globally-oriented in nature. The productive circuit is thus centred around interlocked and extended circuits of capital aimed at the production of hydrocarbons and energy-intensive industries. This has shaped the nature of domestic capitalist accumulation in the productive circuit. Domestic capitalist firms in the Gulf are not directly involved in the production of crude oil – which remains largely the purview of the state and ruling family – but are heavily involved in the downstream production of petrochemicals, aluminium, steel and cement, power production and other infrastructure needs.

In the commodity circuit, large Gulf capitalists are characterized by their position as import agents and distributors for foreign commodity capital. This is reinforced by the bias within the Gulf productive circuit towards hydrocarbons and energy intensive industries, which weights the Gulf commodity circuit towards a reliance on the advanced capitalist countries for the external provision of basic consumer goods. As the commodity circuit expands and the levels of surplus capital in the region increase, Gulf capital has extended their involvement beyond a simple agency role into the ownership of retail outlets and malls.

The finance circuit of the Gulf is structured by the financialization of advanced capitalism. The large revenues flowing through the Gulf finance circuit (itself a reflection of the role of the Gulf productive circuit within the global economy) are critical to the stability of global capitalism and the maintenance of US hegemony. For this reason, the finance circuit occupies a disproportionate weight within the overall Gulf circuit of capital and is an important element in the formation of the dominant sections of the Gulf capitalist class. Every privately controlled commercial bank in the GCC is dominated by large domestic capital, often closely linked to state pension funds and investment authorities, which provide another mechanism for shifting capital flows originating in the hydrocarbon sector into the circuits of accumulation.

The form taken by the capitalist class around these circuits is typically that of large capitalist conglomerates – often established by merchant families or individuals close to the ruling family – that are strongly interpenetrated with the state structures. These conglomerates are generally active across all moments of the circuit of capital – the productive circuit (construction, energy-rich commodities such as aluminium, steel, concrete); the commodity circuit (agents and distributors of imported commodities, malls and shopping centres); and the financial circuit (banks, investment and private equity companies). This class has emerged alongside the state itself, benefitting from state contracts, agency rights, land grants and positions within the government bureaucracy.

Class formation is not solely a process of capital accumulation: it is necessarily accompanied by the development of a working class. The structure of the GCC working classes, once again, reflects the specific nature of the Gulf within the world market. Precisely because of the centrality of the GCC to contemporary capitalism, the GCC working class is strikingly characterized by temporary migrant labour.[45] In all GCC states, the majority of the labour force is constituted by migrant labour drawn from surrounding peripheries (such as India, Sri Lanka, Pakistan, Egypt, Yemen and the Philippines). This labour has a precarious and temporary existence; not only is it heavily exploited through differential conditions and wages, it is deportable at any sign of popular discontent. While this particular reliance on temporary migrant labour was made *possible* by the GCC's own low levels of population and skills shortage, its *actuality* needs to be seen as a particular form of social control. In such an environment, the possibilities for sustained class struggle or political organization become extremely difficult. In this sense, this particular structure underpins not only the continued reproduction of capitalism in the GCC, but also that of the Gulf's position in the world market as a whole. The contrast of this class structure with that found in neighbouring Iran and Iraq – energy rich states that do have their own indigenous working classes with rich histories of anti–imperialist struggle – indicates why the GCC has been so critical to the constitution of the capitalist world market.

The other feature of the region's class formation is the conjoining of the GCC ruling classes within a US-dominated 'power bloc'. The GCC state and capitalist classes have been very much incorporated – as a junior partner – into the projection of US power across the Middle East as a whole. This is reflected in their complete dependence upon US military protection. Indeed, the formation of the GCC in 1981 was, to a large extent, supported and promoted by the US as a means of bringing the Gulf Arab states under their military sphere of influence.[46] The headquarters of US Fifth Fleet, one of the most important US navy bases in the world, is located in Bahrain. And in 2003, the US announced that it was moving US Central Command (CENTCOM) forward headquarters — responsible for all US military engagement, planning and operations across 27 countries – from Florida to Qatar. Through these and other bases, GCC states have acted as the geographical hinterland for the US invasions of Afghanistan and Iraq.[47]

There is one further element to class formation in the GCC that is important to emphasize in the current context. Over the past decade, there has been a pronounced internationalization of GCC capital itself linked, as is always the case, with financialization processes. This is true at two scales. First, the GCC regional integration project is an institutional form that has encouraged the interpenetration of the GCC's own circuits of capital. The large capitalist conglomerates that have arisen within each of the GCC states are themselves internationalizing through the GCC space. This is shown in many sectors: cross-border activities of GCC construction companies, investments in petrochemical projects, share ownership on the regional stock markets, and – most markedly – in the development of private equity and other financial companies that bring together the largest GCC companies within single ownership structures. This process of internationalization is occurring around a Saudi–UAE axis and is indicative of a developing pan–GCC capitalist class.[48]

The second scale at which this internationalization has developed is the Middle East as a whole. GCC companies have aggressively expanded across the region taking large stakes in Middle East stock markets, real estate projects and banks. Indeed, investments from the Gulf in the Middle East and North Africa surpass those from any other region in the world, including North America and Europe.[49] In Iraq, for example, more than half of all FDI between 2003 and the end of 2009 came from the GCC.[50] GCC banks control four out of the six Iraqi banks with majority foreign ownership.[51] In Syria and Lebanon, FDI from the GCC was more than 70 per cent of the country's total FDI in 2008. For Jordan, GCC investors hold approximately 20 per cent of all market value on the Jordanian stock exchange.[52] This internationalization of Gulf capital proceeded in conjunction with the aggressive promotion of neoliberalism through the decade of the 2000s. Neoliberalism – with its associated policies of privatization, deregulation and market opening – was a necessary prerequisite to the expansion of Gulf ownership across the Middle East. In practice, this means that the region's capitalist classes are more and more tied to the reproduction of capitalism in the Gulf itself.[53]

THE GLOBAL CRISIS

The significance of this class structure was amply demonstrated following the 2008 economic crisis. Initially, the rapid drop in oil and other hydrocarbon prices from July to December 2008, accompanied by a reduction in the volume of oil sold, significantly reduced GCC government revenues. Current account surpluses plunged by half in most GCC states, and became deficits in the UAE and Oman. The value of foreign-held assets dropped as share and real estate markets in the US and elsewhere collapsed. Paralleling other regions of the world, there was a reversal of the financial flows that had gone to the GCC in the years preceding the crisis. These outflows were reinforced as GCC asset bubbles, particularly in real estate, began to deflate and investors attempted to move funds to safer and more stable investments outside of the region.

In response, GCC states pursued an economic strategy that aimed chiefly at supporting the position of the large Gulf conglomerates. As oil prices turned upwards in the second half of 2009, governments directed surpluses to assist these conglomerates and state entities. A range of massive construction and real estate projects were launched, most notably in Saudi Arabia. Precisely because of the internationalization of capital through the GCC, this project expansion acted to support construction companies from all GCC states. Companies that had previously been active in the UAE, for example, shifted their focus to Saudi Arabia to take advantage of expected projects in the Saudi market. These plans encompassed $1.4 trillion worth of projects from 2009 to 2015 – more than the combined GDP of the GCC countries in 2008.[54] At the same time, all GCC governments moved to support financial institutions against exposure to bad loans and the withdrawal of capital flows.

Alongside these measures, the particular structure of the GCC's working class – reflecting its high composition of temporary migrant labour – allowed firms to reduce their work forces (and halt the hiring of new labour) without concern to the possible impact of unemployment. Because residency rights in the GCC are explicitly linked to employment, it is impossible for a worker to remain in the GCC for any significant amount of time once they lose their job. As a consequence, thousands of temporary migrant workers returned home in the wake of the crisis, precipitating fears of a devastating drop in remittance flows to surrounding peripheries. Those workers remaining in the GCC frequently found that their working conditions deteriorated – as cuts in wages and benefits disproportionally targeted migrant labour. This was reflected in the large number of suicides of migrant workers across the Gulf. In Kuwait during March 2010, migrant workers were committing suicide at the rate of one every two days.[55] According to data compiled by Nepalese embassies in the Gulf, over 130 Nepalese workers killed themselves in the GCC in 2010.[56]

POLITICAL IMPLICATIONS AND FUTURE TRAJECTORIES

A clear implication of the above analysis is that the character of the Gulf's insertion into global circuits of accumulation will, to a very significant extent, shape the future trajectory of the world market. Moreover, the political, military and economic domination of the Gulf will be a central determinant of the ability of any state to project their power at the global scale. The GCC is thus an essential element (arguably *the* essential element) in assessing the possible course of US hegemony within the world system and the outcome of any challenges from rival claimants.

Possible scenarios for the development of both the Gulf's commodity exports and financial surpluses confirm this assessment. First, the Gulf's energy and petrochemical exports are likely to become ever more significant to capitalist production over the coming decades. The increased Chinese reliance on Gulf hydrocarbons is matched by the simultaneous dependence of the US, Europe and other key states on these same imports. More than one half of all the oil and gas consumed in the United States is imported –

close to one-fifth (19 per cent) of US consumption comes from the Middle East, mostly from Saudi Arabia (11 per cent of total imports).[57] For the EU, 90 per cent of oil needs and 70 per cent of gas needs will be supplied by imports by 2020 according to official estimates.[58] The EU already draws 45 per cent of its oil imports from the Middle East and in 2000 an EU commission remarked that there was an 'acute case of ... dependence' and that 'geographic diversification will not be as easily achieved as for natural gas, since the world's remaining oil reserves will increasingly be concentrated in the Middle East'.[59] India also depends heavily on Middle East oil, with the country predicted to overtake Japan to become the third largest oil importer by 2024, behind the United States and China.[60] Some 67 per cent of India's imports come from the Middle East, with the largest supplier, Saudi Arabia, accounting for 25 per cent of Indian crude oil imports. Overall, more than half of the world's energy comes from oil and gas and it is predicted that the share of the GCC in world oil production will increase to around 25 per cent by 2030. Likewise, GCC production of natural gas (mostly produced in Qatar) is estimated to meet around one-fifth of the expected increase in world demand over the coming years.[61]

The Gulf's financial surpluses will also undoubtedly increase. One set of estimates predicts, for example, that by 2013 the value of foreign assets held by the GCC would increase by around 77 per cent to the $3.8 trillion range if oil prices averaged at the $70 level of early 2010. This would be comparable to the value of foreign assets held by China. Even with a modest estimate of oil selling for USD $100 per barrel by 2013 (and there is a good chance it may well be higher), GCC foreign assets could reach $5.7 trillion by 2013, an increase of over 160 per cent from 2008 levels and exceeding China's foreign assets by around $1 trillion.[62] Foreign asset holdings of all 'petrodollar countries' (i.e. including Russia, Norway and oil producers in Latin America and Africa) will exceed those of the three other 'powerbrokers' (East Asia, hedge funds and private equity) in all scenarios. The GCC is distinguished, however, from all other surplus zones in the world market by its tight dependence upon US military and political support and the relative lack of domestic social pressures given the unique class structure that underpins capitalism in the region. For this reason, it is arguably the most important of all the surplus zones.

Given these trends, the interdependence of the GCC ruling elites and US interests is one of the most decisive relationships in the world today, and is the over-riding consideration in the making of US foreign policy in the Middle East. The importance of this relationship was well confirmed by the most intense and widespread of the 2011 uprisings in the GCC – that of Bahrain. Bahrain differs in many respects from the rest of the Gulf due to the more proletarianized character of its citizen population. The country relies heavily upon migrant labour but many of its Shia majority remain poor and face discrimination from the largely Sunni elite. This distinctive class structure has given Bahrain a longer history of trade union and left-wing struggles, which have overlapped with religious–sectarian differences (although, it must be emphasized, Bahraini opposition groups have been very careful to work across any sectarian divides). In this context, the uprising was viewed as not just a challenge to the ruling Al Khalifa monarchy but also to fundamental US interests in the GCC. The US government extended its explicit support to Bahrain's King Hamad Ibn Isa Al Khalifa, and undoubtedly gave the go-ahead for Saudi troops to intervene to suppress the protests on behalf of the Bahraini monarchy. The hundreds of Bahrainis who subsequently disappeared into torture chambers – some of whom lost their lives while imprisoned – were largely ignored by the Western media. For the US government, the maintenance of Al Khalifa rule was seen as synonymous with its own interests.

It may be difficult to imagine a significant rupture of the US-GCC relationship (particularly given the overwhelming US military hegemony in the area), but the structural interdependencies between the US and GCC ruling classes do not preclude a potential challenge to regional influence. Despite US military dominance of the GCC there are growing indications that China and other Asian states are developing greater economic weight in the region. An increasing proportion of GCC imports are sourced from Asia, while the share of US-GCC trade is dropping (it should be noted, however, that the EU continues to dominate exports to the GCC). Moreover, Asian companies (particularly South Korean, Chinese and Taiwanese) are now the leading force in the Gulf's lucrative engineering sector. It was noted above that Saudi oil exports to China now exceed those to the US, and by 2025 Chinese oil imports are predicted to reach three times US imports from the Gulf. In early 2010, a spokesperson for the world's largest oil producer, Saudi Arabia's Aramco, made the dramatic announcement that the Kingdom's 'eyes are focused on China'. It is almost certain that these trends foreshadow deeper political relationships between Asia and the GCC, potentially at the expense of the US.

Similarly, there are increasing financial links between the GCC and Asia. GCC companies – led by Aramco and SABIC – have made important strategic investments in Chinese petrochemical plants. In banking, one of the global centres of Islamic finance is Asia (particularly Malaysia), and GCC banks have extremely strong ties with Asian banks in this sector. These financial linkages portend a possible shift away from GCC investments in US markets towards those in Asia, and indeed, Nasser Saidi, the chief economist in Dubai's International Financial Centre, remarked in early 2010 that the Gulf 'will be dancing to a Chinese tune; this is a tectonic shift in economic and political power eastwards… this is where our future lies'.[63] SWF investments from the GCC confirm this prediction, with the world's largest fund, the Abu Dhabi Investment Authority (ADIA), announcing in 2010 that it had up to 20 per cent of its investments in Asia – up from a likely 10 per cent about a decade ago.[64]

However, a full appreciation of these contradictory rivalries and trends needs to take into account three essential factors. First, as this essay has repeatedly emphasized, the GCC should not be viewed in isolation from the neighbouring region to which it adjoins. The Gulf is viewed by all states competing for influence in the region as part of a larger energy-rich zone that encompasses Iraq, Iran and the Central Asian states. This zone is estimated to possess close to half of the world's total oil and gas reserves, as well as the largest areas of unexplored potential supplies.[65] The domination of this broader region is at the core of US foreign policy and the orientation of potential rival powers (such as China and Russia) towards Afghanistan, Iraq and Iran. The future direction of political development in the GCC will be partly played out through the lens of struggles in – and over – this wider area.

Second, and this is a vital point, the rivalries of competing states in the capitalist world market need to be seen alongside their shared interests. This essay has argued that the incorporation of GCC ruling classes into the leading hierarchies of the world market has been a necessary element to the way contemporary capitalism has formed; the position of these ruling classes is therefore supported by all advanced capitalist states regardless of conjunctural rivalries. Class formation in the GCC is deeply interpenetrated with the development of capitalism as a whole, and the greatest fear of any of the leading states in the world market – and this, it should be stressed, *includes* China and Russia – is a significant challenge to that class structure. It is, in other words, a shared concern of all leading capitalist states to ensure that the GCC remains fully aligned with the interest of world capitalism.

This brings us to the third key element in understanding the future trajectory of the GCC – the potential development of class struggles across the Middle East as a whole. A key theme of this essay has been the necessity of approaching the Middle East in its unity – with the GCC states located at the core of regional capitalist accumulation. Neoliberalism in the Middle East has emerged alongside (and acted to facilitate) the internationalization of

Gulf capital within this regional system. Gulf capitalist classes and ruling elites not only stand *with* the concentration of power and wealth that characterizes the Middle East today; they are a constitutive force of that concentration and necessarily stand *against* the vast majority of people in the Middle East. For this reason, it is impossible to treat the national and regional scales as two distinct political spheres – what appears at first glance to be 'national' struggles that are contained within individual nation-states, inevitably grow to confront the construction of these broader regional hierarchies and the Gulf's place within them.

A CHALLENGE TO CAPITALISM?

It is important for understanding the popular movements that swept the Arab world in the first half of 2011 to realize that the struggles to overthrow Ben Ali and Mubarak were not solely aimed at dictators in Tunis and Egypt: their logic also inevitably challenged the dominant relations of power across the region as a whole. This argument is not meant simply in the sense of 'contagion' or 'inspiration', as if the effects of these struggles were purely psychological in form. Rather, the social structures that characterized political rule in Egypt, Tunisia and elsewhere are themselves part of how the GCC – linked to the domination of broader internationalized capital – established its place atop the hierarchies of the regional market. This explains the furious attempts by the GCC states to hold back and derail these uprisings. It is also a further reminder of the inseparability of the 'political' and 'economic' spheres under capitalism. The struggles against despotism that the uprisings represented are, simultaneously, intertwined with the way that capitalism has developed across the region and, in this sense, are also struggles *against* the Gulf.

The salient feature of these uprisings is found precisely in what potentially lies beyond this challenge to the GCC states and the regional system. The logic of these struggles has raised the significance of wider unity in the Middle East, reversing the colonially-driven fragmentation of nation-states that only acts to reinforce the massively uneven development of the region. A glimmer of this powerful vision could be witnessed – albeit briefly – in the moment that Egypt, Tunisia and Libya were all seeming to move in a coherent revolutionary direction, raising the possibility of a contiguous, united North Africa for the first time in decades. The ever-sharpening polarization of wealth that characterizes the Middle East as a whole – accentuated, as discussed above, by the effects of the global economic crisis – can only be fully addressed through such a unified Middle East. This requires a genuinely revolutionary process that places the vast resources of the Middle East under the democratic and popular control of the working classes and poor of the region. This vision holds the sole possibility of exit from the decades-long cul-de-sac that has seen wealth and power concentrate in the hands of the ruling elites of the Gulf, supported by imperialism and the assortment of despotic regimes across the Middle East. This outcome represents not only a break with imperialist domination but, precisely because of the way that the GCC has formed alongside and within the world market, a fundamental challenge to capitalism at the global scale. It is this *revolutionary* potential of the Arab uprisings for the world market as a whole, which embodies the greatest fear of both the GCC ruling classes and all the imperialist states.

NOTES

1   This included assistance to the despised Ben Ali and Mubarak regimes in Tunisia and Egypt (Saudi Arabia eventually playing host to Ben Ali after his departure); a role as the main interlocutor between the US government and the Saleh regime in Yemen (attempting to blunt any fundamental challenge to Yemen's role as a client-state of the US); and the GCC's vocal call for NATO intervention in Libya. These initiatives made up the public face of GCC policy – much more is likely hidden in the phone calls, secret cables and diplomatic visits that co-ordinated the US, Europe and the Gulf along a largely single track in the first half of 2011.

2   A range of Marxist and radical thinkers have explored the relationship between oil and imperialism: some have argued that oil is increasingly critical to US power in an environment of declining supplies and tight supply, others place more emphasis on the potential profits that can be drawn from the control of this commodity, and a third set of arguments views oil as a 'potential chokehold on other leading powers', Alex Callinicos, 'Iraq: Fulcrum of World Politics', *Third World Quarterly*, 26, 2005, p. 599. For different approaches to the question of oil and imperialism, see: Simon Bromley, *American Hegemony and World Oil*, Cambridge: Polity Press, 1991; Simon Bromley, 'The United States and the Control of World Oil', *Government and Opposition*, 40(2), 2005, pp. 225–55; Michael Klare, *Resource Wars: The New Landscape of Global Conflict*, New York: Owl Books, 2002; John Bellamy-Foster, 'The New Age of Imperialism', *Monthly Review*, 55(3), 2003; David Harvey, *The New Imperialism*, Oxford: Oxford University Press, 2003, pp. 593–608; Doug Stokes, 'Blood for Oil? Global Capital, Counter-Insurgency and the Dual Logic of American Energy Security', *Review of International Studies*, 33(2), 2007, pp. 245–64.

3   When approaching the question of oil we need to be wary of a form of 'commodity fetishism' through which the nature of the Middle East is seen to be shaped by — to paraphrase Marx — a 'mystical' and 'grotesque' commodity divorced from the social relations in which it is embedded.

4   Marx notes, for example, that 'the transformation of the labour embodied in the product into social labour ...is only [possible] on the basis of foreign trade and of the world market. This is at once the pre-condition and the

result of capitalist production'. Karl Marx, *Theories of Surplus-Value,* Volume III, Moscow: Progress, 1971 [1862-3], p. 253; See Kevin Anderson, *Marx at the Margins: On Nationalism, Ethnicity, and Non-Western Societies,* Chicago: University of Chicago Press, 2010, for a discussion of how Marx's views of colonialism were premised on a conception of Britain, Ireland and the Southern slave-holding states of the US as existing within a single economy. Lucia Pradella, 'Imperialism and Capitalist Development in Marx's Capital', *Historical Materialism* (forthcoming 2012), makes a highly important contribution to this view of Marx's understanding of the world market, drawing upon an analysis of Marx's writings and notebooks on colonialism and pre-capitalist societies.

5   There is no space here to adequately deal with the extensive Marxist debate around internationalization and what this means for the nature of class and state formation at the level of the world market. An important point to emphasize, however, is that internationalization should not be interpreted as simply the increasing traversal of capital across nation-state borders. As Christian Palloix pointed out in the 1970s: 'Such a definition would then be purely descriptive and not theoretical. The "internationalization" of the self-expansion of social capital is defined by the fact that the process of converting the functional "money" form into the commodity form and into the productive form (and vice versa) can no longer be fully realized inside of a single capitalist social formation. In effect, the central element in this process of transformation, the commodity, is no longer produced in one nation. It is no longer limited in this way. The commodity, or rather the commodity-group, can only be conceptualized, produced, and realized at the level of the world market.' Christian Palloix, 'Conceptualizing the Internationalization of Capital', *Review of Radical Political Economics,* 9(2), 1977, p. 20.

6   Karl Marx, *Grundrisse,* Harmondsworth: Penguin Books, 1973, p. 539.

7   Ibid., p. 534.

8   Credit, in this sense, aims to bring about 'circulation without circulation time'. Roman Rosdolsky, *The Making of Marx's Capital,* London: Pluto Press, 1977, p. 393.

9   Leo Panitch and Sam Gindin, 'Finance and American Empire', *Socialist Register 2005,* p. 64.

10   Christian Palloix, 'The Internationalization of Capital and the Circuit of Social Capital', in H. Radice, ed., *International Firms and Modern Imperialism: Selected Readings,* Harmondsworth: Penguin, 1975, p. 76.

11   Nigel Grimwade, *International Trade: New Patterns of Trade, Production, and Investment,* New York: Routledge, p. 119.

12   The petrochemical industry depended upon petroleum and natural gas as the primary feedstock, in contrast to pre-war production that had utilized coal. See Peter Spitz, *Petrochemicals: The Rise of an Industry,* New York: John Wiley, 1988 and Keith Chapman, *The International Petrochemical Industry: Evolution and Location,* Oxford: Blackwell, 1991, for detailed histories.

13   Bromley, *American Hegemony,* p. 82.

14   Figures for oil production from BP, 'Annual Statistical Review', 2007, available at http://www.bp.com.

15   See Bromley, *American Hegemony*, for an excellent account. For more detailed histories of individual GCC states, see Jill Crystal, *Oil and Politics in the Gulf: Rulers and Merchants in Kuwait and Qatar,* Cambridge: Cambridge University Press, 1995; Kiren Chaudry, *The Price of Wealth: Economies and Institutions in the Middle East*, New York: Cornell University Press, 1997; Rosemary Zahlan, *The Making of the Modern Gulf States*, London: Ithaca Press. 1998; Alexei Vassiliev, *The History of Saudi Arabia*, London: Saqi Books, 1998; Robert Vitalis, *America's Kingdom: Mythmaking on the Saudi Oil Frontier*, Stanford: Stanford University Press, 2007.

16   See Barry Eichengreen, *Globalizing Capital,* Second Edition, Princeton: Princeton University Press, 2008 for an account of these processes.

17   Bromley, *American Hegemony*; Anthony Sampson, *The Seven Sisters. The Great Oil Companies and the World They Made*, New York: Bantam, 1976; Pierre Terzian, *OPEC, the Inside Story*, Translated by M. Pallis, London: Zed Books, 1985.

18   David Spiro, *The Hidden Hand of American Hegemony: Petrodollar Recycling and International Markets*, Ithaca, NY: Cornell University Press, 1999; For an account of the development of Eurodollars, see Heather Gibson, *The Eurocurrency Markets, Domestic Financial Policy and the International Instability*, London: Macmillan, 1989.

19   Ngaire Woods, *The Globalizers: The IMF, The World Bank, and Their Borrowers*, Ithaca: Cornell University Press, 2006.

20   Panitch and Gindin, 'Finance and American Empire', pp. 54-55.

21   Internal US Treasury memo from Assistant Treasury Secretary C. Fred Bergsten to Treasury Secretary W. Michael Blumenthal, entitled, 'Briefing for Your Meeting with Ambassador to Saudi Arabia, John C. West', 10 March 1978 (cited in William Clark, *Petrodollar Warfare: Oil, Iraq and the Future of the Dollar*, Gabriola Island, British Columbia: New Society Publishers, 2005).

22   Spiro, *The Hidden Hand*, pp. 105-126.

23   Ibid., p. 109.

24   Ibid., pp. 122-123.

25   Congressional Budget Office (CBO), 'The Effect of OPEC Oil Pricing on Output, Prices, and Exchange Rates in the United States and Other Industrialized Countries', Washington, DC: CBO, 1981, p. 35.

26   International Energy Agency (IEA), *World Energy Outlook 2007: China and India Insights,* France: IEA, 2007, p. 54.

27   IEA, *World Energy Outlook*, p. 325.

28   Saudi Gazette, 'Aramco: China Overtakes US as Largest Customer', 6 April 2010.

29   Nexant Chem Systems, 'Outlook for the Petrochemical Industry: Good Times Ahead', Argentina: Instituto Petroquimico Argentino, 2004, p. 31.

30   SABIC is the largest company in the Middle East and ranks as the world's largest producer of many basic petrochemical products. It is the third largest polyethylene manufacturer, the fourth largest polyolefins manufacturer and the fourth largest polypropylene manufacturer.

31   Isabel Ordonez, 'Exxon VP: Global Petrochemical Trade To Double In 10

Years', *Dow Jones Newswire*, 29 April 2010.

32   McKinsey Global Institute, *The New Power Brokers: How Oil, Asia, Hedge Funds, and Private Equity Are Shaping Global Capital Markets*, San Francisco: McKinsey Global Institute, 2009, p. 2, available at http://www.mckinseyquarterly.com.

33   David Lubin, 'Petrodollars, Emerging Markets and Vulnerability', *Economic and Market Analyses*, Citigroup, 19 March 2007, p. 8.

34   International Monetary Fund (IMF), *World Economic Outlook,* Washington, DC: International Monetary Fund, 2007, p. 29.

35   Institute for International Finance (IIF)', Summary Gulf Cooperation Council Countries', 6 November 2008, p. 2.

36   McKinsey, *The New Power Brokers*, p. 7. McKinsey Global Institute estimates that four countries held most of the GCC's foreign assets in 2008: Saudi Arabia ($780 million), UAE ($870 million), Kuwait ($300 million) and Qatar ($140 million).

37   Rami Tolui, 'Petrodollars, Asset Prices, and the Global Financial System', *Capital Perspectives*, PIMCO, 2007, p. 7.

38   Martin Wolf, 'The Brave New World of State Capitalism', *Financial Times,* 16 October 2007.

39   Estimates are from Karim Solh, 'The Emergence of Regional and Global Investment Leaders out of Abu Dhabi', paper presented on behalf of Gulf Capital to the Abu Dhabi Economic Forum 2008 Emirates Palace, Abu Dhabi, February 3-4, p. 9 and Brad Setser and Rachel Ziemba, 'GCC Sovereign Funds: Reversal of Fortune', Council on Foreign Relations Working Paper, January 2009.

40   See Setser and Ziemba, 'GCC Sovereign Funds', for a discussion of these issues.

41   Michael Sturm, Jan Strasky, Petra Adolf, and Dominik Peschel, 'The Gulf Cooperation Council Countries, Economic Structures, Recent Developments and Role in the Global Economy', European Central Bank, Occasional Paper Series, No. 92, July 2008, p. 42.

42   Ibid., p. 43.

43   This concept of 'internal relations' is based upon Bertell Ollman's reading of Marx's philosophy. Ollman argues that we should not see 'things' as being discrete, but rather, any object under study needs to be seen as 'relations, containing in themselves, as integral elements of what they are, those parts with which we tend to see them externally tied'. See Bertell Ollman, *Dance of the Dialectic: Steps in Marx's Method*, Illinois: University of Illinois Press, 2003, p. 25.

44   For a detailed analysis of the process of class formation in the GCC states, see Adam Hanieh, *Capitalism and Class in the Gulf Arab States*, New York: Palgrave-MacMillan Publishers, 2011.

45   This argument is fully developed in ibid.

46   At the time, with the Iran-Iraq war ongoing through the 1980s, the US encouraged Saudi Arabia to host four US Air Force Airborne Warning and Control Aircraft (AWAC), which provided refuelling capacities for US aircraft. Other Gulf states bought air systems from the US that could be connected

with the AWAC network, thus establishing a pan–GCC air defence system under US control. (Joe Stork and Martha Wenger, 'US Ready to Intervene in Gulf War', *MERIP Reports*, 14(6-7), 1984, p. 45). By 2005, according to a US congressional report, over 100,000 US military personnel were located in the Gulf states (in addition to the approximately 130,000 in Iraq or security personnel operating under civilian firms). See Kenneth Katzman, 'The Persian Gulf States: Issues for U.S. Policy', Washington, DC: Congressional Research Service, Library of Congress, 2006, p. 10.

47   Moreover, the GCC (particularly Saudi Arabia and the UAE) are among the largest purchasers of US military equipment in the world (illustrated in 2010 when the US government announced its biggest ever military sale – $60 billion of hardware to Saudi Arabia). This military equipment is maintained and dependent upon US contracts, thus further tying the GCC within a US military umbrella.

48   See Hanieh, *Capitalism and Class*, 2011.

49   World Bank figures recorded that Gulf countries were responsible for 36 per cent of the total foreign investments in the area in 2008, surpassing those of North America (31 per cent of total investments), Europe (25 per cent), Asia (4 per cent), and the other MENA countries (3.5 per cent). See: World Bank, *From Privilege to Competition Unlocking Private-Led Growth in the Middle East and North Africa*, Washington, DC: World Bank, 2009, p. 56.

50   Dunia Frontier Capital (DFC), 'Private Foreign Investment in Iraq', 2009, p. 4, available at http://www.dfcinternational.com.

51   National Investment Commission (NIC), 'Investment Overview of Iraq', Republic of Iraq, 2009, p. 82.

52   Calculated by author from analysis of Amman Stock Exchange data.

53   For an analysis of this in relation to the Palestinian West Bank, see Adam Hanieh, 'The Internationalization of Gulf Capital and Palestinian Class Formation', *Capital & Class,* 35(1), 2011, pp. 81-106.

54   McKinsey, *The New Powerbrokers*, p. 6.

55   Documentation of these deaths was not widely covered in the media, the only online source that drew attention to these deaths was http://www.migrant-rights.org.

56   'Over 800 workers died abroad, 160 suicides', *The Himalayan Times*, 13 January 2011.

57   Iraq, Algeria and Kuwait are also among the top Middle East oil exporters to the US according to data drawn from US Department of Energy, Energy Information Administration, available at http://eia.doe.gov.

58   European Commission (EC), *Green Paper – Towards a European Strategy for the Security of Energy Supply*, Luxembourg: Office for Official Publications of the European Communities, 2000, p. 18.

59   Ibid., p. 20.

60   IEA, *World Energy Outlook*, p. 495-6.

61   Institute for International Finance, 'GCC Regional Overview', 28 September 2009, p. 9.

62   McKinsey, *The New Powerbrokers*, p. 46.

63 Nasser Saidi, 'Our Future Lies to the East', *Arabian Business*, 15 February 2010, p. 34.

64 'Abu Dhabi ADIA Sees Substantial Risk to Global Economy', *Khaleej Times*, 11 January 2010.

65 Bernard Gelb, 'Caspian Oil and Gas: Production and Prospects', Washington, DC: Congressional Research Services, 2006, p. 3.

THE SINGULARITIES OF LATIN AMERICA

CLAUDIO KATZ

At a time of global turbulence created by the recent economic crisis, the disturbances in Latin America have been relatively limited. The global recession had a strong impact in 2009, but 2010 has been a year of recovery. In contrast with the terrible convulsions of the 1980s and 1990s the banks were able to tolerate the upheaval; there were no significant bankruptcies or modifications in public or private debt. The currencies continued to appreciate, and the stock markets reflected the sustainability of business activity in the region. The growth rate once again exceeded 5 per cent. Exports are also up, and foreign investment is on the rise.[1] The localization of the crisis in the developed countries and the European periphery could have not only material but also important political and ideological consequences for Latin America.

But nobody knows if this respite will persist. The continued price increases for raw materials support the current growth but recreate a vulnerable model based on basic exports, under the leadership of the most transnationalized dominant classes. Moreover, in a highly unequal regional context, there is always the possibility of an abrupt return to the severe impacts endured in the past. The attenuated repercussions of the tremor in South America were not as moderate elsewhere in the region. Because of its close dependence upon the US market, Mexico suffered a strong recession, and the small economies of the Caribbean are seeing a decline in remittances. The climate of uncertainty that prevails in Mexico is in stark contrast to the capitalist euphoria that exists in Brazil.[2]

Furthermore, while the greatest comfort from the relative buoyancy at the macro-economic level is felt by the dominant classes, it has not resulted in significant improvements in employment or income for the majority of the population. Structural poverty and labour precariousness continue to widen the social gap in the region. Latin America still has the highest international indices of inequality, and this inequity tends to grow during phases of both economic growth and recession. The class polarization this signals intensifies social deterioration, as is evidenced in the increase in the crime rate, the destruction of agrarian communities, the massification of urban marginality and the collapse of the public school system.[3]

Yet as we shall see in this essay, the specific class effects of the crisis have played themselves out in very different ways in right-wing, centre-left and more radical governments of the left, and in the different contexts of popular advances and retreats.

THE IMPACT OF DESYNCHRONIZATION

The limited regional impact of the current crisis is, first and foremost, the result of large adjustments Latin America had already undergone through previous crises at various points over the previous three decades, including a significant cleansing of banks, a major restructuring of companies and a brutal devalorization of the labour force, which restored the profitability of the principal firms. But the attenuated effect of the crisis is also to some extent the result of the different impacts the upheaval brings to bear on the centre, the periphery and the semiperiphery of capitalism. While in developed economies recession becomes widespread and in the outer periphery impoverishment continues, a group of intermediate countries – of which Brazil is the leading one in Latin America alongside China and India in Asia – are in an advantageous position in the global production chain and can benefit from the new importance of their natural as well as human resources, which shows up today in the sustained rebound in the prices of raw materials.

These changes in the context, cycle and objective location of the crisis create a regional respite, which orthodox economists attribute to other causes. They argue that the moderate nature of the convulsion is thanks to fiscal discipline. They point to reserves that exceed the historical average and a falling level of foreign debt. They contend that the prosperity of the period from 2003 to 2008 allowed tax revenues to be accumulated, which are now used to sustain the current level of economic activity.[4] But the existence of these resources is not a reward for moderation. Rather, it is the result of earlier social adjustments over the past thirty years that so severely affected the majority of the population. Neoliberals also ignore the unstable and ephemeral nature of recent economic fortunes, which can quickly be reversed if the stock market, real estate or currency bubbles created by the entry of foreign capital burst.

Heterodox economists offer a different explanation. They consider that the limited regional nature of the crisis is a result of state intervention by progressive governments, which were able to sustain demand and consumption with policies not included in the neoliberal recipe book.[5] But in reality, governments of all political stripes reacted to the global recession in a similar fashion, combining Keynesian short-term stimulus initiatives with longer-term austerity measures of fiscal balance. This state regulation has offset the crisis, but it is not of a clear anti-neoliberal nature.

A broader perspective is required to understand what is taking place in Latin America today. It is clear that the recession, having started in the United States – with mortgage failures, bankruptcies in the world of finance and troubles with public debt – has persisted there despite the supremacy of the dollar and the global importance of the Federal Reserve. It is also worthy of note that Japan is being hit by deflationary troubles and that Europe cannot establish a continental state that can guarantee the strength of its currency. This localization of the crisis in the imperial centres refutes the enduring myth that Latin America is responsible for every tremor. All the neoliberal arguments that attribute the economic troubles in the region to the lack of discipline, irresponsibility or corruption of the Latinos are losing credibility.

The searing impact of the crisis on the European periphery recalls what Latin America experienced in the 1980s and 1990s. The kinds of liquidity and commodity surpluses that the United States used to export to its neighbours in the South have come to be exported by Germany and France to the most fragile economies of the peripheral states of Europe. Taking advantage of very similar forms of public indebtedness, metropolitan surpluses were unloaded on the two dependent regions, and this displacement undermined their fiscal stability. Similarly, the kinds of adjustments the United States imposed in its backyard are now being imposed on the weakest countries in Europe, requiring the peripheral states to take on the insolvency of their domestic capitalists, and the people to bear the entire cost of rescuing the creditors. The same taxes that Uruguay, Bolivia and Ecuador once endured are now being imposed in Iceland, and the same recipes that the IMF unleashed upon Venezuela and Peru are now applied to Portugal and Ireland. Just as social democrats as well as conservatives in Latin America undertook to destroy earlier social gains so do we now see this being replicated in Portugal, Ireland, Greece and Spain.[6]

The most striking comparison is Argentina in 2001 and Greece in 2010, not just in terms of the uncontrolled amount and fraudulent nature of the public debt, but in terms of the neoliberal reorganization of the economy involving very similar policies of privatization and labour flexibility. The loss of monetary sovereignty has been similar, as has the disastrous effects of trade openness on national production. If the Greek economy continues down the same path that Argentina did, it will end up defaulting on its debt as well. These repetitions of the Latin American precedent demonstrate the roving nature of recent crises, as they move across different regions of the planet provoking unspeakable suffering. These convulsions are the consequence of intrinsic imbalances in contemporary capitalism. Since they are not merely a result of excess speculation, they cannot be resolved just with greater regulation.

UNIFORMITY AND DIVERSITY

Many factors have a bearing on how mild the crisis has been so far in Latin America. But the most influential one is the boost supplied by the high international prices of raw materials, which are mainly due to China's ongoing demand for primary products. This increase in prices stimulates growth, but in the medium term it consolidates the role of Latin America as a supplier of primary goods, moving it away from the industrialization seen in Asia. The old regional dependency on international fluctuations in the prices of metals, foods and fuel is thus consolidated, reinforcing the dominance of the extractive model. This is why large infrastructure projects tend to guarantee exports with little added value and only minor processing. Foreign investment validates this tendency by being heavily concentrated in the production of basic goods.[7]

Orthodox economists observe this development and assume that Latin America's passive adaptation to its 'comparative advantages' will favour regional development. On these grounds they call for additional neoliberal measures to draw in imports as well as further liberalize the financial system. Their fascination with the illusory benefits of the export model reprises a two-century long tradition of free trade delusions under the hegemony of the region's old oligarchic elite and its foreign trade practices. What is new is the support that heterodox economists offer to this system. Their support goes against the industrialist trajectory of a current of thought – led by CEPAL (the Economic Commission for Latin America) – that has always challenged the disastrous consequences of the agricultural and mining export model. Now they are forgetting about the damaging effects of being dependent upon the sale of primary products. They forget that this dependency increases the vulnerability of the region.

The dominance of primary exports perpetuates poverty and drives out the rural population, without creating jobs in urban areas. These old problems are aggravated by the environmental devastation caused by open-pit mining, deforestation and the irrational use of the soil to further extend monocultures.

The renewed dominance of the extractive model is being seen throughout the region, but in each country it is played out under different conditions. This variation is not only a result of economic factors. It is also a result of the different processes that are reconfiguring the profile of the dominant classes, under specific governments and multiple forms of popular resistance.

It is in this diversity of national situations that the transformation of the large capitalist groups is taking place. This change has consolidated the replacement of old national bourgeoisies, who promoted the domestic market, with new local 'interior bourgeoisies', who prioritize exports and their associations with transnational companies. One manifestation of this change is the importance attained by the new multinational companies, which operate with mixed (foreign and domestic) capital to exploit primary resources.[8]

This transnationalization is taking place in two different ways, one (especially in Mexico) involving stronger ties with the United States and the other (particularly in Brazil and Argentina) an increasing diversification of clients, trading partners and markets. We have not seen the economy placed entirely in foreign hands nor simple transnational domination in any of these cases. New forms of association prevail between concentrated domestic groups and the foreign financial sector. The bloc of bankers, agribusinesses and manufacturing exporters, which replaced the old industrial bourgeoisies of Brazil, Argentina and Mexico, promote closer relations with the central economies and support a range of investment treaties to guarantee the mobility of capital. The recent incorporation of these three principal countries of the region into the G-20 illustrates the strengthening of this alliance. Another manifestation of the same convergence is the resigned acceptance of the IMF's role in the management of the global crisis. Mexico has already requested a new loan, Brazil contributed new capital and Argentina is negotiating a return to the organization. All this is part of the region being open for business even if this is aimed at attracting new trading partners.

The limited way in which the crisis has presented itself has so far not produced the typical financial turbulence that periodically shakes the region. But this apparent calm hides two important potential imbalances. On one hand, the increasingly foreign-owned regional financial system is a time machine, as foreign institutions become an automatic channel for the flight of capital in moments of instability. On the other hand, the financial stability scenario is a double-edged weapon, as it creates dangerous bubbles. Short-term capital arrives in the region in order to make a profit out of the ups and downs of stocks, currencies and real estates. The well-known destablizing effects generated by the arrival of speculative capital have led to the establishment of new restrictions (especially in Brazil). But if these operations maintain their profitability, barriers may be overcome by other means.

GOVERNMENTS AND FORMS OF RESISTANCE

At the political level, regional diversity is more pronounced. After its two decade-long run, the right-wing neoliberal consensus no longer holds sway in the region. There are neoliberal, repressive, pro-American administrations opposed to any social improvements (Mexico, Colombia, Peru). There are also centre-left governments that maintain ambiguous relationships with the United States, tolerate democratic victories and utilise large-scale social programmes (Brazil, Argentina). Alongside these two more or less pro-establishment types of administration, a new type of reformist government has emerged that not only pursues popular goals but mobilizes the masses in confrontations with imperialism and the local dominant classes (Venezuela, Bolivia).[9]

The pre-eminence of any one of these three types of administration is heavily influenced by the degree of mobilization (or demobilization) displayed by the workers, peasants and 'precarious' people in each country. Despite Latin America's current reputation as a great hotbed of anti-neoliberalism, the entire region has not been affected by the uprisings that generated such an image. These actions exceeded national borders, but their impacts were principally felt in Bolivia, Ecuador, Venezuela and Argentina, where we have seen large rebellions behind revoking privatizations, nationalizing natural resources and democratizing political life. These uprisings reflected the vitality of anti-imperialist, democratic and anti-capitalist traditions, they widely surpassed the normal conventions of social protest, they improved conditions for securing popular victories, and they have enabled the partial reversal of the series of popular defeats upon which neoliberalism was established. But they did not involve challenges to the capitalist nature of the state, nor develop forms of popular power or military outcomes that characterize social revolutions.

The same type of rebellion was seen in the resistance employed by the oppressed in Honduras to oppose the coup d'état, and an extension of such forms of mass action can currently be seen in the defence of natural resources. These mobilizations could take on the same weight that the battle against the IMF and the payment of the debt had a decade ago. Bolivia's 'gas war', the Amazonian protests in Peru against the privatization of the forests and the struggles in Argentina against the pulp mills exemplify this new tendency. But this vigour displayed by social movements in several parts of the hemisphere coexists with a context of social movement retreat in countries of great size and regional importance. In some areas, this decline is due to the intensity of state repression (Colombia), and in others it is because of successive defeats (Mexico). In some cases, this regression is a political consequence of the stabilization that conservative and social-democratic governments have successfully been able to establish (Brazil).

The current singularities of Latin America are therefore determined by shared tendencies toward extractive models on the economic level and by similar processes of transnational ties among the dominant classes. But both processes have developed under different governments and levels of popular resistance. This combination also determines how the crisis is currently being dealt with, following three different approaches to regional integration and economic policy.

FREE TRADE ORTHODOXY

Under the new international conditions, right-wing governments have reaffirmed their strategy of free trade and neoliberal orthodoxy. They attempt to strengthen their ties to the United States by signing bilateral trade agreements. Following the failure of the Free Trade Area of the Americas (FTAA) initiative, the world superpower has once again taken up several agreements of this nature in order to secure its supply of Latin American resources. The United States is attempting to recreate its pre-eminence in a region that is crucial for absorbing many of its manufacturing exports. The giant of the North needs to be able to rely on the markets in its own backyard in order to offset the devaluation of the dollar with significant increases in its foreign sales.[10] The natural wealth of Latin America has become internationally disputed terrain which the United States does not wish to share with its rivals. The US thus seeks to recover ground it has lost to European capital – capital that without challenging the military pre-eminence or political leadership of the US has increased its business in the region. The current crisis is seen, then, as an opportunity to take back this influence, especially by minimizing the role of the Spanish firms, which acquired services, banks and oil deposits during the wave of privatizations.

The United States is also trying to curb the incursion of China into a region far from its sphere of action in the East. As the presence of China represents a very serious challenge to the hegemony of the North, the State Department is pushing the ratification of new trade agreements, especially with its partners on the Pacific coast. Mexico, Colombia, Peru, Chile and several small Central American countries accept this US strategy of recomposition while reconfiguring its dominance in Latin America.

The continuity of orthodox economic policies of privatization and labour deregulation strengthens this endorsement. Mexico insists on maintaining the financial dictatorship of its central bank and on sustaining a system of dependency upon its neighbour. This relationship is based on industrial *maquilas* with low competitivity, fragmentary technologies and brutal forms of exploiting the labour force. This model has caused the disarticulation of the old Mexican manufacturing framework and the consequent consolidation of the country as an oil supplier for its powerful client.[11]

The same policy of continued neoliberalism predominates in Colombia, Peru and Chile. These countries are increasingly being established as suppliers of raw materials based on the export of minerals. The dependency of some Andean countries on copper, silver and gold extraction is once again reaching the proportions of the colonial era. But, as the overall level of economic activity is increasing in tandem with this looting, a climate of acceptance has been created around this model. Government officials and ruling-class ideologues promote this legitimation, concealing the exclusive benefits that accrue to foreign companies and their domestic partners. The media play a decisive role in communicating these justifications. They have converted all the myths of neoliberalism into accepted beliefs among significant segments of the population. These deceptions are renewed with the systematic manipulation of information. Newspapers, the radio and the television set the political agenda, stimulate conservative values and foster middle-class resentment toward more impoverished sectors.

The close alliance between conservative governments and the United States that sustains this ongoing process of neoliberalism includes an inescapable military component. The Pentagon resurrected the 4th Fleet in the Caribbean and installed new military bases in Colombia to reinforce a rapid intervention system throughout the region. It aims to forestall the destabilizing consequences of current economic policies. The invasion of Haiti following the earthquake is an example of this type of action. It illustrates how the marines take control of a territory with humanitarian pretexts in order to prevent the entry of refugees into the US.

The coup in Honduras is just one more example of this same tendency, as it would have failed in just five minutes without the support of the American embassy. This demonstrated that coups are not a relic of the past, but still can be used in critical situations to introduce new 'post-Banana Republic' dictatorships. It also illustrated how local dominant elites resort to US military support to neutralize any possibility of political or social reform. The terrible militarization created by the advance of drug trafficking in Mexico can be understood as part of the same process.[12]

The increasing deployment of American troops in Latin America is forging a network of protection for capital, preparing to face the adversities that a future crisis could present. The marines are not only there to defend the interests of US companies. They prop up their local partners and construct barriers to contain the flow of emigration of the dispossessed toward the North. But these policies of free trade and repression no longer have the same support they were able to count on in the early days of neoliberalism. They are facing greater economic limits and growing political opposition, especially in South America.

REGIONALISM AND HETERODOXY

The centre-left governments support a different regional plan, which combines capitalist regionalism and more heterodox economic policies. They seek to develop the trade integration created with the MERCOSUR (Southern Common Market) in order to favour the interests of the principal dominant classes of the region. Brazil has always led the way on this path, but we are now seeing a new strengthening of this country as a regional power. Though in recent years the Brazilian economy has sustained a slow rate of growth, the expansion of its multinational firms is apparent. Most of the business of these companies combines traditional agricultural exports and the new production of soybeans and ethanol. To defend these interests they have prevented all inklings of agrarian reform, and to extend the international placement of their products they promote opening up the domestic market to imported goods.

But unlike the rest of the region, Brazil maintains a significant industrial structure. Though its manufacturing network does not operate with the latest technology – not only in comparison with the central economies but also with its Asian competitors – it has managed to establish itself in the region. This foundation enables it to manufacture the basic products it exports to all the economies of South America. The expansion of the Brazilian multinationals has awoken certain expectations with respect to the eventual consolidation of an economic driving force for regional development. Yet such hopes will run up against the transnational character of these companies and the conflicts that result from the everyday operation of these firms. Far from displaying more benevolent behaviour than their counterparts in Europe and the United States, these companies spark strong tensions with the region's small countries. These conflicts in turn fuel important internal tensions among the Brazilian elites between those in favour of unmitigated support and those that urge only conditional support for these companies.[13]

Brazil's capitalist expansion has its geopolitical correlate in increased military spending. Those governing the country must demonstrate a capacity to act at the regional level and with sufficient force to protect the wealth of the Amazon. They need to project this image in order to lend weight to their repeated attempts to gain a seat on the United Nations Security Council. Brazilian diplomacy works in two directions simultaneously, undertaking initiatives both with greater autonomy and with stronger ties to the United States. It is at once driving the development of an OAS without the world's superpower and engaging in a military occupation of Haiti in close contact with the Pentagon. Brazil's dominant class hopes to fill the spaces opened up by the US crisis in order to bolster its influence in hegemonic cooperation and coordination with American power.

This behaviour is analogous to that developed in Asia, Europe and Africa by other rising, mid-sized economies. But Brazil has neither nuclear arms nor a tradition of military expansion. Furthermore, its economic and strategic relationship with the United States is not as problematic as that of Russia, China or India. It is clear that Brazil continues to be quite a distance from the leadership of the western giants, but it has already left behind its former condition of being a politically subordinated and economically subjugated country.[14]

Brazil's regional influence is consistent with the volume of its production and the size of its domestic market. But a strong contributing factor has been the continuity and durability of the neoliberal economic orientations of the dominant groups, which are implemented by the state bureaucracy. This has been evident in the multiple connections between the explicit neoliberalism implemented by Fernando Henrique Cardoso and the toned-down neoliberalism implemented by Lula. To be sure, this latter administration reduced the dominance of the financiers in favour of a greater balance with agribusiness and industrial exporters.[15] And in order to prevent social tensions, Lula also extended social assistance. Yet under this form of social-liberalism, the principal economic groups maintained high rates of profitability at the expense of the majority of the population. Lula preserved the country's scandalous inequality, while securing political stability and the distancing of Brazil from the South American propensity for popular rebellions.

Argentina shares its neighbour's capitalist regionalism. But the more vicious neoliberal surgery it underwent led it to try the current neo-developmentalist economic course. The government is seeking to restore the old industrial infrastructure corroded by two decades of giving overwhelming primacy to the export sector. This effort to revitalize industry is sparking strong tensions with agribusiness, in a context that makes it quite difficult to resume investment. After a dramatic process of concentration and increasing foreign ownership of its industry, reversing this disarticulation of production is not simple.

The Argentinian bourgeoisie has also faced a convulsive social climate that has modified the balance of forces with the oppressed. It has been forced to grant significant concessions that have not redistributed income, but have limited the brutal impoverishment created by the crisis in 2001.[16] In this sense, there is a clear contrast with Brazil. While Brazil's rulers were able to consolidate their social-liberal orientation by neutralizing popular aspirations, in Argentina the powerful must govern with a watchful eye on the reaction of the oppressed.

In this complex South American context, different variations of heterodox economic policy have emerged. These visions are often associated with the emergence of a post-neoliberal phase. But the use of this concept is very controversial, as it implies a break with the neoliberal era that has not been accomplished by any centre-left government. To date, the neo-developmentalist orientations – explicit in Argentina and possible in Brazil – exhibit more elements of continuity than of rupture with the preceding period. Not only do they maintain social inequality and the unwillingness to nationalize strategic economic sectors, but they display less industrial ambition than did classic developmentalism. The repeated use of progressive discourse has the effect of masking this lack of radical departures and the continued existence of many areas of convergence with economic orthodoxy.

COOPERATION AND DISTRIBUTIONISM

The third regional project is promoted by the reformist governments of Venezuela and Bolivia. By means of the ALBA (Bolivarian Alternative for the Americas), they attempt to combine measures of anti-imperialist cooperation and forms of economic distributionism. They aim to transform trade integration in a process of Latin American political unity.

The ALBA emerged as a proposal of exchange grounded in solidarity, in opposition to the FTAA and different from the MERCOSUR. It seeks to create types of transactions based more on parameters of shared development than on criteria of profitability. But as it is being driven by very underdeveloped and poor countries, its initiatives have significant objective limitations. The new association has tried to overcome these difficulties by increasing the number of member countries, creating its own bank, signing trade agreements and creating a shared export and import company. Amidst very adverse international conditions, it has managed to maintain principles of solidarity with Cuba. But to date, the ALBA's initiatives have more weight than do its accomplishments.

These initiatives include promoting an autonomous lending structure in order to establish mechanisms of protection from the global crisis. The emergence of regional currencies is encouraged with a monetary stabilization fund, which would support the liberation of the region from the reign of the dollar. But these ideas are discussed without any significant concrete steps being taken. The establishment of a Bank of the South is still, for example, blocked by delays imposed by Brazil. Brazil resists the emergence of a financial entity that could rival its own institutions. Though its leaders accept certain criteria of equality among members in the operation of the bank, in practice they have limited its funding. They also impede the materialization of cooperative, community and social projects in conflict with the priorities of the multinational companies.[17]

The impact of the ALBA at the geopolitical level has been more convincing. It has directly repudiated imperialist aggressions and has energetically condemned US complicity in the coup in Honduras. Moreover, it has proposed clear measures of resistance to the installation of military bases in Colombia, which were subsequently neutralized in the assemblies of the UNASUR (Union of South American Nations). ALBA's anti-capitalist declarations also made a strong impact at the climate gathering in Copenhagen and at the later summit in Cochabamba. The ancestral defence of the land was vindicated in opposition to the environmental degradation created by capitalism. Drastic initiatives were also proposed to stop pollution by introducing immediate emission cuts, creating an International Climate Justice Court and carrying out a global referendum in defence of nature. These initiatives form part of an eco-socialist perspective, which may take the form of clear proposals. If the ALBA deepens this process of intervention, it could become a radical point of reference for all the social movements in Latin America.[18]

But the problems are much more complex at the national level. In Venezuela and in Bolivia, reformist governments have been consolidated that combine neo-developmentalist objectives with income redistribution measures favouring the popular majority. For the first time in the history of Venezuela, the powerful have not been the only beneficiaries of the oil bonanza. The bulk of the population felt a significant improvement in their standard of living following a large increase in social spending.[19] Bolivia is facing greater obstacles to implementing these moves as a result of its serious level of backwardness. But hydrocarbon revenues have been used to introduce new forms of social protection for children, income for retired people and subsidies for pregnant women.[20]

However, these measures are only starting points to overcoming longstanding social problems. None of the initiatives adopted to date are sufficient to resolve the structural problems of these two very peripheral and dependent economies. Only with drastic initiatives that would include nationalizing basic resources could a modern industry be built that would create jobs in countries historically governed by the rent-seeking bourgeoisie. The resources generated by the hydrocarbons constitute a key instrument for reducing social inequality and developing a process of industrialization. However, to use these resources it will be necessary to avoid the dilapidation of public funds by paying compensations as part of the nationalization process. It will also be necessary to develop a centralized public investment plan in order to offset the lack of private investment. It is clear that capitalist groups are not willing to risk a single cent of their fortunes while popular economic measures prevail. The same process of transformation also demands democratizing the management of companies with forms of worker and social control. It has been demonstrated that the old state bureaucracy obstructs the regular working of public companies and facilitates the accumulation of wealth by private groups with close links to these companies.

The contradictions and ambiguities that can be seen in Venezuela and Bolivia are a threat to the deepening of popular achievements. They could even lead to a quagmire of political conflicts with the dominant classes, without significant advances in meeting the basic needs of the masses. As time passes, the inherent dilemma of the current process will become more and more apparent, forcing either a move toward revolutionary ruptures or the consolidation of different forms of state capitalism. These two antagonistic perspectives are symbolized in Latin American history by the paths followed by the Cuban revolution (1960) and the Mexican revolution (1910). The first path allowed popular social transformations to be implemented, and the second created a new layer of oppressors out of the very centre of the state apparatus.

The dilemmas involved in choosing between popular protagonism and top-down control is seen in Venezuela in official measures that either favour or conflict with the new 'Bolivarian bourgeoisie' – commonly now called the 'Boli-bourgeoisie'. The government's electoral victories over the last 12 years enabled all of the attempts to restore the influence of the right to be contained. But there are signs that the masses are becoming tired, placing the process in the crossroads between a renewed leap or sudden burnout. The same thing is occurring in Bolivia. The steps that would strengthen the conquests from below conflict with the plan to create an 'Andean-Amazonian capitalism'. The paths that lead toward industrialization and land reform conflict with initiatives to put the richest oil deposits in foreign hands and accept adverse contracts with multinational companies.

It has been difficult to extend this kind of alternative to the current context in Ecuador, as the political process there includes many additional components that defy classification. The so-called Citizen's Revolution brought about social improvements (minimum wage, control of precarious labour), in a context of increasing social assistance. A debt audit was also carried out that was followed by a restructuring of liabilities. But there is still no sign of the beginning of a turn toward a popular economy, nor are there any significant projects for social transformation.[21] These ambiguities coincide, furthermore, with the presence of strong tensions between Andean governments and social movements around the management of natural resources. In Bolivia, there is disagreement about how to exploit zinc, lead and copper deposits, which mining companies have their eyes on and indigenous peoples seek to protect. In Ecuador, there are disputes about the use of water resources and the future of oil wealth. The great challenge is to find a balance between the traditional demands for clean water and fresh air and the new objectives of using the minerals for the development of the two countries. Nationalization processes also constitute a precondition for reconciling the two objectives.

CAPITALISM OR SOCIALISM OF THE 21st CENTURY

The limited impact of the current crisis on Latin America is significantly different from what happened in recent decades. The capitalist tremor affected several countries, but without the same devastating effects as the convulsions of the 1980s and the 1990s. At that time, the entire region was sinking due to the explosion in public debt, bursts of inflation and catastrophic social deterioration. It was under these conditions that the introduction of neoliberalism was consolidated, but later this unleashed a great degree of popular resistance, which sparked alternative processes in the region. These experiences constitute a great shared resource for the world's social movements, and they are especially useful for the youth and the workers, who are currently taking to the streets to protest cuts in several cities across Europe.

The battles waged in Latin America suggested ways of successfully responding to right-wing attacks. In the battle against the assaults by the IMF, banners were hoisted by the social movements at peak moments of the crisis calling for moratoria on debt payments, debt audits, nationalizing the banks and alliances among debtor countries to take on the lenders.[22]

In most cases, these proposals did not prosper or they were adopted only very partially. But they opened up a path for popular victories, which created new settings for struggling against neoliberalism.[23] This legacy offers fruitful lessons for the people of the first world, who are now personally experiencing the consequences of the capitalist crisis.

These same experiences will return to the forefront of the Latin American reality if the effects of the global convulsion become less tempered. The respite could continue if the Asian and mid-sized economies remain disconnected and the price of raw materials remains high. But the opposite scenario of a Latin American setback could also emerge if the depression spreads to the global level. Both of these scenarios are feasible. In both situations, demands for employment, wages, education and health will return, and the capitalist system will not be able to meet them. A system based on competition for benefits as a result of exploitation condemns the majority to endure long-lasting hardships, both during times of prosperity and during times of recession. Thus, popular movements must not dodge the strategic debates about the social system of the future.

Current strategic discussions continue to be dominated by the belief that the only feasible option in the face of neoliberalism is the development of 'a different (neo-developmentalist, distributionist, humanitarian, equitable) capitalism'. But in Latin America, an alternative vision has emerged that may alter this assumption – a call to build the socialism of the 21st century. This call is very vague and still lacks specific meaning. But the significance it holds for the anti-capitalist agenda is clear – it redeems its basic ideal. The mere mention of socialism has been subjected to scorn, censure and defamation in recent decades. In the face of such discrediting, the rehabilitation of the term is important.

In Latin America there are several signs that a new ideological battle is underway to inject content into a contemporary project of emancipation. In Bolivia, the meaning of communitarian socialism is under discussion. In Venezuela, proposals to build socialism from the top down conflict with initiatives that build from the bottom up. In Cuba, there is debate about how to renew the goal of equality with greater democracy and without losing what has been achieved.

But most important is the existence of a new generation of activists, social movements and organizations of the left, developing socialist thought and practice within the tradition of Latin American Marxism. This construction is in its early stages, but it holds out the promise of welcome surprises.

NOTES

1   The latest information compiled by the Economic Commission for Latin America and the Caribbean (ECLAC) shows a 6 per cent growth for 2010 and a 4.2 to 5 per cent forecast for 2011. The report underlines that the region has recovered its pre-crisis commercial volumes and that both imports and exports have improved in volume as well as in prices. Direct foreign investment has shown a 30 to 35 per cent increase, after a drop of over 40 per cent in 2009. The ECLAC report is available at http://www.eluniverso.com.

2   A comparative analysis of these effects can be found in Pierre Salama, 'Argentine, Bresil, Méxique, face a la crise internacional', 16 December 2008, available at http://socio13.wordpress.com. More general analyses are developed in José Antonio Ocampo, 'La crisis económica global', *Nueva Sociedad*, 224 (November/December), 2009; Luis Maira, '¿Cómo afectará la crisis la integración regional?', *Nueva Sociedad*, 224 (November/December), 2009.

3   Some information about this deterioration is presented in Francisco Rojas Aravena, 'Siete efectos políticos de la crisis internacional en América Latina', *Nueva Sociedad*, 224 (November/December), 2009; Hugo Fazio, 'Las grandes crisis latinoamericanas de los últimos 15 años', in H. Fazio et al., eds., *La explosión de la crisis global: América Latina y Chile en la encrucijada*, Santiago: LOM, 2009.

4   This perspective is presented by Ricardo Arriazu, 'América Latina logró ser menos vulnerable', *Clarín*, 21 September 2009; Julio María, Sanguinetti, 'Misteriosa América Latina', *La Nación*, 26 June 2010.

5   See CEPAL, 'Panorama de la inserción internacional de América Latina y el Caribe', 10 December 2009.

6   A comparison of the Latin American crises and those of the European periphery is developed in Daniel Munevar, 'Europa y la Crisis de la Deuda: Repitiendo los errores de América Latina', available at http://www.cadtm.org.

7   Two convincing critiques of this model are presented in Alberto Acosta, 'Los gobiernos progresistas no han puesto en tela de juicio la validez del modelo extractivista', 10 September 2009, available at http://www.ecoportal.net; Eduardo Gudynas, 'Inserción internacional y desarrollo latinoamericano', *Observatorio de la Globalización*, 7 December 2009.

8   The role of these new countries is analyzed by *The Economist*. Economist Intelligence Unit, 'Las Hijas de la globalización', *La Nación*, 7 April 2007; Igor Ojeda and Luis Brasilino, 'Las venas cada vez más abiertas de América Latina', *ALAI*, 10 March 2008.

9   We develop these categories in Claudio Katz, *Las disyuntivas de la izquierda en América Latina*, Buenos Aires: Ediciones Luxemburg, 2008.

10   For a general evaluation of these agreements, see Osvaldo Martínez, 'Por la integración de los pueblos', presentation at the Hemispheric Gathering for the Struggle against the FTAs, Havana, 3 May 2007.

11   Cogent evaluations of these processes are presented in Alejandro Valle Baeza, 'México, del estancamiento a la crisis', May 2009, available at http://

www.razonyrevolucion.org; Svenja Blanke, 'México: una crisis sin (grandes respuestas)', *Nueva Sociedad*, 224 (November/December), 2009; Francisco Colmenares, 'México: Saldos de la crisis económica y del petróleo', *OSAL*, 26, 2009.

12   Different aspects of this context of militarization are discussed in Atilio Boron, 'Prólogo', in M. A. Gandasequi, ed., *Crisis de hegemonía de Estados Unidos*, Mexico: Siglo XXI, 2007; James Cockcroft, *América Latina y Estados Unidos. Historia y política*, Mexico: Siglo XXI, 2001; Rick Rozoff, 'Estados Unidos intensifica los planos de guerra', *Memoria*, 238 (October/November), 2009; Greg Grandin, '¿Cómo será la doctrina Obama?', *Memoria*, 238 (October/November), 2009.

13   Complete report in *The Economist*, 'Special Report on Business and Finance in Brazil', 14 November 2009. A critical analysis in Mathias Luce, 'La expansión del subimperialismo brasileño', *Patria Grande*, 9 December 2008.

14   A comparative inquiry into Brazil's role in this context is presented in José Luis Fiori, *O poder global e la nova geopolitica das nacioes*, Sao Paulo: Editorial Boitempo, 2007.

15   This change is analyzed in Armando Boito Jr, 'As relacoes de classe na nova fase do neoliberalismo no Brasil', in G. Caetano, ed., *Sujetos sociales y nuevas formas de protesta en la historia reciente de América Latina*, Buenos Aires: CLACSO, 2006.

16   We analyse this issue in Claudio Katz, *Batalla de Ideas*, 1(1), September 2010, Buenos Aires.

17   A complete analysis is presented in Eric Toussaint, *El Banco del Sur y la nueva crisis internacional*, Madrid: El Viejo Topo, 2008.

18   We analyze this perspective in Claudio Katz, *El rediseño de América Latina, ALCA, MERCOSUR y ALBA*, Buenos Aires: Ediciones Luxemburg, 2006.

19   An evaluation of these tendencies is presented in Víctor Álvarez R., *Hacia dónde va el modelo productivo?*, Caracas: Editorial Centro Internacional Miranda, 2009.

20   For a general analysis, see Mark Weisbrot, Rebecca Ray and Jake Johnston, 'Bolivia: La economía bajo el gobierno de Morales', Centro de Investigación en Economía y Política, Washington, DC, December 2009. Available at http://www.cepr.net.

21   On these problems see Rosero Andrés. 'El proceso político en perspectiva', 30 January 2008, available at http://correosemanal.blogspot.com.

22   For the meaning of this resistance, see Modesto Guerrero, 'Señales de un continente en movimiento', *Página/12*, 8 November 2008.

23   The Ecuadorian debt audit experience, the debt payment suspension in a popular uprising context that took place in Argentina and the partial nationalizations of Venezuelan banks are three particularly instructive examples of these actions. We have analysed this subject in Katz, *El rediseño*.

SINOMANIA: GLOBAL CRISIS, CHINA'S CRISIS?

HO-FUNG HUNG

At a time when the global economic status quo seems to be crashing down, the seemingly endless hyper-capitalist growth of China has spurred such admiration and even euphoria from a wide circle of observers as may indeed justify use of the term Sinomania.[1] While many corporate CEOs look to China's strong recovery from the crisis as representing a vast, new, and limitless frontier to profit from just when business profitability in the global North sees little room for expansion, many left intellectuals take it as proving once and for all that China will successfully challenge the West's global capitalist domination. Martin Jacques, the former editor of *Marxism Today*, says as much when he looks forward to 'when China rules the world' and celebrates 'the birth of a new global order' amidst 'the end of the Western world'.[2]

Just as eighteenth-century Sinomania among Enlightenment intellectuals reflected cursory, exotic, and sometimes deliberately distorted information about China compiled by Jesuit missionaries, so has the latest celebration of the Chinese miracle been informed by superficial understanding of China's political economy. Within China, ironically, the excitement about the prospect of endless economic growth has long been offset by anxiety about a looming economic crisis even before the global financial crisis erupted in full in 2008. In 2007, the Chinese Academy of Social Science warned that China was witnessing an unsustainable expansion of an asset bubble reminiscent of what Japan experienced in the 1980s.[3] At a press conference during the annual plenary session of the National People's Congress in March 2007, Premier Wen Jiabao himself characterized the current path of development in China as 'unstable, unbalanced, uncoordinated, and unsustainable'. Although the Chinese government's stimulus programme of 2008–09 staved off the free fall of the economy that would have been caused by the collapse of the export engine, it at the same time opened the floodgate of lax lending by state banks, aggravating overinvestment that had already been worsening before the crisis. The hyper-investment spree and liquidity creation via lax lending in post-crisis China has already generated a mega bubble. The bursting of this bubble can be the trigger of a second wave of the global financial crisis.[4]

OVERACCUMULATION WITH CHINESE CHARACTERISTICS

What made the Chinese miracle possible was, first, the capacity of subnational states to promote local economic growth in a single-minded manner and, second, the capacity of the national party-state to repress labour's demands and the growth of civil society. While the autonomy and competitive pressure among local states perpetually goaded them to increase their individual attractiveness, and hence China's overall attractiveness to global capital, the authoritarian national rule kept discontent at bay without requiring large-scale income redistribution through taxation and wage increases. These two processes, when unfolding on the vast geographical and demographic scale of China, made China the most dynamic centre of capital accumulation in the world system. But this same sociopolitical framework also has been cultivating an economic imbalance that poses a threat to the sustainability of the miracle itself: while the decentralization of economic governance accelerated overinvestment, unchecked social polarization constrained the growth of domestic consumption power.

This imbalance is particularly notable when China's pattern of growth is compared with the other 'Asian Tigers' at comparable stages of development. First, the decentralized nature of the Chinese developmental state makes the problem of overinvestment more severe in China than in earlier Asian Tigers. During the initial economic ascendancy of Japan, South Korea, and Taiwan, central governments played a key role in mobilizing and allocating precious financial and other resources to support the growth of strategic industrial sectors. This 'pick the winner' process was crucial not only to success in the early stages of industrial takeoff but also to the subsequent industrial upgrading of these economies.[5] The decentralized economic growth in today's China deviates from the model of a centralized developmental state.[6] Many local states in China act 'developmentally' in that they proactively facilitate growth of selected industrial sectors, and these developmental efforts are often well planned and executed at the local level. The totality of these efforts combined, however, to create anarchic competition among localities, resulting in uncoordinated construction of redundant production capacity and infrastructure. Foreign investors, with the expectation that the domestic and world market for Chinese products will grow incessantly, also raced with one another to expand their existing industrial capacity in China. Though export-oriented foreign investments consistently yielded decent profits on the world market, and the US market in particular, investments made by many state-owned, domestic-market-oriented enterprises, particularly state-owned enterprises, became increasingly excessive and unprofitable.

Idle capacity in such key sectors as steel, automobile, cement, aluminum, and real estate has been soaring ever since the mid-1990s.[7] It was estimated in 2006 that more than 75 per cent of China's industries were plagued by overcapacity, and that fixed asset investment in industries already experiencing overinvestment accounted for 40 to 50 per cent of China's GDP growth in 2005.[8] The build up of excess capacity was exacerbated by the lack of geographical and intersectoral mobility of domestic enterprises, which increases their propensity to invest in already saturated localities and sectors. On the one hand, many provincial or municipal governments erected protectionist barriers against investment from other provinces or cities. This created a 'one country, thirty-two economies' malaise.[9] One survey found that 85.8 per cent of state-owned enterprises invested only in a single city and that 91.1 per cent invested only in a single province.[10] This was partly due to the underdevelopment of financial markets that has made it difficult for enterprises to divert their savings to invest in other sectors or regions.[11]

To make matters worse, major state-owned banks, rather than discipline enterprises and direct them away from excessive and low-return investments, have encouraged these investments through lax lending practices. These banks, as the financial arms of the central and local governments, have delivered easy credits to insolvent or profligate state-owned industrial enterprises, of which roughly 40 per cent incurred losses in 2006, according to government figures.[12] In contrast, private enterprises, even very successful ones, were at a disadvantageous position in obtaining financial support from major state banks. This set China apart from the developmental experiences of other East Asian developmental states.[13]

The state banks' motivation in extending loans to keep unprofitable state-owned enterprises afloat was to maintain social and political stability by slowing massive layoffs. In addition, these loans were often made at the behest of local party bosses, who command overwhelming influence over local branches of state banks and are inclined to fuel local investment booms to boost local growth figures and short-term government revenue gain. This magnified the sectoral overinvestment into a generalized risk to the economy through the pileup of nonperforming loans in the financial system.[14] As the Bank for International Settlement remarked, 'In China, the principal concern must be that misallocated capital will eventually manifest itself in falling profits, and that this will feed back on the bank system, the fiscal authorities and the prospects for growth more generally. After a long period of credit-fuelled expansion, this would be the classic denouement. Indeed, this was very much the path followed [before the prolonged crisis in the 1990s] by Japan.'[15]

The ratio of nonperforming loans to all outstanding loans was reduced after the 1990s largely as a result of massive government bailouts, the transferring of these loans to state-owned asset-management companies, and deliberate under-reporting of nonperforming loans.[16] Major state banks continued to lend without taking into account the profitability and risk of their borrowers.[17] As Nicholas Lardy pointed out, this continuous reckless lending could renew the accumulation of bad debt and 'erase some of the very hard-won progress in bank reform in the last eight years'.[18] Many seemingly 'good' loans at times of rapid economic growth could swiftly deteriorate into bad ones when the economy slowed, leading to an explosion of nonperforming loans, similar to what Japan underwent in the early 1990s.

The second problem that has plagued China's developmental model is underconsumption. All East Asian Tigers at their initial stage of industrial takeoff were governed by authoritarian regimes. But these regimes were disciplined by Cold War geopolitics. Just next door to Communist China, they were anxious to root out any significant socialist influence among the lower classes. They achieved this goal through pre-emptive redistributive policies such as land reform and provision of free education as much as through repression of independent labour and peasant organizations. By letting the fruits of economic expansion trickle down to the lower classes, in particular the rural population, these authoritarian regimes became economically inclusive, even though they were highly exclusive politically.[19] The reduction in income disparity and rising income among the lower classes helped create sizeable domestic markets in these newly industrializing economies that buffered them against the vagaries of the world market, in addition to providing infant industries with sufficient internal demand before they could compete internationally.[20]

In contrast, China's party-state in the 1990s single-mindedly pursued rapid economic growth without much success in alleviating the subsequent social polarization, which was aggravated by the government's draconian suppression of dissenting voices from below. Class, urban-rural, and regional inequalities expanded hand in hand with the economic miracle. Poverty intensified in the rural inland area, and the old bastions of state industry were besieged by extensive unemployment.[21] As jobs created by export-oriented capital could not catch up with the jobs disappearing from battered state-owned factories, China appears to have experienced a net loss of manufacturing jobs after the mid-1990s, with the share of manufacturing in total employment never reaching the levels found at the peak of manufacturing employment in the smaller newly industrializing economies.[22] The peasants-turned-workers in the coastal boom towns did not fare much better. Owing to the colossal size of the pool of surplus labour and the 'despotic factory regime' under the auspices of the party-state, manufacturing wage growth amid China's economic miracle was dismal in comparison with the growth in other East Asian newly industrializing economies during their 'miraculous' moments.[23]

During the most explosive phase of takeoff, Taiwan's Gini coefficient declined from the range of 0.5 to 0.6 in the 1950s to the range of 0.3 to 0.4 in the 1970s, China's Gini coefficient ascended from 0.33 in 1980 to more than 0.45 in 2007. The increasingly skewed distribution of income constrained expansion of the mass-consumption market. The share of wage income in China's GDP declined from 53 per cent in 1998 to 41.4 per cent in 2005, leading one Wold Bank study to comment that 'the declining role of wages and household income in the economy are the key driver behind the declining share of consumption in GDP'.[24] The growth of consumption in China was hardly stagnant, but it did not keep pace with the exuberant growth in investment.[25]

Although the earlier 'East Asian developmental miracles' were known for their high investment and low consumption rates, they were dwarfed by China's. China's fixed asset investment rate, which has been above 40 per cent of GDP and reached 45 per cent in 2009, was far higher than Taiwan's and South Korea's rates at their peaks of industrial growth in the 1970s (25 to 35 per cent). Its private consumption rate, which has been below 40 per cent and dropping since 2004, on the other hand, was much lower than Taiwan's and South Korea's rates in the 1970s (60 to 70 per cent for Korea and 50 to 60 per cent for Taiwan).

The increasing overinvestment and underconsumption of the Chinese economy made China increasingly reliant on the global market to export its excess capacity. It in turn made China very vulnerable to any protracted global economic downturn. China's ratio of gross fixed capital formation to final consumption expenditure exceeded the level that most other Asian economies reached on the eve of the 1997 Asian financial crisis.[26] This escalation of the investment-to-consumption ratio is reminiscent of what the United States witnessed on the eve of the Great Depression in the 1930s and what Japan also did just before the 'lost decade' of the 1990s, both of which were preceded by debt-financed expansion of excess industrial capacity, asset inflation, sluggish domestic demand, and falling profitability in the production sectors.[27]

From a Marxist perspective, a capitalist economy is said to encounter an overaccumulation crisis when the rate of capital accumulation surpasses the level that could not prevent rate of profit from falling, either because of the build up of excess production capacity or lack of consumption.[28] Overinvestment and underconsumption in China's economic miracle should, theoretically speaking, precipitate such a crisis and ultimately lead to collapse of profit and growth. But, in reality, this did not happen and the Chinese economy roared ahead uninterruptedly for more than two decades. This paradox needs to be understood in terms of China's ability to export its excess capacity through booming exports.

Besides making the Chinese economy vulnerable to the vicissitudes of the global economy, China's export sector could maintain its cost competitiveness in the world market by not allowing much of their gains to improve the living standards, and hence the consumption power, of the working classes. These Chinese enterprises could turn most of their increasing profits into corporate savings instead of wage increases for their employees. These enterprise savings constituted a large proportion of the aggregate national saving, which in turn helped fuel a credit boom from the bank and aggravated overinvestment.[29]

The accumulation of excess industrial capacity, gluts, and relatively sluggish consumption growth did lead to falling prices of finished products in key industrial sectors and falling profit margins in key industries over the 1990s.[30] The growing economic imbalance and concern about profitless growth led many to question the sustainability of the boom and to anticipate an economic crisis to come. This worry heightened in the aftermath of the Asian Financial Crisis of 1997/98.[31] The signs of fatigue of the Chinese miracle back then included soaring non-performing loans in state banks that started to threaten the stability of the financial system. It also included plummeting industrial profits, particularly among state enterprises, under a deflationary spiral.

The fear about a serious economic crisis was soon allayed by a new round of robust economic expansion driven by FDI inflow and export growth after 2000. These upward trends were not unrelated to the heightened optimism about China's export-driven economy at home and abroad, enlivened by China's entry into the WTO, its successful bid for hosting the 2008 Olympics, and the real estate bubble and debt-financed consumption spree in the US and Europe that sustained thriving markets for Chinese exports. The rising state revenue given by this export-led economic boom enabled the state to bail out the state banks and state enterprises.

China became ever more dependent on its booming export sector to neutralize the increasing peril posed by its excessive capacity in the domestic-market-oriented sector dominated by state enterprises. As Table 1 shows, the profit rate of large state-owned industrial enterprises and limited liability corporations owned by the state, despite all the policy favours, subsidies, and low-interest loans from state banks, stood at 4.81 per cent in 2007 and was far below the national average of 7.69 per cent, while private industrial enterprises and foreign-funded joint venture industrial enterprises enjoyed profit rates of 9.48 per cent and 8.26 per cent respectively, much higher than the national average.

Table 1. Profit Rate in Various Types of Industrial Enterprises, 2007 and 2009

Type	Profit rate 2007 (%)*	Profit rate 2009
All	7.69	7.09
State-owned enterprises	4.81	3.77
Limited liability corporations with state funding only	4.57	3.85
Private enterprises	9.48	10.94
Joint-venture enterprises with		
Hong Kong, Taiwan and Macao capital	8.26	7.60
Other foreign capital	8.72	7.21

* profit rate = total annual profits/total assets
Source: National Bureau of Statistics.

Ballooning foreign reserves resulting from rapid export growth fuelled a credit expansion in the banking sector, boosting debt-financed investment further and in turn exacerbating the build up of excess production capacity to be countervailed by further export growth. A cycle of surging export and surging investment ensued.[32] In sum, China's pattern of economic growth on the eve of the global crisis of 2007-08 remained marked by a high (and ever-increasing) dependence on export and debt-financed investment on the one hand, and low domestic consumption on the other.

It was already at that time doubtful whether China's formidable export engine, so far the economy's single most profitable component as well as the key component that neutralizes the risk of an overaccumulation crisis, could last indefinitely. The success of the export-led development strategy of the Asian Tigers rested mainly on the fact of so few small developing economies pursuing the strategy. The exports of these economies were easily absorbed in the world market. But when many more developing countries adopted the strategy in the 1980s and 1990s, the world market, flooded with cheap manufactured exports, became even more volatile. Given its economic size and export volume, China was exceptionally vulnerable.[33] Worse, China's exporting trade was highly concentrated in the US consumer market, which absorbed more than 30 per cent of China's total exports (including re-exports via Hong Kong).[34]

CRISIS AND STIMULUS

China's developmental model, driven by hyper growth in its export sector at the expense of the growth of its domestic consumption, was thus exceptionally vulnerable to any major contraction of consumption demand in the Global North. The compulsion of Chinese and other Asian governments to employ their foreign reserves to purchase US debt was not just a result of the presumably stable and safe return of the US Treasury bonds, but is also due to a conscious effort among Asian central banks to finance the US's escalating current account deficit and hence to secure the continuous increase in US demand for their own exports.

Viewed from this perspective, the growth of China's export engine, as well as the growth of its financial power in the form of the accumulation of US debts, was closely linked to the consumption spree in the US. The onset of the US economic crisis, which badly affected China's exports by setting off a free fall of export growth rate from 20 per cent in 2007 to -11 per cent in 2009,[35] together with what many feared might be the imminent collapse of the dollar and Treasury bonds, seem to be the worst nightmare coming true.

Before the financial crisis struck, the Chinese government was experimenting with different ways to diversify and increase the return of its foreign reserve investment. It had tried investing in foreign equities and financing state-owned companies' acquisition of transnational corporations, but nearly all attempts ended in embarrassing failures, such as Lenovo acquisition of IBM PC and the acquisition of major stakes in Blackstone, a private equity fund, by China's sovereign wealth fund.[36] These failures were more a result of the constraint posed by the exceptional size of China's foreign reserve than bad investment decisions per se. Given the size of China's foreign reserve, it was difficult for China to move in and out of certain financial assets freely without disrupting the global market for those assets. And no other market except the US debt market had liquidity deep enough to absorb China's gigantic reserves. Paul Krugman was not exaggerating when he claimed that China had been caught in a 'dollar trap', in which it had few choices other than to keep purchasing US debts and other dollar assets to help perpetuate the hegemonic role of the dollar.[37]

The expansion of the US consumer market hinged on an unsustainable, debt-financed consumption spree and created a mega-current account deficit. The US was forced into a deep adjustment following the bursting of its real-estate bubble and collapse of its debt-financed consumerism in 2008. This readjustment of China's main export outlet is occurring alongside the escalating pressure for substantial appreciation of the Chinese yuan and the rise of protectionist measures in the US and other economies. This conjuncture of events put great pressure on the profitability of China's export sector.

In late 2008 and early 2009, China's export engine stalled and its export-dependent manufacturing sector contracted sharply across the board. In response, the central government immediately (in November 2008) attempted to arrest a free fall of the economy by rolling out a mega fiscal stimulus package amounting to US$ 570 billion (including both government spending and targeted loans from state-owned banks) to revive growth. Many initially celebrated this massive stimulus as a precious opportunity to accelerate the rebalancing of the Chinese economy into a more domestic consumption driven mode, and expected that the stimulus would be constituted mainly by social spending, such as financing of medical insurance and social security, that could further raise the disposable income and hence purchasing power of the working classes.

To the disappointment of many advocates of structural rebalancing of the Chinese economy, the stimulus package in fact carried no more than 20 per cent of social spending, while the major fraction of the spending went into investment in capital assets such as highway construction and expansion of sectors already plagued by overcapacity such as steel and cement.[38] Since the stimulus package did not bring much benefit to social welfare institutions and small and medium labour-intensive enterprises, it was not able to generate much increase in disposable income and employment. Worse, seemingly horrified by the sudden collapse of the export sector, the central government retreated from the rebalancing efforts and restarted a number of export promotion measures, such as a cutback in value-added taxes and halting of yuan appreciation. Vested interests in the export sector even made use of the crisis to call for a suspension of the New Labour Contract Law for the sake of the survival of export manufacturers.[39]

The massive fiscal stimulus, despite its impressive size, would do little to rebalance the Chinese economy via promoting domestic consumption and hence reducing China's export dependence.[40] Though a larger part of the stimulus fund was directed to the Western provinces and helped redress the development gap between coastal and inland areas, the mostly capital-intensive, urban-oriented growth under the stimulus, such as increasing production capacity in the steel industry and construction of the world's longest high-speed rail system, aggravated rural-urban polarization which was one of the underlying causes of underconsumption. Urban-rural household income per capita ratio continued to surge and reached the historic height of 3.33 in 2009.[41]

Figure 1. Purchasing Manager Index of China (Official and HSBC indices)

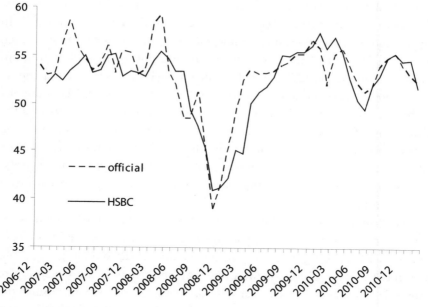

Source: China National Bureau of Statistics and HSBC.[42]

The massive spending actually did keep the economy roaring with a state-led investment spurt in the short run while waiting for the export market to turn around. By the summer of 2009, the fiscal stimulus had successfully stalled the free fall of the Chinese economy and fostered a decent rebound of the economy (as shown in Figure 1). But at the same time, more than 90 per cent of GDP growth in all of 2009 was solely driven by fixed asset investments fuelled by the loan explosion and government spending under the stimulus programme.[43] Initial figures for 2010 indicates this investment-driven growth became even more entrenched, as fixed investment growth for 2010 exceeded 23 per cent, while overall GDP grew only 10.3 per cent. Most of these investments are of low quality and repetitive, with dubious profitability.[44] In the words of a top Chinese economist, this mega stimulus programme is like 'drinking poison to quench the thirst'.[45] As Figure 2 shows, new income generated by each unit of fixed asset investment has been falling as the investment spree financed by lax lending fostered increasingly inefficient investment. Table 1 also showed that the profit rate across the economy, particularly in the investment-driven state sector, dropped significantly under the stimulus-fuelled rebound of the economy.

Figure 2. Increase in National Income Generated by One Unit of Fixed Asset Investment

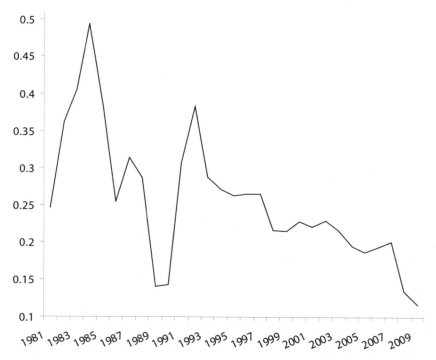

Source: China National Bureau of Statistics.

The latest available data shows that fixed asset investment had picked up the slack left by the sluggish recovery of exports in driving the Chinese economy after the crisis of 2008, while private consumption, despite all the publicized efforts of the central leadership in stimulating domestic consumption, had not shown any significant growth.

Figure 3. Share of Export, Consumption, and Investment in China's GDP

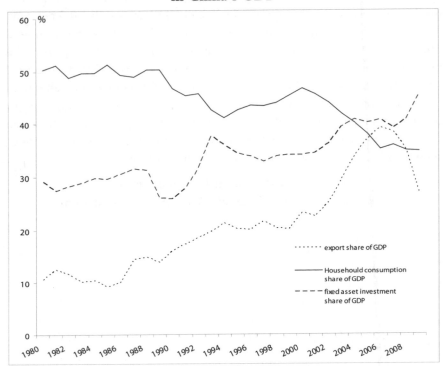

Source: China National Bureau of Statistics.

It is still very possible that the fiscal deficit, nonperforming loans, and exacerbation of overcapacity created by the stimulus will generate a deeper downturn in the medium and long run. And to gain the financial resources necessary for bailing out the banks and state-owned enterprises, the government may be forced to resort to heavier tax levies, which will further curtail the growth of private consumption. This scenario is increasingly likely with the sluggish and jobless recovery of the US and the deepening crisis in the eurozone.

If the current course of response to the global crisis continues, China is likely to waste the crisis. Only a shift to more balanced growth based on greater domestic consumption can turn China into a genuinely autonomous economic powerhouse.

The working-class solution

The key to reducing China's dependence on exports is to boost the consumption power of the working classes through measures that redistribute larger portions of income from enterprises to employees. The Chinese Communist Party elite know this very well. As an impetus to rebalance China's development, the central government has tried since about 2005 to fuel a takeoff of China's domestic consumption by boosting the disposable income of the peasants and urban workers, even at the expense of China's export competitiveness. The first wave of such initiatives included the abolition of agricultural taxes, an increase in the government procurement price of agricultural products, and an increase in rural infrastructure investment. Though this redirection of attention to raising rural living standard was no more than a small step in the right direction, its effect was instantaneous.

The slightly improved economic conditions in the rural–agricultural sector slowed the flow of rural–urban migration, and a sudden labour shortage and wage hike in the coastal export-processing zones ensued, inducing many economists to declare that the 'Lewis turning point', that is, the point at which rural surplus labour was exhausted, had finally arrived in the Chinese economy.[46] This sudden tightening of the labour market was reflected in the steep increase in the Chinese manufacturing wage as a share of the US manufacturing wage after 2005. The livelihoods of workers were further protected by the introduction of the New Labour Contract Law, which, even if not implemented effectively by local governments, became a new weapon workers could wield in their fight for concessions from employers.[47]

The effect of such measures was immediate. Concomitant to the rising peasant income and industrial wage was an unprecedented growth in retail sales on the eve of the current global crisis.[48] But when the government took the first step away from excessive export dependence and toward a domestic consumption driven growth, vested interests in the coastal export sector loudly complained about the grim prospect that the new policy initiatives brought to them. They asked for a compensation policy to safeguard their competitiveness, and attempted to sabotage further initiatives of the central government to elevate the living standards of the working classes.

In 2010, a wave of labour unrest and resistance, including strikes and collective suicides, swept through China's industrial sunbelt in the South. This had a serious impact on some of the largest employers in the region, including Honda and Foxconn. These instances of unrest were widely reported in China's and foreign media and seemed to successfully force the foreign capital concerned to make significant concessions in improving workers remuneration and reducing the length and intensity of work on the shop floor. In April 2011, the National People's Congress of China, seemingly out of concern for the economy's imbalances and the rising tide of labour unrest, approved a new Five Year Plan that pledged more proactive policies to raise workers' wage share in GDP and enhance the social and workplace protection of workers.

But such pledges are nothing new and their precedents repeatedly turned out to be less than met the eye. Labour organizations have already found signs that the compromises that foreign investors made to the contentious workers last year were on paper only, as many of them sought to shift their production to inland areas with harsher labour practices as well as exact new deductions from workers' nominally raised salaries to compensate for the losses incurred by the compromises.[49] Nouriel Roubini, who rightly predicted the Great Crash of 2008 and has recently paid close attention to Chinese political economy, has notably remarked that '[d]espite the rhetoric of the new Five-Year Plan – which, like the previous one, aims to increase the share of consumption in GDP – the path of least resistance is the *status quo*. The new plan's details reveal continued reliance on investment'.[50]

China therefore has never amounted to the autonomous economic powerhouse representing an alternative force to the US-led world economic order that so many have perceived it to be. On the contrary, China was a constituent part of the mega financial bubble in the US that led to the latest global crisis. As with the US itself, the response by the Chinese government to the crisis, in the words of Martin Hart-Landsberg,[51] has been to 'maintain the status quo' of the world economy. The state elite is betting on the full recovery of the export sector for a solid recovery of the economy in the medium and long run. As the full recovery of the export sector depends on the revival of consumption growth in the US, it is no accident that China's central bank did not hesitate to increase its purchase of US Treasury bonds amidst the crisis, despite all the anxiety that China expressed about the risk of US Treasury bonds as an investment vehicle.[52]

Since the origins of China's economic imbalance, which contributes largely to the global economic imbalance, lies in China's low-wage regime of manufacturing, this is essentially a class power as well as a distributive issue. Rebalancing the Chinese and world economy will require a political solution which could bring improvement of the working classes' share of economic growth. Such a political solution will not transpire automatically, though escalating labour unrest and the seeming readiness of the current leaders to yield to such unrest do give us reason to be optimistic.[53] In any event, the prospect of the economic rebalancing in China via a shifting balance of power between capital and labour in the country is where analysis ends and action begins.

NOTES

1   Perry Anderson, 'Sinomania', *London Review of Book*, 28 January 2010.
2   Martin Jacques, *When China Rules the World: The Rise of the Middle Kingdom and the End of the Western World*, London: Allen Lane, 2009.
3   *People's Daily*, 13 January 2007.
4   In a Bloomberg survey of 1,000 investors, analysts, and traders in January 2011, 45 per cent of respondents expect a major financial crisis in China in the next five year, while another 40 per cent believe there will be a crisis after 2016. See 'China will Face Crisis within 5 Years, 45% of Investors in Global Poll Say', *Bloomberg News*, 26 January 2011.
5   Robert Wade, *Governing the Market: Economic Theory and the Role of Government in East Asian Industrialization*, Princeton: Princeton University Press, 1990; Stephen Haggard, *Pathways from the Periphery: The Politics of Growth in the Newly Industrializing Countries*, Ithaca: Cornell University Press, 1990; Peter Evans, *Embedded Autonomy: States and Industrial Transformation*, Princeton: Princeton University Press, 1995.
6   Alvin So, ed., *China's Developmental Miracle: Origins, Transformations, and Challenges*, Armonk: M. E. Sharpe. 2003.
7   Thomas G. Rawski, 'Will Investment Behavior Constrain China's Growth?', *China Economic Review,* 13, 2002, pp. 361-72.
8   Raghuram G. Rajun, 'Financial System Reform and Global Current Account Imbalances', Presentation at the American Economic Association Meeting, Boston, 6 January 2006, available from http://www.imf.org; Andy Xie, 'China: What Next?', Global Economic Forum, Morgan Stanley, 3 February 2006, available at http://www.morganstanley.com; Yasheng Huang, 'Between Two Coordination Failures: Automotive Industrial Policy in China with a Comparison to Korea', *Review of International Political Economy*, 9(3), 2002, pp. 538-73; Rawski, 'Investment Behavior', pp. 364-5; *Xinhuawang*, 14 November 2005.
9   Yasheng Huang, *Selling China: Foreign Direct Investment during the Reform Era,* Cambridge, UK: Cambridge University Press, 2003, pp. 140-48.
10   Lisa A. Keister and Jin Lu, 'The Transformation Continues: The Status of Chinese State-Owned Enterprises at the Start of the Millennium', *NBR Analysis*, 12(3), 2001, p. 26.
11   Rajan, 'Financial System Reform'.
12   Bank for International Settlement, *77th Annual Report*, Basel: Bank for International Settlement, 2007, p. 56.
13   Kelli S. Tsai, *Back-Alley Banking: Private Entrepreneurs in China,* Ithaca: Cornell University Press, 2002, pp. 29-35; Victor Shih, 'Dealing with Non-Performing Loans: Political Constraints and Financial Policies in China', *China Quarterly,* 180, 2004, pp. 922-44.
14   Nicholas Lardy, *China's Unfinished Economic Revolution*, Washington: Brookings Institution Press, 1998; Rawski, 'Investment Behavior', pp. 364-5; *The Economist*, 29 October 2005.

15 Bank for International Settlement, *76th Annual Report*, Basel: Bank for International Settlement, 2006, p. 144.

16 *New York Times*, 15 November 2006; Wendy Dobson and Anil K. Kashyap, 'The Contradiction in China's Gradualist Banking Reforms', *Brookings Papers on Economic Activity*, Fall, 2006, pp. 103-48; Barry Naughton, *The Chinese Economy: Transitions and Growth*, Cambridge, MA: MIT Press, 2007, pp. 460-67.

17 Richard Podpiera, 'Progress in China's Banking Sector Reform: Has Bank Behavior Changed?', IMF Working Paper, 2006, available at http://www.imf.org.

18 *The Economist*, 8 April 2006.

19 Fedric C. Deyo, 'State and Labor: Modes of Political Exclusion in East Asian Development', in F.C. Deyo, ed., *In The Political Economy of the New Asian Industrialism*, Ithaca: Cornell University Press, 1987, pp. 227-48; Haggard, *Pathways from the Periphery*, pp. 223-53.

20 Richard Grabowski, 'The Successful Developmental State: Where Does It Come From?', *World Development*, 22(3), 1994, pp. 413-22.

21 Shaogang Wang and Hu Angang, *The Political Economy of Uneven Development: The Case of China*, Armonk: M. E. Sharpe, 1999; Carl Riskin, Renwei Zhao, and Shi Li, eds., *China's Retreat from Equality: Income Distribution and Economic Transition*, Armonk: M. E. Sharpe, 2001.

22 Peter Evans and Sarah Staveteig, 'The Changing Structure of Employment in Contemporary China', in Deborah Davis and Feng Wang, eds., *Creating Wealth and Poverty in Post-Socialist China*, Stanford: Stanford University Press, 2008.

23 Ching-kwan Lee, *Gender and the South China Miracle*, Berkeley: University of California Press, 1998; Andrew Glyn, 'Imbalances of the Global Economy', *New Left Review*, 34, 2005, pp. 22; Ho-fung Hung, 'Rise of China and the Global Overaccumulation Crisis', *Review of International Political Economy*, 15(2), 2008, p. 162.

24 He Jianwu and Louis Kuijs, 'Rebalancing China's Economy--Modeling a Policy Package', *World Bank China Research Paper*, 7, 2007, pp. 11-12, available at http://www.worldbank.org.cn.

25 Hung, 'Rise of China', p. 164.

26 Ibid., p. 165.

27 Michel Aglietta, *A Theory of Capitalist Regulation: The US Experience*, London: Verso, 1979; James N. Devine, 'Underconsumption, Over-Investment, and the Origins of the Great Depression', *Journal of Radical Political Economics*, 15(2), 1983; Walden Bello, 'East Asia: On the Eve of the Great Transformation?', *Review of International Political Economy*, 5(3), 1998, pp. 424-44; Robert Wade, 'Wheels within Wheels: Rethinking the Asian Crisis and the Asian Model', *American Review of Political Science*, 3, 2000; Taggard R. Murphy, 'Japan's Economic Crisis', *New Left Review*, 1, 2000, pp. 25-52; Korkut A. Erturk, 'Overcapacity and the East Asian Crisis', *Journal of Post Keynesian Economics*, 24(2), 2002; Ravi A. Palat, '"Eyes Wide Shut": Reconceptualizing the Asian Crisis"', *Review of International Political Economy*, 10(2), 2003.

28 David Harvey, *The New Imperialism,* Oxford: Oxford University Press, 2005.

29 National Development and Reform Council of China, *Zhongguo jumin shouru fenpei niandu baogao,* 2005 (annual report of Chinese resident's income distribution).

30 Emma X. Fan and Jesus Felipe, 'The Diverging Patterns of Profitability, Investment, and Growth of China and India, 1980–2003', Center for Applied Macroeconomic Analysis, Australian National University Working Paper, 2005; Shan Weijian, 'The World Bank's China Delusions', *Far Eastern Economic Review,* 169(7), 2006, pp. 29–32; Shan Weijian, 'China's Low-Profit Growth Model', *Far Eastern Economic Review,* 169(11), 2006; Nazrul Islam, Dai Erbiao, and Hiroshi Sakamoto, 'Role of TFP in China's Growth', *Asian Economic Journal,* 20(2), 2006, pp. 149–54; Hung, 'Rise of China', p. 166.

31 John G. Fernald and Oliver D. Babson, 'Why Has China Survived the Asian Crisis So Well? What Risks Remain?', Board of Governors of the Federal Reserve System, International Finance Discussion Papers, No. 333, 1999; Justin Y. Lin, 'The Current Deflation in China: Causes and Policy Options', *Asian Pacific Journal of Economics and Business,* 4(2), 2000.

32 *Washington Post,* 17 January 2006.

33 Walter Russell Mead, 'Needed: A New Growth Strategy for the Developing World', *Development Outreach,* World Bank, Summer 1999; Thomas I. Palley, 'A New Development Paradigm: Domestic Demand-Led Growth', *Foreign Policy in Focus,* September 2002; Asian Development Bank, *Asian Development Outlook 2005,* Manila: Asian Development Bank, 2005.

34 Stephen Roach, 'The Fallacy of Global Decoupling', Global Economic Forum, Morgan Stanley, 2006. Available at http://www.morganstanley.com; Stephen Roach, 'China's Rebalancing Imperatives: A Giant Step for Globalization', *Morgan Stanley Research Global,* 1 December 2006.

35 World Bank 2010, 'China Quarterly Update', Beijing: World Bank Beijing Office, March 2010, p. 10.

36 Ho-fung Hung, 'America's Head Servant? PRC's Dilemma in the Global Crisis', *New Left Review,* 60, 2009, pp. 17–18.

37 Paul Krugman, 'China's Dollar Trap', *New York Times,* 2 April 2009.

38 'Siwanyi neiwai' (inside and outside of the four thousand billion), *Caijing,* 16 March 2009.

39 See 'jiuye xingshi yanjun laodong hetong fa chujing ganga' (severe unemployment jeopardize labor contract law), *Caijing,* 4 January 2009.

40 'Zhongguo GDP zengzhang jin 90% you touzi ladong' (nearly 90% of China's GDP growth was driven by investment), *Caijing,* 16 July 2009.

41 Manufacturing PMI (purchasing managers' index) is a monthly estimate of manufacturing activities based on a sampled survey of manufacturing establishments. An index above 50 signals expansion of manufacturing activities while an index below 50 signals contraction.

42 Hung, 'America's Head Servant?', Table 3.

43 'Investment contributes over 90% to China's GDP growth: NBS', *Xinhua News,* 2 February 2012.

44   Michael Pettis, 'More Public Worrying about the Chinese Stimulus', blog entry at China Financial Markets, 24 July 2009, available at http://mpettis.com.

45   The comment is from Xu Xiaonian at the China Europe International Business School in Shanghai. See 'China Stimulus Plan Comes Under Attack at "Summer Davos"', *China Post,* 13 September 2009.

46   Cai Fang and Du Yang, eds., *The China Population and Labor Yearbook, Vol. 1: The Approaching Lewis Turning Point and its Policy Implications*, Leiden: Brill, 2009.

47   Virginia Emily Ho, 'From Contracts to Compliance? An Early Look at Implementation of China's New Labor Legislation', Unpublished manuscript, Indiana University, Bloomington – School of Law, 2008.

48   Hung, 'America's Head Servant?', Figure 9.

49   Students and Scholars Against Corporate Misbehavior (SACOM), 'Foxconn and Apple Fail to Fulfill Promises: Predicaments of Workers after the Suicides', SACOM, Hong Kong, 16 May 2011, available from http://sacom.hk.

50   Nouriel Robini, 'China's Bad Growth Bet', *Project Syndicate*, 14 April 2011, available from http://www.project-syndicate.org.

51   Martin Hart-Landsberg, 'The US Economy and China: Capitalism, Class, and Crisis', *Monthly Review*, 61(9), 2010.

52   Chinese holding of US Treasury bonds jumped from US$ 618 billion in Sept of 2008 to US$ 1,160 billion in December of 2010 according to US Treasury data.

53   Beverly Silver and Lu Zhang, 'China as an Emerging Epicenter of Labor Unrest', in Ho-fung Hung, ed., *China and the Transformation of Global Capitalism*, Baltimore, MD: Johns Hopkins University Press, 2009; Dorothy Solinger, *States' Gains, Labor's Losses: China, France, and Mexico Choose Global Liaisons, 1980-2000*, Ithaca: Cornell University Press, 2009.

EASTERN EUROPE:
POST-COMMUNIST ASSETS IN CRISIS

JAN TOPOROWSKI

During the 1980s, in the final years of communism, Eastern European economists and politicians were easily persuaded by the myth that removal of the petty restrictions on private business would allow private enterprise to flourish. The idea of a permanent state of capitalist dynamism is rooted in the notion that finance spontaneously backs industrial enterprise. As Michał Kalecki put it: 'Many economists assume, at least in their abstract theories, a state of business democracy in which anybody endowed with entrepreneurial ability can obtain capital for starting a business venture. This picture of the 'pure' entrepreneur is, to put it mildly, unrealistic. The most important prerequisite for becoming an entrepreneur is the *ownership* of capital'.[1] This romantic view, that the inconvenience of doing business is the most effective obstacle to capitalism (a view most ardently subscribed to by inconvenienced businessmen), may be found even among the best-informed circles. The World Bank's *Doing Business in 2009* highlighted the achievement of nearly two decades of setting up capitalist institutions in Eastern Europe. The World Bank pointed out that it now takes on average 21 days to register a business in Eastern Europe, compared with 49 days in East Asia.[2] This relative inconvenience of doing business in East Asia has not prevented that region from being the most dynamic – at times the only dynamic – region of the capitalist world in the last decade. Capitalism is not set in historical motion by its conveniences, but by the accumulation of capital.

CREDIT AND A NEW CAPITALIST CLASS:
THE FINANCIAL LEGACY OF COMMUNISM

The collapse of the communist system induced a financial crisis of the state and its enterprises. Under communism, the balance sheets of state enterprises, consisting of productive assets matched by state financing, were integrated in the balance sheets of the government in an elaborate system of automatic cross-subsidy that may have been at times inefficient, but was at least financially stable.[3] The balkanization of the state-controlled economy, and the separation out of individual enterprises that were now supposed to be self-financing, or generate their own financing, plunged that system into financial crisis as newly autonomous enterprises struggled to secure financing for current production and new investment. Out of that came a rushed privatization that enriched those individuals and firms that could buy enterprises cheaply from the state and then resell them at a higher price, or float them on the stock market. The greatest damage was experienced by the heavy industry that had been privileged under Stalinist industrialization. Such industry required continuous high capital expenditures to maintain or modernize its equipment so that, by the time the Communist system collapsed, engineering, machine tools, shipbuilding, mining and energy were operating with badly dilapidated equipment. Masses of workers were laid off in those industries as state companies were sold off to multinational companies at negligible prices in the hope that foreign capital would re-equip the former state enterprises.[4] But the profits from such ventures were speculative rather than productive: they came from buying assets cheaply and re-selling or re-financing them at a higher price, rather than from the profits of production. The various schemes for distributing new shares to workers or to citizens, like privatisation in the West, only ever made any money through resale in merger or takeover.

The business success of the capitalists from emerging markets, notably the Russian oligarchs, even Arcelor Mittal, the Indian multinational that has bought up the steel industry of Slovakia, comes from their financial enhancements rather than the development dynamic of capitalism. By financial enhancements is meant here access to financial markets and operations within those financial markets.[5] Two operations in particular are at the heart of the way in which finance operates in the modern and emerging capitalist system. The first of these is secured lending, that is loans secured against assets. This allows banks, in practice, to overcome all those problems of asymmetric information to which New Keynesian theorists like Joseph Stiglitz and Frederic Mishkin attribute all banking problems.[6] If an asset is held as security against a loan then, providing that the value of the asset does not fall below the value of the loan repayments, there is no risk of default: should the borrower not pay, then the asset may be seized.

The difficulty in emerging markets and in the post-communist economies was that, until asset markets had developed, assets seized through non-payment could not be easily sold. Indeed, in the first years of transition, such was the 'liquidity hunger' among businesses, that obtaining a loan against an asset owned by a business and then defaulting on the loan became a way of acquiring liquid capital. The credit equivalent of the loan was, in effect, seized by the borrowing business and the bank given in return an illiquid asset.

Once asset markets develop, the second key credit operation becomes crucial to business success. This is using credit to buy assets that are appreciating in value because credit is coming into the markets for those assets through secured lending. Appreciating assets allow their owners to make a profit from capital gain. Notable here are real estate markets that have enjoyed a boom throughout Eastern Europe, until recently. Once financial markets are established then the obvious assets to use for this kind of speculation are financial assets. Real estate capital can be turned over more rapidly than industrial capital; financial assets can be turned over even more rapidly than real estate.

The developmental benefit of finance comes from its application to industrial production. Initially it was thought that the emergence of capitalism was being constrained by the lack of commercial banking and finance. However, even when this was successfully established, in most of the post–communist countries by the mid–1990s, the indigenous industrial capitalists were still missing. The reason was financial development. This keeps asset markets liquid, which in turn allows the balance sheets of companies to be far more liquid than the balance sheets of industrial capitalist producers operating with illiquid capital equipment.

Banking and finance develop in this way, forcing corporate finance towards speculation, because the turnover of capital is the alpha and omega of capitalist reproduction. Marx made this explicit in his analysis of circuits of capital, where he gave production the key intermediate role, because production generates surplus value, which financial market operations cannot create. Nevertheless, in a credit economy capital gains are profit and claims on surplus value. Moreover, once finance disengages from production, capital can be turned over much more rapidly and massively in financial markets. This disengagement is a key feature of today's finance-dominated capitalism.

Economic and financial liberalization in transition and emerging economies complicate the situation in those countries by allowing their indigenous proto–capitalists (or, more correctly perhaps, proto–rentiers) access to the financial markets of the financially advanced capitalist countries, in Western Europe and North America. This has greatly increased the scope for turning over capital in far more sophisticated markets. It again explains why such liberalization has failed to produce an effective industrial capitalist class, other than among small and medium-sized enterprises. Indigenous capitalists who can command credit prefer to use it to generate faster and easier profits in financial speculation. Small and medium-sized enterprises, with limited access to financial markets, can only accumulate capital through production. But that accumulation depends on the reinvestment of modest and precarious profits that are also needed as reserves, in the form of liquid assets, against the extreme fluctuations in business that have been experienced in Eastern Europe since 1990.

Apart from indigenous capitalists, another class of capitalist enterprise has also been active in Eastern Europe. These are multinational companies. They have entered Eastern Europe attracted less by cheap labour and more by mineral resources (oil, gas and metals) during a period of rising commodity prices in the 1990s and up to 2008. In the larger Eastern European countries the major attraction has been the size of the market. Many multinationals have entered Eastern Europe as a result of foreign direct investment (FDI). But little of that has been in the form of fixed capital investment. Most such FDI has been buying former state companies, usually at very low prices from financially-pressed governments. Far from upgrading and improving the capital equipment of former state companies, multinationals have tended to reduce industrial activity to assembly operations, concentrating production in home countries. The scandal of the Polish turbine producer which was taken over by ABB and run down, before being completely shut down, is a case in point.[7]

FINANCIAL CRISIS TODAY

As Marx showed, capitalist financing is about lending against assets. Since the late 19th century, through into the twentieth century, capitalist financing had come to be about financing productive assets. The value of those productive capital assets is then determined by the stream of income that they may be used to generate. This kind of financing is apparent in Marx's analysis of *interest-bearing capital* in *Capital*, as well as in Keynes's *General Theory*. In effect these analyses postulate financing against streams of future *income* flows generated by the application of finance to profitable ventures. Actual financing from the late nineteenth century developed in a different direction, towards advancing credit against an increase in the value of an asset: a change in *stock* value rather than a flow. The increase in asset value depends on the liquidity of the markets in those assets for its realization or conversion into money.

The difference between financing against assets whose value is determined by income streams, and financing against assets, especially real estate or financial assets, whose value is determined by the credit coming into asset markets, provides the vital clue to understanding the financial crises that emerged in Eastern Europe, in Latvia, Estonia and Hungary, in the wake of the American crisis of 2007-08. The transitional economies were encouraged to open up their financial systems to asset-based lending and to FDI. Foreign direct investment hardly made up for the collapse in state-financed investment and the drastic squeeze imposed by self-financing on state enterprises. Eastern Europe languished in slow growth and periodic financial and economic crisis. Hyperinflation in the early 1990s was dealt with by market forces, reducing the incomes and employment from those on the lowest incomes upwards. This was a prolonged process because many more on the lowest incomes have to lose their jobs and incomes to obtain a given reduction in market demand, than if those with higher incomes are squeezed. When lower incomes are reduced, so is consumption, and this immediately affects the retail sector and companies serving the consumption sector. In turn, this affects the quality of bank loans advanced to those companies. Latvia and the Czech Republic experienced a first round of banking crisis around 1993.

In the economic and financial crises that followed the collapse of the communist regimes, the aspirations of the working class and its allies for a more democratic socialism were thwarted by the drive of the International Monetary Fund (IMF), the World Bank, and numerous private sector consultants to create a model of free-market capitalism on the ruins of the communist economy.[8] The failure of the new democracy to satisfy the aspirations of the mass of working people involved not only an ideological shift but also bred social divisions. Nationalist sentiments that had been suppressed under communism were now acceptable and legitimized hostility to ethnic and religious minorities, generally Jews and gypsies – more specifically Hungarians in Slovakia, Turks in Bulgaria and Russians in Latvia. Extremes of nationalism were reached in Yugoslavia as Western encouragement to secession fomented a frenzy of killing that reduced a once-prosperous multinational federation into micro-states under international supervision.

The entry in 2003 of Poland, Hungary, the Czech Republic, Slovakia, Slovenia and the Baltic States into the European Union (EU) brought a degree of stability and renewed financing for economic and social infrastructure. The apparent stability encouraged asset-based lending and foreign direct investment. Industrial production recovered slowly from the crises of the 1990s. But the largest growth in demand came from the consumption of the middle classes, whose confidence in capitalism (even though few of them were capitalists) was revived by rising real estate markets, new means of financing desirable durable goods and visa-free travel.

The stabilization of Eastern European economies through FDI and EU support stabilized their banking systems, helped by the emergence of proper asset markets in real estate and financial securities. The middle classes and the political and business establishments in Eastern Europe reassured themselves that pampering the middle classes and asset inflation were stable and 'normal' ways in which capitalism functions. However, the apparent stabilization masked continuing weak capital accumulation in the region. Consumption-led growth, with underlying industrial stagnation, in Eastern Europe, as in North America and the UK, resulted in a widening foreign trade deficit. In Latvia, by 2006, the trade deficit had reached a staggering 25 per cent of Gross Domestic Product (GDP).

In mercantile capitalism, a trade deficit gives rise to the depreciation of domestic currencies, as more imports have to be purchased without an increase in foreign currency inflow. However, with a liberalized capital account, inflows of foreign direct investment (FDI) may cover the foreign trade deficit, allowing the exchange rate to be stabilized. With the collapse of their manufacturing industry and the stabilization of middle-class incomes and consumption, the foreign trade of most countries in Eastern Europe went into deficit, making those countries dependent upon foreign capital inflows to cover their deficits in trade. Without such capital inflows there is a tendency for the local currency to lose its value (or depreciate) against the foreign currency needed to buy imports, because the supply of foreign currency from exports is inadequate. Governments of the new member countries of the EU, and aspiring new members, sought this kind of exchange rate stabilization, through attracting foreign capital, as a prelude to entry into the European Monetary Union (which all new member governments of the EU have to join). The crisis that has hit Hungary and Latvia came as a result of the failure of those FDI flows in the wake of the collapse of Lehman Brothers in September 2008.[9] As international financial markets froze up because of fears of non-payment on international financial commitments, capital flows to Eastern Europe fell off, reducing the inflows of foreign currency that had previously kept exchange rates stable.

While the course of the crisis in many Eastern European countries has varied according to the different circumstances of each country, there are certain common features. For example, the Hungarian crisis of 2008 arose out a speculative selling in the foreign exchange market of the local currency, the forint, with its government's finances heavily exposed by having the highest per capita foreign debt in the region.[10] The Latvian crisis, by contrast, arose in an economy that had pegged its currency, the Lat, to the euro, only to find that the local rate of inflation, due to buoyant local demand and asset inflation, made Riga one of the most expensive cities in Europe. The reaction of banks in both countries was to discourage lending, causing economic activity to slow down. The Latvian Government's difficulties were made worse by a taxation reform that had introduced flat rate taxes on property (real estate) and business. The reform was supposed to encourage enterprise, while keeping the effective tax rate on labour income at a staggeringly high 59 per cent. Needless to say, this highly skewed and regressive tax regime encouraged employment to go into the informal cash economy, with the result that, when business activity slowed down and government expenditure on welfare rose, tax revenue rapidly fell away and the fiscal deficit rose sharply. Government debt, which had been just 7.9 per cent of Latvia's GDP in 2007, shot up to 74 per cent in 2010, much the same level of indebtedness as that of Hungary.[11] Both the Latvian and the Hungarian governments rapidly embraced International Monetary Fund financing packages, with the usual strict conditionalities imposing reductions in government expenditure and raising taxes. IMF loans were substantially reinforced by loans from other European governments. In the case of Latvia, only $10 billion came from the IMF. Some $18 billion came from the European Union, the Nordic countries, Estonia, Poland and the Czech Republic.

Both Hungary and Latvia resisted the devaluation of their currencies against the Euro. Such a devaluation would have caused FDI to dry up, while raising inflation in countries that depend on imports for most (in the case of Latvia virtually all) of their consumption of manufactured commodities. In the region, the abandonment of exchange rate pegs would have exposed other countries with similar pegs to the Euro (most notably Slovakia and Estonia) to similar runs on their foreign exchange, and brought to a standstill the eastward expansion of the Eurozone. This is why the European Bank for Reconstruction and Development and the European Central Bank have all offered assistance, but on tough banking terms that require governments to generate fiscal surpluses in the future in order to repay the loans.

One curious point about the assistance from the IMF is that much of it is in the form of lending to international banks rather to the governments in trouble. Under a little-known agreement with international banks at the end of March 2009, known as the Vienna Initiative, those banks are supposed to continue to lend to private customers through their subsidiaries in the countries affected, in order, ostensibly, to prevent credit markets in those countries from freezing.[12] The Vienna Initiative is crucial for the countries in crisis. A notable feature of the countries of Eastern Europe is the takeover of their banking systems by foreign banks, leaving only a small minority of bank lending in the hands of locally-based banks. Foreign ownership of banks now represents a major change in the financial systems of those countries. The money market operations of central banks in those countries are in effect conducted with foreign banks. The commitment of those foreign banks to the post-communist countries was strong while asset markets in those countries were rising. Those markets are now falling. Moreover, those foreign banks (notably Italy's UniCredit and Vienna-based Raiffeisen International, and France's Société Générale, all of which have benefitted from the loans given by the IMF) are now under twin pressures to increase their lending in their home countries and to raise their capital ratios (the ratio of capital to risk-weighted assets). The easiest way of raising their capital ratios is reducing the lending that is deemed to be risky. Given the increased financial risks now attendant upon lending in peripheral markets, such as the post-communist ones, it is perhaps inevitable that those banks will reduce their lending to Eastern Europe, blaming the usual policy errors of governments in that region.

The international financial establishment has identified 'macroeconomic imbalances' (i.e., foreign trade and government deficits) as to blame for the financial crisis in Eastern Europe. These imbalances were created by the new features of those countries' financial systems; that is the way in which liberalized financial systems favour asset inflation and middle-class consumption without any corresponding increase in local production. The most striking example of such features is the United States, which has pioneered massive deficit financing of its government expenditure and its foreign trade. Indeed, its deficits are essential for the financial stability of the rest of the world because the deficits provide the flow of dollars to service the international credit and debt system. The misfortune of the post-communist states in crisis, and most other countries in the world, is that they are unable to finance deficits through the export of their domestic currencies. At the same time, fiscal deficits are a problem in the EU because their central banks are not allowed to regulate government bonds markets in the way other central banks – most notably the United States Federal Reserve and the People's Bank of China – effectively do so.

Moreover, it would be wrong to take at face value the economic diagnoses offered up by economists representing financial interests, the IMF or the World Bank. They not only got it disastrously wrong in advance of the crisis of 2007-09. They have also offered up contradictory advice, urging

Keynesian stimulus in 2008, only to criticize the growing indebtedness of governments two years later. An ugly class bias is now apparent in the view gaining ground, among central banks and in finance ministries, that the revival of economic activity in Eastern Europe can only now be obtained by a structural adjustment in the labour market. The painless way to obtain this is by devaluation of the domestic currency against the Euro. This would exclude for the foreseeable future membership of the European Monetary Union, to which all new member states are supposed to be committed. The alternative way is what is euphemistically called 'reducing the wage-price ratio', i.e., cutting real wages, as a way of generating 'international competitiveness'. This view confuses the economics of individual firms with the economics of whole countries. For a country as a whole, a fall in real wages reduces domestic demand and actually increases unemployment, rather than decreasing it. Any increased economic activity due to greater competitiveness must, if it is to be effective, exceed the initial fall in demand due to lower real wages.

The rationale for increasing 'competitiveness' in this way is that it may attract FDI again, bringing in much-needed foreign currency and spearheading economic revival. This is unlikely because falling demand discourages FDI inflows rather than encouraging them. FDI is only attracted by low wages if there is a growing market nearby. But the largest markets for Eastern European business are in Western Europe, and those markets are stagnant because of financial crisis and falling real wages. Finally, the very mechanism of international capital flows is now crippled because of the financial crisis, and the reduced investment of key multinationals (e.g., Arcelor Mittal) since 2008.

There is a further reason for resisting the adjustment of 'macroeconomic imbalances' through the labour market. This is the existence of debt in modern credit-based economies – debt being the balance-sheet counterpart of credit. As Europe's national financial systems have become more integrated, much as globally financial systems have become integrated around the US dollar and American financial markets, the solution that seems obvious to capitalists of reducing wages in countries in crisis, while they rise in the apparently more stable countries such as Germany and Scandinavia, would actually make those imbalances worse. Since prices follow wages, this solution would cause inflation in Germany and Scandinavia, and deflation in the peripheral, crisis-hit countries. Rising prices would then cause a reduction in the real value of German and Scandinavian business debt, while falling prices in Greece, Hungary and Latvia raise the real value of business debt in those countries. This means that, far from redirecting production from higher cost Germany and Scandinavia to countries now affected by debt crises, the reflation of those higher cost countries will concentrate production even more in those countries.[13]

The fiscal programmes being inflicted upon all governments in Eastern Europe, but obviously with greatest urgency on the governments in crisis in Hungary and Latvia, all involve reductions in expenditure. This contrasts with the 'Keynesian' policies adopted in Poland, whose government has avoided crisis at the expense of only token reductions in its expenditure. When asked about the cost in unemployment of his fiscal austerity package, the Hungarian Prime Minister, Viktor Orban, on a visit to London in October 2009, referred to grants being given by the European Commission and multilateral agencies to support social welfare programmes, and increased reliance on foreign remittances. As Western Europe succumbs to the crisis, remittances are if anything likely to fall rather than rise, while the 'contracting out' of social services to NGOs and multilateral agencies threatens the welfare state foundation of modern social democracy.

CLASS AND POLITICS

The politics and social complexion of Eastern Europe is determined, as elsewhere, by the balance of class forces in the countries of that region, and also, to an unusual extent, by the region's historic economic, financial and political dependence on powerful neighbours. In domestic politics, this has placed nationalism in opposition to class politics. Under communism, political dependence on the Soviet Union brought a degree of industrial and social progress (in women's rights and cultural policy, for example). But it always had a tendency to reinforce backwardness, through the incorporation of traditional leaders who became ruling party secretaries when communism took over, most notably in the Central Asian parts of the Soviet Union, or later under Brezhnev, when social policy took a distinctly conservative turn. The legacy of this backwardness is the political immaturity of the 'new democracies'. They aimed at playing off the great powers, seeking membership of the EU but, at the same time, using American military interest in pursuit of regional rivalries, as in the case of the Anti-Ballistic Missile installations that aroused the anti-Russian interest of Slovak and Polish governments. The EU, in particular, became the new pole of attraction after the collapse of the Soviet Union. Social progress was put on hold because, after years of 'goulash socialism', consumption has become the focus of individual and social aspiration.

The main casualty of the polarization of nationalist and communist politics has been class politics. Communism in backward Russia, with a narrow social base for the working-class movement, could only survive using dictatorial methods which were then imposed on the rest of Eastern Europe. Ironically, communist governments got the working class that they deserved: in Poland, the Solidarity movement had a socialist and syndicalist core, but it also showed clericalist and nationalist influences. By the end of the 1980s, the inability of communist governments to sustain living standards and democratic engagement led to their downfall.

But post-communist governments have not done very well. After an initial period of democratic enthusiasm, they got the capitalism that they deserved: a large-scale rentier capitalism operating in financial markets rather than applying finance to expanded reproduction, contrasting with the many petty capitalists in small and medium-sized enterprises eking out a precarious living in services or small-scale production. The result is that industrial employment has not recovered to the levels reached in the final years of communism.

The biggest social change has been the rise of unemployment, virtually unknown under communism. This rose dramatically immediately after the fall of communism, and subsequently fell in the early years of this century, as economic activity stabilized, especially among the new member countries of the EU, and in Russia after its crisis of 1998 and its subsequent commodities boom. The key cause of the first rise in unemployment was the breakdown in industrial cross-subsidies in the previous centrally planned system. The imposition of a hard budget constraint, before firms had had a chance to accumulate reserves of liquid assets (as capitalist firms in the West have) was bound to have a devastating effect on economic activity and employment.

In the end, unemployment was managed by the expansion of the middle classes and services (especially financial and business services), 'forced' self-employment or entry into precarious small business activity, part-time or casual employment, and emigration, most commonly to the EU. But this has been accompanied by immigration to the new member EU countries from non-EU countries. In any case, these changes in employment have had a devastating effect on the working-class movement, reducing its most important concentrations in large factories and other places of work. Large factories are most at risk in the shift to raw materials production (in Russia) and services (in all the countries of Eastern Europe).

The main beneficiaries of the fall of communism may be found among the middle classes. The 'free' professions of law, medicine and accountancy, had their incomes and professional independence reduced under communism. After 1990 their business burgeoned as authority shifted from the political authorities to the courts and private medicine flourished. More importantly, their ranks were joined by a whole new stratum of business and financial services personnel. This stratum expanded with the introduction of a new business of consultancy, giving advice on a range of questions from the organization of a business, through financing of that business, and its (possibly) eventual dissolution in the periodic crises that have plagued the post-communist economies. To this must be added a growing profession of banking, as households moved over to operating with bank accounts and borrowing for house purchase, and as financial development allowed firms to make money from turning over their balance sheets in the new financial markets. Another segment of the middle class – those employed in public services, such as teaching, health care and public administration – did not do so well. Falling real wages and reduced staffing contributed to insecurity and a deterioration in conditions of work.

INDUSTRIAL VERSUS FINANCE CAPITAL

The collapse of communism in 1989-90 was an opportunity for the labour movements in those communist countries to install social democracy and capitalism directed by social priorities.[14] That collapse gave Eastern Europe democracy, weakened by feeble class politics, and two decades of speculative financial capitalism, in which businessmen turn capital over in financial markets and pretend that they are capitalists, and multinational companies buy companies in Eastern Europe and pretend that they are investing while in reality running them down. Both local and multinational companies benefit from the access that financial liberalization gives to the more sophisticated markets in the major financial centres of the world. But that has also weakened the productive impetus of the 'new capitalists' and exposes Eastern Europe to the crisis of those financial centres.

The working class in Eastern Europe faces the current crisis of accumulation in the region handicapped by the absence of a socialist alternative. In countries that have managed to evade recent financial difficulties, such as Poland and the Czech Republic, workers with jobs view their continuing employment as the just reward that capitalism bestows for their effort and loyalty, while looking anxiously at countries in the region hit by crisis. However, even the relative stability of the fortunate countries cannot hide the rising youth unemployment, reaching up to 40 per cent in certain regions. For the young unemployed the only vent is the traditional one of emigration. Indeed, on 1 May 2011, German restrictions on labour immigration from Eastern Europe expired. This is how the present regional macroeconomic imbalances will be resolved through the labour market.

The political elite in Eastern Europe, supported by the conservative establishments in central banks, the International Monetary Fund and the European Commission, will offer solutions to local crises restricted to 'technical questions' of exchange rates and the refinancing of bad debts, and making workers pay for the crisis. Their solutions will at best revive asset inflation, instead of reviving productive economic activity, and distort still further the problems of uneven development in European capitalism. The financial crises in their neighbourhood have made this political elite even more sensitive to the financial interest in their local capitalism. This essay's historical and comparative perspective reveals those crises to be merely the latest stage of the confrontation between finance capital, which creates luxury, but cannot create value, and industrial capital, which can generate value, but is corrupted by luxury. All over the world, except perhaps in China, finance confronts industrial capitalism to sap the dynamism of capital accumulation with the prospect of easy profits from financial operations rather than production. Eastern European industry remains a legacy of state-sponsored industrialization. Only in Eastern Europe does industrial enterprise enter the confrontation with finance bearing the stigma of communism.

NOTES

This paper is in large part a personal reflection on my discussions with Tadeusz Kowalik, whose wisdom and insight into the problems of the post-communist countries far exceeds mine. The author is grateful to the participants in a *Socialist Register* workshop in Toronto in February 2010 for helpful suggestions and comments on an earlier draft. Their generosity leaves the author entirely responsible for the remaining errors.

1   Michał Kalecki, *Selected Essays on the Dynamics of the Capitalist Economy 1933-1970*, Cambridge: Cambridge University Press, 1971, p. 109.
2   World Bank and International Finance Corporation, *Doing Business in 2009*, Washington: World Bank, 2008.
3   T.M. Podolski, *Socialist Banking and Monetary Control*, Cambridge: Cambridge University Press, 1973; Kazimierz Poznanski with Joanna Poznanska and Hai Yue Liu,'
4   Peter Gowan, 'Neoliberal Theory and Practice in Eastern Europe', *New Left Review*, 213, 1995. See also European Bank for Reconstruction and Development, *Transition Report 1994*, London: EBRD, 1995 and Jan Toporowski, 'Neo-liberalism: The Eastern European Frontier', in Alfredo Saad-Filho & Deborah Johnston, eds., *Neoliberalism: A Critical Reader*, London: Pluto Press 2005.
5   Jan Toporowski, 'The Transnational Company after Globalisation', *Futures*, 42(9), 2010, pp. 920-25.
6   Ricardo M. Bebczuk, *Asymmetric Information in Financial Markets*, Cambridge: Cambridge University Press, 2003.

7   B. Domański, 'Poland, Labour and the Relocation of Manufacturing from the EU', in G. Gradev, ed., *CEE Countries in EU Companies' Strategies of Industrial Restructuring and Relocation*, Brussels: European Trades Union Institute, 2001.

8   Peter Gowan, 'Neoliberal Theory and Practice in Eastern Europe', captures the constructivist ardour of Western diplomats, academics, and financiers, although it exaggerates the consistency of their aspirations. George Soros, for example, has devoted much of his philanthropy to the establishment of democratic institutions in Eastern Europe. However, in 1998, he shamed the West into providing financial support for Russian democracy, support that enabled the Russian Government to repay loans outstanding to Soros.

9   Grzegorz Gorzelak and Chor-Ching Goh, *Financial Crisis in Central and Eastern Europe: From Similarity to Diversity*, Leverkusen Opladen: Verlag Barbara Budrich, 2011.

10   László Andor, 'Hungary's Boomerang Effect', *The Guardian*, 29 October 2008.

11   Michael Hudson and Jeffrey Sommers, 'World Economic Crisis', *Global Research*, Centre for Research on Globalization, 15 February 2010, available from http://www.globalresearch.ca.

12   European Bank for Reconstruction and Development, 'The Vienna Initiative – Moving to a New Phase', May 2011.

13   Jan Toporowski, *Why the World Economy Needs a Financial Crash and Other Critical Essays on Finance and Financial Economics,* London: Anthem Press, 2010.

14   Tadeusz Kowalik, *Współczesne systemy ekonomiczne*, Warszawa: Wydawnictwo Wyższej Szkoły Przedsiębiorczości i Zarządzania im. Leona Koźmińskiego, 2000, chapter 10.

WHEN BANKS CANNIBALIZE THE STATE: RESPONSES TO IRELAND'S ECONOMIC COLLAPSE

PEADAR KIRBY

Even though for a period in the 1850s and late 1860s, Ireland was seen by Marx and Engels as holding the key to a revolution in England, the country has since attracted little more than passing attention from socialist analysts internationally.[1] Despite the revolutionary origins of the independent Irish state, politics since has been dominated by a bourgeois nationalism that gave way in the 1960s to an extreme subservience to global capital as the country opened to foreign investment. The Irish Labour Party, a party with the weakest of social democratic credentials, traditionally played the role of the half party in Ireland's 'two and a half party system', having to coalesce always with conservative parties, particularly Fine Gael, to oust the dominant Fianna Fáil party from power. Where socialist parties emerged to the left of Labour, they remained miniscule and failed to win any representation at national or local level until the 1980s. Furthermore, the dominance of Irish society by an authoritarian and conservative Catholicism, coupled with the fact that the 'national question' (namely how to address the partition of the island) deeply divided the left, meant that Ireland proved very barren soil for socialist ideas to take root. Conflict in Northern Ireland, which re-emerged in the late 1960s and persisted until the peace agreement of 1998, tended to puzzle rather than attract socialists as it by and large seemed a throwback to late 19th and early 20th century independence struggles. As a result, at no time up to the present has Ireland shown any promise to challenge global capitalism.

As the title to this paper indicates, however, this may be changing. Following the seeming dramatic success of the years of the Celtic Tiger boom (1994-2007), the even more dramatic collapse of the Irish banking system since 2008 has, as stated by senior Labour politician Pat Rabbitte, a former party leader and currently Minister for Communications, Energy and

Natural Resources, come to threaten the solvency and stability of the Irish state itself.[2] Not only has this led to a significant breakthrough for the left in the February 2011 general election, but it has raised serious questions about the sustainability of the extreme free-market road to development followed by successive Irish governments. As a member of both the European Union (EU) and the eurozone, the Irish crisis furthermore threatens the cohesion of the Union and the longer term viability of the common currency. After decades when free-market capitalism seemed unassailable, Ireland is showing the economic and social cost of promoting the market as the motor and arbiter of what constitutes development. From being the poster child of success in the era of globalization, Ireland has now become a warning signal.[3]

When the International Monetary Fund (IMF) issued its first annual report on Ireland subsequent to the economic and financial collapse of September 2008, it wrote in its measured way that the Irish crisis 'matches episodes of the most severe economic distress in post-World War II history'.[4] At the time, this was taken as something of an exaggeration. After all the then Minister for Finance, Brian Lenihan of the Fianna Fáil party, in announcing a state guarantee covering customer deposits and the banks' own borrowings to a total of €440 billion early in the morning of 30 September 2008 to avert what was feared would be the imminent collapse of at least one bank, had described his government's approach as providing the cheapest bailout in history. Yet, as became ever clearer over the subsequent thirty months, what the government had done was to hand Irish taxpayers the bill for the reckless practices of the Irish banking sector during the economic boom, a bill that grew exponentially over that period resulting in a budget deficit in 2010 of 32 per cent of GDP as the economy experienced its worst contraction in the state's history and unemployment grew to 14.7 per cent by early 2011.

While the economic collapse was severe in itself, what heightened its impact on the Irish people was that it came in the wake of the country's greatest economic boom with its high growth rates in the late 1990s and early 2000s earning it the title of 'Celtic Tiger'. This was achieved through Ireland's success in winning very high levels of foreign direct investment in key sectors such as information and communications technology (ICT), pharmaceuticals, medical devices and financial services. The principal policy tool was widely seen as Ireland's low level of tax on corporate profits, which is set at 12.5 per cent. The use of low tax rates generated a widespread consensus during the boom years towards the reduction of tax, particularly on capital gains and on incomes, which left the state's finances in a very vulnerable position once growth collapsed in 2008. The low-tax model also failed to invest in social provision for the most needy thus leaving severe social deficits that badly need significant public investment if they are not to worsen further.

One result was a more critical evaluation in public debate of what had been widely regarded as very successful economic policies. Indeed, the collapse prompted a lively public debate on the need for extensive reforms of the electoral and political system, reforms that dominated the campaign for the February 2011 general election. This election saw Fianna Fáil, the populist party that had dominated Irish politics since its foundation in 1927, never being out of power for more than one term and always being the largest party even when in opposition, reduced to a rump as its vote collapsed from 41 per cent in 2007 to 17.4 per cent and losing 58 of the 78 seats it had won in the previous election. Fine Gael, which had always remained the smaller of the two dominant parties, supplanted Fianna Fáil as Ireland's largest party with 76 seats in the 166-seat Dáil or lower house of parliament. Labour was returned with its largest vote ever and 37 seats. Apart from Labour's success with 19.4 per cent of the vote, a number of parties to the left of Labour made substantial gains, including Sinn Féin (14 seats), the United Left Alliance (comprising the Socialist party and other left-wing groups) (5 seats)[5] and some vocal left-wing independents (6 seats); this marks by far the largest left-wing block ever elected to an Irish parliament, with over 60 seats and some 43 per cent of the popular vote. In March Fine Gael and Labour formed a coalition government with the largest majority in Irish electoral history.

CRISIS, WHAT CRISIS?

The first signs that Ireland's growth economy was faltering appeared in 2007 as prices in the booming housing market began to fall. But it was not until mid 2008 that it became clear that the economy was entering into a deep recession. Even then most forecasters were predicting a return to growth in 2009, expecting that an upswing in the global economy would increase demand for Irish exports. The collapse of Lehman Brothers in September 2008, however, exposed the vulnerability of the Irish banking sector as a gap of around €200 billion between what the banks had lent (largely to property developers) and deposits taken in had been bridged by borrowing in international markets. Access to these markets began to dry up. The bank most exposed to the property market, Anglo Irish Bank, started losing deposits of around €1 billion a day as international depositors withdrew their money. Within days it became clear that most other Irish banks were also in difficulties. This prompted the €440 billion Irish government guarantee of the banking system after an all-night crisis meeting between the government and the heads of the largest Irish banks.

While the government guarantee avoided the collapse of any Irish bank, it failed to resolve the banking crisis largely because the Fianna Fáil government drastically underestimated its depth. Indeed, the period since September 2008 witnessed five different attempts to estimate the final bill for bailing out the Irish banks: the tab grew from €5.5 billion in December 2008, to €11 billion in March 2009, to €35 billion in March 2010, and to €46 billion in September 2010. It was the loss of credibility and the steady downgrading by rating agencies of both the state's and the banks' credit ratings, that made the Irish banking system increasingly dependent on day-to-day support from the European Central Bank (ECB). The extent of this support set alarm bells ringing in Frankfurt and Brussels, forcing the Irish government to accept a rescue package from the EU, the ECB and the IMF at the end of November 2010. Finally, severe 'stress tests' of the banking system at the end of March 2011 led to an estimate of €70 billion to recapitalize the banks. This announcement by the new government within a month of it taking office, coupled with a plan to restructure the banking system, now almost entirely in the hands of the state, was calculated to draw a final line under the crisis and win badly needed credibility in financial markets.

With the financial system seizing up, the Irish economy sharply contracted, with GDP declining by 3.5 per cent in 2008, a further 7.6 per cent in 2009, and 1 per cent in 2010.[6] Growth forecasts for 2011 have been revised downward on a number of occasions by authoritative agencies; for example, in early 2011 the IMF was predicting growth of a mere 0.9 per cent for 2011 and 1.9 per cent for 2012. By the end of 2009 the government budget deficit had widened to 14.6 per cent of GDP. But various measures to cut spending (including two cuts to the incomes of public servants) and some modest tax increases had reduced it to 11.9 per cent by late 2010. However, once the full cost of supporting the banks is factored in, the budgetary deficit is in the order of 32 per cent of GDP as of 2010. This deficit can be traced to two causes. On the one hand, tax receipts fell from €40.7 billion in 2008 to 33 billion in 2009 reflecting the fact that, during the economic boom, the composition of tax revenue had shifted gradually from stable sources of taxation, like personal income tax and VAT/excise taxes, to cyclical taxes, such as corporation tax, stamp duty and capital gains tax. The tax revenues from these sources collapsed once the recession hit. The share of these taxes had reached 30 per cent of tax revenue in 2006, while in the late 1980s it had amounted to only 8 per cent. On the other hand, current expenditure had grown faster than nominal GDP in each year from 2001 to the onset of the crisis, reflecting the fact that the share of Irish public spending in GDP had been well below the European average.[7]

The combined banking collapse and rupture in public finances greatly constrained government action, effectively forcing the Irish state to adopt a series of austerity packages to try to calm markets and reassure the European Commission (EC). This culminated in a four-year austerity plan, entitled *The National Recovery Plan 2011-2014*, setting out in detail how Ireland planned to return the budget deficit to 3 per cent of GDP by 2014 as demanded by the EC. Announced in November 2010, it specified cuts in public spending totalling €10 billion and tax rises of €5 billion over four years. Cuts are spread widely and include reducing the number of public servants by 25,000 from the current level of 307,000, cutting the pay of new entrants to the public service by 10 per cent, public service pensions by up to 12 per cent, and cutting spending on health, education and social welfare. One controversial proposal was to cut the minimum wage by €1 an hour (although this was reversed by the new government in May 2011).

On the tax side, most of the proposals hit low and average-income earners rather than high-income earners, as the central measure was a reduction in the income levels at which people begin to pay tax from €18,300 to €15,300 by the end of the plan. A modest tax on housing and water charges are to be introduced for the first time. In contrast, very modest adjustments to capital gains tax and no increase in corporation tax are proposed. Value Added Tax (VAT) is to rise from 21 to 23 per cent in the final two years of the plan, a measure that will especially hit lower-income households since they spend higher percentages of their incomes on goods and services than do those on higher incomes. This ongoing policy of austerity had the predictable effect of deepening the recession. Unemployment has been rising continuously – and reached almost 15 per cent of the labour force by mid 2011. Ireland's tradition of extensive emigration has begun to re-emerge, with the Economic and Social Research Institute predicting that 120,000 mostly skilled young people would emigrate between 2010 and 2012,[8] though this has been disputed by some experts.

Meanwhile, as a way of trying to resolve the banking sector's heavy exposure to residential and commercial real estate, the prices of which were in freefall since 2007 with no sign of them bottoming out by mid 2011, the state had established the National Asset Management Agency (NAMA) in April 2009 to manage the sector's non-performing loans. Altogether it expected to buy €73 billion worth of non-performing loans from the five banking institutions and for these to pay around half the original value of the debts. In the first six months of 2010, for example, NAMA paid €8.4 billion for property loans with a nominal value of €16.4 billion, paying the banks with bonds which they can then exchange for cash with the ECB. Through relieving the banks of their bad debts, it had been hoped that they could raise fresh capital and so begin lending again. However, the extent of the 'haircut' – as the discount on the value of loans is called – further damaged the balance sheets of the banks. The new government stopped any further transfer of loans to NAMA. In time, the agency hopes to sell the property it has now acquired at a profit, though it is expected to have to simply knock down and return to vacant sites some of the unfinished 'ghost estates' it now owns, particularly those in small towns where demand for housing is unlikely to grow for a very long time. Many of those who did buy property during the boom now find themselves with a serious problem of negative equity. A report by a government-appointed expert group in late 2010 estimated that 70,000 mortgages, or 8.9 per cent of the total, are in arrears – an increase from just under 14,000 or 1.4 per cent in mid 2008. Some observers fear that mortgage delinquency could become a lot worse putting further pressure on the banking sector.[9]

A final and revealing point about the particularities of the Irish economic crisis is that it is entirely a recession of the domestic economy as the foreign-owned sector continues to boom. This is revealed in the performance of Irish exports: these are primarily constituted by goods and services produced by multinationals, the value of which in February 2011 was higher than at any time since 2002 and had risen by 11 per cent over the previous 12 months.[10]

SAVING EUROPE'S BANKS: THE ROLE OF THE EU

The European Union and the European Central Bank have played a major role in the Irish crisis in bolstering the strategy to underwrite the banking system. Public opinion in Ireland about their objectives has tended, however, to become more critical over the course of the crisis, as revealed by an incident in January 2011. This began with comments in the European Parliament by the Socialist Party MEP for Dublin, Joe Higgins, who attacked the EC/ECB/IMF rescue package for Ireland, calling it a mechanism to turn Irish taxpayers into vassals for European banks. Higgins went on to question the morality of transferring to taxpayers the responsibility for the bad debts of the banks. It was, he said, no more than a tool to cushion banks from the consequences of reckless speculation. Clearly angered, the Commission President, José Manuel Barroso, replied that 'the problems of Ireland were created by the irresponsible financial behaviour of some Irish institutions and by the lack of supervision in the Irish market'.[11]

What made this exchange particularly interesting was the letter written soon afterwards by former Taoiseach and former EU ambassador to Washington,

John Bruton, to the Commission President telling him his criticisms of Irish institutions were fully justified. However, Bruton also argued that he was only telling one part of the story as British, German, Belgian and French banks (not to mention banks of other EU countries) as well as American ones, 'lent irresponsibly to the Irish banks in the hope that they too could profit from the Irish construction bubble' and that they 'must take some share of responsibility for the mistakes that were made'. Furthermore, referring to the responsibility of the European Commission for supervising the Irish economy, he wrote: 'You ought to have acknowledged that responsibility of your own institution, which the Commission shares with ECOFIN'.[12] He added that the ECB kept interest rates low 'pursuing interest rate policies that were unsuitable for Ireland'.[13] This letter, from a strongly pro-European senior Irish politician, accurately reflects the widespread view in Ireland that the country has been unfairly treated by both the Commission and the ECB.

Three aspects of Europe's role in the Irish crisis require attention. The first relates to the role of the euro in creating the conditions for the crisis; the second to the actions and advice of European institutions and leaders, particularly the ECB, during the crisis; and the third to the impact of interest rate rises on Ireland's ability to emerge from the crisis. In a report on Ireland's banking crisis commissioned by the Irish Minister for Finance, international financial experts Klaus Regling and Max Watson pose the question: 'Was it a coincidence that Ireland's economic fundamentals began to deteriorate when Ireland joined the euro area?'[14] They argue that certain aspects of EMU membership 'certainly reinforced vulnerabilities in the economy. Short-term interest rates fell by two thirds from the early and mid 1990s to the period 2002-07. Long-term interest rates halved and real interest rates were negative from 1999 to 2005 after having been strongly positive'. This situation contributed to the credit boom in Ireland since low interest rates encouraged borrowing and the removal of exchange rate risk facilitated the banks in accessing foreign funding, ensuring the flow of credit could continue. The authors conclude that policy instruments such as fiscal policy, bank regulation and incomes policy 'were not used to offset the well-known expansionary effects of EMU membership on the macroeconomic environment or even fuelled the fire, in particular tax policies'.[15] But Regling and Watson add that being a member of a large monetary union 'helped Ireland to survive better the global financial crisis' since without it funding problems for the banking sector would have become bigger, firms and households would have borrowed more in foreign currency and so would have been exposed to greater risks (as happened in Iceland), and coordination problems for national central banks would have been significant. They add that 'none of the interlocutors in Ireland and abroad, with whom the authors of this report talked, questioned that EMU membership for Ireland has been, on balance, highly beneficial'.[16]

Once the crisis hit, the lender of last resort role played by the ECB in the Eurozone took on growing importance for Ireland, which by early 2011 had required some 20 per cent of the ECB's total lending to prop up its banking sector, reaching some €140 billion. Murphy argues that it was the ECB's desire for a new mechanism to relieve it of some of this burden that prompted a major change in its monetary policy in mid November 2010: 'As a result the Irish crisis, which has been initially a fiscal/funding crisis as highlighted by the bond markets, shifted to a full-scale crisis about the liquidity and solvency of the Irish banking system'.[17] It was its decision to discontinue lending to Irish banks and seek a new arrangement from the European Commission and the IMF to provide an alternative bailout strategy that forced the Irish government to negotiate in November 2010 an €85 billion package of financial assistance. This was made up of €10 billion for re-capitalization of the banks, a €25 billion bank contingency fund and a €50 billion sum to support the state's borrowing requirements for the next three years. Of this, €22.5 billion comes from the IMF, €22.5 billion from the EU Commission, €17.5 billion from the European Financial Stability Fund and a total of €5 billion in bilateral loans from the UK, Sweden and Denmark.

Controversially, the Irish state is also to contribute €17.5 billion, €12.5 billion of it from the National Pension Reserve Fund, effectively depleting this last financial reserve that the government had as its disposal. The average interest rate on these loans is 5.85 per cent. The agreement endorses many of the measures contained in the Irish government's four-year austerity plan and involves intrusive oversight by officials of the three institutions of Irish budgetary and expenditure decisions. In an interview in April 2011, the former Minister for Finance, Brian Lenihan, substantially supported the claim that it was the ECB rather than the European Commission that precipitated the Irish rescue package and that the Bank did so as Irish banks grew more dependent on its short-term liquidity funding. Prior to November 2010, the ECB had been 'rather disinterested in Ireland', Lenihan said.[18] In the same interview, Lenihan was very critical both of the high rate of interest included in the rescue package and of ECB plans for the Irish banking system, which he described as 'unimplementable'.

The package was extensively criticized in Ireland for the high interest rate, of course, but also for the failure of the European institutions to share any of the burden of adjustment. The influential *Irish Times* columnist Fintan O'Toole, for example, wrote that the package 'is much more [Treaty of] Versailles than Marshall [Plan]. There is no sharing of the burden. There is no evidence of a single thought for the consequences of mass unemployment, mass emigration and war on the most vulnerable. There is no European solidarity… The sadistic pleasures of punishment have trumped the sensible calculation that an Ireland enslaved by debt is not much use to anyone'.[19] In his April 2011 interview, Lenihan stated that the government sought to impose losses on the banks' senior bondholders but that the option was ruled out by the troika of the EC, the Bank and the IMF. 'I discussed the matter with Dominique Strauss-Kahn [IMF managing director] himself and Monsieur Trichet [ECB president], but it was clear to me there was no budge on this whatsoever in the discussions'.[20] The new government promised to negotiate a reduction of the interest rate and less onerous conditions. But European leaders continued to insist that Ireland offer something in return, with French President Sarkozy and German Chancellor Merkel mentioning the need for Ireland to increase its 12.5 per cent corporation tax. This measure is completely refused by Irish politicians.

The final dimension of Europe's role relates to interest rates. If low interest rates throughout the Eurozone were a contributory factor to Ireland's property bubble, it is now paradoxical that the rising interest rates which the ECB began to implement in March 2011 are likely to hinder further any Irish recovery. On the one hand, they will add yet another obstacle to attempts to get Irish banks lending again thus stimulating demand in the economy. On the other, they will add to the burden being carried by many mortgage holders and will further dampen consumer spending. It can be concluded, therefore, that if Europe is widely seen to have contributed to Ireland's economic development over the decades since joining the then European Community in 1973, then its role in the banking crisis is now seen as protecting the interests of Europe's banks at the cost of placing a huge burden on Irish taxpayers and making the prospects of economic recovery more difficult.

AN IRISH ALTERNATIVE?

What then might be an alternative way of dealing with the crisis? The very question presents particular challenges in the Irish case because political life since independence has been dominated by two right-of-centre parties, Fianna Fáil and Fine Gael, originally distinguished from one another by the former's more radical separatist nationalism and the latter's more moderate constitutional variety. In recent decades little has distinguished their positions on the broad content of economic and social policy. The absence of a strong social democratic party has meant that public debate in Ireland has tended to lack a sustained input influenced by any version of socialism. Those lone voices or small parties arguing from such positions have been very easily marginalised. It is significant, therefore, that the period since 2008 has seen a sustained attempt to develop a more left-wing alternative to the approach implemented by the Fianna Fáil-Green coalition government, backed in its essential features by the employers' and business organizations and by many influential economists. This alternative finds some expression in the programme for government of the Fine Gael-Labour coalition that took office in March 2011. Though Fine Gael has tried to distinguish its position from that of Fianna Fáil for electoral reasons, in essence it is closer to the mainstream position than to the alternative one.

This alternative is to be identified primarily in the positions put forward by the Labour Party and by the Irish Congress of Trade Unions (ICTU), with significant contributions on banking, economic and social policies being made by the left-wing think tank, TASC (Think tank on Action for Social Change), and some academics and commentators. The civil society group, Claiming Our Future, has emerged as a key group building a social movement around central ideas of this alternative. A distinct and more critical left-wing position is expressed by Sinn Féin, the Socialist Party and the United Left Alliance which now form a vocal bloc in the Dáil. This bloc distinguishes itself by its rejection of the EC/ECB/IMF rescue package and by its refusal to consider putting any more money into supporting the banking sector. However, the lack of detail as to how such actions might succeed in resolving Ireland's severe crises has presented a major credibility problem for this position.

In the immediate term, the principal issue that divides the neoliberal mainstream from the alternative option relates to the issue of austerity versus stimulus. The neoliberal view has been that severe cuts in public spending and increases in taxation will restore not just the state finances to some kind of sustainable footing but will also restore export competitiveness and so contribute to a return to economic growth, though proponents of this view differ on when this might happen. In contrast, the alternative view argues strongly for the need for a stimulus package to limit job losses and to help invest in small and medium-sized domestic enterprises so as to boost production and to stimulate spending in the economy. According to this view, austerity deepens the crisis and heightens the possibility of prolonging it and the failure to return to growth after three years of austerity is seen as supporting evidence.

Closely linked to the question of austerity versus stimulus is a second difference over expenditure cuts versus tax increases. Those espousing the neoliberal view place the burden of the adjustment on cutting public spending; they are prone to maintain as far as possible the commitment to a low-tax economy. Both of these were strongly promoted by Fine Gael during the 2011 election campaign and, indeed, when in opposition the party proposed even more severe cuts than were being implemented by Fianna Fáil. The alternative option, in contrast, sees much more room for increasing taxes, particularly on the well-off in Irish society, as well as on Irish tax exiles.

This, then, marks a third point of fundamental difference: in the neoliberal view economic recovery is seen to come from the private sector and it has little positive to say about the role to be played by the public sector. For the alternative view, the public sector has a vital role to play through, for example, re-skilling workers, intervening in key sectors of the economy to stimulate development (the telecoms sectors is mentioned) and developing greater capacity to manage expenditure. This more interventionist stance would extend to a fourth difference in terms of the restructuring of the banking sector. From the beginning the Labour Party was a lone voice among political parties in the Dáil in opposing the 2008 blanket guarantee for the banking sector and the establishment of NAMA. It advocated a much more hands-on approach by the state through nationalisation to restructure the banking sector.

A final and major difference between both approaches relates to the need for social investment. Both the Labour Party and ICTU emphasize the need for using stimulus spending or resources generated by a National Recovery Bond to invest in education, infrastructure and better public services. Overall, the alternative approach sees the need for a much more radical break with the past. Paul Sweeney, the ICTU's economic advisor, has written that 'the solution must go far deeper than simply addressing the public finances … We require a fundamental realignment of our economy and society'.[21] And the Labour Party, following other social democratic parties, calls for an end to 'crony capitalism' and supports a new code of practice for corporate governance. How these critical notions will be transformed to policy and practice is hardly clear (particularly given the experiences of the social democratic governments in Greece, Spain and Portugal).

The Programme for Government of the Fine Gael–Labour coalition that took power in March 2011, to provide a particular illustration, cannot be clearly located within either of the alternatives outlined above. It is an amalgam of both parties' policies and lacks any clear strategic departure.

The coalition gives prominence to several commitments: stimulating the economy with the promise of a Jobs Fund within its first 100 days in office; 15,000 places for the unemployed in training, work experience or education; additional resources for a national housing retrofitting plan; and the acceleration of capital works, including schools and secondary roads. These measures come within the constraints of the austerity package for 2011-12 already implemented by the previous government. On the role of the state, it includes key features such as a strategic investment bank and other new developmental state agencies, particularly in bio-energy. But other proposals entail extensive reliance on the private sector, particularly in areas such as upgrading to a new generation telecoms network, developing Ireland as a 'digital island' with particular emphasis on cloud computing, agri-food, home and renewal energy programmes and financial services.[22] Some of this may hold promise for establishing some new growth sectors. But it remains far from certain that the foundations for a new model of productive economy can so easily emerge from the wreckage of financial collapse of the 'Celtic Tiger' without far bolder departures in economic policy.

Indeed, the very narrowness of the coalition government programme against the severity of the Irish financial crisis makes it impossible not to mention the option of default on the debt as a viable – and necessary – option. As the crisis has deepened over the past three years, and with sovereign debt expected to stabilize at somewhere between 110 and 125 per cent of GDP (depending on levels of economic growth achieved), a broad range of opinion acknowledges that such a debt burden will never be repayable and that European and international banks and institutions will have to take significant 'haircuts' on their holdings. If there is a left-right divide on this issue, it concerns whether any default would be unilateral or negotiated. While there is much public talk of 'burning the bondholders', it is 'negotiated burden-sharing' which dominates the discourse of the Fine Gael-Labour coalition. But even this mild compromise runs directly against the position enforced by the ECB and the hardening of opinion within the EU, not only among leaders but also among electorates such as the German and Finnish. In June 2011, the Minister for Finance, Michael Noonan, announced in Washington that he had won IMF support to impose substantial losses on senior bondholders in the two banks whose lending had been most reckless and which are in the process of being closed down – Anglo Irish Bank and Irish Nationwide Building Society. However, he added that he needed to win ECB support for this move and his announcement unnerved the financial markets. This led to his immediate clarification that no moves against bondholders in the other Irish banks were being contemplated. ECB sources also made clear that the Bank was not going to change its opposition to such a move.

The one area on which a consensus for radical reform emerged during the 2011 election relates to the political system. The banking and economic crises revealed serious weaknesses in policy-making. This could be traced back to the electoral system which tends to elect to parliament people more interested in local than national issues, and the weakness of mechanisms of accountability within the legislature. Parties vied with one another as to the extensive reforms they promised the electorate, including a continental-style electoral list system, stronger powers for parliamentary committees, banning corporate donations to political parties, greater transparency and an independent advisory council to oversee government fiscal policy. Labour proposed a constitutional convention to draft a new Constitution with wide-ranging reforms to the political system within 12 months of taking office. *The Irish Times* editorialized that these changes would lead to 'seismic changes in our system of constitutional democracy' of a kind not seen since the foundation of the state.[23] These changes now form a central part of the programme of the new government. Such reforms, if substantially implemented, are likely to result in greater parliamentary oversight over executive decisions and greater public transparency; however, nothing in them concerns the content of economic or social policy.

WHAT NOW FOR THE IRISH MODEL?

The 'Irish model', as it came to be known internationally during the Celtic Tiger boom, liked to present itself as a form of negotiated governance using corporatist type mechanisms. It was commonly labelled 'social partnership' and was meant to achieve a broad consensus among the 'social partners' (which included a range of domestic NGOs beyond the unions) on the central tenets of economic and social policy. This was seen as the key to the successful policies that drove the boom.[24] It was paradoxical, however, that when the banking sector and economy collapsed so, too, did the social partnership as both the government and employers' groups effectively deserted it. Instead of being seen as a key element of success, social partnership came instead to be seen as part of the cosy consensus that had failed to identify and address the weak regulation of the banking sector or the many subsidies and tax breaks that were fuelling the property bubble. Yet, largely under pressure from the trade union leadership, the former government in early 2010 negotiated an agreement on public sector reform which was ratified by most unions in June of that year. Unions which opposed it, including some teachers' unions, were effectively brought into line when the government threatened additional pay cuts on those workers who had not signed up to it. Under the Croke Park Agreement (as it is known after the place where it was negotiated) the unions accepted the need to cut costs in the public sector, largely through the phased reduction of the labour force, and the liberalization of working practices in exchange for a promise of no more pay cuts (but this was conditional on the state not facing a further major funding crisis). The first annual report on the agreement, presented in June 2011, showed that targets on reducing the public pay bill were exceeded (payroll savings of €289 million against a target of €251 million), largely through over 5,000 staff leaving, and that significant non-pay savings of €308 million and productivity gains had also been achieved. Yet, the government insists that further significant cuts – both in expenditure and in the numbers employed in the public service – remain necessary. While being initially very controversial, the Croke Park Agreement has been reluctantly accepted by many workers as offering a phased and negotiated basis for cutbacks that otherwise might be more draconian.

In the run-up to the February 2011 election, attention turned from the Croke Park Agreement to reforming the political system to make it more effective in formulating and implementing policy. What had previously been held up as a successful model of growth came instead to be seen as 'crony capitalism'. The close and mutually beneficial overlapping relationships among elite figures in banking, the construction industry and Fianna Fáil had undergirded some of the speculative excesses of the banking system (this was symbolized by the close personal relationship between successive leaders of Fianna Fáil and the former chief executive of Anglo Irish Bank, Seán Fitzpatrick). This fuelled the public anger against Fianna Fáil, resulting in its catastrophic performance in that election.

However, none of these developments necessitates fundamental changes in the Irish model, which has three fundamental features. The first is the extensive reliance on foreign direct investment as the motor of economic growth. This results in a significant percentage of the value of what is produced in Ireland leaving in the form of profit repatriation, hence the remarkable gap between GDP and GNP in the Irish case, with the latter some 18 per cent less than the former over recent years. This has the consequence not only of a constant haemorrhaging of resources from the Irish economy but of fostering an extreme deference to global corporations on the part of the Irish state. As one leading economist has written, Ireland inverted the normal process of development – instead of generating a wealth-building strategy for the Irish nation, the state simply adapts to the needs of the global firms it seeks to attract to establish in Ireland.[25] The same reflexive dependence on multinationals has now come to characterise the one area of state policy that is seeking to build innovative capacity, namely extensive state investment in research and development (R&D). While this is showing positive results, it is largely benefiting multinationals located in Ireland rather than building capacity in domestically-controlled firms.[26]

The second feature of the Irish model is its commitment to low taxes as an incentive to attract multinational companies, particularly a low level of corporation tax. As a result, Ireland has one of the lowest levels of tax receipts and of public expenditure in the OECD, evident in low spending on health and education, and on public infrastructure, by comparison with the EU or OECD average. This feature of the Irish model led even Garret FitzGerald, a former Fine Gael Taoiseach, to ask just before the collapse: 'why have our governments failed so miserably to deploy the vast resources thus created [during the Celtic Tiger boom] in such a way as to give us the kind of public services we can clearly afford and desperately need?'[27]

The third feature of the Irish model was the creation of a remarkably market-friendly state, what Peter Nyberg in his report for the Department of Finance described as 'the general acceptance of the paradigm of efficient markets'.[28] In practice in Ireland, this meant favouring the private sector both in the non-intrusive forms of regulation it established and in the many tax breaks and subsidies it put in place. As amply documented in reports on the recent crises commissioned by the government, this also meant permitting the state's own economic and policy-making capacity to be eroded for market regulation as opposed to market-building.[29]

The crucial question then is the extent to which currently proposed reforms will change these essential features of the Irish model. The staunch defence of the state's low corporation tax across the political spectrum in Ireland (going so far as to insist that clinging to this policy is a matter of national sovereignty even in the face of intense pressure from key European leaders to raise it) is one illustration of the extent to which the foreign-owned sector remains the priority for political leaders and policy makers. Though support for small and medium-sized enterprises (SMEs) is promised by the new government, there is nothing to indicate that there will be any re-balancing of economic development policy in a way that would, for the first time in half a century, give priority to the development of domestically-owned companies, as opposed to foreign capital, not to speak of building a nationalized state sector. Neither is there any evidence of a commitment to develop a taxation system that would both be more equitable and raise levels of state revenue to something closer to the OECD average. This is despite the widespread consensus that the tax base had been dangerously eroded by a consistent policy of tax-cutting during the boom and pressure by EU leaders for Ireland to adopt more normal European levels of taxation. Indeed, Fine Gael, now the largest party in the Dáil with 76 seats, portrayed itself during the 2011 election campaign as being the low-tax party while Labour dropped its previous policy of introducing a higher band of income tax for high-income earners. While there is a pledge to reform the taxation system, there is nothing in government proposals or discourse to suggest that this will go beyond modifying some of the blatant weaknesses that were allowed to develop during the boom years.

It is the overtly market-friendly state that holds the greatest promise for reform from the coalition with the introduction of a more intrusive and better resourced regulatory system, at least for the banking sector, and a more capable and efficient political system that breaks from the worst cronyism of the Fianna Fáil regimes. While such reforms might provide the state with greater capacity and effectiveness, how they are deployed will determine the future of the 'Celtic Tiger' growth model. The evidence strongly suggests that the Fine Gael-Labour coalition will deliver a more capably managed version of the low-tax Irish model. Ireland will remain heavily dependent on capturing and maintaining at any cost some of the world's leading multinationals in the ICT, pharmaceutical, medical devices and financial services sectors.

While the collapse has bankrupted some leading construction entrepreneurs and generated public outrage at the extravagantly paid senior staff of Irish banks, the Irish economic elite has been little damaged. The *Allianz Global Wealth Report*, for example, shows that the Irish share of global financial assets amounts to €307 billion and these had a 7.1 per cent year-on-year growth from 2008 to 2009. This amounted to financial assets per capita of €68,060, the eighth highest of the 50 countries included which comprise 87 per cent of global GDP.[30] A report on Ireland's 300 wealthiest individuals published by the *Sunday Independent* newspaper revealed that their collective wealth had increased by €6.7 billion between 2010 and 2011 to a total of €57 billion. The number of Irish billionaires had increased from six in 2006, to nine in 2010 and 11 in 2011. The sources of this wealth include music, culture and sport, but most is derived from finance, investment or industry, with technology, telecoms and media businesses, commodities like gas, oil, gold, copper and food, and global construction and retail all listed.[31] Furthermore, despite gains by the left in the 2011 election, it is difficult to argue that there has been a fundamental change in Irish political elites. Fine Gael replaced Fianna Fáil as Ireland's largest party but not only is it a right-of-centre party, it has traditionally represented the professional and commercial elites of Irish society. By contrast Fianna Fáil has always managed to maintain solid bases of support among urban and rural workers while developing close links with emerging economic elites, particularly in the construction industry.

MORE OF THE SAME?

Behind the dramatic collapse of the Celtic Tiger and the remarkable political upheavals of the 2011 general election, a closer examination reveals just how little has really changed in Ireland's political economy and the ruling Irish, European and global elites that benefit from it. Ireland remains a highly dependent liberal market economy, distinguished primarily by the extent of multinational control of the leading sectors of its economy. While some argue for pursuing a more Nordic-style social democratic model, most notably the general secretary of the Irish Congress of Trade Unions, David Begg,[32] this has had minimal impact on public debate in Ireland. It is conventional liberal market precepts which still dominate: the need to get a functioning banking system operating to help stimulate activity in the economy, and the imperatives to cut costs in order to restore competitiveness and reduce the budget deficit. The general expectation therefore is for a return to the fundamentals of the Irish model of growth.

Yet, while the structural features of the Irish economy and society remain largely unchanged, there is widespread anger at the actions of economic and political elites, and a new spirit of intellectual and cultural debate and questioning. For the first time in Irish history, left-wing voices are now gaining a hearing, since their critique of free-market capitalism rings true to many who are suffering from the collapse. The greatly strengthened presence of the left in the Dáil gives added weight and influence to anti-market and anti-capitalist criticisms. Civil society in Ireland is more mobilized than it has been for decades with a new attempt to develop a broad-based movement for radical change.[33] There are spaces opening that may take on greater importance if, as many predict, the crisis proves quite intractable and the recovery fleeting. A new social volatility is already evident in political life, and a decisive move to the left over coming years cannot be ruled out. The crisis is proving a powerful educator in its revelation of how political and capitalist elites have used their power for private gain at the expense of the common good. Out of this may well emerge a new culture of contestation that could begin a real challenge to elite dominance of Irish society and to the Irish economic model that so benefits these elites. The severe financial crisis of the present may be turned into an opportunity for fundamental changes. But if it is, it will only happen through the determined struggle of the Irish working people.

NOTES

1   Ellen Hazelkorn, *Karl Marx and Frederick Engels on Ireland: An Annotated Checklist*, Dublin: DIT, 1980, available at http://arrow.dit.ie.

2   In a debate in the Dáil [lower house of parliament] on 17 November 2010 on the European Commission, European Central Bank and International Monetary Fund rescue package for Ireland, Rabbitte, then in opposition, said: 'Whatever emerges from the discussions with the IMF, the talks had better ensure that this is the last bailout, unless the Government is going to permit the banks to cannibalise the State'. 'Bank Guarantee Scheme: Motion (Resumed)', *Dáil debates*, 17 November 2010, available at http://www.kildarestreet.com.

3   For some left-wing analyses of the Irish boom and bust, see Kieran Allen, *Ireland's Economic Crash: A Radical Agenda for Change*, Dublin: Liffey Press, 2009; Peadar Kirby, *Collapse of the Celtic Tiger: Explaining the Weaknesses of the Irish Model*, Basingstoke: Palgrave Macmillan, 2010; Denis O'Hearn, *Inside the Celtic Tiger: The Irish Economy and the Asian Model*, London: Pluto Press, 1998; Daniel Finn, 'Ireland on the Turn? Political and Economic Consequences of the Crash', *New Left Review*, 67, 2011; Julie L. MacArthur, 'Mortgaging Irish Independence: From Financial Crisis to Socialist Resistance', *Monthly Review*, 62(1), 2011.

4   IMF, 'Ireland: IMF Country Report No. 09/195', Washington, DC: International Monetary Fund, 2009, p. 28.

5   The ULA emerged in the period before the 2011 election as an alliance of three left-wing groups – the small Socialist Party led by Joe Higgins, formerly a leader of the Militant tendency within the Labour Party who went on to electoral success following his expulsion from Labour, the People Against Profit activist group, and a left-wing campaigning group in Tipperary. Some smaller Trotskyist groups remain outside the ULA. The ULA's tally of five Dáil seats is made up of two for the Socialist Party, two for the People Against Profit group and one in Tipperary.

6   GNP is regarded as a more accurate measure of Irish growth since it excludes the profits of multinational companies taken out of the economy; it contracted by 3.5 per cent in 2008, a further 10.7 per cent in 2009 and 2.1 per cent in 2010.

7   Karl Whelan, 'Policy Lessons from Ireland's Latest Depression', *The Economic and Social Review*, 41(2), 2010, p. 246.

8   ESRI, *Quarterly Economic Commentary, Summer 2010*, Dublin: Economic and Social Research Institute, 2010.

9   One researcher who has accurately predicted the scale of the property and banking crises over recent years caused a minor panic in late 2010 when he predicted mass mortgage defaults which would plunge the country into an even deeper and long-lasting recession. See Morgan Kelly, 'If You Thought the Bank Bailout was Bad, Wait Until the Mortgage Defaults Hit Home', *The Irish Times*, 8 November 2010, p. 11.

10 CSO, 'External Trade', Dublin: Central Statistics Office, April 2011.

11 Arthur Beesley, 'Angry Barroso Points Finger of Blame at Irish Institutions', *The Irish Times*, 20 January 2011, p. 1.
12 ECOFIN is the Economic and Financial Affairs Council of the EU and is composed of finance ministers.
13 John Bruton, 'A Letter to President Barroso of the European Commission', January 2011, available from http://www.johnbruton.com.
14 Klaus Regling and Max Watson, *A Preliminary Report on the Sources of Ireland's Banking Crisis*, Dublin: Government Publications, 2010, p. 24.
15 Ibid., pp. 24–5.
16 Ibid., p. 25.
17 Antoin Murphy, 'ECB Shift from Lender of Last Resort Casts Doubt on Independence', *The Irish Times,* Business This Week supplement, 26 November 2010, p. 3.
18 Dan O'Brien, 'Banking on Europe: The True Story Behind Ireland's Bailout', *The Irish Times*, 23 April 2011, p. 11.
19 Fintan O'Toole, 'Abysmal Deal Ransoms Us and Disgraces Europe', *The Irish Times*, 29 November 2010, p. 11.
20 Dan O'Brien, 'Lenihan Warned EU Tough Bailout Terms Could Spark Unrest', *The Irish Times*, 25 April 2011, p. 1.
21 Paul Sweeney, 'What We Need for Recovery is a Major Keynesian-Style Stimulus Package', *The Irish Times*, 31 January 2009, p. 15.
22 Department of the Taoiseach, 'Programme for Government, 2011', Dublin: Department of the Taoiseach, 2011.
23 Leader, *The Irish Times*, 8 February 2011.
24 For a critical overview of social partnership, see Kirby, *Collapse of the Celtic Tiger*, pp. 179–82; Kieran Allen, *The Celtic Tiger: The Myth of Social Partnership in Ireland*, Manchester: Manchester University Press, 2000; and Niamh Gaynor, *Transforming Participation? The Politics of Development in Malawi and Ireland*, Basingstoke: Palgrave Macmillan, 2010.
25 John Bradley, 'The Computer Sector in Irish Manufacturing: Past Triumphs, Present Strains, Future Challenges', *Journal of the Statistical and Social Inquiry Society of Ireland*, XXXI, 2002.
26 Kirby, *Collapse of the Celtic Tiger*, pp. 153–56.
27 Garret FitzGerald, 'Public Services Make a Shabby Contrast with National Wealth', *The Irish Times,* 22 March 2008, p. 14.
28 Peter Nyberg, *Misjudging Risk: Causes of the Systemic Banking Crisis in Ireland*, Report of the Commission of Investigation into the Banking Sector in Ireland, Dublin: Department of Finance, 2011, p. 95.
29 Patrick Honohan, *The Irish Banking Crisis: Regulatory and Financial Stability Policy 2003-2008,* A Report to the Minister for Finance by the Governor of the Central Bank, Dublin: Department of Finance, 2010; Rob Wright, *Strengthening the Capacity of the Department of Finance*, Report of the Independent Review Panel, Dublin: Department of Finance, 2010; Regling and Watson, *A Preliminary Report*; Nyberg, *Misjudging Risk*.
30 Gabriele Steck, et al., *Allianz Global Wealth Report,* Munich: Allianz, 2010, p. 81.

31 Nick Webb, 'The Rich Got Richer', *Sunday Independent*, 13 March 2011.
32 David Begg, 'Dangers of Worshipping False God of Self-Regulating Markets', *The Irish Times*, 3 October 2008, p. 14.
33 Peadar Kirby and Mary P. Murphy, *Towards a Second Republic: Politics after the Celtic Tiger*, London: Pluto Press, 2011.

SYMPOSIUM ON THE EUROZONE CRISIS
AND LEFT STRATEGIES

FROM SUBPRIME FARCE TO GREEK TRAGEDY: THE CRISIS DYNAMICS OF FINANCIALLY DRIVEN CAPITALISM

ELMAR ALTVATER

At the beginning of his essay on 'The 18th Brumaire of Louis Bonaparte', Karl Marx refers to Hegel: all events in history happen twice, and he adds, once as a tragedy, the second time as a farce.[1] That is because people make their history, but not under conditions of their own choosing. It is equally possible to move from farce to tragedy. The farce started in what had appeared to be a minor segment of the US financial system in 2007, the real estate subprime market.[2] Initially, it seemed as if the crisis would be limited to the real estate sector in the US and the most vulnerable victims – the over-leveraged 'NINJA' subprime, mortgage-holders with no income, no job, no assets.[3] Even critical economists in Europe were convinced that the US subprime crisis would not cross the Atlantic and disrupt Europe's 'real economy'.[4] It was unimaginable that member states of the eurozone like Ireland, Portugal and Greece, and even heavyweights like Spain and Italy, could be pushed to the brink of bankruptcy; or, after half a century of progress, the European integration project brought to the brink of failure. But the mechanisms of the contemporary financial crisis quickly transformed a regional farce into a crisis of the global capitalist formation. This is nowhere better exemplified today than the tragedy of the debt crisis plaguing Greece, and the implications of this for the world's most important currency union, the eurozone.

FIRST LEHMAN, THEN GM, AND ALWAYS THE STATE

The financial turmoil of capitalism over the past five years has been an expression of underlying contradictions in the process of capital accumulation on a global scale. These contradictions have centred around the structural imbalances between countries with huge surpluses and others with huge deficits in their current accounts. These imbalances can partly be explained by the regressive redistribution of incomes and wealth in favour of the capitalist and professional classes.

The negative effects on the US working classes in particular were mitigated for years by means of an expansion of consumer and subprime credit,[5] which were in turn used to sustain American imports from China and Germany. The 'structural imbalances' in trade are the counterpart to the regressive redistribution of income and the blowing up of debt and asset bubbles destined to burst.

Notably, crises of the international capitalist system in the 1850s, 1907 and 1929 also had their epicentre in the US; soon after the shock waves also reached the 'old continent' where they did tremendous economic damage.[6] And it is not by accident that the crisis broke out in the real estate sector of a thoroughly financialized US capitalism. In previous eras, the industrial cycle of the 'real economy' always had ramifications in financial markets and, from the very beginnings of the capitalist world system, international reach.[7] In today's finance-driven 'globalized' capitalism, a crisis begins as a financial crisis, but quickly escalates into a crisis of the real economy. First Lehman Brothers and then General Motors.

As long as the profit rate is above the interest rate, such a finance-driven system may be relatively stable. But the profit rate has a tendency to fall, while concomitantly the interest rate and the yield curve of financial investment tend to rise due to financial innovations in disembedded financial markets. These divergent developments push the capitalist system first into a financial crisis and then into a crisis of the real economy, both as expressions of a more general crisis of capital accumulation.[8] Hence, the original subprime crisis in the financial sphere also transforms labour relations in the 'real' sphere. The number of unemployed workers, for example, grows as does the precarity of work and the spread of the informal economy.

Socially protected labour in many countries is often perceived today as a privilege of a minority of workers. The impact of the crisis is uneven, and this weakens the political power of the working class and their organizations. This is a key reason why in Europe severe austerity measures could be imposed to shift the distribution of income and wealth in favour of the capitalist class. Even mass protests in many European countries have not yet been able to inhibit this process. One bitter consequence is that the ensuing frustrations fuel right-wing populism.

As the crisis persists, it returns to the world of finance, but now as a fiscal crisis of the state and thus as a sovereign debt crisis. The reason is simple. In a finance-driven system, as monetary wealth and yields increase, financial claims on the one hand, and debt and debt service on the other, also must increase. But over the course of a financial crisis the opposite happens: huge amounts of claims belonging to private monetary wealth owners are devalued and hence become 'toxic assets'. In order to keep the system running, it becomes necessary to find new and solvent financial investors. New private investors, however, are not willing to 'throw good money after bad'. The good debtors that financial investors need to regain solvency are to be found with sovereign debtors. After 2008, states and central banks created 'good assets' which were substituted for the 'toxic assets' on the balance sheets of private financial institutions, which were dumped into 'bad banks' in the public sector.

In transferring the credit risk from the private to the public sector, the state as the government functions as the *'borrower of last resort'* whereas the state as the central bank functions as the *'lender of last resort'*. Private financial institutions are bolstered by 'good money' at low or no cost (at nearly a zero nominal interest rate in the US and in Europe at a rate of only 1.25 per cent). In the last instance, the economic system of modern financialized capitalism only works so long as the state supports the credit–relation on both sides as lender as well as borrower.

The principal actors in the contemporary crisis in the eurozone are the Greek government and population, the Greek banks and other European banks, and international institutions like the International Monetary Fund (IMF), the European Central Bank (ECB) and the European Commission (EC). The latter three form the powerful 'Troika' managing the crisis of indebted European states, sharply impinging on the national sovereignty and democratic institutions. Each of the actors in the Greek tragedy proposes solutions to prevent the further outbreak of the crisis. But whatever their good intentions, they are aggravating the crisis by transforming it into a social and political crisis.

A BAD RATING

Under normal conditions, sovereign debtors are good debtors as they have access to tax revenues not dependent on risky rates of real returns on capital above the interest rate. So long as the sovereign tax burden is accepted by the citizens as legitimate and not felt as too high and thus intolerable, there is no budgetary problem. If the servicing of the debt requires too much of the surplus of the primary budget, neither the debt stock nor servicing will be accepted as fair. In any case, and even more serious in the long run, the primary surplus will never be sufficient to reduce the debt burden. The sovereign debt load will then unleash a vicious circle. Real economic growth rates will be below the level necessary 'to grow out of debts' and, moreover, the debt grows as the refinancing requirements reduce economic growth rates. The debt burden as a share of GDP inevitably increases, and consequently the levels of debt service. In the European sovereign debt crisis, according the ECB's own data, the government debt to GDP ratio in all indebted countries is growing – in Greece from 105.4 per cent in 2007 to 142.8 per cent in 2010, in Portugal from 68.3 per cent in 2007 to 93.0 per cent in 2010, in Ireland from 25.0 per cent in 2007 to 96.2 per cent in 2010.

For creditors and investors, sovereign indebtedness is well-collateralized as it is backed by public property. In a default, sovereign debt can be swapped against public goods, economic assets, public real estate, or 'nature'. The exit strategy of swapping political sovereignty against private property was already used during the debt crisis of Third World countries in the 1980s. Debt-for-nature swaps, debt-for-equity swaps, debt-for-public-goods swaps, were widely transformed into practice by using the facilities of the Brady Plan.[9] Such swap deals are again on the agenda in order to save the value of assets of private monetary wealth owners (banks and financial funds) against defaulting sovereign debtors.

The Troika has presented official justification of these swap deals. The chief economist of the ECB, Jürgen Stark, estimates Greek real estate property at 300 billion euro that must be 'mobilized' for debt servicing, while Lorenzo Bini Smaghi, a member of the Executive Board of the ECB, argues that the Greeks 'have assets they can sell and reduce their debt'.[10] The popular version of debt-swap-proposals is the advice to be found in German tabloids: 'Greeks, swap Your debts for Your Acropolis and some of Your islands and beaches...'.[11] The privatization of public assets is nothing less than dispossession and expropriation in order to push the process of accumulation ahead and the Greek population into austerity. It is an assault on the democratic rights of a sovereign people.

The economic crisis triggered the fiscal crisis of the state due to shrinking tax revenues and new fiscal expenditures caused by the crisis. Welfare expenditures for a growing number of unemployed or short-term workers or impoverished former house owners were less important, however, than the huge rescue packages for private banks and subsidies for hard-hit corporations. The role of the state as 'lender of last resort', and as 'borrower of last resort', resulted in a drastic increase of public debt. The fiscal deficit's origins lay in neoliberal tax reforms and tax competition between European countries that led to a considerable reduction of income and wealth taxes in the EU. The tax burden of mobile factors of production (capital) decreased whereas the taxes on immobile factors of production (labour) remained constant or even increased.

The figures for the fiscal deficit and government debt (as a share of GDP) in Europe are telling. From 2006 to 2010, public debt in the eurozone rose from 68.4 per cent to 79.2 per cent.[12] The binding Maastricht criteria introduced some 20 years ago set a maximum debt level of 60 per cent of GDP (about the level of debt at the time). Over the course of the crisis, average public deficits in the eurozone rose by a factor of almost five from 1.4 per cent to 6.3 per cent (with the Maastricht limit set at 3 per cent). The crisis of private banks and real estate debtors has thus morphed into a crisis of European sovereign debtors and of the euro area as a whole. The spread of the crisis across Europe is by no means astonishing when we consider the nature of modern credit-money. While a single national money might command the circulation of a broad variety of commodities, in foreign exchange markets money necessarily exists in a plurality of currencies. The crisis of a 'small' currency may be contained as a monetary crisis of a single country, but a financial crisis of an important and powerful currency such as the euro affects all other currencies and the global monetary system. This has an inevitable 'global fallout'.[13]

A comparison of the eurozone with other currency areas may be useful for a better understanding of the influence of indebtedness on the economy. In the US, the UK and even more so in Japan, public debt is larger as a proportion of GDP than in most euro-countries. The US budget deficit in 2010 stands at US$ 1,537 billion, some 10.4 per cent of GDP. California, both in absolute as well as in relative terms, is significantly more indebted than any single European country. Nonetheless, speculators are targeting the eurozone by attacking the weakest link in the chain in the European periphery, but also core countries like Spain and Italy. Their debts are national debts and not European ones, and the Maastricht Treaty explicitly contains a 'no bailout rule'. The corresponding loans are largely due to financial institutions in other European states. From 2013 on, a European Stabilisation Mechanism is to guarantee the creditworthiness of EU member states, but it is unclear whether this will work. As long as loans between EU countries and institutions are perceived not as domestic loans occurring in a single currency area (comparable to Japan and the US), global financial markets expect turbulence and thus opportunities for financial speculation against individual states of the eurozone, often aided by the bond rating agencies. The effect is to weaken member states, put pressure on the euro and place in peril the entire eurozone.

The level of debt servicing depends not only on the debt stock, but also on the maturity schedule of annuities and, especially, the interest rate. The debt burden to be transferred depends, moreover, on the inflation rate and the real growth rate of GDP. In indebted countries like Greece, Portugal and Ireland, growth prospects have been declining as a direct consequence of severe austerity programmes. The interest rate of official IMF credits is modest at 3 per cent; and EU credits are less favourable at between 5 and 6 per cent. But private loans on capital markets for countries like Greece are prohibitive due to the rating grade and the country spread on the market interest rate. The Deutsche Bundesbank has shown that until the outbreak of the crisis in 2008, there was no sharp divergence of interest rates on state bonds in the eurozone: Greek loans were no more expensive than German or French ones. But after 2008 a bifurcation occurred such that yield returns on state loans with mostly private investors in mid-2011 were about 2.5 to 3 per cent for Germany, whereas Greece had to pay yields of up to 18 per cent.[14]

When governments fail to service the debt, they are blamed as the culprits who are causing the crisis of the currency union. The argument is as simple as it is false and demagogic. Money is an asset, and vice versa; in fact, *only assets are money*. Debts are the opposite of assets and therefore they are interpreted not as money but as a betrayal of the foundations of the European Monetary Union (EMU). Highly indebted states with no chance to liquidate debts in a reasonable time-span are evaluated as states short of money and lacking assets. This is the reason why rating agencies downgrade indebted states. But money is a social relation and therefore the default of debtors immediately has consequences for creditors as they must write off some of their assets. This, in turn, overwhelms credit insurers and hence the resilience of the financial system. Financial turmoil transforms into a financial tsunami.

European leaders like French President Sarkozy and German Chancellor Merkel (along with most economists) cannot understand that money is always a mutual and contradictory social relationship. The responsibility to adjust is not only on the side of the debtors. Current public debt levels cannot simply be blamed on 'loose' fiscal and budget policies in today's crisis-ridden eurozone countries (although this might be justified). Responsibility also lies with the policies of increasing current account surpluses in countries like Germany, and the redistribution that encouraged the formation of large private asset holdings that were then invested in government bonds that national states now have to service.

It is a modern form of the money fetish that monetary and financial relations are not understood as necessarily including creditors and debtors, financial claims and debt service. In discourses on finance and in political debates, the social relation between a creditor and a debtor is in principle understood as asymmetric. During discussions on the solution of the Greek crisis, for example, Merkel and Sarkozy opted for 'voluntary' not obligatory participation of the private bank creditors in the 'rescue package' of several hundred billion euro. In contrast, the IMF and the EU, with the support of the rating agencies, have imposed severe 'conditionalities' on Greece as the debtor. The debtor takes all the blame for the problems of the financial relation between debtor and creditor. Consequently, the debtor country alone bears the necessary sacrifices through reductions of transfer incomes, elimination of infrastructural spending, wage cuts and a flexibilization of the labour market, tight anti-inflationary fiscal policy, and other fiscal cuts. In other words, the austerity measures imposed to meet the demands of creditors in effect contribute to a worsening of living conditions, an increase in unemployment, and even to an impoverishment of a broad stratum of the population.

The debtor countries in Europe under stress have been subject to the 'conditionality' provisions of the EU and the IMF, as well as the rules of the 'debt brake' agreed to in the German parliament in 2010. The tenets of the 'Washington consensus' have been reanimated by the European crisis. These measures continue the 'accumulation by dispossession' characteristic of times of systemic crisis. The fiscal cuts imposed on Greece amount to 10.5 per cent of GDP for 2010 and 2011, and another 9.9 per cent until 2014. The consequence of this austerity is a drop in real GDP in Greece of more than 4 per cent in 2009 and 2010. This Greek tragedy is likely to continue in the coming years.

After the decision of the Troika and the European Council on the rescue package for Greece and its acceptance by the Greek Parliament in June 2011, the rating agency Standard & Poor's contended that the requested voluntary participation of creditors in the restructuring of Greek debt is nothing other than the write-off of assets. Such a 're-profiling' of Greek debts must be interpreted as a credit default, and Greek sovereign debt must be downgraded to default. The message was simple and clear: Greece is bankrupt.

The asymmetry in the relations between debtor and creditor is again clearly exposed. Governments as 'lenders of last resort' were allowed to save private banks from collapse to the acclaim of the rating agencies. But now indebted governments are not allowed to demand from rescued banks a contribution to the restructuring of sovereign debts.[15] Rating agencies are providing obstacles in the way of a solution to the debt crisis. The downgrade of sovereign debt by rating agencies can push countries like Greece and Portugal over the edge.[16] The assessment of the creditworthiness of assets and debts and of the quality of the policy of a government is an important prerogative of democratic institutions. But this rating is surrendered to private institutions who autocratically decide on a country's standing on financial markets and hence on the debt-service levels to be paid out of the budget. Rating agencies are a key determinant of the necessary surplus of the primary budget to meet interest payments, and thus implicitly the amount of revenues which remain to finance all other state expenditures – from social services to infrastructure.

THE CRISIS OF THE EURO

The sovereign debt crisis of a single member country of the eurozone has repercussions for the euro as a lead currency. Being a lead currency depends on, first, international availability for trade and investment flows and for the circulation of finance and, second, on security. Both can be interpreted as public goods which have to be provided by the nation-state and international institutions. Availability and security are prerequisites for the acceptance of a lead currency as a value store (reserve currency), as a means of circulation (trade) and of payments (credit). The availability of the reserve currency on global markets is dependent on the ability of the central bank, and also of private banks, to create money; and on the geographical extension and penetration of global markets by a national banking system. The US financial system, for example, is able to provide the financial infrastructure for the global circulation of the US dollar as a lead currency.

The double role of the lead currency as a national and a global vehicle – being both secure and available – is the basis for the so-called 'Triffin dilemma'.[17] The successful regulation of the dilemma is decisive for acceptance as a lead currency on global financial markets. Further, political influence and military power to secure and enforce private property rights, protect trade flows, direct investments and secure energy and raw materials are crucial to supporting a lead currency. The US is still better able to meet these requirements than Europe or China, and thus the US dollar rather than the euro or the renminbi is still the hegemonic currency.

At the end of 2010, the IMF tally of global official foreign exchange reserves was US$ 9.3 trillion, of which 5.2 trillion are allocated reserves, with 3.1 trillion denominated in US dollars and 1.3 trillion in euro-reserves. This means that 26.3 per cent of global reserves today are euro-denominated (as opposed to the 17.9 per cent in 1999 when the euro was formed). The share of the Chinese renminbi held in reserves is still small: China is a great economic power, but it lacks the other characteristics necessary to provide the lead currency. The Chinese leadership is fully aware of this deficiency.

The governor of the People's Bank of China, Zhou Xiaochuan, in a pivotal speech in March 2009, noted that the 'Triffin dilemma' 'still exists' in the contradiction that 'the issuing countries of reserve currencies cannot maintain the value of the reserve currencies while providing liquidity to the world'. Zhou concluded that an international reserve currency should be created 'that is disconnected from individual nations and is able to remain stable in the long run, thus removing the inherent deficiencies caused by using credit-based national currencies'.[18] If Special Drawing Rights (SDRs) are to form the basis of a new reserve currency and substitute for the US dollar, China could exchange parts of its huge US dollar holdings into SDRs and reduce its dependence on the dollar by approximately two-thirds because the dollar contributes less than 40 per cent to the currency basket that would be the value base of the SDRs.

Since this proposal, like Keynes's proposed Bancor during the Second World War, has gone nowhere, China's only other viable strategy is to buy the state bonds of European countries. This has several advantages. First, China gets rid of excess US dollar holdings and hence can reduce its dependence on the US. Second, China has less pressure to revalue its currency and jeopardize its competitiveness. Finally, European markets are opened to Chinese goods and FDI. The crisis of the euro is, therefore, not a matter to be resolved only in Europe, but a global issue. As acknowledged by the World Bank, multipolarity in 'the new global economy' would lead to a larger role for the euro and, in the long term, for the renminbi. [19]

Although the use of the euro as a reserve currency was enlarged, it had an Achilles heel insofar as the relation between individual EU states and the common currency was unsettled. The downgrade of a single sovereign European debtor country by private (and nearly exclusively US) rating agencies can result in a devaluation of the common currency of the seventeen eurozone countries. This is why the Troika of the ECB, the EC and the IMF is stepping in to 'reinforce economic governance in the euro area', as an ECB paper proposes.[20] The loss of confidence in the euro as a reserve currency, and its subsequent devaluation, inevitably strengthens the US dollar. But currency conflicts are hegemonic struggles waged in many arenas: in the financial, economic, political and military spheres, which is why rating agencies are welcome allies. Implicitly, the Troika are addressing constitutional questions of democratic rights of citizens under the economic pressures of a crisis-ridden European capitalism.

ASYMMETRICAL RELATIONS

After 2008, the financial rescue strategies for private financial institutions by European states created new business opportunities for banks that only a short time ago had been 'non-performing institutions'. The rescue strategies restoring the liquidity of ailing banks had two central counterparties: governments under financial stress and debtors willing to take on new debts in order to refinance subsidies and other elements of the rescue packages. Eurozone governments had to sell bonds to the same banks that had just been saved. The reason for this *quid pro quo* is one of the many defects of the EMU. The Maastricht Treaty forbids governments to go directly into debt with the ECB. The consequence is that governments are highly indebted vis-à-vis private banks, much more so than before the liberalization of financial markets.

As privileged actors, private banks take cheap money from the ECB (at 1.25 per cent in June 2011) in order to lend it out to governments at the market rate of 5 per cent or more.[21] The size of the interest rate spread is strongly influenced by rating agencies: the higher the risks of a certain loan, the lower the grade of the rating, the higher the spread. Downgrading a loan or an investment can, therefore, be a good deal for financial institutions (and a bad one for sovereign debtors). As long as a country is not defaulting on its foreign debts, the extremely high risk premium (in the Greek case up to about 15 per cent) is a formidable and secure business for banks. The credits to the stressed European states engineered by the Troika guarantee the flows for servicing the debt. And government austerity attempts to ensure that, in the last instance, citizens as taxpayers transfer an increasing part of their income to private banks.

Credit default swaps (CDS) are a financial insurance instrument designed to spread the risk of a sovereign bankruptcy. The more likely a default, the higher the costs of CDS 'risk insurance'. As a result of the banks being saved by public funds, the credit default risk for financial institutions is reduced, while the default risk for the public sector is increased. An ECB report explicitly speaks of a 'credit-risk transfer from the banking sector to the government'.[22] Since 2008, CDSs have become ever cheaper for banks, while governments have been forced to pay ever more. Whenever debts are being rescheduled, governments have to pay correspondingly higher risk premiums.

There are many arguments for Warren Buffett's judgement of CDSs as 'financial weapons of mass destruction': CDS markets are not transparent; they are dominated by an oligopoly of a few traders; deals are nearly exclusively 'over the counter'; and they are highly leveraged.[23] CDSs are perfect instruments not for reducing the risk of default, but for speculation on defaulting sovereign debts. Speculation is not just the outcome of financial manipulation by legendary figures like Buffett, Madoff and Soros today; as a systemic feature of capitalist financial systems speculation also has positive functions. The mechanisms of finance, however, do not allow the system to work smoothly for a long period of time. A disembedded financial system creates financial innovations which, as a rule, are designed to increase the yields of monetary wealth without connection to the production process and capital accumulation, for example, with respect to the scarcities of natural resources. The rules of this game are set not by societal norms and natural boundaries of the real world, but by financial speculation itself. Indeed, financial innovation takes on 'autopoetic', or self-sustaining, features of continual origination and shuffling of financial claims. Financial flows are channelled from places where yields are comparatively low to places where they are more promising. This is the reason why finance flows from low interest rate countries like the US or the core countries of the EU, into emerging markets like China, India, Brazil, and Russia. These countries might then suffer from overheating and currency revaluation.

Financial asset holders do not take into account that the monetary riches they appropriate must eventually have a counterpart in really produced values, or else asset bubbles form that necessarily must burst. In any case, debtors will reach the limits of real growth of the budgetary surplus out of which debts are to be serviced. Paradoxically, as indebted states pay ever more to service their debt to the point of sovereign bankruptcy, private financial market actors pay ever less. The ECB demonstrated this in its expressively titled report, *The Janus-Headed Salvation*.[24] After the collapse of Lehman Brothers in September 2008, distressed banks dumped most of their worthless assets into publicly financed 'bad banks' – in essence the state was guaranteeing their bad debts. In addition, the balance sheets of banks were bolstered by injections of public funds, without governments socializing any control over their business operations. These measures were a political act of privatization of public wealth.

For their part, the banks have used access to cheap money from the ECB to extend their engagement in interest and exchange-rate arbitrage. They have shifted money into emerging markets where interest rates and yields on financial investments, especially on real-estate assets, are comparatively high. The persistence of structural imbalances of current accounts continues to contribute to exchange rate volatility and encourage speculation. In its *Annual Report* for 2010, the BIS warns that the evolving situation in the emerging markets in 2011 is comparable to that of the northern core countries immediately before the crisis exploded in 2007.[25] This is, in fact, a striking concession that the stabilization of the financial system has not been successful, unless these policies are understood as a means for implementing a regressive redistribution of income, wealth and power from those at the bottom to those on the top.

Among the structural adjustment measures under the old Washington consensus that cannot be imposed on European debtor countries are devaluation of the currency and a severe monetary policy contraction. Monetary and exchange rate policies are in the hands of the ECB and not at the sovereign disposal of nation-states. Only if an indebted country opts for exit from the euro or if it is thrown out of the currency union by the other members could this change. These remedies are proposed by reactionary neoliberals as well as by some on the Left, because the unequal distribution of income and wealth in Europe, taken together with the assessments of the bond rating agencies, generates large interest rate differentials between the indebted and 'wealthy' countries, to whose banks they are indebted. They do not really help. Greece's debt is mostly to financial institutions based in France (€75bn), Switzerland (€60bn) and Germany (€43bn); in Spain, it is German, French, Dutch and British banks holding the bulk of claims; in Portugal, banks from Spain are the major creditors, followed by banks from Germany and France; and of Ireland's almost US$ 1 trillion total debt, German and British banks hold about $200bn each.[26] The public debt of European peripheral states thus corresponds to claims by private banks of roughly the same amount; and hidden behind the banks are vast sums of private money wealth, shielded by the archaic 'banking secrecy' laws of the EU. For this reason, as well as the danger of a broader financial and economic crisis it would cause, the remedy of throwing the peripheral states out of the eurozone is hardly an attractive one for the wealthier countries of Europe.

MONEY, VOICE OR EXIT

What measures might reduce money wealth as a counterpart to the repayment or to the cancellation of parts of the debts owed by the highly indebted countries of Europe? A first would be a 'haircut' – getting creditors to play their part in the reduction of debt. Creditors have to be made to shoulder some of the burden for which they are co-responsible; and it should be clear that the 'haircut' is more than just a quantitative reduction of debt and hence wealth. It is a corollary that financial institutions will have to be fundamentally restructured as, in many cases, a balance sheet contraction will be necessary. If banking institutions are smaller after the 'haircut', this will also change the 'systemic relevance' of banks used to justify billions of public aid. In the case of the indebted European countries, a 'radical haircut' is the only alternative to a chaotic bankruptcy. The haircut is part of the necessary restructuring of public and private debt – so long as the rating agencies accept it as an orderly restructuring of debt and not as a debt default. A default assessment would lead to a ratings downgrade and an increase of the servicing costs on the remaining debt. A haircut is only possible, therefore, in combination with a disempowerment of rating agencies.

A second measure would have to be the reintroduction of wealth taxes in all European countries. During the era of booming financial markets, the financial lobby successfully pushed for wealth taxes to be reduced or completely abolished across Europe. It is necessary to move away from the ruinous and politically corrupting process of tax competition between EU countries. Within the eurozone, the expense side of government budgets is tightly regulated by the Maastricht criteria, even if the budgetary impact of the financial crisis has been to disrupt significantly the guidelines. The revenue side, on the other hand, is subject to regulatory arbitrage in favour of investors. Limiting wealth taxes frees up money wealth that is, in turn, used for speculation in financial markets.

A third measure must be to cut the claims of financial investors and thus the debts of debtors, as two typical ways of getting rid of debt are closed. Private debtors normally can go bankrupt and disappear from the market. But the solution to the financial crisis has been to socialize debt and debt servicing. Sovereign debtors cannot disappear because they are political institutions as well as economic actors. In this capacity, they follow the rules of the national constitution and of international law and global governance, whereas private firms are subject to economic criteria. Since social and political resistance and environmental limits simply do not allow an increase in the growth rate to match interest rates set by absurd risk spreads, the only way out is to reduce the claims of the investors.

These ways out of the financial crisis have been closed because they are not acceptable to the dominant neoliberal coalition of finance, big capital, conservative governments and economic brain trusts. As a result another solution has been pushed to the centre of the political agenda: austerity, the peoples shall pay. As a condition for getting new credits from the financial system, the state budget is to be cut. But in the midst of an economic crisis and weak demand conditions, these cuts provoke a deeper recession and ultimately the bankruptcy of sovereign debtors. This impact of austerity can be seen with respect to Greece, but the contagion will spread to Portugal, Spain and others.

A complete breakdown of the eurozone is not impossible. There are historical examples of currency unions which existed over substantial periods of time before falling apart, as with the Latin monetary union in Europe in the late 19th century. But the euro is something quite different: it is a globally strong currency, and a failure of the euro project could trigger chaos in all of Europe and beyond. Although it was one of the objectives of the Economic and Monetary Union plan in the mid 1980s, the move to set up a currency zone in Western Europe might not have happened at all except for the adventurous bravado that came with the breakdown of the Soviet bloc. In 1991 at the signing of the Maastricht Treaty, the differences in competitiveness between the participating countries were great, and there clearly was insufficient democratic regulation of the European economy to reduce the divergences. The eurozone was in no way an 'optimal currency zone'.[27] Twenty years later, the euro is still no 'optimal currency', but it is a European *factum*, whether *brutum* or *bonum* is not important.

There are only two paths in Europe right now. They lead in opposite directions: one towards the disintegration of the eurozone; and a second towards the strengthening of 'European statehood' because a currency union without fully functioning political institutions is hard to imagine in the long run. Conservative and neoliberal economists and politicians are toying with the idea of splitting the monetary union into two or even more groups, into a Europe of 'different velocities'. A core Europe of Germany, France and a few other countries would continue using the euro (or a common currency with another name), while a European periphery might have Greece reintroduce the drachma, Italy the lira, Portugal the escudo, and so forth.

There are also Left positions that point in this direction. In these views, exit from the euro creates new space for political action; better national conditions for overcoming the crisis can be enforced; and a break from the neoliberal integration project becomes possible.[28] But what is likely to happen if the eurozone fails?[29] Unlike the 1970s, today we are dealing not merely with the equivalent of the disintegration of the Bretton Woods regime of fixed exchange rates into its component parts of national currencies with flexible exchange rates. Instead, this would be a collapse of an actual monetary union that has existed for nearly two decades. The component parts – national currencies – would have to be reinvented. As conditions within the eurozone vary widely, this process would be extremely controversial, not the least because the 'old' economies existing within the borders of the nation-state do not exist anymore. Sovereign territories as spaces of regulation are no longer consistent with the reach of transnational corporations or of financial speculators.

A new currency issued by an indebted country exiting the euro, for example, would likely suffer an immediate drop in value. But euro-denominated debts would still need to be serviced in euros but now purchased by a non-euro currency. Rating agencies would likely further downgrade the credit rating and the financial crisis would be exacerbated. While the devaluation allowed by a non-euro currency would increase monetary competitiveness, this advantage is limited if real competitiveness does not increase as well. Many of the indebted European countries lack the relevant export industries. On the other side, the remaining eurozone will likely undergo currency appreciation. This revaluation would limit the competitiveness of industrial capital and further encourage financial capital to speculate on the euro. The 'equilibrium' that would result across Europe, after such a period of economic turbulence, is impossible to predict.

It was a historical mistake on the part of the European Left, perhaps related to its confusion in the years of the breakdown of actually existing socialism, to accept the formation of the European Monetary Union as regulated by the Maastricht Treaty.[30] Since it only stipulated market mechanisms to address economic imbalances and to smooth social contradictions, and since exchange rates were fixed and interest rates would be set by the ECB, only wages, salaries and government expenditures could vary in order to adjust diverging 'real' economies in a single currency area. This meant a permanent pressure on workers and their organizations to respect the laws of competitiveness. We see this today in the harsh conditionalities imposed by the Troika as they try to salvage the common currency area.

In order to improve the efficiency of market adjustments, the President of the ECB, Jean-Claude Trichet, has launched a proposal to set up a European Ministry of Finance endowed with the power to override national governments that fail to fulfil their financial stability obligations. The Ministry would also have executive powers over the European banking system on such matters as owner's equity and solvency rules. The proposal only targets the workings of the financial system, and does not take account of the asymmetry between creditors and debtors. Trichet does not address the fact that the European Union is also a political and social union that citizens seek to have a voice in constituting.

If the eurozone is to have a decent future (to the extent that this can be achieved under capitalist conditions), it is a very new type of 'European statehood' that needs to evolve from the market-oriented one that its establishment proponents have always envisaged. Interventionist policies have to work towards reducing the real economic divergences that exist within the eurozone and the genuine construction this time of a social Europe. This goes beyond making the case that the European Union must become a 'transfer union', although we can see that even in Trichet's technocratic neoliberalism, the necessity for more fiscal cooperation is seen as irrefutable.

It is a ridiculous by-product of the neoliberal worship of the market that the most unqualified, politically undemocratic and economically inefficient institutions in the form of the debt rating agencies sit in judgement on the creditworthiness of countries, on the quality of democratically elected governments and on the value of the currency. These monsters of the neoliberal financial market are more powerful than a state like Greece, with more than two thousand years of history and a population of more than 10 million. This intolerable state of affairs has to be changed.

NOTES

This paper is the revised version of a contribution to a manifesto on the European crisis presented by the Scientific Council of Attac-Germany in February 2011. Linguistic support has been given by Braden Kohn.

1   Karl Marx, *Der achtzehnte Brumaire des Louis Bonaparte*, Marx-Engels-Werke, Volume 8, Berlin/DDR: Dietz Verlag, 1960, pp. 111-207.

2   Bank for International Settlement, *78th Annual Report*, Basel: BIS, 2008, p. 3

3   The subprime crisis was a catastrophe for individual house owners as well as for municipalities and cities hit by the real estate crisis. See Margit Mayer, 'Das neue Elend der US-Städte: eine avancierte Form des Klassenkampfes von oben', *PROKLA - Zeitschrift für kritische Sozialwissenschaft*, June 2011, pp. 253-72.

4   Arbeitsgruppe Alternative Wirtschaftspolitik, *Memorandum 2008: Neuverteilung von Einkommen, Arbeit und Macht. Alternativen zur Bedienung der Oberschicht*, available at http://www. memo.uni-bremen.de.

5   This is one of the core arguments in John Bellamy Foster and Fred Magdoff, *The Great Financial Crisis. Causes and Consequences*, New York: Monthly Review Press, 2009.

6   On this see Leo Panitch and Sam Gindin, 'Capitalist Crises and the Crisis this Time', *Socialist Register 2011*, Pontypool: Merlin Press, 2010.

7   This already was an important issue in Karl Marx's analysis of crisis-ridden capitalism, especially the discussion on interest-bearing capital in Volume 3 of *Capital*. Karl Marx, *Das Kapital*, 3 Band, Marx-Engels Werke, Band 25, Berlin: Dietz, 1968.

8   This has been analyzed in more detail in Elmar Altvater, *Der große Krach*, Münster: Westfälisches Dampfboot, 2010.

9   The plan facilitated the exchange of debts into 'Brady Bonds' which could be used as debt-collateral for creditors. In the Greek case, Greek bonds should be exchanged against euro bonds.

10   Ralph Atkins, 'Achieving an Orderly Debt Restructuring is a "Fairytale"', *Financial Times*, 30 May 2011.

11   The Rosa Luxemburg Foundation published a small pamphlet against the

demagogic demands to sell natural and cultural commons to banks and funds in order to reduce the sovereign debt of Greece: *Sell Your Islands You Bankrupt Greeks*, Berlin: RLF, June 2011, available at http://www.rosalux.de.

12   The data are from publications of the ECB, http://www.ecb.europa. eu. A more detailed analysis of debts and assets in the European economy can be found in Hans-Jürgen Bieling, 'Vom Krisenmanagement zur neuen Konsolidierungsagenda der EU', *PROKLA*, June 2011, pp. 173-94.

13   *Financial Times*, 7 June 2011.

14   Deutsche Bundesbank, Renditedifferenzen von Staatsanleihen im Euroraum, *Monatsberichte der Deutschen Bundesbank*, June 2011, p. 31.

15   See the articles in *Süddeutsche Zeitung*, 5 July 2011, on the decision of Standard & Poor's to downgrade Greek debts.

16   Kevin Gallagher, 'The Tyranny of Bond Markets', *Guardian*, 9 April 2010.

17   Edoardo Campanella, 'The Triffin Dilemma Again', *Economics. The Open Access, Open Assessment E-Journal*, Discussion Paper No. 2009-46, 2009.

18   The speech, 'Zhou Xiaochuan's Statement on Reforming the International Monetary System', 23 March 2009, is available from http://www.cfr.org/ china.

19   World Bank, *Multipolarity: The New Global Economy*, Washington: World Bank, 2011.

20   A report of a task force to the European Council presents the main discussion: 'Strengthening Economic Governance in the EU, 21 October 2010, available at http://www.consilium.europa.eu.

21   The debt burden is dependent on the profit rate to be charged and on the real growth rate of GDP. Therefore, an interest rate of 1.25 per cent may be rather high and economically detrimental when the rate of profit and the growth rate are below 1.25 per cent or even negative.

22   Jacob W. Ejsing and Wolfgang Lemke, *The Janus-Headed Salvation: Sovereign and Bank Credit Risk Premia During 2008-2009*, European Central Bank, Working Paper Series No. 1127, December 2009.

23   See the analysis of Deutsche Bundesbank, Entwicklung, Aussagekraft und Regulierung des Marktes für Kreditausfall-Swaps, *Monatsbericht*, December 2010, pp. 47-64.

24   Ejsing and Lemke, *The Janus-Headed Salvation*.

25   Bank for International Settlement, *81ˢᵗ Annual Report*, Basel: BIS, 2010.

26   For a detailed table see: Bieling, 'Vom Krisenmanagement', p. 182.

27   Robert A. Mundell, 'A Theory of Optimum Currency Areas', *American Economic Review*, 51, 1961, pp. 657-65.

28   See the debate with Costas Lapavitsas and Michel Husson in this volume.

29   Financial Times columnist Wolfgang Münchau has suggested that the eurozone may have no future. Wolfgang Münchau, 'Warum die Euro-Zone zerbricht', *Financial Times Deutschland*, 2 December 2010.

30   This was an argument against the critique of European monetary integration à la Maastricht in Elmar Altvater and Birgit Mahnkopf, *Gewerkschaften vor der Europäischen Herausforderung. Tarifpolitik nach Mauer und Maastricht*, Münster: Westfälisches Dampfboot, 1993.

DEFAULT AND EXIT FROM THE EUROZONE: A RADICAL LEFT STRATEGY

COSTAS LAPAVITSAS

The world crisis that began in 2007 has summed up contradictions, tensions and imbalances accumulated in the course of the financialization of capitalism.[1] The crisis originated in mortgage lending to the poorest and most marginal workers in the US; it assumed a global dimension because of securitization and related innovations by financial capital; it became a recession that was exacerbated by the relative weakness of productive capital in the US and the UK; it affected developing countries severely through collapse of exports and tightness of credit; it then turned into a crisis of private and public debt in the eurozone, revealing the unbalanced character of the European Union (EU) as that is reflected in its common currency.[2]

The eurozone crisis is thus an integral part of the world crisis of 2007 which is an event of rare historical significance in the development of capitalism. State intervention in 2008-09 pacified the banking crisis and ameliorated the recession in the US and other parts of the developed world. But the eurozone crisis, which burst out in 2010 and became progressively worse in 2011, showed that the malaise of financialization is deep and structural. As peripheral eurozone states approached default, the prospect of a renewed and global financial crisis could no longer be discounted. A generalized banking crisis, in turn, threatened to usher in economic depression.

The eurozone has become the weak point of the world economy for reasons associated with its exploitative and unequal nature. For the same reasons, the attempt by several European powers collectively to create a new form of world money has effectively failed. The euro in its current form is untenable and might even collapse altogether. The economic, social and political unrest that has emerged offers to the left the opportunity to shift the balance of forces against capital and in favour of labour. For the left to succeed, however, it must propose radical solutions for the crisis. This requires a break with the hold of Europeanism that has dominated left thinking for decades.

A PECULIAR FORM OF WORLD MONEY
SHAPES THE CRISIS IN EUROPE

For Marxist monetary theory, the crisis-ridden nature of capitalist economies is summarily captured by world money (or international reserve currency in mainstream economic terminology), that is, by the means of payment and hoarding (reserve) operating in the world market.[3] The euro is a form of world money created to serve the interests of large European industrial and financial capital under conditions of financialization. Its peculiarity as a form of world money is that it has been created *ex nihilo* by a group of states, rather than originally being the national money of a particular state. The purpose of the institutional mechanisms of the European Monetary Union (EMU) has been to ensure the ability of the euro to act as a world means of payment and hoarding and thus also as a stable unit of account, given the peculiarity of its provenance.

Briefly put, an independent European Central Bank (ECB) has been created, with complete command over monetary policy and obliged by its statutes to ensure the stability of the euro as a unit of account. The ECB sits atop a homogeneous money market in which European banks are able to obtain liquidity that is acceptable across the world. The purpose of the eurozone's 1997 Growth and Stability Pact, on the other hand, has been to provide requisite fiscal discipline by imposing arbitrary limits on budget deficits and aggregate public debt. But since the euro has been created by an alliance of states, responsibility for compliance and for honouring public debt has been largely left to each sovereign state − a weakness that has been the catalyst of the current crisis. Given this monetary and fiscal framework, competitiveness in the internal market has relied on productivity growth and labour costs. The result has been to create a 'race to the bottom' for workers' wages and conditions across the eurozone.

German capital has been particularly adept at squeezing the wages and conditions of German workers, and has therefore emerged as the dominant force within the eurozone. Its rising competitiveness has generated current account surpluses, reflected in current account deficits of peripheral countries. The necessary counterpart to this imbalance has been the enormous indebtedness of the periphery, financed by capital flows (generally in the form of bank lending) from the core. Debt has also accumulated domestically in the periphery as banks took advantage of the homogeneous European money market to expand their credit operations.

Consequently, the main form taken by the world crisis in Europe has been that of a crisis of debt − both private and public − in the periphery of the eurozone. Enormous debt has meant that Greece, Ireland, Portugal, and even

Spain are currently facing default. Such an event would put the solvency of the banks of the core in doubt, and would probably lead to renewed banking crisis across the world.[4] The ability of the euro to act as world money would be immediately compromised. Core eurozone countries, therefore, were forced to confront peripheral debt out of fundamental self-interest. Their overriding concern has been to rescue the banks and to protect the euro.

The ECB has thus provided abundant liquidity to banks even to the extent of accepting huge volumes of peripheral debt as collateral. The ECB has also ignored its own statutes by purchasing peripheral debt to stabilize the secondary markets. In addition, core countries have put together rescue packages for states that have been cut off from bond markets. A European stabilization mechanism and a European financial stabilization facility were created, capable of borrowing in the open markets under joint government guarantees to fund loans to countries in difficulties. The loans have been supplemented and advanced jointly with the International Monetary Fund (IMF). In 2013 these ad hoc arrangements will presumably become a permanent mechanism dealing with sovereign bankruptcies.

It should be mentioned here that the role of the IMF has been supplementary to that of the EU and the ECB. The IMF has provided substantial funds, technical support, the mechanism of conditionality, and periodic examinations of the performance of countries in receipt of emergency lending. But the Fund has been fully aware of the difficulty of imposing tough adjustment programmes on countries that cannot have a simultaneous devaluation of the domestic currency. The EU and the ECB have been much larger lenders than the IMF, insisting on punitive interest rates, the imposition of harsh austerity, and the adoption of further liberalization, in the name of protecting the euro. The true defenders of neoliberal orthodoxy in the eurozone crisis have been the EU and the ECB, not the IMF.

The price paid by peripheral countries for EU/ECB/IMF assistance has been exorbitant interest rates, often with spreads of 2–3 per cent for every euro lent by the so-called rescue institutions. Not a penny has been given for free to countries in difficulties; instead the providers of emergency lending made healthy profits in 2010–11. Equally, the price has been the imposition of austerity and liberalization not only across the periphery but also the core. Peripheral countries have been forced to cut social spending, public investment, wages, and pensions. Deregulation of labour and other markets has been promoted and privatization has been encouraged. In March 2011 it was even proposed permanently to institutionalize austerity and liberalization in the form of the Pact for the euro. This plan would give Germany control over the fiscal deficits of others as well as pressuring labour to improve competitiveness. The repercussions of these measures on the periphery are not hard to ascertain: in the last quarter of 2010 and the first quarter of 2011, Greek GDP and the rate of unemployment worsened to rates comparable to the Great Depression in the US in the 1930s. Even worse, recession has exacerbated the burden of debt, thus raising the risk of insolvency.

Yet, there is method to the madness of eurozone policy. First, austerity and liberalization are entirely consistent with the treaties that have sustained the creation of the euro. Neoliberalism has always been the dominant ideology of the eurozone: the destruction of welfare provision is a natural response and not an aberration. Second, the imposition of austerity fits the narrow interests of the German ruling class, which has openly acknowledged its ascendancy within the eurozone in the course of the crisis. On the one hand, it has been keen to preserve the euro as a world money, which means avoiding a major banking crisis. On the other, it has not been prepared to bear the cost of peripheral default, which could run into hundreds of billions of euro. Quite rationally, therefore, it has opted to supply banks with liquidity, while imposing austerity on peripheral countries. The risks are high but, if the strategy succeeds, Germany could become the undisputed master of European capitalism, in command of the second most important form of world money.

The counterpart to German ascendancy will be economic, social and national decay for the periphery. If peripheral countries are to remain in the eurozone, they will have to continue indefinitely with austerity that undermines their productive base and leads to high unemployment. In contrast to the 2000s, there will not be cheap borrowing from abroad to ease the pressures generated by the common currency. Inequality will increase and social tensions will rise. The only beneficiary is likely to be a thin layer of the domestic ruling class – typically connected to the financial system but also comprising elements of industrial capital – which has accepted its subordinate position and wishes to remain within the eurozone at all costs.

A 'GOOD EURO'?

Opposing these policies requires abandoning the notion that the European Monetary Union could be reformed in the interests of working people, or that a 'good euro' could be created. The advocates of this view can be split into two currents, both of which are prominent within the newly formed Party of the European Left but also more broadly across Europe.[5] One current consists of ardent Europeanists who typically disregard the class and imperial interests at the heart of monetary union. For them, 'Europe' is a transnational integration that presumably fosters welfare and association among the people of Europe. Social progress makes no sense independently of this transcendental 'Europe', which would presumably be at risk if the euro failed. The task that ardent Europeanists set for themselves, consequently, is to prevent collapse of the monetary union, even if that involved alliances with parts of the bourgeoisie that were also keen to rescue the monetary union.

The other current comprises reluctant Europeanists who are aware of the class interests at the heart of the eurozone, though not necessarily of the full implications of creating a new world money. This group is worried about the dangers of nationalism and isolationism should the eurozone project collapse. The drive toward monetary union might have been ill-conceived, but now that the people of Europe have found themselves within the reality of the union, it is not advisable to break out of it. Indeed, this argument appeals to both groups.[6] But for some reluctant Europeanists it leads to a further argument that might be called 'revolutionary Europeanism'. Namely, the strategy for the left should be to fight for the revolutionary overthrow of capitalism on the 'privileged terrain' of European integration.

Whether ardent or reluctant, Europeanist proposals to create a 'good euro' demonstrate considerable convergence. There is general agreement that austerity and liberalization ought to be resisted, and that Europe needs major redistribution of income and wealth. There is also agreement that a European policy of investment would be desirable to raise productivity in the periphery and to restructure the European economy. But then, who among the left would oppose these ideas which, moreover, have been around for a long time? Essential as they are, they do not go to the heart of the current crisis.

Europeanist proposals become more acute when the issue of debt is considered. It has eventually been accepted by all that the burden of debt on several peripheral countries must be lifted for economies to recover. Beyond this point, however, agreement is hard to find. Ardent Europeanists tend to favour consensual restructuring of debt, or rather creditor-led default, which would lower the level of peripheral debt without upsetting the mechanisms and institutions of the eurozone. The trouble is that creditor-led default is unlikely significantly to reduce peripheral debt. Lenders are not generally known to welcome losses. Reluctant Europeanists, consequently, tend to favour radical restructuring of debt, often at the initiative of the borrower. The trouble is that they propose to write debt off unilaterally while remaining within the framework of the eurozone, the main powers of which will have to take the losses. Quite how this will be achieved has yet to be explained.

Against this background, the advocates of the 'good euro' have collectively engaged in making specific proposals to deal with the debt crisis. Here the ground becomes treacherous because it leads to the outer reaches of actual policy-making by the governments of Europe. The proposals made by various parts of the 'good euro' left have typically revolved around lending by the ECB and issuing eurobonds, both of which are already practiced in the eurozone to a certain extent.

Summarizing ruthlessly and across a variety of suggestions, the general idea appears to be that the ECB should expand its current practice of purchasing public debt in secondary markets (and lending against collateral of peripheral public debt). The ECB should acquire much of the existing debt of peripheral countries and it should also finance the borrowing of eurozone states in the future. It is further suggested that the issuing of eurobonds – a limited variant of which is already undertaken by the European Financial Stabilisation Facility (EFSF) to obtain funds for lending to countries in difficulties – should be expanded to meet the regular lending needs of eurozone states.[7] Nothing precludes crossbreeding between these suggestions, including the notion that the ECB should be financing the public debt of the eurozone itself by issuing eurobonds. Such proposals appear as the analogue of the operations of the Federal Reserve in the US, and thus an important step toward creating fiscal as well as monetary homogeneity within the eurozone.

Unfortunately, there are underlying problems with these proposals, which help explain why they have generally been given short shrift by the eurozone establishment. One problem relates to the losses from bad peripheral debt. If, for instance, the ECB were to acquire existing peripheral debt at a deep discount, the capital of banks would have to be replenished to prevent failure; if debt was acquired at face value, the eventual losses of the ECB would have to be made good. The ECB does not possess a magic wand to make bad debts vanish – public funds would have to be used for the purpose, and this means drawing on the tax income of core countries. Similar considerations apply to the issuing of eurobonds through which to replace existing peripheral debt. And that is without even mentioning the additional cost to core countries from borrowing at higher interest rates, if they were to issue eurobonds jointly with peripheral countries.

But there is an even deeper problem in this regard, which is often not appreciated by those who aim to eliminate the imbalance between fiscal heterogeneity and monetary homogeneity within the eurozone. The financial sphere of the eurozone is not nearly as homogeneous as is often imagined. There is indeed a common money market, which homogenises the terms of borrowing for banks, but the ownership of banks remains resolutely national. When bank solvency becomes problematic, banks can only seek recourse to their own state, as was shown in the case of Ireland in 2009-10 and Belgium in 2008-09. There are no European mechanisms to deal with the losses that European banks would inevitably make if peripheral debt was written off. Nor is there any obvious way in which German or French workers could be made to accept higher taxes to rescue, say, Italian banks.

Finally, the suggestion that the ECB should systematically acquire peripheral debt and, even more, that it should have an open commitment to finance the future borrowing of eurozone countries is deeply problematic for the euro as world money. There is no comparison between the dollar and the euro in this respect. The former is the incumbent form of world money that draws on established institutional and customary mechanisms for its acceptability; the latter is a pretender with barely ten years of existence. If the ECB were to begin financing the regular borrowing of all eurozone countries, the acceptability of the euro would decline in world markets, not least because the stability of the ECB would be immediately in doubt. This is reason enough for the German ruling class to reject such a prospect.

A RADICAL LEFT STRATEGY

A radical left strategy should offer a resolution of the crisis that alters the balance of social forces in favour of labour and pushes Europe in a socialist direction. This would be impossible without challenging the class and imperial relations at the heart of the eurozone, something that the 'good euro' generally avoids. In short, the left urgently needs a distinctive independent position on the structural crisis of European capitalism, which implies that the left must recapture some of its radicalism. The point of departure of a radical strategy ought to be that working people in both core and periphery have no stake in the success of the EMU. On the contrary, the attempt to create a world money that serves the interests of European capital has meant worsening labour conditions at the core and major crisis in the periphery of the eurozone.

The division between core and periphery means that a radical left alternative would necessarily present itself differently across the eurozone. For workers at the core, particularly in Germany, it would be vital to break the relentless pressure on wages entailed by monetary union. But note that it is a fallacy to think of higher wages as a means of rescuing the euro by rebalancing competitiveness and boosting domestic consumption in the core. There is no capitalist class that would systematically aim at raising the wages of its own workers since it would then be ruined in competition. If wage restraint was broken in Germany, the monetary union would become a lot less attractive to the German ruling class, raising the issue of its own continued euro membership. After all, Germany has had long experience in deploying the Deutschmark strategically to improve its share of world production and trade.

The strategy for the left in core countries ought to include further steps that could complement the push to break wage restraint while confronting the failure of monetary union. An important element would be control over the financial system. Tax and other impositions to rescue banks from their foolish exposure to the eurozone periphery ought to be resisted. Indeed, the left ought to make the case for bank nationalization that could act as a lever to rebalance core economies. Above all, the weight of the German economy ought to be shifted away from exports and toward improving domestic consumption, public provision, and infrastructure. For this, it would be necessary to recapture command over monetary policy from the ECB and to impose controls on capital flows.

In the periphery, in contrast, the immediate focus of a radical alternative must be to confront the burden of public and private debt. Dealing with debt would inevitably raise the issue of eurozone membership. Public debt, in particular, has to be renegotiated with the aim of writing off its greater part. To this purpose there should be debtor-led default drawing on grassroots participation. There are certainly costs to defaulting and unilaterally writing off debt, including being shut out of financial markets for a period and paying higher interest rates in the future. But even mainstream literature points out that, to its surprise, these costs do not seem to be very substantial.[8] Debtor-led default would be immeasurably strengthened by establishing independent Audit Commissions on public debt across peripheral countries. They would facilitate workers' participation in confronting the problem of debt, not least by allowing for independent knowledge of the causes and terms of indebtedness. The Commissions could make appropriate recommendations for dealing with debt, including debt that is shown to be illegal, illegitimate, odious, or simply not sustainable.

Debtor-led default in the periphery would immediately raise the issue of eurozone membership, given that the lenders are core countries. Exit is an important component of a radical left strategy that could deal with austerity while restructuring economies in the interests of labour. But changing the monetary standard is a major shock that would require a broad programme of economic and social change. The most important concern would be to prevent the monetary disturbance from turning into a banking crisis, for then the repercussions on the economy could be severe. It follows that banks would have to be placed under public ownership and control, protecting depositors and creating a framework to restructure the economy. Needless to say, it would also be necessary immediately to impose capital controls.

The new currency would inevitably depreciate, putting added pressure on banks borrowing abroad, but also removing the shackles from the productive sector and boosting exports. Regaining command over monetary policy while defaulting on the debt would also immediately remove the stranglehold of austerity on the productive sector. But rising import prices would put pressure on workers' incomes, thus necessitating redistributive measures through tax and wage policies. On this basis, industrial policy would be introduced to restore productive capacity in the periphery and to create employment. Finally, to bring about such a dramatic shift in the balance of social forces in favour of labour it would be necessary to have democratic restructuring of the state improving tax collection and dealing with corruption.

A radical left strategy for both core and periphery entails measures that would not necessarily be socialist in the first instance. The precise character of the strategy would depend on the social forces that would be mobilized and on the types of struggle that would emerge. But there is no doubt that it could change the balance of forces in favour of labour, creating better conditions to resolve issues of distribution, growth and employment in the longer term. In this respect, a radical left alternative would comprise transitional demands in the most profound sense of the term. It could create a favourable environment for social change in a socialist direction by improving the social and economic conditions of workers. There is no need for such a strategy to lead to isolationism and nationalism, provided that the European left regained a modicum of confidence in itself and in its historic arsenal of socialist ideas. For this, it would be necessary to abandon Europeanism, the imperial ideology that has for years haunted its collective mind.

NOTES

1   There is a broad literature on financialization. For the approach implicitly adopted here, see *Historical Materialism*, 17(2), 2009, which examines various aspects of financialization and the crisis. For further discussion of financialization see also several publications and discussion papers of Research on Money and Finance (RMF) at http://www.researchonmoneyandfinance.org.

2   The causes and mechanisms of the crisis were established in full detail in two RMF reports in 2010. See: C. Lapavitsas, et al., *eurozone Crisis: Beggar Thyself and Thy Neighbour*, Research on Money and Finance, Occasional Report 1, March 2010; and *The eurozone between Austerity and Default*, Research on Money and Finance, Occasional Report 2, September 2010. Both are available at: http://www.researchonmoneyandfinance.org.

3   World money is discussed briefly by Karl Marx in *Capital*, Volume 1, London: Penguin, 1976, pp. 240-4.

4   The two RMF reports noted above have shown that, at the end of 2009, the total debt of Spain, Portugal and Greece was nearly €7 trillion. Of this, €2.5 trillion was owed abroad, including more than €1 trillion to core banks. The total capital of the latter was not far in excess of €0.6 trillion in 2009. A combined default of the periphery would be devastating.

5   Both were very much in evidence at the conference 'Public Debt and Austerity Policies in Europe: The Response of the European Left', held in Athens in March 2011, the proceedings of which can be found at http://athensdebtconference.wordpress.com.

6   Witness, for instance, ATTAC-Germany, *Manifesto on the Crisis of the Euro*, March, 2011, available at http://www.alternative-regionalisms.org; and Michel Husson, 'A European Strategy for the Left', *Socialist Resistance*, 29 December 2010, available at http://hussonet.free.fr/@bibi.htm.

7   The idea of systematically issuing Eurobonds gained considerable influence when proposed by the official voices of J.C. Tremonti and G. Juncker, 'Eurobonds Would End the Crisis', *Financial Times*, 5 December 2010. But it had already been circulating among left currents for some time.

8   As is repeatedly noted by, for instance, F. Sturzenegger and J. Zettelmeyer, *Debt Defaults and Lessons from a Decade of Crises*, Cambridge, MA: MIT Press, 2007.

EXIT OR VOICE?
A EUROPEAN STRATEGY OF RUPTURE

MICHEL HUSSON

The course of the economic crisis that erupted in late 2007 can be simply summarized as follows: during the two decades preceding the crisis, capitalism has been reproducing itself by accumulating a mountain of debt. To avoid the collapse of the system, states have taken over some of these debts, in transferring from the private to the public sector. The project of the ruling classes is now to present the bill to citizens through budget cuts, increases of the most unfair taxes and frozen wages. In a nutshell, the majority of the population – as workers and pensioners – must sacrifice through austerity to ensure the realization of the fictitious profits accumulated over many years.

THE WORM IS IN THE FRUIT

In Europe, the effort to build an economic integrated area via the European Union (EU) with a single currency in the form of the euro, but without a matching budgetary capacity, was not a coherent project. A truncated monetary union became an economic framework to generate heterogeneity and divergence in the countries of Europe. Countries with above average inflation and below average productivity lose competitiveness, and are encouraged to base their growth on overindebtedness; while countries with below average inflation and above average productivity gain competitiveness and sustain structural surpluses.

In retrospect, the choice of the euro (with its launch in 1999) had no obvious advantage over a common currency system – a convertible euro for relations with the rest of the world, and adjustable currencies inside the zone. The euro was designed as an instrument of budgetary and above all wage discipline (following on the EU's Growth and Stability Pact): the use of devaluation is no longer possible, and the wage becomes the only adjustment variable for addressing competitiveness and external imbalances.

In practice, the Economic and Monetary Union also worked through overindebtedness and, at least initially, the decline of the euro against the dollar. These expedients eventually had to run out. Things started to go off-track with the German policy of wage deflation through the 2000s which has led to an increase of Germany's market share in Europe. Although the euro area was broadly in balance with the rest of the world, the gap has widened between the German surpluses and the deficits of most other countries in Europe. As a result, the growth rates inside the euro zone have tended to diverge, right from the first introduction of the euro.

This market configuration inside Europe has proven, not surprisingly, unsustainable. The crisis has sharply accelerated the process of fragmentation and financial speculation and it has exposed the tensions inherent within neoliberal Europe. The crisis has deepened the polarization of the euro area. On the one hand, Germany, the Netherlands and Austria enjoy trade surpluses and their fiscal deficits have remained moderate. On the other, the famous 'PIGS' comprised of Portugal, Italy, Greece and Spain (Ireland being partly another case) are in a reverse situation: high trade deficits and fiscal deficits above average and rapidly climbing. Although the depth of the economic crisis has led to an increase in fiscal deficits everywhere, it has been much less in the first group of countries.

The sovereign debt crisis has accelerated the move toward austerity which was, in any case, already the neoliberal policy of adjustment and the planned policy response as the economic crisis stabilized. Speculation against Greece, then Ireland and Portugal, has been possible because no systematic measures have been taken to regulate banks in the wake of the crisis. The pooled management of the debt on a European scale, through the European Financial Stabilisation Mechanism and the European Financial Stability Facility, remained partial and always came late in the day. The central banks themselves have provided ammunition for this speculation by lending to banks, at a very low interest rate, money which the banks in turn lent to governments at the higher rates paid on sovereign debt, neatly pocketing the difference.

As sovereign debt takes over from private debt, the financial crisis moves into the public sector. The bailouts of the peripheral European countries under attack from financial capital are, in fact, the bailouts of European banks (concentrated in Germany, France and Britain, with US banks also implicated) that hold much of their debt. Speculative attacks are used as an argument in favour of moving quickly to drastic austerity plans, as in the cases of Greece and the Iberian countries. This strategy is a nonsense that can only lead to another recession, including in Germany, whose exports to emerging markets outside Western Europe might not offset its losses internal to European markets.

European governments and the European Commission have had one overriding goal: to return as quickly as possible to 'business as usual'. This goal is, however, out of reach, precisely because everything that had helped manage the contradictions of the flawed form of European integration, such as peripheral Europe indebtedness and internal European trade imbalances, has been rendered unusable by the crisis. These elements of the analysis of the current European economic conjuncture are now quite widely shared. However, they lead to quite opposite predictions and orientations, particularly on the Left: the bursting of the euro area, or overhaul of the pan-European political project.

FOR A REFOUNDATION OF EUROPE

The main objective of any Left alternative for Europe must be the optimal satisfaction of social needs. The starting point is, therefore, the distribution of wealth. From the capitalist point of view, the way out of the crisis requires a restoration of profitability through additional pressure on wages and employment. But that approach does not take into account the real causes of the crisis. It is the decline of wage share which has fed the financial bubble. And the neoliberal fiscal counter-reforms have deepened deficits, even before the erruption of the crisis.

The political equation for the Left is simple: we will not emerge from the crisis on top without a radical change in income distribution. This question comes before economic growth. Certainly, higher growth in itself could lead to more employment and higher wages, although such a growth-fixated strategy needs to be assessed from an ecological point of view. In any case, we cannot rely on growth if, at the same time, income distribution becomes increasingly unequal.

We must therefore squeeze inequalities from both sides: by an increase in the payroll for workers and by a tax reform. The upgrading of the wage share could follow *the rule of three thirds*: one third for direct wages, one third for socialized wages (or welfare) and one third to create jobs by reducing working hours. This rise of wages would be at the expense of dividends, which have neither economic justification nor social utility. The fiscal deficit should be gradually reduced, not by cuts, but by a re-fiscalization of all forms of income (bringing them back into public finances), which have gradually been exempted from taxes. The immediate cost of the crisis should be borne by those responsible: this means that the debt should be in large part cancelled and the banks nationalized and socialized.

Unemployment and job insecurity were already two of the most serious social ills of neoliberalism and the capitalist system. The crisis worsens both of them as the austerity plans hit the living conditions of the poorest. Here again, a return to some hypothetical new growth regime should not be considered as the solution – producing more in order to create more jobs. This is to take things in reverse. What is needed is a total change of perspective that takes the creation of useful jobs as a starting point. Whether by reduction of working time in the private sector, or by *ex nihilo* creation of public jobs, the objective must be to respond to social needs, and create 'true wealth', not necessarily in the form of commodities. Such an approach is both economically coherent and consistent with environmental concerns: the priority to free time and useful employment are two essential elements of any radical programme to fight against climate change.

The issue of income distribution is the correct starting point for a socialist response to the crisis based on the simple – but entirely correct – principle: 'we will not pay for their crisis'. Such an approach has nothing to do with a Keynesian 'wage stimulus', but with a defence of workers' wages, employment and social rights, none of which should be a matter of discussion. A socialist strategy would then also highlight the complementary notion of control: control over what they (the capitalists) do with their profits (dividends versus jobs) and control over the use of taxes (subsidize banks or finance public services). Such an approach would allow, in turn, the indictment of the private ownership of the means of production, and the central anti-capitalist message to acquire a mass audience in Europe.

As Özlem Onaran puts it: 'A consensus among the anti-capitalist forces for a strategy against the crisis is emerging across Europe around four pillars: i) resistance against austerity policies and all cuts; ii) a radically progressive/redistributive tax system and capital controls; iii) nationalization/socialization and democratic control of banks; and iv) debt audit under democratic control followed by default'.[1]

LEAVING THE EURO?

It is certainly true that the merging of national currencies within the eurozone has removed a crucial adjustment variable, namely the exchange rate. Countries with declining price competitiveness have no other options than a wage freeze and fiscal austerity or a further headlong rush into overindebtedness. Still, the 'exit from the euro' scenario is inconsistent economically and politically miscalculated.

Leaving the euro would not solve the issue of sovereign debt loads in peripheral Europe, but worsen it insofar as the debt owed to non-residents would be immediately increased by the rate of devaluation. The return to a national currency would directly expose the countries with a large external deficit to speculation. In any case, the debt restructuring should be made in the first place.

Devaluation makes a country's exports more competitive, at least against the countries which do not devalue. It is a non-cooperative solution in which a country seeks to gain market share against its trading partners. Moreover, by increasing the price of imports devaluation leads to inflation, which partly offsets the initial gains in competitiveness. Jacques Sapir, a French economist who supports the exit from the euro for France, acknowledges that inflation will impose 'devaluations every year or every 18 months to keep the real exchange rate constant'.[2] This means accepting an endless inflation-devaluation loop Yet, a country's competitiveness depends on many other elements: productivity gains, innovation, industrial specialization, and so forth. To suggest that the manipulation of exchange rates may be sufficient to ensure competitiveness is an illusion, and, by the way, a central postulate of the 'Pact for the Euro'.[3] There is little or no experience of devaluation that has not resulted in an increase in austerity that ultimately falls on workers.

A different distribution of income and an alternate mode of growth require as a prerequisite a profound change in the relation of social forces: this cannot be achieved by a currency devaluation. Taking devaluation as a starting point is equivalent to the reversal of priorities between social transformation and exchange rates. It is an extremely dangerous mistake. In his essay, Sapir stresses that the 'new currency should be embedded in the changes in macroeconomic policies and institutions... if it is to give all the desired effects'.[4] Among these changes, he cites a recovery of wages, the perpetuation of social systems, strict control of capital, requisition of the Bank of France, and state control over the banks and insurance companies. But all these measures should be imposed *before* any political project for leaving the euro.

A government of social transformation would, indeed, commit a terrible strategic mistake by leaving the euro, exposing itself to all kinds of speculative retaliation. The political risk that it would give legitimacy to the programmes of the far right is great. In France, the exit from the euro is one of the cornerstones of the National Front. The exit strategy revives a national-socialist logic that combines xenophobia and a discourse denouncing European integration as the ultimate cause of all economic and social ills.

While it is true that globalization and neoliberal European integration has strengthened the balance of power in Europe in favour of capital, it is not the only factor. It is, therefore, a fundamental error to suggest that an exit from the euro would spontaneously improve the balance of power in favour of workers. It is enough to consider the British example: the pound keeps Britain out of the European Monetary Union and the euro, but that has not protected the British people from an austerity plan which is among the most brutal in Europe.

Supporters of the exit from the euro advance another argument: it would be an immediate measure, and relatively easy to take, while the strategy of a refoundation of the European project would be out of reach. This argument misses the very possibility of a national strategy that does not presuppose a simultaneous rupture in all European countries.

FOR A STRATEGY OF RUPTURE AND EXTENSION

As often put, the dilemma seems to be between a risky adventure of 'exit' from the euro and a utopian European harmonization giving 'voice' to workers' struggles. The central political issue for socialists is to get out of this false choice. The main distinction here is between ends and means. The objective of a programme of social transformation is to guarantee to all citizens a decent life in all its dimensions – employment, health, retirement, housing, and so on.[5] These can be achieved by a change in the primary distribution of income between profits and wages and by tax reform. But advancing the struggles for these goals implies the questioning of dominant social interests, their privileges and their power. This confrontation takes place primarily within a *national* framework. But the resistance of the dominant classes and their possible retaliatory measures *exceed* the national framework.

The only viable strategy is to rely on the legitimacy of progressive solutions that arise from their highly cooperative nature. All neoliberal recommendations are ultimately based on the search for competitiveness, such as reducing wages, trimming social contributions, and cutting taxes to win market share. As European growth levels will continue to be weak in the period that has opened up with the crisis in Europe, the only way for any individual country to create jobs will be by competing for them with neighbouring countries, especially since the largest part of foreign trade of European countries is within Europe. This is true even for Germany as the second largest world exporter: it cannot rely only on emerging countries. The neoliberal way out of the crisis is inherently non-cooperative: you can only win against the others, and this is the ultimate cause of the deepening crisis of European integration.

In contrast, progressive solutions are cooperative; they will work even better if they are generalized to a larger number of countries. For example, if all European countries reduced working time and charged taxes on capital income, such coordination would avoid the backlash that the same policy would undergo if adopted in only one country. It is incumbent, therefore, that a government of the radical left follow *a strategy of extension*:

(1) 'good' measures are implemented unilaterally as, for example, with the taxation of financial transactions;

(2) accompanying plans for protection such as capital controls are adopted;

(3) the political risk of breaking European Union rules to implement these radical, initially nationally-based, policies is accepted and challenged;

(4) the proposition is made to amend these rules by extending them on a European scale to allow these measures to be adopted by member states, for example, in the extension of a European tax on financial transactions; and

(5) the political showdown with the EU and other European states is not avoided and thus the threat of exit from the euro is not excluded as a viable option.

This strategic scheme acknowledges that the making of a 'good' Europe cannot be the precondition to the implementation of a 'good' policy. The retaliation measures must be neutralized through counter-measures which effectively involve resort to a protectionist policy arsenal if needed. But the strategy is not protectionism in the usual sense: this protectionism defends an experience of social transformation emerging from the people and not the interests of the capitalists of a given country in their competition with other capitalists. It is, therefore, a *'protectionism for extension'*, whose very logic is to disappear once the 'good' measures have been generalized across Europe.

The rupture with European rules is not based on a petition of principle, but rather on the fairness and legitimacy of measures that correspond to the interests of the majority and are equally proposed to neighbouring countries. This strategic challenge for change can then rely on social mobilization in other countries and hence build a relation of forces that can influence EU institutions. The recent experience of the neoliberal rescue plans implemented by the ECB and the European Commission has shown that it is quite possible to bypass a number of the provisions of the EU Treaties.

For this strategy of rupture, exit from the euro is not a prerequisite. It is rather a weapon to use in the 'last resort'. The immediate break should proceed on two points which would allow real room for manoeuvre: the nationalization of banks and the restructuring of debt.

The first point of support is the ability to harm capitalist interests: the innovating country can restructure its debt, nationalize foreign capital, and similar steps, or threaten to do so. Even in the case of a small country, such as Greece or Portugal, the capacity of response is considerable, given the intertwining of economies. Many could lose; the showdown is not wholly unequal. But the main point of support lies in the collaborative nature of actions taken. It is a profound difference than the classic strategy of protectionism which occurs on the plane of a single state striving to succeed against its competitors.

Quite the contrary, all progressive measures are most effective when they are generalized to a larger number of countries. This strategy of rupture is ultimately based on the following discourse: we affirm our will to tax capital and we take the necessary protective measures to do so. But we propose the extension of this measure to the whole of Europe. It is on behalf of another Europe that the rupture with really existing Europe would be initiated. Rather than seeing them as opposing courses of action, we must consider the relationship between the rupture with neoliberal Europe and a project for the refoundation of Europe.

THE PROJECT AND THE RELATION OF FORCES

A programme aimed only at regulating the capitalist system at the margins would not only be undersized but insufficiently motivating. Conversely, a radical perspective can seem discouraging because of the sheer magnitude of the tasks at hand. What we need, as socialists, is somehow to determine the optimal degree of radicalism in this conjuncture. The difficulty is not, as so often suggested, to develop technical devices: such capacities are obviously essential and many of these capacities well advanced. But no clever measure can avoid the inevitable political clash between conflicting social interests.

Concerning the banks, the strategic range of possible departures stretches from full nationalization to more or less restrictive regulations, through the establishment of a public financial entity. Similarly, public debt could be cancelled, suspended, renegotiated, all along innumerable lines. Full nationalization of banks and the renunciation of public debt are measures that are both legitimate and economically viable. But they seem out of reach, due to the current balance of forces. Herein lies the real debate: what is the degree of radicalism in the strategy of rupture that is most capable of mobilizing workers and the political movements? It is clearly not for economists to decide. That is why, rather than proposing a complete set of economic measures and plans, the emphasis here has been to ask questions of method and highlight three essential ingredients for a radical Left response to the crisis: (1) a radical change in the distribution of income; (2) a massive reduction of working time; and (3) a rupture with the capitalist world order, starting with 'really existing' Europe.

This debate cannot – and should not – be summarized as an opposition between anti-liberals and anti-capitalists, or between Europeanists and progressives. These distinctions obviously have a sense, depending on whether the project is to get rid of finance or of capitalism. But this tension should not prevent us from beginning a long journey together, with the Left leading this debate. Such a 'common programme' as presented here could be based on the will to impose other rules on the functioning of capitalism. And this is, indeed, a dividing line between the radical Left and the social liberalism of centre-left political forces. The priority today for the radical Left is, in any case, to build a common European horizon as a basis for a genuine internationalism.

NOTES

1   Özlem Onaran, 'An Internationalist Transitional Program Towards an Anti-Capitalist Europe: A Reply to Costas Lapavitsas', *International Viewpoint Online*, 435, 2011, available at http://www/internationalviewpoint.org.
2   Jacques Sapir, *S'il faut sortir de l'Euro*, Document de travail, 6 avril 2011, at http://gesd.free.fr/sapirsil.pdf.
3   The 2011 'Pact for the Euro' was a demand, led by the German and French governments, that member states make concrete political commitments to improve fiscal positions (via austerity) and competitiveness (via cutting labour costs) as a condition for increasing funds for financial stability. See: 'The Euro and the European Union: Can Angela Merkel Hold Europe Together?', *The Economist*, 10 March 2011.
4   Sapir, *S'il faut sortir de l'Euro*.
5   For further analysis along these lines see, among others, my: *Un pur capitalisme*, Lausanne: Éditions Page Deux, Collection Cahiers Libre, 2008; 'Toxic Capitalism', in Raphie De Santos, et al., *Socialists and the Capitalist Recession*, London : Resistance Books, 2009 ; 'La nouvelle phase de la crise', *ContreTemps*, 9, 2011; 'A European Strategy for the Left', *International Viewpoint Online*, 432, 2011.